The Long Decade

The Long Decade

How 9/11 Changed the Law

Edited by David Jenkins
Amanda Jacobsen
Anders Henriksen

OXFORD
UNIVERSITY PRESS

OXFORD
UNIVERSITY PRESS

Oxford University Press is a department of the University of Oxford. It furthers the University's objective of excellence in research, scholarship, and education by publishing worldwide.

Oxford New York
Auckland Cape Town Dar es Salaam Hong Kong Karachi Kuala Lumpur Madrid
Melbourne Mexico City Nairobi New Delhi Shanghai Taipei Toronto

With offices in
Argentina Austria Brazil Chile Czech Republic France Greece Guatemala Hungary
Italy Japan Poland Portugal Singapore South Korea Switzerland Thailand
Turkey Ukraine Vietnam

Published in the United States of America by
Oxford University Press
198 Madison Avenue, New York, NY 10016

Library of Congress Cataloging-in-Publication Data

The long decade : how 9/11 changed the law / edited by David Jenkins, Amanda Jacobsen, Anders Henriksen.
pages cm
Includes bibliographical references and index.
ISBN 978-0-19-936832-7 (hardback)
1. Terrorism—Prevention—Law and legislation 2. Terrorism—Prevention—Law and legislation—United States. 3. War on Terrorism, 2001-2009. I. Jenkins, David (Christopher David) editor of compilation. II. Jacobsen, Amanda, editor of compilation. III. Henriksen, Anders, editor of compilation.
KZ6795.T47L66 2014
344.05'325—dc23

2013035239

Note to Readers
This publication is designed to provide accurate and authoritative information in regard to the subject matter covered. It is based upon sources believed to be accurate and reliable and is intended to be current as of the time it was written. It is sold with the understanding that the publisher is not engaged in rendering legal, accounting, or other professional services. If legal advice or other expert assistance is required, the services of a competent professional person should be sought. Also, to confirm that the information has not been affected or changed by recent developments, traditional legal research techniques should be used, including checking primary sources where appropriate.

(Based on the Declaration of Principles jointly adopted by a Committee of the American Bar Association and a Committee of Publishers and Associations.)

CONTENTS

LIST OF CONTRIBUTORS

Iain Cameron is a Professor of Public International Law at Uppsala University. He has been a member of the Council of Europe Commission on Democracy through Law since 2005. He has also been a Rapporteur for the journal *European Public Law* (1995–2009) and an expert in the Commission of Inquiry into U.N. and E.U. Sanctions. He is the author of several books, including *An Introduction to the European Convention on Human Rights* (2011), *International Criminal Law from a Swedish Perspective* (2011), and *National Security and the European Convention on Human Rights* (2000).

Oren Gross is a Professor of Law and the Director of the Institute for International Legal & Security Studies at the University of Minnesota Law School. He was a member of the faculty of the Tel Aviv University Law School in Israel from 1996 to 2002. Between 1986 and 1991, he served as a senior legal advisory officer in the international law branch of the Israeli Defense Forces' Judge Advocate General's Corps. In 1998, he served as the legal adviser to an Israeli delegation that negotiated an agreement with the Palestinian Authority's senior officials concerning the economic component of a permanent status agreement between Israel and Palestine.

Anders Henriksen is an Associate Professor of International Law at the University of Copenhagen, Faculty of Law. He holds a Ph.D. in international law from the University of Copenhagen and was affiliated with the Danish Center for Military Studies before joining the University. He has written extensively on international law and national security. His 2009 book in Danish, *Arven efter Bush: Præsidentembedet og krigen mod terror*, focused on the legal legacy of the George W. Bush presidency; his 2010 book, *Krigens folkeret—og international væbnet terrorbekæmpelse*, dealt with the international regulation of armed counter-terrorism; and his 2011 book, *Antiterrorismen, retsstaten og demokratiet*, discussed various international and constitutional law aspects of Danish counter-terrorism legislation.

Amanda Jacobsen is a Research Fellow at the University of Copenhagen, Faculty of Law. She is licensed to practice law in the United States and acts as habeas corpus counsel for Abu Zubaydah, a former CIA prisoner, now being detained in Guantanamo Bay, Cuba. Before coming to the University, she worked in private practice in Washington, DC, primarily in government contract litigation. She has also previously worked as a legal researcher for the Office of the Prosecutor at the U.N. International Criminal Tribunal for Rwanda.

David Jenkins is an Associate Professor of Comparative Law at the University of Copenhagen, Faculty of Law. He is an attorney at law in the United States, and earned his J.D. from Washington and Lee University School of Law. In addition to M.A.s in both history and political science from Marshall University, he holds the LL.M. and Doctor of Civil Law (D.C.L.) degrees from McGill University's Institute of Comparative Law in Montréal. He has published multiple articles regarding comparative constitutional law, with a focus on emergency theory, anti-terrorism measures, and the separation of powers.

Amnon Lev is an Associate Professor at the University of Copenhagen, Faculty of Law. He has advanced degrees in both law and philosophy (cand. jur et phil., Ph.D.) and studied law and philosophy in Copenhagen, Freiburg im Breisgau and Paris. His research interests include transformations of sovereignty, natural law, and constitutional politics.

Fiona de Londras is a Professor at Durham Law School in the United Kingdom. Prior to her appointment at Durham, she was a Lecturer at University College Dublin. Dealing primarily with the relationship between counter-terrorism, human rights and constitutionalism, her work has been published in leading internationally peer-reviewed journals including *Human Rights Quarterly*, the *Modern Law Review*, and the *Journal of Law and Society*. Her latest book, *Detention in the "War on Terror": Can Human Rights Fight Back?* was published by C.U.P. in 2011. She is one of the editors of *Legal Studies*, the scholarly journal of the Society of Legal Scholars, and co-editor in chief of the *Irish Yearbook of International Law*.

Victor V. Ramraj is an Associate Professor in the Faculty of Law, National University of Singapore. From 2006 to 2010, he served as the Faculty's Vice-Dean for Academic Affairs, and in 2010–2011, as a Faculty Co-Director of the Center for Transnational Legal Studies in London. He has qualifications in law (LL.B., Toronto; LL.M., Queen's University Belfast) and philosophy (B.A., McGill; M.A., Ph.D., Toronto) and is a member of the Law Society of Upper Canada (Ontario). Before joining the N.U.S. Faculty, he served as a law clerk at the Federal Court of Appeal in Ottawa and as a litigation lawyer in Toronto. He has edited several books with Cambridge University Press, including *Emergency Powers in Asia* (2010), *Emergencies and the Limits of Legality* (2009), and *Global Anti-Terrorism Law and Policy* (2nd ed., 2011), and *Fundamental Principles of Criminal Law* (LexisNexis, 2005).

Kent Roach is a Professor of Law and holds the Prichard-Wilson Chair of Law and Public Policy at the University of Toronto, Faculty of Law, with cross-appointments in criminology and political science. He is a former law clerk to Justice Bertha Wilson of the Supreme Court of Canada and has been editor-in-chief of the *Criminal Law Quarterly* since 1998. His book, *The 9/11 Effect: Comparative Counter-Terrorism*, was published by Cambridge University Press in 2011. In 2010, he authored *The Unique Challenges of Terrorism Prosecutions: Towards a Workable Relation between Intelligence and Evidence*. He has also co-edited *Global Anti-Terrorism Law and Policy* (2nd ed., 2011), and *Taking Remedies Seriously* (2010).

Gabor Rona is the International Legal Director of Human Rights First, where he advises on questions of international law and coordinates international human rights litigation. Previously, he was a Legal Advisor to I.C.R.C. in Geneva, where he was focused principally on the application of international humanitarian and human rights law to counter-terrorism policies and practice. In addition, he represented the I.C.R.C. in connection with the establishment of international and other criminal tribunals, including the International Criminal Court. He has also taught International Humanitarian Law and International Criminal Law in several academic settings, including Columbia University in New York; the International Institute of Human Rights in Strasbourg, France; and the University Centre for International Humanitarian Law in Geneva, Switzerland.

Jens Elo Rytter is a professor of constitutional law at the University of Copenhagen, Faculty of Law. His Ph.D. thesis from 2000 concerned fundamental rights and the role of courts in upholding them against the legislature. He is the author of two textbooks on human rights law and has published numerous articles on national and European human rights law and on the constitutional role of the judiciary, including several articles concerned with counter-terrorism measures.

Martin Scheinin is a Professor of International Law and Human Rights at the European University Institute in Florence, Italy. He was also the first United Nations Special Rapporteur on Human Rights and Counter-Terrorism. He was selected for this position after serving for eight years (1997–2004) as a member of the United Nations Human Rights Committee. A few of his recent publications include *International Protection of Human Rights: A Textbook; Monitoring Human Rights Obligations and the Fight against Terrorism: Whose Obligations? And Monitored How?; Security and the Law—Facing the Dilemma*; and *The Impact of Human Rights Law on General International Law*.

Kaarlo Tuori is a Professor of Jurisprudence at the University of Helsinki, Faculty of Law, where he is also the Director of the Centre of Excellence in Foundations of European Law and Polity. He has been a member of the Venice Commission (European Commission for Democracy through Law) since 1998, and its Vice-Presidence since 2007. In jurisprudence, his main work is *Critical Legal Positivism* (Ashgate, 2002). He is currently preparing an English version of a monograph called *Ratio and Voluntas in Law*, which has already appeared in Finnish in 2007.

Mark Tushnet is the William Nelson Cromwell Professor of Law at Harvard Law School. He served as a law clerk to Justice Thurgood Marshall. Some of his most recent books include *The Routledge Handbook of Constitutional Law* (2012); *Why the Constitution Matters* (Yale University Press, 2010); and *The Constitution of the United States of America: A Contextual Analysis* (Hart Publishing, 2009). Some of his most recent articles include "The Rise of Weak Form Judicial Review" (2011), "How Different Are Waldron's and Fallon's Core Cases for and against Judicial Review?" (2010), and "A Political Perspective on the Theory of the Unitary Executive" (2009).

Adrian Vermeule is the John H. Watson Professor of Law at Harvard Law School. He is a graduate of Harvard College and Harvard Law School. Vermeule was on the faculty of the University of Chicago Law School from 1998 to 2005, and of Harvard Law School from 2006 onward. His writings on terrorism and national security include "Our Schmittian Administrative Law," *Harvard Law Review* (2009); *Terror in the Balance: Security, Liberty and the Courts* (Oxford University Press, 2007, with Eric A. Posner); and *The Executive Unbound: After the Madisonian Republic* (Oxford University Press, 2011, with Eric A. Posner). He is also the author of, *The System of the Constitution* (Oxford University Press, 2011).

Clive Walker is Professor of Criminal Justice Studies at the School of Law, University of Leeds, where he has served as the Director of the Centre for Criminal Justice Studies (1987–2000) and as Head of School (2000–2005, 2010). He has written extensively on terrorism issues, with publications not only in the United Kingdom but also in several other jurisdictions, especially the United States, where he has been a visiting professor at George Washington and Stanford Universities. In 2003, he was a special adviser to the U.K. Parliamentary select committee and scrutinized what became the Civil Contingencies Act 2004, from which experience he published *The Civil Contingencies Act 2004: Risk, Resilience and the Law in the United Kingdom* (Oxford University Press, 2006). He has also authored a comprehensive study of *Terrorism and the Law* (Oxford University Press, 2011).

ACKNOWLEDGMENTS

This book grew out of the contributors' participation in an academic colloquium of the same title, held at the University of Copenhagen Faculty of Law in Copenhagen, Denmark on August 11–12, 2011, which commemorated the tenth anniversary of the terrorist attacks of September 11, 2001. The event was hosted by the Centre for European Constitutionalization and Security (CECS; since renamed the Centre for Comparative and European Constitutional Studies) at the Faculty of Law, in collaboration with the Centre for Advanced Security Theory (CAST), located in the University of Copenhagen Department of Political Science. The editors of this volume, who organized the colloquium, thank the Faculty of Law, CECS, and CAST for their support and financial sponsorship of that meeting. The editors also thank the Dreyers Foundation and Knud Højgaards Foundation, both based in Denmark, for their generous financial contributions to the project, without which this book would have been impossible. Finally, special thanks go to The Rt. Hon. Lord Hoffmann, former Lord of Appeal in Ordinary, for his valuable contributions to the discussions in Copenhagen.

Introduction

CHAPTER 1

The Long Decade

DAVID JENKINS*

It is well over twelve years since September 11, 2001, when the airplanes hit the World Trade Center and the Pentagon, killing nearly three thousand innocent people—around the same number as the worst night of the London Blitz in 1941. Indeed, London itself has not been spared tragedy since "9/11." On July 7, 2005, Britain's "7/7," terrorists detonated bombs in central London, killing fifty-two people and injuring over seven hundred more. Throughout the ensuing years, there have been more attacks by radical Islamists: in Madrid, Bali, Mumbai, Glasgow, Stockholm, and other places outside of the Middle East. The Western response to such terrorism has been forceful. The United States, United Kingdom, and their allies have carried out two wars and lengthy occupations in Afghanistan and Iraq. The United States and its accomplices have imprisoned without trial, abducted, and even tortured suspected terrorists, while targeted killings of Islamic militants by American drone strikes—with much "collateral damage"—have become regular in the Middle East. Many countries have implemented tough anti-terrorism laws. Nevertheless, the so-called "war on terrorism" is no closer to being won.

Instead, we live in a "long decade" of 9/11, where terrorists and the state press against us from both sides with little sign of relenting. If the contemporary globalized world has indeed become an intrinsically insecure and unpredictable place, as some have suggested, the state has likewise adapted quickly to meet its security obligations to its populace. This period has accordingly been—and continues to be—a time of significant political and legal transformation throughout the West, but where an emphasis on security threatens to destabilize and perhaps even replace other constitutional values. A lingering fear of terrorism, the rise of militant democracy, and an increasing turn to extraordinary legal measures now challenge many of our assumptions about liberal constitutionalism, built as they are on notions of limited, accountable government and individual rights.

This chapter looks at how these post-9/11 trends threaten to become the "new normal," if they are not halted. Of course, many commentators have already expressed concerns about just such a normalization of exceptional responses to crisis situations and the attendant dangers of permanently increased executive powers, reduced democratic transparency, ever more assaults on individual rights, and—with those—a lasting damage to the rule of law. Although this chapter is negative in outlook, it does not go so far as to say that fear, militant democracy, and extraordinary legal procedures have yet become so severe or permanent as to have fatally damaged liberal constitutionalism; such a claim would be an exaggeration. Yet, these changes have been significant and they present, certainly in theory, serious challenges to pre-9/11 liberal norms. Furthermore, because these challenges will be ongoing for the foreseeable future as a condition of our new, insecure global community—and hence, just why the decade after 9/11, still with us, continues to be a long one—their dangers lie not only in whatever damage they might already have done. Rather, it is their strength as ongoing, still slowly developing trends that should be of special worry to defenders of liberal constitutionalism.

Characterizing the "long decade" in this way, this chapter draws support from and introduces the rest of this book, which is comprised of contributions by participants who took part in an international conference held at Copenhagen University in August 2011. These chapters, like those scholarly discussions, examine more specific legal changes that occurred over the long decade and have had lasting effects on international law and many national legal systems. Although this introduction does not presume that all contributors agree with everything about its characterization of the "long decade," it nonetheless suggests that they implicitly lend support to its identification of this period's major trends of fear, militant democracy, and the use of extraordinary legal procedures. The structure of the book is loosely based on this premise.

Part I of this book explores the conflict between security and rights resulting from panics and fear, and considers the difficulty of crafting anti-terrorism measures that succumb neither to irrational fears nor alternative political agendas. Part II then closely follows with discussions of the challenges to international law and transnational governance in the post-9/11 world, as both states and the international order adapt to new security threats. In Part III, the book then looks at how terrorism has stressed legal and political models of constitutionalism in the United States and United Kingdom, and how it has forced those countries to make choices about their political stakeholders and the targets of their counter-terrorism measures. Part IV follows up on these themes with a couple of case studies of how the United Kingdom and Sweden have taken more proactive counter-terrorism measures that increasingly bypass criminal procedures. Part V then critiques how, over the past decade, extraordinary legal procedures, military or intelligence operations, and counter-terrorism efforts generally have challenged democratic accountability and human rights protections in ways that could harm the rule of law. Although the contributors to this volume take varied approaches on a variety of topics, this introduction argues that they all nevertheless lend various degrees of support to the main contention of this chapter and, along with it, this book: the years following 9/11 have witnessed significant, lasting legal changes throughout the world, and those changes continue in ways that pose risks to liberal democracy as we have known it. Security has bred insecurity. In this sense, the long decade just keeps getting longer.

FEAR

From Panic to Fear

There was, it is fair to say, a widespread panic in many countries—not only in the United States—in the weeks and months after 9/11. The apparent randomness, scale of destruction, and callousness of those attacks (even as compared to past acts of terrorism) touched a chord in the international community in a way that other ones had not. There was a palpable feeling of solidarity across the globe and a sense among much of its population that these attacks were not directed solely at the Americans. The resultant anxiety was perfectly natural and understandable. Nevertheless, anxiety and caution—indeed, even fear—are not the same as panic. Merriam-Webster's English dictionary defines panic as: (1) "a sudden overpowering fright; *also*: acute extreme anxiety," and (2) "a sudden unreasoning terror often accompanied by mass flight."[1] Although some of the reaction to 9/11 by the public and governments of many liberal democracies was sensible, much of it was indeed overpowering, extreme, and unreasoning.

This post-9/11 panic spurred an important reaction in the minds of politicians and the public throughout North America and Europe: that is, there was *us*, the innocents and potential victims of violent circumstance, and then there were *the others*, the unknown attackers lurking in hidden places, waiting to blow us apart to achieve their own fanatical, suicidal martyrdom. The role of panic in the construction of the "other," as well as in knee-jerk, poorly imagined legal responses, has received considerable attention by legal scholars, including two contributors to this volume. Fiona de Londras, in her book *Detention in the "War on Terror,"* draws on the work of sociologist Stanley Cohen to call attention to the concept of the "folk devil" in the creation of a post-9/11 "us-versus-them" panic mentality. Such a mentality opens a space through which the rhetoric of exceptionalism enters, as the only viable alternative to deal with the new threat to the community. In his chapter in this book, Oren Gross similarly recognizes the power of panic and the tendency to demonize unpopular groups when bad things happen.[2] The result is all too often a cognitive dysfunction on the part of both decision-makers and the public that targets the "other," accepts (or even demands) greater executive power, excuses rushed legislation, and generally distorts assessments of the actual risks in question. Thus, in many places—not just the United States—popular imagination after 9/11 went into overdrive, imagining more, even greater atrocities to be committed by shadowy "evil-doers," as President Bush put it.[3] Executive measures such as immigrations roundups, extraordinary rendition, and unwarranted wiretaps in the United States, as well as rushed anti-terrorism legislation there and in other places such as the United Kingdom, were among the ill-considered responses to this shadowy threat. Unpopular minorities bore (and continue to bear) the brunt of popular hostility, official suspicion, and special government powers. *Our* panic was a collective one and *we* desperately sought a collective enemy, against whom we could lash out decisively, all too often after insufficient reflection.

This initial panic eventually subsided, but it did not entirely go away. Rather, as the months turned into years, temporary panic gave way to lasting fear. This was not the fear of the moment, as one would have expected following any terrorist attack. This was instead an existential fear that free societies were now under prolonged siege from dark forces without and infiltrated by those within. While panics can certainly produce poor judgments and injustices, such tragedies are not unknown (the Japanese-American internments during World War II are a case in point). The cyclical nature of crisis and "normalcy" at least means that the injustices usually will last only as long as the panic and, in calmer times, we can eventually recognize and learn from our mistakes.[4] Fear, from this perspective, poses a different threat from panic. Whereas fear might suggest a lesser degree of anxiety (and, indeed, might even be more reasonable) than panic, fear is also something that can remain with us, demanding long-term (if perhaps less dramatic) adjustments to life, in ways that short-term panics might not. Thus, whereas panic is by definition a temporary hysteria, fear can be both internalized and lasting.

What is even more insidious about fear, as opposed to panic, is that it must not necessarily lead to either a folk devil or cognitive dysfunction (although it often does). It also cannot easily justify ad hoc, crisis-provoked infringements of liberty norms, as contemplated by the "tradeoff thesis" posed by Adrian Vermeule and Eric Posner in *Terror in the Balance* (and defended by Vermeule in his contribution to this volume).[5] Rather, what fear can do—and very quietly over a prolonged period—is actually shift the security-liberty frontier described by Vermeule and Posner. Because their conception of the frontier is normatively weak, it offers little resistance against shifting norms that might challenge previously accepted views about just what the precise relationship between security and liberty must be in a healthy, value-rich liberal democracy. Fear therefore has a transformative power that panic does not, in that it can provoke (sometimes even thoughtful) consideration that what once was normal and desirable is no longer sufficient or wanted in an increasingly risk-conscious society. In the short-term—and consistently with Kent Roach's worries about mission amnesia and mission creep, as discussed in his chapter in this book—fear (like inertia or other misjudgments) might persuade us simply to retain even panic-induced policies, even though they no longer have utility, or expand their application in ways not originally intended. In the long-term, however, fear can prompt slow, imperceptible transitions in underlying norms themselves, conceivably in ways that could reshape liberal democracy, as considered below. So, long after the post-9/11 panic has passed, it is a great concern that a *fear* of terrorism remains.

The Age of the Suicide Bomber

Still, just as liberal democracies have seen (and survived) panics, they have also known pervasive fear during the Cold War. In his chapter to come, however, Amnon Lev makes the critical point that the existential fear of terrorism is qualitatively different than the one we knew during the Cold War.[6] Indeed, seeing 9/11 as a breaking point from the post–Cold War world is crucial to understanding the long decade. During the Cold War (now seeming almost quaint in its simplicity), two nuclear-armed, ideological camps opposed each other. Whatever side of the Iron Curtain one might have been on, one knew the enemy and what it wanted. Everyone knew the consequences of actions and the stakes in play. Moreover, even with the horrid threat of total nuclear annihilation, the political game being played was not altogether different from that of centuries past. The Cold War, for all of its ideology and risk of doom, was the ultimate culmination of Great Power politics, where sovereign nation-states—now divided into two great and precariously balanced ideological blocs—vied for power and threatened to clash by great force of arms, whether conventional or nuclear. What kept both sides in check was fear of the mutually assured destruction that might follow any warming-up, perhaps however slight, of the Cold War.

Unlike the religious fanaticism behind the 9/11 attacks, this ideological struggle and global balance of power was worldly, in which the hoped-for victories and dreaded defeats were ones of either hegemony or total eclipse; although both the United States and the USSR pushed one another here and there or conducted proxy wars in far corners of the globe, neither side dared to misbehave too badly for fear of the ultimate consequence. The capitalist and the communist both feared their own earthly passing. Moreover, the prospect of civilian deaths—an inescapable fact of total war, much less nuclear holocaust—was still fundamentally conceived of as horribly tragic, but nonetheless collateral damage. The bombs on Hiroshima and Nagasaki, or Dresden, proved that this moral distinction could quickly turn into a self-deceiving charade; yet, the distinction still remains at the core of international law applying to armed conflicts (as seen, for example, in the Geneva Conventions and human rights law). Indeed, the European holocaust and the Pacific atrocities—as with twentieth-century totalitarianism generally—were partly so shocking because they were intentional, methodical campaigns of degradation and murder *directed at* civilians. These campaigns of death were not even for the most contrived military purposes, but simply to annihilate human beings.

Although the human carnage of 9/11 obviously could not compare to the latent, destructive potential of the Cold War, those attacks possibly exceeded it in their nihilism. The men who hijacked the planes not only intentionally targeted civilians, but they perversely *used* them as the instrument of their own and others' destruction. The hijackers also had no concern for their own survival; indeed, they embraced their deaths as acts of martyrdom, much like the Kamikaze pilots so feared by Allied sailors in the Pacific war. Although terrorists had blown themselves to bits before, something about 9/11 and its sheer audacity was especially shocking. When and where would it happen next? Who would be the attackers, and what would they want? What if they got their hands on weapons of mass destruction? As Lev writes later in this book, the "end of history" had indeed come with the fall of communism, but its meaning was not rightly understood at the time. The old, bipolar Cold War world had passed away, but the promising period of peace, freedom, and prosperity that followed was only its quiet epilogue. On the morning of September 11, before any of us had realized it, we awoke in the new age of the suicide bomber.

In this age, we can no longer trust in centuries-old habits and wisdom to allay our fears. Armies, navies, and air forces no longer guarantee us real security—even less so than they did with the Cold War risk of nuclear escalation. Nuclear weapons can also no longer ensure the peace, ironically, through their ability to destroy our planet. Diplomats have no one with whom they can talk, argue, or make peace as they did with nation-states. Indeed, the suicide bomber instilled panic and a lingering fear precisely because no one knows for sure who he or she is, or what he or she wants—and even if we can begin to surmise concrete goals, the demands can appear so dystopian or fanciful that they are not ours to give, as Lev suggests. This uncertain state of affairs challenges not only the ability of the nation-state to keep us safe, but the integrity of the international order and modes of global governance; these are increasingly dependent on cross-border networks and societies shaped by the movement of people and the free flow of information, as well as cross-cultural communication and understanding—characteristics of globalization that enable terrorism while being its targets. As Victor V. Ramraj and Kaarlo Tuori discuss in their contributions to this book,[7] new modes of international cooperation have accordingly struggled to adapt to terrorism. The result, as Tuori points out with reference to constitutional developments in the European Union, has been the "securitization" of much transnational political cooperation—a process similarly at work within nation-states themselves and that has uncertain long-term consequences.

The State under Siege

Can the nation-state, then, protect us in this age of terror? This was uncertain shortly after 9/11, as the state struggled to retain its political preeminence in this strange, new world. If terrorism is both a product of and a threat to globalization, it is just as symptomatic of the weakening hold of the nation-state on both violence and individual political identity. Citizenship, for example, has not guaranteed loyalty as people might have once assumed. For example, the bombers of the London transit system in July 2005 were young *British* Muslims. So too was Richard Reid, the "shoe bomber," who tried to board a plane with explosives in his shoe. Such incidents of national betrayal are not only a byproduct of an increasingly borderless world, but a homegrown pathology in liberal, open societies that are ever less demanding of conformity and allegiance. When applied to the 7/7 bombers, Reid, or other "traitors," citizenship has only a nominal legal function, as these individuals self-identified with a radical, pan-Islamist movement—itself a product of globalization, as well as a challenger to the dominant, post–Cold War (and essentially Western) model of the liberal, democratic state. Old assumptions about citizenship have therefore failed, as disaffected individuals can choose their loyalties; this has happened at the same time as the state's monopolies on both violence and political discourse have given way.

Consequently, a radical reorientation in the relationship between the individual and the state seems to be occurring—themes to which I will return at the end of this chapter. As I suggest in my later chapter in this volume, the American government and courts have doggedly held on to old legal doctrines about citizens' rights and the sanctity of national territory (and the vulnerability of foreigners). This has been a reactionary attempt to shore up the nation-state and reinforce its political community, and in the process to define the "other" in legal terms. Although clear legal rules about such things might send a message about what the state itself expects, their wider normative force is now in question. However, a legal rejection of the privileges of citizenship seems no more attractive, when one looks at the United Kingdom after the House of Lords' decision in the famous *Belmarsh Case*:[8] everyone, citizen or not, is now a potential security risk subject to state monitoring and control. In any case, what is clear is that as political loyalties and immensely destructive violence have become denationalized and individualized, it has become increasingly difficult for us to tell our friend from our foe, and to trust in the state to protect us as it once did.

Thus, although a construction of the "other" prompted a strong government response in the crisis moment after 9/11, it ironically masked the weakness of the state and our faith in its protective power. As discussed further below, the "us-versus-them" rhetoric and the state's struggle for meaning have both municipal and global implications not yet fully realized. We — who are caught between a borderless world and a liberal-minded, civic society (and international order) still premised on the model of the constitutional nation-state—are partly still afraid, not only because we do not know when or from whom the next attack will come, but because we doubt the ability of the nation-state to protect us from it. The state cannot easily defeat an enemy we do not know, cannot limit to a distinct territory or population, or ascribe concrete political objectives to as we did our enemies of yore. Indeed, the very danger of the suicide bomber is itself a testimony to the state's contemporary inability to awe the individual and monopolize violence. Nonetheless, our fear and stubborn attachment to the nation-state—the only protector we have known for a very, very long time—demands that the state respond, even if we must adjust the norms by which it acts and governs. Accordingly, the long decade has seen the rise of an emerging power to confront the threat—militant democracy.

MILITANT DEMOCRACY

The Discourse of War

The American and British reactions to the September 2001 attacks were militant from the start. As President Bush addressed the American public on September 12, 2001: "The deliberate and deadly attacks, which were carried out yesterday against our country, were more than acts of terror. They were acts of war."[9] Indeed, war seemed to be the natural state of affairs between us, the victims, and the "terrorists" and their sympathizers: the swift rhetorical move toward the "folk devil" accompanied a simultaneous rhetorical move toward war. In the same speech of September 12, the president described the enemy as one who "hides in shadows and has no regard for human life. This is an enemy who preys on innocent and unsuspecting people, then runs for cover."[10] Bush's speech set the tone for the upcoming decade, and other world leaders quickly joined in the war talk. "Whatever the technical or legal issues about a declaration of war," Prime Minister Blair said a few days after President Bush's remarks, "the fact is we are at war with terrorism."[11] The initial post-9/11 panic thus led not only to a discourse of the "other," but to a discourse of war; politicians seized the chance to show their mettle with strong martial actions.

The American and British response to 9/11, then, was not going to be a search for criminals and murderers, no matter how evil they might be portrayed; instead, this was war against an enemy to be vanquished. On September 14, the U.S. Congress passed a joint resolution authorizing the president to use all necessary force against Al Qaeda and any others responsible for the September 11 attacks. The Authorization for the Use of Military Force was broadly worded; the federal courts have since given it a permissive interpretation as constituting congressional approval under the Constitution for a wide array of executive actions taken against terrorism. Congress' action in passing the resolution evidenced a commonly held perception across the political spectrum that 9/11 required an exceptional state response that the criminal law was unable to provide. Legally, the Authorization conflated the power to take action and identify the new enemy in a worrying way: the president himself could determine both who was responsible for the 9/11 attacks and what countermeasures were necessary. Such executive-legislative concurrence, and the increased executive authority flowing from it, was not only an American phenomenon. Prime Minister Blair, able to exercise the Crown's prerogative for war-making and backed by a party majority in the House of Commons, had similar political leverage for a militant response to terrorism—only more so after 7/7.

This discourse of war had important long-term political and legal consequences in both the United States and the United Kingdom. President Bush's constitutional authority was at its maximum, including all that he possessed in his own right plus all that Congress could delegate;[12] Mr. Blair also had a wide discretion to manage the "war on terrorism" under the Crown's prerogative and by commanding a strong party majority in the House of Commons. Such an increase in executive power was a worrying state of affairs from a constitutionalist viewpoint: it destabilized the normal separation of powers in the American and British political systems. Congress and Parliament, as well as the American and British courts, would often (but not always, as seen below) assume deferential postures toward the executive actions and legislative agendas in the "war on terrorism." Yet, such deference has usually been the case in times of war and national emergency: legislative and executive checks weaken, just when vigilance against invigorated executive powers becomes most necessary.

However, unlike wars of the past, the "war on terrorism" was not to be a temporary, acute period of political stress; rather, it was a potentially permanent state of affairs in an insecure globalized world. The institutional imbalance brought about by the "war on terrorism" threatened to remain as long as the public's fear of the suicide bomber did. The growth of executive power was the most visible symptom of this problem, but it was not the only one, and was perhaps not even the most important from a wider point of view. As de Londras and Mark Tushnet point out, the constitutional stress born of the "war on terrorism" also revealed tensions between models of legal and political constitutionalism that defined just what that institutional balance (and so the role of law and the courts) *ought* to be. According to Tushnet, this instability in constitutional orientation makes sense of both the policy consistencies and differences between the Bush and Obama administrations in ways that the Supreme Court's decisions on Guantanamo Bay do not. It also explains the significant impact of British judicial decisions, such as the *Belmarsh Case*, that effectively limited a government supported by a sovereign Parliament.[13]

Furthermore, as de Londras argues, institutional and partisan conflicts in the United States over the conduct of the "war on terrorism" revealed even more worrisome problems with the condition of American politics itself; that is, many inter-branch and inter-party disputes over counter-terrorism measures were not principled debates about either best policies or constitutional practice, but were instead unprincipled bickering and political maneuvering in the worst sense.[14] What should have been debates about the power of the state (especially the executive) to take exceptional measures instead deteriorated into arguments about *who* (as in which person or party) was making decisions. Important constitutional questions became obscured or, even worse, influenced by petty politics. Either way, the ensuing constitutional stress in the United States and United Kingdom—brought about not just by terrorism, but by the discourse of war in response to it—upset normal assumptions about the separation of powers, while raising difficult questions about the role of law in constraining state power in times of crisis.

Therefore, with their discourse of war, President Bush and Prime Minister Blair seized the political initiative and shaped the American and British responses to 9/11 for the foreseeable future. The war on terrorism was to be an existential struggle. We were under siege from dark forces beyond our walls and infiltrated by secretive evildoers within them. This discourse did more than respond to the immediate post-9/11 panic; it tapped into the public's deeper, widely held fears and anxieties about insecurity in the globalized world. Importantly, then, this rhetorical move was only successful because of widespread support. The United States and United Kingdom—their executive officers, their legislatures, and probably a great percentage of their people—considered themselves at war: not with a sovereign state, not even with a fast ideology such as fascism or communism, but with an unknown, unseen enemy—the suicide bomber. Osama bin Laden and Al Qaeda were the closest anyone could come to putting a face and name to this unconventional enemy. The full significance of this martial discourse has become only more apparent over the course of the last decade and beyond, as security has become the primary objective of the militant democracy.

The Security Agenda

For over ten years after 9/11, the American and British governments would use the discourse of war to implement a security agenda that would prioritize security over individual rights. As discussed in more detail below, the state would pursue an aggressive foreign policy in defending its national security interests, while the prevention of terrorism quickly took precedence over its criminal punishment. This is not to say that rights are no longer important considerations in either government policymaking or judicial decisions. As Jens Elo Rytter argues, courts have generally been protective of rights even in the face of government national security claims.[15] Nonetheless, in "balancing" rights with security, the latter has come to weigh much heavier now than before 9/11. Whether this reweighing represents an actual trade-off of security and rights, in the way described by Vermeule, or is rather a new way of reconciling the two, is perhaps not as important as the overall effects that the security agenda has had on both politics and law. Over the past decade, this agenda has significantly and negatively transformed the way in which many elected officials and members of the public have come to perceive the state, as it has struggled to respond to terrorism and protect the public; that is, the role of government has shifted from a benevolent enforcer of individual rights—a view shaped by the post–World War II human rights era—to become an ominous provider of collective security in the dangerous post-9/11 world. If we all now lived in the age of the suicide bomber, many of us also found ourselves in an emerging militant democracy, as the state adapted to wage the unconventional war against terrorism.

The British newspaper *The Guardian*, for example, recognized the British government's increasingly aggressive attitude after the 7/7 bombings, an attitude illustrative of the militant democracy's new resolve:

> Tony Blair last night signalled a turning point in British postwar liberalism when he announced plans to deport extremist foreign Muslim clerics without appeal, close down mosques preaching hate, proscribe extremist Muslim groups and extend the use of control orders [described below] to British nationals advocating terrorism.
>
> The prime minister also promised to wage a battle with the British and European courts, warning that he would amend the Human Rights Act if necessary to override likely judicial objections to the proposed deportation regime.[16]

In response to critics, Mr. Blair responded: "Let no one be in any doubt that the rules of the game are changing."[17] Indeed, one sign of the emerging militant democracy was a fundamental shift in official attitudes toward "the rules" as a result of events such as 9/11 or 7/7—an official attitude that possibly reflected normative shifts in some segments of the population at large and so, as pointed out below, illustrates the dangers of transformation within liberal democracy itself. Unlike World War II or the Cold War, the war against terrorism quickly became a popular "dirty war" of sorts, with no clear enemy, victory, or end—and no options off the table. If the smoking Twin Towers are the image of the age of the suicide bomber, the shackled, hooded prisoner has become that of the militant democracy.

This militant democracy—seen ever more plainly in the United States and the United Kingdom over the long decade—has not been afraid to "get chalk on its cleats," "take the gloves off," or "work on the dark side."[18] Government readiness to push legal and moral boundaries in the name of security has sadly led to many well-publicized abuses with uncertain constitutional implications. The list of complaints—government eavesdropping on private communications and massive collections of personal data, the doctoring of intelligence, and the misleading of national legislatures and the public in the mad run-up to the Iraq invasion, as well as prisoner mistreatment and even torture—could get quite long. It was not only the Americans and the British that went too far in some cases: many European countries, for example, were complicit in the Bush administration's "extraordinary rendition" of suspected terrorists, buying into the administration's "with us or against us" diplomacy. Several more examples could be given, but such excesses showed that many liberal democratic states had become increasingly willing after 9/11 to do whatever was believed necessary to keep the public safe and hunt down terrorists, wherever or whoever they might be. With militant democracy, to use a phrase, a new sheriff was in town.

Characteristics of Militant Democracy

There are three characteristics of the militant democracy as it has emerged over the long decade: the defense of liberal values at home, the use of force to advance national security aims abroad, and a focus on risk prevention to stop terrorism or other harms before they occur. First, the militant democracy sets clear boundaries of acceptable and unacceptable political behavior, prohibiting the latter to keep democracy safe from those who do not share the same liberal values as the mainstream public. Of course, no democracy can tolerate overt political violence, but the militant democracy tightens restrictions on political rights such as speech, association, and assembly, so that they exclude illiberal content. It then strictly enforces these limits on political behavior, for the reason that they now represent normative boundaries beyond which no individual can go and the state is no longer prepared to be tolerant. Policing these boundaries therefore goes beyond enforcing the criminal law, as such, for the purpose of preserving public peace and order, or even punishing disloyalty through old-style sedition or treason laws. Instead, the defense of normative values—as opposed to the mere punishment of bad behavior—becomes an existential project, like the war on terrorism itself. The militant democracy, however, always risks falling into the contradiction of overly restricting the very civil liberties it aims to protect. As discussed below, this project also eventually impels the state to take preventive action not just against individuals who cause concrete harm, but against all those who exhibit risk factors suggesting they might be hostile in the future to liberal society.

Of course, the idea of policing democracy by seeking out and neutralizing its enemies is nothing new.[19] During the red scares after the First and Second World Wars, for example, American law enforcement authorities hunted down suspected communists and Congress outlawed political parties that had, as their aim, the violent overthrow of the U.S. government. These postwar periods were times of panic and fear over the Bolshevik threat, and police actions notoriously descended into persecution of those unpopular political views and ethnic minorities considered to be "un-American." Nevertheless, the idea was to protect democracy by rooting out its ideological enemies before they could cause any further mischief by proselytizing their beliefs or fomenting violent resistance. There are other examples, notably in Europe. In Germany, the *Grundgesetz* permits the *Bundesverfassunggericht* to declare, upon government petition, that a political party is unlawful for being an antidemocratic party, having the aim to undermine or destroy Germany's democratic system. The National Socialist Party was banned almost immediately after the founding of the West German republic, quite understandably, as was the Communist Party. More recently, the German government has attempted to ban (so far unsuccessfully) the NDP, a far-right and allegedly neo-Nazi party. In relation to terrorism, the U.S. Congress has made it a crime to provide "material support" to terrorists,[20] while the U.K. Parliament has gone further by criminalizing the "glorification" of terrorism—a legal offense of unclear meaning and scope.[21]

Although any laws restricting political activities are problematic in a democracy, the goal of defending it from political extremism is understandable. Tellingly, such political extremism is not protected under the European Convention on Human Rights, for example. Article 17 proclaims that "nothing in this Convention may be interpreted as implying for any State, group or person any right to engage in any activity or perform any act aimed at the destruction of any of the rights and freedoms set forth herein...," while Article 10 guarantees freedom of expression subject to certain public interest limitations (as do the articles protecting rights to association and belief). Both within and outside of Europe, legal prohibitions against hate speech and Holocaust denial in some countries protect democratic values of racial or religious equality by restricting the rights of bigots to say or print prejudiced things. As has often been said, a constitution is not a suicide pact, meaning that it does not create a liberal, democratic order only to allow its enemies to abuse tolerance to democracy's ultimate destruction. The idea of the democratic state defending itself against illiberal forces is an old one, but many such governments have done so with increasing gusto against Islamic fundamentalism during the long decade.

A second characteristic of militant democracy, especially seen in American and British foreign policy since 9/11, is greater government willingness to use military force in the pursuit of national security aims. These goals are often infused with a new ideological drive, such as forcing democratization in foreign countries or reconstructing so-called "failed states." NATO's military intervention in Libya might be seen as a benign manifestation of the its willingness to support freedom fighters in the Arab world, with the long-term aim of achieving security through regional political stability. The U.N.-sanctioned post-9/11 military action against the Taliban in Afghanistan is an even better example of the use of force not only to attack Al Qaeda and its Taliban supporters, but to rebuild the country and promote human rights in order to eliminate a breeding ground of terrorism. Of course, a more problematic example is the invasion of Iraq in 2003, which the American and British government sold to the public as a campaign to eliminate Saddam Hussein's weapons of mass destruction (later found not to exist). Thus, it cannot be said that the militant democracy always ignores more immediate and less idealistic national self-interests: oil no doubt had some role to play in both Iraq wars. Nevertheless, some governments (most notably the American and British) seem to be increasingly guided by ideological considerations, such as democracy-building, in articulating and forcefully pursuing their national security goals.

Although moral purpose in foreign policy is not a bad thing, it can lead to perverse results when pursued in a utilitarian fashion. As with the Cold War's realpolitik, an ends-means analysis has figured into the post-9/11 foreign policy and national security strategies of many democratic states, like the United States and United Kingdom. Taken too far, this way of thinking justifies states in doing whatever is necessary to protect themselves from present and future threats. Thus, as the second invasion of Iraq showed, governments can tout righteous goals in support of politically unwise or even morally questionable foreign policy choices. Even if, for sake of argument, a war against a dictator suspected of harboring chemical weapons was morally justifiable, it cannot overshadow the ethically questionable ways in which both the American and British governments actually laid the preparatory political groundwork for the invasion. For example, the Blair government's doctoring or "sexing-up" of intelligence information to inflate the risk posed by Iraq was a serious violation of public trust and a constitutionally inappropriate misleading of Parliament. However, both the Blair government and the Bush administration seemed to bet that, after finding Saddam's stockpiles of chemical weapons (none were found), we, too, would understand that the ends had justified the means.

The second Iraq War also illustrates the third characteristic of the militant democracy: its fear-driven impulse to *prevent*, rather than simply react to, perceived threats to a democracy, whether they originate from within or without its borders. The primary excuse given by the American and British governments for the invasion of Iraq was to prevent Saddam Hussein from acquiring weapons onf mass destruction (WMDs), which he could then use in the future to threaten the United States and United Kingdom or which could fall into the hands of terrorists. As Iraq had not attacked the United States, United Kingdom, or their allies, this was not a classic case of national self-defense. However, the U.S. administration, based on a theory of preemption of foreseeable future threats, formulated the so-called "Bush doctrine": a country could defend itself by removing these potential threats, without having to wait until they had become imminent or an actual attack had occured. To wait, this argument ran, would be too late in an age of suicide bombers and rogue states armed with weapons of mass destruction. That this doctrine was inconsistent with international law on the use of force did not stand in the way of either the Bush administration or the Blair government. However, both governments also advanced an alternative justification: a controversial and not very convincing interpretation of the Security Council Resolutions sanctioning Iraq, which would have allowed military enforcement by Member States in the event of Iraq's noncompliance with a prohibition of WMDs. Nevertheless, this interpretation similarly rested on a presumption that the Security Council had considered Iraq's mere (suspected) possession of such weapons to be a serious threat inviting preemptive military strikes.

The fact that no WMDs were later found in Iraq did not necessarily undermine this preemption theory to its hawkish proponents; it was a natural response to the lingering post-9/11 fear and prioritized national decision-makers' assessments about the existence, severity, and likelihood of a particular threat. If leaders found a sufficiently dangerous threat to exist (proximity in time and likelihood of occurrence were less important than expected destructive capability), the state was not only justified, but obligated to its own citizens and even the global community to remove that threat however it was best able to do so. This security imperative not only trumped international law and human rights, if necessary, but also possibly foreclosed more cautious and proportional, but less decisive, options than military force. Moreover, the militant democracy's turn toward speculative risk prevention was not limited to foreign policy and military intervention abroad. Rather, over the long decade, it has also taken forceful preventive measures against security risks among its own population. It has done so through extraordinary legal measures that expand the state's powers within the national legal system to limit the freedoms of those suspected of posing a future threat. To do this, the militant democracy has increasingly refashioned the law from a shield of individual rights to a proactive weapon of the state.

EXTRAORDINARY LEGAL MEASURES

Preventive Law

Militant democracy—the state's adaptive form to provide security from the fear of terrorism—is characterized by the aggressive defense of democracy's liberal values, greater use of force abroad in national security matters, and focus on threat prevention. Although the militant democracy also pursues the latter through its foreign policy, at home it develops and uses extraordinary legal measures to manage security risks within its own borders. As a general proposition, such measures permit the state: (1) to deprive an individual of personal liberty or other rights, not for any crime actually committed, but for things which he or she *might* do that could harm the national security; and (2) to do so pursuant to special procedures that favor government's subjective risk assessments and limit the individual's rights of defense. In-so-far as such measures depart from normal legal practices, they challenge pre-9/11 assumptions about rule-of-law requirements. In some circumstances, courts have resisted some of these extraordinary legal measures (but certainly not all), thus mounting an internal institutional challenge of sorts to militant democracy's turn toward them. Nevertheless, such measures continue to become more commonplace in many liberal, democratic legal systems. Although there are many examples of such measures over the long decade, a few suffice to illustrate just how the militant democracy has used the law as a tool of risk prevention.

Laws targeting terrorist financing are good examples of extraordinary legal measures designed to prevent terrorism and the rule-of-law problems they raise. Such laws typically allow the executive to restrict financial transactions or impound the funds of groups and individuals it suspects of supporting terrorism. Executive designations and freezing orders often afford limited opportunities for subsequent legal challenge after they have taken effect. Terrorism financing laws are now common in many countries, and the United Nations has even sought to impose such measures on its Member States. However, courts have occasionally resisted these moves toward procedural shortcuts and expansive executive discretion. In 2008, for instance, in the well-publicized *Kadi* case,[22] the European Court of Justice annulled an E.U. Council of Ministers regulation that implemented U.N. Security Council requirements to impose financial restrictions on anyone associated with Al Qaeda. The regulation was procedurally defective under European law, the European Court of Justice found, because it allowed the European Council to freeze the assets of individuals and entities on a U.N. proscription list without affording them an adequate opportunity to be heard, to know the evidence against them, or to petition for removal from the list altogether.

Many national laws against terrorist financing have followed this model and have been widely criticized for reasons similar to those given by the E.C.J. Laws that allow the state to designate a person as a supporter of terrorism without actual wrongdoing—thereby resulting in a loss of reputation, property, and perhaps livelihood—seriously challenge the presumption of innocence and right to a fair hearing that the rule of law requires. These kinds of measures increase the chances for injustice to innocent parties, racial or religious discrimination, and government abuse, while having a chilling effect on an individual's exercise of such rights as those of speech and association. Furthermore, because terrorism financing laws and many other extraordinary legal measures are administrative rather than punitive in form (as they do not purport to prosecute actual wrongdoing), they confuse long-standing distinctions between civil and criminal legal proceedings in a way that allows the state to strip an individual of important rights without the benefit of a proper trial. Whatever their value in preventing terrorism (and this is contested), such laws can have a devastating impact on innocent people's lives, due to their weak procedural safeguards.

This concern over the possibility of injustice is especially acute when the militant democracy uses extraordinary legal measures to deprive individuals of their personal freedom. For example, since 9/11, the British Parliament has reintroduced preventive detention schemes in the United Kingdom for the first time since the Troubles in Northern Ireland. Not surprisingly, these have been controversial and have led to legal challenges in the courts. Thus, in the 2004 *Belmarsh Case*, the House of Lords declared that a statutory provision allowing the indefinite detention of aliens suspected of terrorism, who could not be deported due to a risk of torture abroad, was incompatible with the European Convention on Human Rights.[23] The Law Lords found that such detention irrationally discriminated on grounds of national origin, because it allowed British citizens suspected of terrorism—who might be just as or more dangerous as alien suspects—to go free unless criminally prosecuted. Indeed, the 7/7 bombers later proved what the House of Lords had predicted: previous assumptions or prejudices about citizenship, race, religion, or political views could not necessarily predict who was now a security threat. Instead, the government was required to treat all persons equally under the law, targeting them solely on the basis of their security risks, rather than their citizenship.

As I point out in my later chapter, however, the *Belmarsh Case* provoked an unexpected response from the Labour government and Parliament, which together contrived a different preventive detention regime designed to comply with the Law Lords' ruling. While repealing the statutory provision for the indefinite detention of foreigners, Parliament passed a new law allowing the Home Secretary to place "control orders" on any person determined to pose a terrorism risk—including a British citizen;[24] by making such an order, the minister could seriously limit the suspect's rights to personal liberty, movement, and association, among other things. Control orders were subject to court approval under shortcut procedures that restricted the individual's access to a lawyer, knowledge of the state's evidence, and right to be present at the court hearing. The later Tory-Liberal Democrat government would eventually replace these control orders with a somewhat less-onerous system of "terrorism prevention and investigation measures,"(TPIMs), although that system continues to use essentially the same procedures as those for control orders. Controversially, the coalition government also proposed using these same procedures in any civil case in which secret evidence would come into question. The United Kingdom's trend in expanding upon these extraordinary legal measures is particularly worrying, because so many countries—such as Canada, Australia, and Denmark—have copied the British example in creating their own preventive detention regimes with special procedures.

In-so-far as extraordinary legal measures such as these permit the state to deprive a person of fundamental rights based on suspicion and without a fair hearing, they present a rule-of-law problem. Sadly, however, some extraordinary legal measures have gone even further and stretched legal boundaries to their breaking point. For example, American military detentions and military commissions uncomfortably straddle the line between a spurious rule-of-law compliance and an outright *extralegal* rule by force, as explained below. For example, in the months after the September 11 attacks, President Bush signed a military order authorizing the military detention and trial of foreigners captured as "enemy combatants." The Bush administration accordingly locked up hundreds of foreigners, seized around the world, in the special prisons at Guantanamo Bay (as well as in military prisons in Iraq and Afghanistan, and secret CIA "black sites" in Eastern Europe). The president even ordered two American-citizen terrorist suspects to be detained in military prisons on the U.S. mainland. The administration tried to deny these detainees legal representation, a criminal trial, and a fair opportunity to challenge their imprisonment in a federal court (some detainees, such as those imprisoned in "black sites," were not even publicly acknowledged). Pursuant to his constitutional role as commander in chief and Congress's Authorization for the Use of Military Force, President Bush claimed legal authority to detain these enemy combatants indefinitely, granting them only a thin veneer of (executive-dominated) legal process—if any at all.

As with courts elsewhere, however, the Supreme Court pushed back against such extraordinary measures in an attempt to uphold the rule of law. In a well-known series of cases, citizen detainees won the right to a fair hearing in challenging their status as an enemy combatant, the Guantanamo prisoners were allowed habeas corpus review in the federal courts, and the president's military commissions were struck down as incompatible with federal law (which the Supreme Court interpreted as incorporating the Geneva Conventions.)[25] Regrettably, however, many other detainees around the world have received no legal redress for their detention or torture. Moreover, the most lasting legacy of the Supreme Court's judgments might resemble that of the *Belmarsh Case* in Britain; that is, the Court's decisions seem to have only goaded the security-obsessed political branches into taking alternative, but no less extraordinary, measures. In the years since these judgments, Congress has denied funding for the closure of the Guantanamo Bay prisons, and has statutorily authorized future military detentions and commissions.[26] The Supreme Court's decisions have also undoubtedly encouraged the Obama administration to detain captured Islamic militants far from American shores or to forgo capture in favor of extralegal measures, such as the shooting of Osama bin Laden or the "targeted killing" of militants abroad (some have been American citizens) by drone strikes.

The Paradox of Militant Democracy

Extraordinary legal measures over the long decade, such as those above, have generally targeted security risks within the domestic population in order to prevent terrorism or, in some cases (as with military commissions), to render "justice" of some sort to terrorist suspects captured abroad. As constructs of municipal legal systems, they therefore pose a different constitutional problem than do extralegal measures, such as drone strikes or torture, that (morally justifiable or not) are brute acts of violence with no pretense of legal process. So, while the militant democracy creates extraordinary legal measures to expand its preventive powers in compliance with the rule of law (or in the attempt to manipulate it) at the municipal level, its extralegal measures are essentially use-of-force decisions (most usually taken abroad) that are fundamentally political in nature. As such, extralegal measures do not interact with or directly impact the state's internal legal norms in the same way as those extraordinary legal measures incorporated into the national legal system itself.

Nevertheless, this distinction between extraordinary legal and extralegal measures should in no way be understood to suggest that the former necessarily comply with the rule of law; rather, as discussed above, they have presented serious rule-of-law problems over the course of the long decade. The distinction also does not mean that extralegal measures taken abroad are ungoverned by international law; they most certainly are. However, unlike with domestic law, the militant democracy has little power to alter international law in its favor. Lacking this legal agency, it can only attempt to justify its uses of force against preexisting and virtually unmovable international standards (an attempt that can sometimes be tenuous, as with drone strikes) or challenge international law directly (such challenges are not only unlikely to produce change, but risk controversy or damage to political prestige, as with the "Bush doctrine"). Accordingly, the distinction between extraordinary legal and extralegal measures rests on: (1) their use of judicial process of some sort, (2) their relationship to the domestic legal system, and (3) the militant democracy's ability to use them to alter existing legal norms at either the municipal or international level. These terms therefore serve a useful analytical function in describing the two ways that militant democracy uses the coercive force of the state for preventing terrorism, as well as how those methods impact liberal values—something that extraordinary legal and extralegal measures can both do.

Importantly, then, this difference in terminology should in no way downplay the seriousness of human rights abuses (whether the state commits them in legal guise or not), and the contradictions that such abuses create between the norms of liberal democracy and the actions of its militant variety. Indeed—whether it has been the militant democracy's use of shortcut statutory procedures that deny an individual a fair hearing before the freezing of his financial assets or the waterboarding of a detainee at a secret CIA facility to extract information—the long decade has witnessed a greater willingness by democratic governments, like the American and British,to employ the coercive force of the state in preventing terrorism and, with it, a hardening attitude toward human rights. Either of these new instincts, whether expressed through or outside of legal forms, can eventually impact the foundational norms of both the liberal democratic state and the liberal international legal order. This is because extraordinary legal and extralegal measures are based upon a common underlying assumption in tension with these norms: with militant democracy, collective security and risk prevention increasingly trump individual rights and government accountability.

Consequently, the militant democracy's use of extraordinary measures of any sort over the long decade—a trend that has gone on regardless of political parties in power—is a cause for worry, if it continues. As Gabor Rona points out in his chapter,[27] although the Obama administration abandoned and renounced torture and rendition, it continued to detain hundreds of individuals in Afghanistan and elsewhere, support the use of military commissions (albeit in a fairer form), and increasingly rely on "targeted killings" using automated drones. Rona's charges of American hypocrisy do more than highlight the new realpolitik discussed earlier; more fundamentally, they point to a troubling lack of commitment to the human rights culture at the heart of the post–World War II international and municipal legal orders, as Martin Scheinin indicates at the beginning of his epilogue to this book.[28] Such hypocrisy also impacts democratic accountability. For instance, Amanda Jacobsen discusses the worsening government habit of attempting to control information and deny "open secrets" in spite of public knowledge.[29] As she explains in her chapter, a state's refusal to release official information is not always a national security imperative, but the lack of transparency can interfere with both the legal and democratic accountability of government officials.

Accordingly, over the long decade, the militant democracy's rule *by* law has become less constrained by the rule *of* law, while its politics is increasingly marked by obfuscations and contradictions: identifiable security risks multiply and become ever more unpredictable, the extraordinary is increasingly ordinary, and human rights are valid only until national security outweighs them. In the securitized world of the militant democracy, the state more readily violates human rights to counter the never-ending threats that only it can see; everyone knows that it does; politicians know that everyone knows that it does; yet both the public and the politicians overlook the contradictions between what the militant democracy says and does in providing security. Over time, these contradictions will only beget more contradictions: a quest for an unattainable peace in spite of permanent war, the protection of a free society through ever-tighter state control, and trust in a state that is ever more militant and less democratic. At present, it is unclear just how much the proliferation of extraordinary measures has actually damaged or already reflects changes in pre-9/11 liberal norms. However, if we do not sort out the resulting contradictions soon, they may well one day collapse into paradox: the militant democracy will become the biggest threat to the security it is meant to provide.

CONCLUSION: THE ENEMY WITHIN US

Behind this paradox lurks yet another, from which we and the militant democracy might find it harder to escape: a fundamental re-conceptualization of the relationship between the individual and the state, with uncertain implications for liberal democracy, as we know it. *If* this long decade stretches further into the future, the greatest danger is that the public itself—obsessed by fear of the enemy among us, forgetting all but the need for greater protection, and becoming utterly inured to now meaningless contradictions between old norms and new realities—collectively becomes both "risk engendering" and "risk running," a process that Clive Walker suggests is already happening.[30] This paradox feeds and is, in turn, fed by the one above, that of the militant democracy that is all at once the provider and destroyer of our security. Faced with the simultaneously risk-engendering/risk-running public that fears and demands protection from itself, the militant democracy has no choice but to give the public what it wants: it must monitor and control its own population. From this perspective, then, Edward Snowden's shocking revelations in 2013 about the massive scale of clandestine American and British data surveillance and collection programs did more than create a political scandal; they previewed the real possibilities of a future, security-obsessed dystopia premised on fear and control.

If Walker is right – and as Edward Snowden's leaks about American and British mass surveillance suggest – we might already be moving beyond the simplistic us-versus-them mentality that arose in the first years after 9/11. It could now be that everyone is on the path to being both a potential victim and a potential terrorist; if so, we really will no longer be able to tell *us* from *them*. Each of us will have then ceased being a morally autonomous stakeholder in a political society, instead becoming mere objects that pose risks and merit collective control under the aegis of the ever-vigilant state. We will have come to fear ourselves and our own freedom. This result is not inevitable, as we—as well as our politicians—can still renew our commitments to liberal values without losing the security that we need from the state, even in a reinvigorated form. Scheinin, in this book's epilogue, is confident that we can achieve this. However, if not, we must then face the conundrum as to whether militant democracy, fully matured, must necessarily be an illiberal one; if total security is ever really possible, the costs might be too terrible to bear. This, then, appears to be the leitmotif of the long decade: the paradoxical insecurity that the anxious quest for safety can bring.

NOTES

* Associate Professor of Comparative Constitutional Law, University of Copenhagen Faculty of Law.

1. Merriam-Webster Dictionary, *online at* http://www.merriam-webster.com/dictionary/panic?show=1&t=1345125035.
2. Oren Gross, "Security vs. Liberty: On Emotions and Cognition," Chapter 3 in this volume.
3. Manuel Perez-Rivas, "Bush vows to rid the world of 'evil-doers'" CNN (16 September 2001), online at CNN,http://edition.cnn.com/2001/US/09/16/gen.bush.terrorism/.
4. See Mark Tushnet, "Defending *Korematsu*?: Reflections on Civil Liberties in Wartime" (2003) *Wisc. L. Rev.* 273.
5. Eric Posner and Adrian Vermeule, *Terror in the Balance: Security, Liberty, and the Courts* (New York: Oxford University Press, 2007); Adrian Vermeule, "Security and Liberty: Critiques of the Tradeoff Thesis," Chapter 2 in this volume.
6. Amnon Lev, "The War on Terrorism and International Law: Towards a Continental Divide," Chapter 5 in this volume.
7. Victor V. Ramraj, "Counter-Terrorism's Engagement with Transnational Legality," Chapter 7 in this volume; Kaarlo Tuori, "A European Security Constitution?," Chapter 6 in this volume.
8. *A and Others v Secretary of State for the Home Department*, [2004] UKHL 56.
9. "AFTER THE ATTACKS; Bush's Remarks to Cabinet and Advisors" The New York Times (13 September 2011), online at http://www.nytimes.com/2001/09/13/us/after-the-attacks-bush-s-remarks-to-cabinet-and-advisers.html.
10. Ibid.
11. "Britain 'at war with terrorism'" BBC News (16 September 2001), online at BBC News, http://news.bbc.co.uk/2/hi/uk_news/politics/1545411.stm.
12. See *Youngstown Sheet & Tube Co.* v. *Sawyer*, 343 U.S. 579, 635 (1952) (J. Jackson, concurring).
13. Mark Tushnet, "Legal and Political Constitutionalism, and the Response to Terrorism," Chapter 8 in this volume.
14. Fiona de Londras, "Guantanamo Bay, the Rise of the Courts and the Revenge of Politics," Chapter 9 in this volume.
15. Jens Elo Rytter, "Terrorist Threats and Judicial Deference," Chapter 13 in this volume.

16. Patrick Wintour, "Blair vows to root out extremism" The Guardian (6 August 2005), online at The Guardian, http://www.guardian.co.uk/politics/2005/aug/06/terrorism.july7.
17. Simon Jeffery, "The rules of the game are changing" The Guardian (5 August 2005), online at The Guardian, http://www.guardian.co.uk/uk/2005/aug/05/july7.uksecurity5.
18. These phrases are attributable, respectively, to the former CIA director Michael Hayden, former secretary of defense Donald Rumsfeld, and former vice-president Dick Cheney.
19. See, for example, Karl Loewenstein, "Militant Democracy and Fundamental Rights, I" (1937) 31(no. 3) *The American Political Science Review* 417, and "Militant Democracy and Fundamental Rights, II" (1937) 31(no. 4) *The American Political Science Review* 638.
20. The U.S. Supreme Court upheld this ban in *Holder* v. *Humanitarian Law Project*, 130 S.Ct. 2705 (2010).
21. Terrorism Act 2006, § 1.
22. *Kadi & Al Barakaat International Foundation v. Council and Commission* (C-402/05 and C-415/05), [2008] ECR I-6351.
23. Anti-terrorism, Crime and Security Act 2001, § 23.
24. Prevention of Terrorism Act 2005.
25. Hamdi v. Rumsfeld, 542 U.S. 507 (2004); Rasul v. Bush, 542 U.S. 466 (2004); Hamdan v. Rumsfeld, 548 U.S. 557 (2006); Boumediene v. Bush, 553 U.S. 723 (2008).
26. See *Military Commissions Act of 2006*, Pub. L. No. 109-366, 120 Stat. 2600 (17 October 2006); *Military Commissions Act of 2009*, Pub. L. No. 111-84, 123 Stat. 2190 (28 October 2009); and *National Defense Authorization Act for Fiscal Year 2012*, Pub. L. No. 112-81, 125 Stat. 1298 (31 December 2011).
27. Gabor Rona, "Views from Mars, Views from Venus: Minding the Gap between What We Say and What We Do on Terrorism," Chapter 15 in this volume.
28. Martin Scheinin, "Human Rights and Counter-Terrorism: Lessons from a Long Decade," epilogue to this volume.
29. Amanda Jacobsen, "Open Secrets in U.S. Counter-Terrorism Policy," Chapter 14 in this volume.
30. Iain Cameron, "The Influence of 9/11 on Swedish Anti-Terrorism Policy and Measures," Chapter 12 in this volume.

PART ONE:

Fear and the Security Agenda

CHAPTER 2

Security and Liberty: Critiques of the Trade-Off Thesis

ADRIAN VERMEULE*

Both before 9/11, and in the decade since, national security and counterterrorism policy have repeatedly encountered security-liberty trade-offs. A few examples:

- The 9/11 Commission found that the attacks could have been prevented by removing the "wall" that blocked intelligence-sharing between law enforcement agencies;[1]
- The Commission also found that more aggressive screening and profiling at immigration points could have prevented the attacks;[2]
- Given a "laxly regulated international market [in] ground-to-air missiles or computer circuits for roadside bombs," stricter regulation of a range of transactions in technology becomes more valuable as the security threats posed by such transactions increase;[3]
- The CIA's former head of counterterrorism, Jose Rodriguez, stated that the use of "enhanced interrogation techniques" produced critical information that made it possible for U.S. forces to kill Osama Bin Laden.[4]

Of these, the first two arose before 9/11, the third and fourth after it; the first, second, and fourth involve trade-offs between security and "civil liberties" as traditionally understood, while the third involves a trade-off between security and economic liberty or free markets. Even if all these examples turned out to be wrong, there are a thousand more waiting in the wings, given the very long history of conflicts between the imperatives of war-making or domestic security, on the one hand, and liberties such as free speech, free political association, and privacy on the other.[5] Security-liberty trade-offs are ubiquitous.

Terror in the Balance: Security, Liberty and the Courts offered a simple framework for understanding such cases: the "tradeoff thesis."[6] Here is the picture:

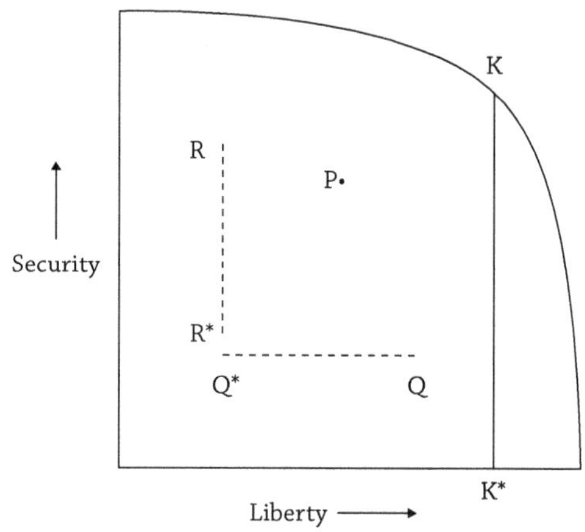

Figure 2.1: The Tradeoff Thesis.

As Figure 2.1 illustrates,[7] just as production and allocation of any two goods in a toy model economy can be depicted as constrained by a possibility frontier, so too counter-terrorism policy can be understood as constrained by a security-liberty possibility frontier. At any point on the frontier, security cannot be increased without corresponding decreases in liberty, and vice versa. At points below the frontier—for example, the point marked as P in Figure 2.1—either security and liberty can be increased without sacrificing any of the other, and indeed both can be improved simultaneously. Points beyond the frontier represent policies that cannot be attained, given currently available technology and resources. In a world of scarcity, there are some combinations of security and liberty, some states that combine expansive freedom with perfect safety, which society will simply be unable to attain.

The level and shape of the frontier are not fixed; they change over time, as exogenous threats wax and wane. Moreover, the level and shape of the frontier may change because society shifts resources toward or away from security policy, thus expanding or contracting the set of feasible measures. When changes of this sort occur, policies that were previously on the frontier (or beyond it, and thus infeasible) might fall below the frontier, and conversely. The trade-off thesis is unaffected by such changes; whatever the level and shape of the frontier at any given time, there will still be some such constraint on feasible security policies.

There are many things the trade-off thesis is not:

- It is *not* an empirical claim that any given security policy or the whole set of policies lies on the frontier. That is, the thesis is entirely compatible with an argument that any given policy lies below the frontier and could thus be improved on both margins. I return to this point shortly;
- It is *not* a normative argument that, somehow, it is a good thing to trade off security and liberty (a bizarre sort of argument to make); of course more of both is better when possible, but we cannot always have more of both. The normative significance of the trade-off thesis is indirect: because the trade-off frontier at any given time constrains the feasible set of security policies, the maxim "ought implies can" will come into play;
- It is *not* a normative argument for evaluating security policy by a moral criterion of consequentialism in general or welfarism in particular. In *Terror in the Balance*, we combine the trade-off thesis with an independent welfarist and consequentialist argument that government ought to choose combinations of security and liberty that maximize aggregate welfare, adjusting security and liberty over time until the marginal contribution of each to aggregate social welfare is equal. However, nothing in the identification of the possibility frontier commits anyone to that approach. One might, for example, hold a deontological theory of rights according to which it is impermissible for society to choose policies such that liberty falls below the line K—K* in Figure 2.1, even if security and (perhaps) aggregate welfare would thereby be increased. For anyone holding such a theory, the significance of the trade-off thesis is entirely unchanged: it is still the case that at some point on the frontier, here the point K, increasing security would require decreasing liberty;
- It is *not* an argument that safety is better than freedom or that safety should be strictly maximized;
- It does *not* presuppose that the government necessarily chooses optimal security policies, or that courts and legislatures should defer to executive branch officials with respect to such policies.

The last argument is one that *Terror in the Balance* does advance—the "deference thesis" holds that "the executive branch, not Congress or the judicial branch, should make the tradeoff between liberty and security"[8]—but analytically the trade-off thesis and the deference thesis are entirely independent. One might well subscribe to the former while denying the latter.[9]

In light of its limited character and purpose, the trade-off thesis ought to be uncontroversial. Oddly enough, it is anything but. A half-dozen leading scholars have criticized the notion of security-liberty trade-offs,[10] arguing that the idea is conceptually incoherent, empirically ungrounded, or normatively pernicious.[11] In some cases, the intended scope or thrust of the critiques is ambiguous; the authors seemingly question the trade-off thesis itself, but then offer more limited claims or in some other way draw in their horns. The aim of this chapter is to understand these critiques, to evaluate them, and to sort the wheat from the chaff.

There is a great deal of wheat to be harvested, or so this chapter claims; the critics of the trade-off thesis make a number of excellent and important points about security policy and the institutions that should be charged with formulating and implementing it. Yet this chapter also claims that these critiques miss their main target (to the extent that it is their main target; again, the precise intention and scope of several of the critiques is ambiguous or unclear). None of them undermine the basic idea that there exists a trade-off frontier that constrains security policy and that sometimes forces policymakers to trade off security, suitably defined, against liberty, suitably defined. The problem with the critiques, excellent though they are in many cases, is that they are all consistent with the trade-off thesis rightly understood, even though their proponents sometimes seem to understand them as posing fundamental challenges to that thesis.

POLICYMAKING BELOW THE FRONTIER

A central theme of many of the critiques is that "the tradeoff thesis implies that whenever liberty is curtailed, security is automatically increased."[12] More generally, the critics portray the trade-off thesis as claiming that "the risk of terror *necessarily* justifies losses in liberty."[13] In fact the trade-off thesis implies nothing of the kind. A glance at Figure 2.1 shows that there are many points such as P that lie below the frontier, and at all these points, security might be increased with no harm to liberty, or even with an increase in liberty. Conversely, beginning with policy at Q and moving along the line to Q*, liberty has been curtailed without any increase in security; and beginning with policy at R and moving to R*, security is reduced without any gain in liberty. There just is no "hydraulic" picture of security and liberty underlying the trade-off thesis.[14]

Analytically, then, this class of critiques beats against an open door. Identifying issues where it is plausible that an alternative policy could improve on both security and liberty (somehow defined),[15] perhaps because current policy is myopic or results from cognitive biases, agency problems, or other political distortions, amounts to identifying points that are below the frontier. However, that is no challenge to the existence of the frontier itself.

Versions of this mistake are ubiquitous.[16] In place of an array of quotations, an article in the *American Political Science Review*, entitled "Is There a Trade-Off between Security and Liberty? Executive Bias, Privacy Protections, and Terrorism Prevention," represents a fair sample of the literature.[17] The article offers a model in which the counter-terrorism agencies are imperfect agents and thus pursue policies that do not maximize social welfare. The model shows conditions under which these strategic agencies might select a policy that lies below the frontier, such that "reducing privacy protections can lead to less security from terrorism."[18] So far so fine, but the article inflates this possibility theorem into a larger claim, insinuating without ever quite stating that—as the article's very title implies—there is something wrong with the "dominant paradigm," which "posits a fundamental trade-off between civil liberties and security from terrorism."[19] Nonetheless, the points that can be derived from the article's model fit comfortably within the trade-off thesis; they are not any sort of threat to it.

Part of the confusion here probably results from stating the issues imprecisely, as when the article describes the claim it means to undermine as holding that "democratic societies and their government face inevitable trade-offs [between security and liberty]," or when another work depicts the trade-off thesis as claiming that "the risk of terror *necessarily* justifies losses in liberty."[20] The trade-off thesis does claim that, in a world of scarce resources, there necessarily exists a frontier at which security-liberty trade-offs are unavoidable. That is *not* the same as claiming that it is necessarily the case that any increase in security requires a reduction in liberty. That further claim would hold only if all policies necessarily lie on the frontier, a bizarre claim to make and one that to my knowledge has never been made.

The best version of this critique might run as follows: "True, it is analytically possible or even necessary that there is a trade-off frontier that constrains feasible security policy. Yet in our world, under our government, most or almost all of the observable policies lie below the frontier; most or almost all of our security policies are badly designed, unnecessarily sacrificing liberty or missing opportunities to increase security without curtailing liberty. We, or some of us, are far more likely to commit the error of believing that policies lie on the trade-off frontier when they do not, than the opposite error of believing that they lie below the frontier when they actually lie on it."

Such a claim is entirely unobjectionable in principle. It yields no critique of the trade-off thesis, but it does helpfully raise the institutional issues that *Terror in the Balance* discussed under the heading of the deference thesis. Similarly, what the model discussed above does show is that there exist conditions under which executive agencies might choose policies that unnecessarily sacrifice privacy or liberty; as such, the model offers a point against the deference thesis, not the trade-off thesis.

DISTRIBUTIVE CONSIDERATIONS

Another important line of critique points out that the trade-off thesis says nothing about the *distribution* of security and liberty.[21] Any given security policy might reduce the liberties of A in order to enhance the security of B, or vice versa. In the most general version of the critique, we must always ask whose security is being traded off against whose liberty.[22] In more specific versions, critics worry that majorities will externalize the costs of security onto ethnic minorities, aliens, or noncitizens, in effect taking the latter groups' liberties for public use (and without just compensation).[23] The ultimate result will be security policies that do not maximize overall welfare or that violate the rights of disfavored groups, or both.

In the general version, the critique rightly underscores a well-known limitation of aggregative social welfare functions, which are in principle indifferent to the distribution of welfare among parties and in that sense do not respect "the distinction between persons."[24] I have nothing new to say about that issue, nor does *Terror in the Balance*. However, this familiar debate has nothing to do with the trade-off thesis, which by itself does not commit one to aggregate welfarism. Respect the distinction between persons as much as you like, and the nature of the world will still be such that scarcity places constraints on the feasible combinations of liberty and security. Moreover, the general version of the point has nothing to do with *security and liberty* in particular. If the relevant goods were guns and butter, the arguments would run exactly the same way.[25] So here too, it is not that the critique is wrong, but it is no critique of the trade-off thesis, and is not well tailored to the context of security policy in any event.

The particular versions of the critique raise two further issues. One issue is whether government agencies charged with formulating security policies will act so as to maximize aggregate welfare or not. The particular versions of the critique offer arguments that, under identifiable and predictable conditions, they will not do so; instead they will pander to majorities, perhaps for electoral reasons, harming minorities in the process. *Terror in the*

Balance discusses that possibility under the heading of "democratic failure," and offers reasons for thinking that the problem is not likely to be a serious one, and that there is nothing that courts can do about it anyway.[26] Whatever the (de)merits of those arguments, they go to the deference thesis and to the institutional allocation of responsibility for security policy, rather than to the trade-off thesis.

The second and deeper issue is the old question about whose rights or welfare government must take into account when making decisions and how. Within the body of citizens, there are many possible distributions of liberty and security. With respect to noncitizens, the question is about the "scope of the demos," in the parlance of democratic theory. Do aliens have interests that must be counted or rights that must be recognized? Does it matter whether they are resident aliens or nonresident foreigners? The questions are legion, but they are also not unique to the trade-off thesis, or for that matter to welfarist or consequentialist policy analysis. Deontological theories have to decide the identity of rights-bearers just as much as consequentialist and welfarist theories have to decide whose welfare will count and for how much.

The questions are also not unique to security policy.[27] When choosing among the feasible combinations of guns and butter, a welfarist social planner must decide whose welfare counts; under certain theories of rights, a government that wishes to respect "positive" individual rights to a certain amount of butter must decide whose putative rights count. None of this implies that, given a suitably specified set of persons whose rights or welfare must be taken into account—a demos—there is no trade-off frontier that constrains the resulting decisions.

BUDGET CONSTRAINTS

A related issue involves budget constraints, or limitations on the amount of resources that society can devote to maximizing the sum of security and liberty. Some commentators reject the trade-off thesis on the ground that with increased resources, particular policies that are not currently feasible might be made so, thereby enhancing security without reducing liberty, or enhancing liberty without reducing security.[28] This is quite true, and helpfully points out that the level and shape of the security-liberty possibility frontier are not exogenously fixed and immutable; both will change as governments shift resource toward or away from (what might be called) the security sector.

In principle, a welfare-maximizing government will shift resources across sectors so as to equalize the marginal contribution of each sector to social welfare. In the real world, government may not do this, because of political distortions or myopia or any number of other pathologies. Whether or not government acts to maximize social welfare, the most that can be done by allocating more resources to the sector is to push the frontier farther out, or to change the rate of trade-off in desired ways at particular points, thus affecting the shape of the frontier; either of these scenarios is entirely compatible with the trade-off thesis. The trade-off thesis does not entail that the frontier at any given moment must be frozen in place; quite the contrary, one of the motivations for the thesis is to focus attention on how exogenous shocks, such as a terrorist attack, or other changes to the political and technological environment affect optimal security policy over time.

Furthermore, it must be said that commentators who (implicitly) relax the budget constraint in the security sector rarely discuss the opportunity cost of shifting resources to that sector. At any given level of social output, doing so requires shifting resources away from other sectors; it would be useful to hear whether those resources are to come from defense budgets, education, social welfare programs, funding for courts and public defenders, or some other sector. Specificity of this sort would clarify the unavoidable "cost of rights"[29] problem that lurks behind proposals to enhance civil or economic liberties, at any given level of security, and would equally clarify the costs of enhanced security, at any given level of liberty.

"SECURITY" AND "LIBERTY"

Many of the critiques point out that liberty is itself a precondition for, or a component of, security.[30] Without liberty, who can feel secure? If one has no civil liberties—if government agents can intrude at will—the consequence will be political subordination, psychological anxiety, and legal insecurity. This is the mirror image of a claim associated with, inter alia, political theorists of the New Deal, including President Franklin Delano Roosevelt himself; these theorists emphasized that without security there is no true liberty.[31]

From the standpoint of the trade-off thesis, all this is entirely unobjectionable. To see why, imagine a version of Figure 2.1 in which the vertical axis is labeled "Security Type I" and the horizontal axis is labeled "Security Type II." Type I security is the sort of security that people want when they are worried about being blown up by Al Qaeda. Type II security is the sort of security that people want when they are worried about intrusions from government officials. The trade-off thesis would then claim that there exists a frontier at which enhancing Type I security requires diminishing Type II security, and vice versa. Alternatively, we might distinguish between security understood as physical safety, on the one hand, and liberty understood as autonomy, on the other, and then analyze trade-offs between safety and liberty (with threats to either value potentially coming from either government or terrorists). Any of these enterprises could be accommodated with suitable reframing of the possibility frontier. Getting the labels for the axes right is conceptually important and of great interest to philosophers, but does not affect the substance of the issues for present purposes.

SECURITY-SECURITY TRADE-OFFS

Another critique points out that there are security-security trade-offs.[32] (The critique is silent about liberty-liberty trade-offs;[33] with appropriate modifications, however, mirror-image points apply). That is, a given policy might increase security against terrorism on one margin, while decreasing it on another. Because of this possibility of countervailing risks, it can be perversely counterproductive to adopt maxims such as "better safe than sorry." This argument applies to security policy a basic point usually offered against so-called "precautionary principles" in the regulation of risks involving health, the environment, and other domains: "erring on the side of safety" is an incoherent program, because there are risks of harm stemming from both action and inaction.[34]

This critique is analytically airtight, but who denies it? Who or what is the target, apart from some muddled pronouncements by that notable decision theorist, Dick Cheney?[35] Needless to say, serious arguments for maximizing "security at all costs" are not cited, for they do not exist. The trade-off thesis certainly does not make any such claim. In Figure 2.1, the vertical axis simply represents *net* security after all relevant consequences of a given policy have been taken into account.

The point about security-security trade-offs is an excellent one, and although it is entirely familiar to theorists of risk regulation, it is an important point in the political sense that figures such as Cheney, with their hands on the levers of power, have committed the conceptual blunder that the point seeks to dispel. Yet it too is entirely compatible with the trade-off thesis, rather than some sort of critique of that thesis.

COGNITIVE LIMITATIONS AND DISTORTIONS

A striking claim in the critical literature is that executive agents might do better precisely to the extent that they respond to emergencies by following rules and preestablished protocols, rather than by improvising measures on the fly.[36] The analogy is to medical workers in an emergency room or to first responders such as paramedics and firefighters, all of whom follow clear protocols despite the extreme urgency of the tasks they undertake. Rules, on this view, are enabling rather than constraining; they help agents to manage their own cognitive limitations.

Although the point is excellent, and raises an issue that *Terror in the Balance* should have recognized and discussed, its ultimate merits are unclear. For one thing, rules and protocols themselves may have to be adjusted as new threats arise over time; when a new infectious disease appears, doctors and nurses may need to adjust their procedures, trading off variables such as speed of treatment for a given patient against the safety of other patients and medical personnel. A trade-off will still be made, whether embodied in a rule-like protocol or in an ad hoc standard. Furthermore, as the literature on rules and standards makes clear,[37] emergency protocols can be cast into rules only for routine threats—routine in the sense of frequently recurring.[38] From the standpoint of most patients a heart attack is a terrifyingly unfamiliar crisis, but for the emergency-room doctors it is just another day at the office. Then the question becomes whether and when counter-terror protocols can be routinized, or whether terrorism threats are so protean and variable that rule-bound decision-making is unlikely to work well.

Without delving any further into the merits of these questions, I note only that this critique too is entirely consistent with the trade-off thesis. If rules work better than standards, meaning rules are more likely to move security policy toward the frontier, then hooray for rules; if not, not. If second-order decisions to set rules in advance are more likely to end up producing policy near the frontier than is ad hoc first-order decision-making, by all means let us have second-order decisions. It is unclear whether this critique is intended to undermine the trade-off thesis or as a point within the framework that the thesis sets up, but much of the tone of the critique implies that the trade-off thesis is fundamentally misconceived, perhaps because it is incapable of recognizing the benefits of rules.[39] Yet any such implication would be wrong.

It is likewise with a more general class of claims that governments and security agencies will suffer from cognitive distortions (whether or not they also suffer from politically induced motivational distortions) that will cause them to make poor decisions about counter-terrorism policies.[40] Arguments of that form, plausible and useful though they are, just suggest mechanisms by which security policy might fall below the frontier. They thus amount to arguments *within* the framework established by the trade-off thesis; they do not contradict or undermine it. *Terror in the*

Balance considered similar arguments[41] and there is no reason to rehash the issues here.

TRADE-OFFS AND DEFERENCE

As many of the foregoing examples illustrate, the critical literature systematically tends to conflate the trade-off thesis and the deference thesis. It is a puzzle why that conflation occurs. Critics who make entirely plausible first-order arguments about the justice or merits of particular security policies, or make entirely plausible second-order arguments about which institutions can best be entrusted with formulating the first-order policies, feel compelled to question the trade-off thesis itself, even though that thesis provides, in many cases, the very framework within which their first-order and second-order points are implicitly couched.

The deference thesis is the ground on which debates over the legal, political, and institutional framework for security policy should occur. The trade-off thesis ought to be uncontroversial. The root of all conflict is scarcity, and the cause of many conflicting arguments in the domain of security policy is that by virtue of scarcity there is inevitably some frontier at which we can no longer increase security without decreasing liberty. Although the level and shape of the frontier can be moved around by reallocating social resources, and although there are many important questions to be answered about which institutions are best able to move policy toward the frontier, some such limitation on our possibilities will always constrain us.

CONCLUSION

More than ten years after 9/11, the academic literature on security-liberty trade-offs is in some conceptual disarray. Many works attempt—more or less explicitly—to question or criticize the "image of balance"[42] or the "dominant paradigm"[43] of security-liberty trade-offs. However, these works invariably end up making analytically distinct points; although those points are, in many cases, excellent and useful ones, they do not amount to critiques of the trade-off thesis, whether taken jointly or severally.

In conclusion, a quotation from Jon Elster captures the sensible way to think about such matters:

> I shall address the post-9/11 choices as involving the tradeoff between liberty and security, assuming in a rather abstract way that an agent—call it "society"—is

victim of a terrorist attack that causes it to readjust "its" security and "its" liberty levels. In many ways, this is an extreme simplification.... I believe, nevertheless, that there is a rough-and-ready sense in which a society as a whole may face a security-liberty tradeoff. In the light of innumerable controversies over civil liberty curtailments in wartime as well as during the Cold War..., I find it hard to imagine anyone denying this proposition.[44]

Although, to be sure, it seems that many do want to deny it.

NOTES

* John H. Watson Professor of Law, Harvard Law School; Thanks to Jacob Gersen, Oren Gross, Anders Henriksen, Eric Posner, Mark Tushnet, and the conference participants for helpful comments, and to Janet Kim and Jon Murray for helpful research assistance.

1. See Eric A. Posner and Adrian Vermeule, *Terror in the Balance: Security, Liberty and the Courts* (New York: Oxford University Press, 2007) at 24–25 and sources cited.
2. Ibid.
3. See Stephen Holmes, "In Case of Emergency: Misunderstanding Tradeoffs in the War on Terror" (2009) 97 *Cal. L. Rev.* 301 at 314–15.
4. See "Ex-CIA Counterterror Chief: 'Enhanced Interrogation' Led U.S. to bin Laden," Massimo Calabresi, *Time Magazine*, 4 May 2011, available online at Time, http://swampland.time.com/2011/05/04/did-torture-get-the-us-osama-bin-laden.
5. See Daniel Farber, ed., *Security v. Liberty: Conflicts between Civil Liberties and National Security in American History* (Russell Sage Foundation, 2008).
6. Posner and Vermeule, *supra* note 1, at 21–41.
7. Figure 2.1 is just a more elaborate version of Figure 1.1 in Posner and Vermeule, ibid. at 27.
8. Posner and Vermeule, ibid. at 5.
9. Oren Gross's contribution to this volume conflates these two logically independent issues at a number of points.
10. See, for example, David Cole, "No Reason to Believe: Radical Skepticism, Emergency Power, and Constitutional Constraint" (2008) 75 *U. Chi. L. Rev.* 1329 at 1335–36; Thomas P. Crocker, "Torture, with Apologies" (2008) 86 *Tex. L. Rev.* 569 at 575, and 579; Oren Gross, "Security vs. Liberty: An Imbalanced Balancing," unpublished manuscript, available online at Social Science Research Network, http://papers.ssrn.com/sol3/papers.cfm?abstract_id=1471634; Stuart Macdonald, "The Unbalanced Imagery of Anti-terrorism Policy" (2009) 18 *Cornell J.L. and Pub. Pol.* 519; Deborah Pearlstein, "Form and Function in the National Security Constitution" (2009) 41 *Conn. L. Rev.* 1549 at 1592–95; Jeremy Waldron, "Security and Liberty: The Image of Balance" (2003) 11 *J. Polit. Phil.* 191 Not all of these explicitly criticize Posner and Vermeule, ibid., although most do; Another frequent target of the critiques is the discussion of security-liberty trade-offs in Richard A. Posner, *Not a Suicide Pact* (New York: Oxford University Press, 2006); Waldron's article, ibid., appeared earlier than either of the two main targets and thus discusses the general idea of balancing security against liberty.

11. An intermediate case is Eyal Zamir and Barak Medina, *Law, Economics, and Morality* (New York: Oxford University Press, 2010) at 128–34, which accepts the basic idea of trade-offs, but repeats some of the standard critiques.
12. Holmes, *supra* note 3 at 317; see also Cole, *supra* note 10 at 1335.
13. Zamir and Medina, *supra* note 11 at 134 (emphasis original). At another point, Zamir and Medina claim that according to the trade-off thesis, the state always operates at the possibility frontier. They cite Posner and Vermeule, *supra* note 1 at 26–27. But see Posner and Vermeule, ibid. at 26 ("Of course, not every issue of security policy presents such a tradeoff.") and 33 ("it is certainly possible that policy might be stuck below the frontier"). What *Terror in the Balance* does argue is the separate empirical thesis that, most of the time, governments in advanced democracies operate at or near the frontier. However, that thesis can be false even if the trade-off thesis is true, as the two theses pose independent issues.
14. See Holmes, *supra* note 3 at 317; Macdonald, *supra* note 10 at 522 (citing Andrew Ashworth, "Security, Terrorism and the Value of Human Rights," in *Security and Human Rights*, ed. Benjamin J. Goold and Liora Lazarus (Portland, Oregon: Hart, 2007) at 203, 208.
15. See, for example, Pearlstein, *supra* note 10 at 1592–95.
16. Gross's contribution to this volume amounts to a protracted example.
17. Tiberiu Dragu, "Is There a Tradeoff between Security and Liberty? Executive Bias, Privacy Protections, and Terrorism Prevention" (2011) 105(1) *American Political Science Review* 64.
18. Ibid. at 66.
19. Ibid. at 73.
20. Zamir and Medina, *supra* note 11 at 134 (emphasis original).
21. See, for example, Waldron, *supra* note 10 at 200–04.
22. See, for example, Holmes, *supra* note 3 at 316.
23. Cole, *supra* note 10 at 1347–52; James McDonald, "Democratic Failure and Emergencies: Myth or Reality?" (2007) 93 *Va. L. Rev.* 1785.
24. John Rawls, *A Theory of Justice*, rev. ed. (Cambridge, Mass.: Harvard University Press, 1999) at 24.
25. See also L. Rush Atkinson, "Guns, Butter and Judges: Judicial Frameworks for Cases Implicating Security-Wealth Tradeoffs" (2010) 85 *N.Y.U. L. Rev.* 587.
26. See Posner and Vermeule, *supra* note 1 at 87–129.
27. The same goes for Gross's attempt to make an issue of "interpersonal comparability" (in his contribution to this volume). This is a stock issue in the literature, but again it has nothing at all to do with security and liberty in particular. The same questions arise with respect to any pair of goods; consistent skepticism about interpersonal comparisons yields the conclusion that all attempts to compare social allocations of goods across persons fail. (I believe that even to state such a conclusion is to refute it, but that goes to the merits of the issues, which I need not enter into here). Gross has really raised a familiar and more general issue that fails to engage the subject of the volume.
28. See, for example, Macdonald, *supra* note 10 at 536–37.
29. Stephen Holmes and Cass R. Sunstein, *The Cost of Rights: Why Liberty Depends on Taxes* (New York: W.W. Norton, 1999) at 48.
30. See the discussion and sources cited in Jeremy Waldron, "Safety and Security" (2006) 85 *Neb. L. Rev.* 454 at 503–06.

31. See Adrian Vermeule, "A New Deal for Civil Liberties: An Essay in Honor of Cass R. Sunstein" (2008) 43 *Tulsa L. Rev.* 921.
32. Holmes, *supra* note 3 at 318–23.
33. See Vermeule, *supra* note 31.
34. See, for example, Jonathan Weiner, "Precaution in a Multirisk World" in Dennis J. Paustenbach, ed., *Human and Ecological Risk Assessment: Theory and Practice* (New York: Wiley-Interscience, 2002); Cass R. Sunstein, *Laws of Fear: Beyond the Precautionary Principle* (Cambridge: Cambridge University Press, 2005).
35. See Holmes, *supra* note 3 at 320–21.
36. Ibid.
37. See Louis Kaplow, "Rules versus Standards: An Economic Analysis" (1992) 42 *Duke L.J.* 557.
38. This is clearly recognized in Holmes, *supra* note 3 at 305–06.
39. See the ambivalent or ambiguous discussion in Holmes, ibid. at 312–18, which acknowledges that "there is something to the idea of a liberty-security tradeoff" (at 314), yet also states that "[t]he 'tradeoff thesis' functions as a mystification" (at 316). See also Stephen Holmes, *The Matador's Cape: America's Reckless Response to Terror* (New York: Cambridge Univ. Press, 2007) at 7–8 ("Is it really possible to increase American security in the war on terror by curbing the right of American citizens to examine and criticize their government? Recent experience suggests the contrary. . . .").
40. Many commentators offer versions of this claim; Gross's contribution to this volume is an example.
41. See, for example, Posner and Vermeule, *supra* note 1 at 61–68.
42. Waldron, *supra* note 10
43. Dragu, *supra* note 17.
44. Jon Elster, "Emotions and Behavioral Economics," unpublished manuscript, available online at Ragnar Frisch Centre for Economic Research, University of Oslo, http://www.frisch.uio.no/behave_seminar/papers/Elster.pdf at 18.

CHAPTER 3

Security vs. Liberty: On Emotions and Cognition

OREN GROSS*

In his contribution to this volume, Adrian Vermeule defends the "tradeoff thesis" that he and Eric Posner developed in their book *Terror in the Balance*.[1] The metaphor of balancing and the use of balancing tests have been invoked so regularly since the terrorist attacks of September 11, 2001, to explain the need for a trade-off between liberty and security that they have become "ambient feature[s] of our political environment."[2] In *Terror in the Balance*, Posner and Vermeule argue similarly that there exists a security-liberty frontier along which trade-offs between security and liberty take place. The allocation of security and liberty anywhere along the frontier is Pareto efficient (i.e., any further increase in one good can only be done at the expense of the other).[3] According to Posner and Vermeule, the problem is one of optimization (i.e., choosing the point along the frontier that maximizes the joint benefits of security and liberty).[4] As is the case with similar social utility frontiers, the security-liberty frontier does not inform us, in and of itself, where the optimal trade-off may lie. It is not concerned with such issues as distributive justice or fairness and equality. Those policies, and the points on the frontier that will correspond to them, are to be determined "entirely [by] the values or preferences of the people in the relevant society."[5] Posner and Vermeule emphasize the significance of possible, indeed inevitable, changes in the shape of the security-liberty frontier over time. Thus, "the balance between security and liberty is constantly readjusted as circumstances change. A well-functioning government will contract civil liberties as threats increase. A government that refuses to adjust its policies has simply frozen in the face of the threat. It is pathologically rigid, not enlightened."[6]

Two general categories of assumptions underlie Posner and Vermeule's trade-off thesis and the claims made by its proponents. Conceptually, the trade-off thesis assumes interpersonal comparability. Security and liberty are comparable (albeit not necessarily monetarily commensurate) inasmuch as individuals can assess the relative worth, to themselves, of increases in one and the concomitant decreases in the other. Security and liberty are also interpersonally comparable in the sense that a loss of one to an individual could be compared to an increase in the other to someone else, thus allowing us to measure the trends of overall social welfare.[7] Empirically and institutionally Posner and Vermeule make the dual claims that government is not necessarily less rational and well motivated in times of emergency than during normal times (rather than making the conceptually stronger, and empirically suspect, claim that government is always rational and well motivated) and that courts are less able to police governmental conduct and potential errors during emergencies than during normal times.[8] In other words, government is unlikely to make more errors in responding to emergencies than it makes in normal times, and to the extent that government *does* make more errors when faced with the need to respond to crises, those mistakes are not systematically biased in one direction (i.e., they are not more security-favorable than liberty-enhancing or vice versa). As Posner and Vermeule acknowledge, what they call the "civil libertarian view" may be justified "only if an additional assumption is made, namely, that errors are biased in favor of security in the first place."[9]

This chapter critically examines the trade-off thesis and challenges its basic assumptions through the prism of cognitive theory of decision-making. It argues that the assumption of interpersonal comparability between security and liberty cannot be maintained as the two are neither comparable, in general, nor are they interpersonally comparable in the sense that Posner and Vermeule suggest. Furthermore, it argues that, when faced with violent states of emergency, public officials are likely to be unable to assess accurately the risks facing the nation. In those circumstances an act of balancing between security and liberty—of optimizing the trade-off between the two—is, in fact, likely to be biased in ways that ought, at the very least, to be recognized and accounted for. Significantly, the pressures exerted by acute exigencies on decision-makers (and the public at large), coupled with certain unique features of crisis mentality and thinking, are likely to result in a systematic undervaluation of one interest (liberty) and overvaluation of another (security) so that the ensuing balance would be tilted in favor of security concerns at the expense of individual rights and liberties. This argument does not depend on a further claim that the presence of risk turns individuals and decision-makers into irrational actors. Rather it is of more modest proportions, suggesting that there are certain challenges to the rational actor model that are exacerbated in the context of responding to violent crises. Those challenges suggest that acts of balancing in this context are likely to be systematically biased and that our ability to analyze and measure risk accurately is prone to suffer from endemic distortions. The systematic nature of those biases suggests that failure to address them may turn such mistakes and errors into cognitive pathologies (i.e., decision methods that are not only mistaken but, indeed, irrational).[10]

COGNITIVE THEORY OF DECISION-MAKING UNDER CONDITIONS OF UNCERTAINTY

Individuals operate under certain cognitive limitations and biases that may prevent them from capturing the real probabilities of the occurrence of certain types of risks and uncertainties. Because accurate risk analysis requires information pertaining to both the magnitude of the risk and the probability of that risk materializing, such cognitive limits color our risk assessment and create a strong tilt toward putting undue emphasis on certain potential risks. Although similar observations hold true in a wide variety of areas, the risks involved in acute national crises, in general, and in violent threats, in particular, coupled with other factors that influence decision-making, have a special tendency to trigger such cognitive limitations and biases due not only to their potential magnitude, but mostly to the manner in which they are perceived.

The concept of "bounded rationality" relates to our limited knowledge and computational imperfections and explains our failure to process information perfectly. As Herbert Simon explains it: "The capacity of the human mind for formulating and solving complex problems is very small compared with the size of the problems whose solution is required for objectively rational behavior in the real world—or even for a reasonable approximation to such objective rationality."[11] In fact, even if we did possess all the relevant (and complex) information that is required to formulate and solve complex problems, we might not be able to formulate or solve these problems. Moments of great consternation and upheaval, such as those invoked by the imagery of war and violent crises, accentuate the problems related to our ability to process information and evaluate complex situations. For example, an important element of information processing and analysis is the time needed to investigate consequences and alternatives. Emergencies that are characterized by sudden, urgent, and usually unforeseen events or situations that require immediate action, often without time for prior reflection and consideration, may exacerbate the problems of insufficient time. Such crises tend to lead to an increased reliance on cognitive heuristics—shortcuts that people use when making decisions—as a means to counter the lack of sufficient time to properly evaluate the situation.[12] Posner and Vermeule acknowledge the "undeniable truth" that "during an emergency, the government does not have as much time for making decisions as it usually does, and as a result will make more errors than it usually does." However, they argue that "these errors will be driven by ordinary cognitive limitations [and] thus . . . will be normally distributed."[13] Indeed, the use of heuristics makes perfect sense as it "reduce[s] the time and effort required to make reasonably good judgments and decisions."[14] Being "cognitive misers" individuals utilize shortcuts in order to minimize the effort involved in processing information and make decisions as expedient and painless as possible.[15] However, common heuristics may create patterns of mistaken assessments.[16] "Ordinary cognitive limitations" do not lead to "normal distribution" in "normal times," but in such times it may be that the deviations from normal distribution in which they result are not significant enough to make a difference (whether this is in fact so is beyond the scope of this chapter). Be that as it may, the "normal" patterns of mistaken assessments are further reinforced and are likely to result in a significantly biased distribution of errors in governmental decision-making when these heuristics are applied in times of crisis.

AVAILABILITY, ASYMMETRIC SALIENCE, AND PANICS

The availability heuristic means that individuals tend to link their assessment of the probability of an occurrence of a particular event to their ability to imagine similar events taking place.[17] The easier it is to recall an event—the more familiar we are with it, for example, from personal experience—the more we are likely to overestimate the likelihood of its occurrence in the future.[18] Such events are not merely abstract notions, but rather are tangible and real and thus perceived as more probable. However, experiential familiarity is not a necessary condition for availability. The stronger, the more vivid, and the more salient the images that are associated with a particular event are (that is, the closer they are in space or time, the more emotionally exciting, or the more concrete and "image provoking" they are), the more such events are going to be perceived as likely to occur in the future, even if not experienced personally.[19] The images linked to the September 11, 2001, terrorist attacks—the planes hitting the Twin Towers, the towers crumbling down, firefighters and police officers battling against time, and people jumping to their death—have been exceptionally powerful. Repeated official warnings of pending attacks, the periodic and at times frequent changes in the ill-conceived and ill-executed official color-coded terror alert level,[20] and the prominence of the wars in Afghanistan and Iraq in the public's mind, have increased further the imaginability of various potential hazards and hence their perceived riskiness and the concomitant sense of individual and national insecurity.

Individuals tend to overestimate the likelihood of dramatic events that attract significant media coverage and attention, and underestimate the risks of "mundane" events that are, in fact, more (perhaps even much more) likely. That being the case, we can expect greater attention and public pressure, and consequently more resources, to be directed at controlling, minimizing, insuring against, or preventing the former.[21] Overestimation of the likelihood of such risks would also mean that when put on the balancing scales and compared to other competing interests, we are likely to perceive such risks as weighing the scales down more than they actually ought.

Posner and Vermeule make two claims in rejecting this argument. First, they suggest that the availability heuristic is poorly understood and the evidence supporting it is merely anecdotal.[22] I have misgivings as to this suggestion when viewed against the significant body of literature on the issue. Second, and more significantly, they argue that "the government's violation of civil liberties . . . are [*sic*] just as salient as the terrorist attacks that provoke them. . . . [T]errorist attacks cause people to overestimate the probability of further terrorist attacks, but civil liberties infringements also cause people to overestimate the probability of further infringements."[23] They contrast this state of affairs with environmental disasters that, although salient, may lead to overregulation, the cost of which does not have salience.

The symmetric salience claim—arguing for symmetry between the availabilities of terrorist attacks and of governmental violation of civil liberties—is linked to Posner and Vermeule's assumption of interpersonal comparability between security and liberty. However, both hinge on shaky foundations. First, although the benefits of counter-terrorism policies are widely shared, their costs for civil liberties are more narrowly borne. If a disproportionate part of the costs to civil liberties due to counter-terrorism policies and measures is imposed on discreet and identifiable groups, then there is no reason to believe that such costs will be any more salient for the general public than the costs involved in environmental overregulation.

Second, even if we accept arguendo the symmetric salience argument, we ought to recognize and account for the fact that certain salient events (but not others) may lead to particularly biased responses and reactions, and that it is more likely that terrorist attacks will do so than infringements on civil liberties. Finally, whereas strong governmental responses against terrorism are perceived by the public as socially beneficial, the longer-term costs to individual rights and liberties tend to be overly discounted, leading, once again, to overemphasis on the former and undervaluation of the latter.

The dialectic of "us versus them" allows people to vent anxiety, fear, and anger in the face of actual or perceived danger, and direct negative emotional energies toward groups or individuals clearly identified as different.[24] It also accounts for the greater willingness to confer emergency powers on the government when the "other" is well defined and clearly separable from the members of the community.[25] We allow for more repressive emergency measures when we believe that such powers will not be turned against "us." The portrayal of the sources of danger as "foreign" and terrorists as "others" who are endowed with barbaric characteristics and who are out to destroy us and our way of life is used further to prove the urgent need for radical measures to meet the threat head-on.[26] In these circumstances, balancing takes place not between security and liberty as such, but rather between *our* security and *their* liberty.[27]

Targeting outsiders is likely to incur little political cost for decision-makers. It may even prove to be politically expedient: although the benefits (perceived or real) of fighting terrorism and violence accrue to all members of society, the costs of such actions are borne disproportionately (even exclusively) by a distinct and ostensibly well-defined group of people. Inasmuch as violent emergencies lead to the targeting of "foreigners" who lack the right to vote political officials out of office, the danger is that political leaders will tend to strike a balance disproportionately in favor of security and impose too much of a cost on the target group without facing much resistance (and, in fact, receiving strong support) from the general public.

Research has demonstrated that when people contemplate their mortality they tend to punish or judge more harshly those who violate (or are at least perceived to violate) deeply held cultural values.[28] The specter of our own mortality tends to lead us to make decisions that reinforce deeply held cultural values. To the extent that "foreign" connotes that which is not part of our group cultural identity and is even perceived to threaten it, it is not hard to see why, in the context of terrorist threats, "foreign" will be particularly targeted.[29] It should be noted that the stigma of foreignness is not limited to the distinction of citizenship. Crises tend to lead to focus on identity and solidarity, rather than the formal legal characteristics of citizenship.[30] Citizens who are somehow identified with the enemy are also seen as outsiders, as the internment of American citizens (together with noncitizens) of Japanese ancestry during World War II demonstrated. "Foreign" connotes, therefore, anything that threatens "our way of life."[31] The links to things and influences from abroad can then be easily made.[32] Race, religion, and eventually ideas and beliefs and associations can, and have been, described as "foreign," mobilizing significant popular forces against particular groups. As William Wiecek notes: "Since the early nineteenth century, Americans have nurtured a consistent fear that alien ideologies, as well as the foreigners who were thought to be their vectors, were invading the pristine American republic."[33]

Of course, the distinction between "us" and "them" is not unique to times of great exigency.[34] However, violent crises lead to heightened individual and group consciousnesses.[35] The lines of ins and outs are more clearly and readily drawn. Heightened levels of concern and widespread anxiety over the behavior of a certain group, coupled with an increased level of hostility toward that group, are significant characteristics of moral panics.[36] The behavior of the clearly identifiable group of "enemies" is seen as harmful or threatening to the values and even existence of the society. Internal conformities within the community are exaggerated, while divergence from "outsiders" is emphasized.[37] The division between "us" and "them" is reinforced further by stereotyping that is employed with respect both to insiders and outsiders, emphasizing good, noble, and worthy attributes of the former, and negative traits of the latter who are depicted as "folk devils" and demonized or otherwise described as inhuman.[38]

Thus, even if we accept Posner and Vermeule's symmetric salience argument, we ought to recognize that certain salient events (but not others) may lead to particularly biased responses and reactions. Indeed, it is more likely that terrorist attacks (especially high profile ones) will do so than infringements on civil liberties (or, for that matter, environmental issues). Some salient events, but not others, may become triggering events of moral panics that, in addition to heightened concern and hostility toward an identifiable group or groups are also characterized by public concern that is disproportionate to the levels of threat and potential harm.[39] Terrorism clearly fits the moral panic framework in ways that environmental risks and infringements of civil liberties generally speaking do not.[40]

Social anxiety about environmental risks and even disasters takes a different form than moral panic, which may well affect the character of the responses to it. By and large, risks that are perceived as inherently connected to modern technology and the social production of wealth are linked to what Ulrich Beck calls the "risk society."[41] Although the management of such risks, and even catastrophes, may lead to the "reorganization of power and authority,"[42] there are notable differences between dealing with such risks-of-modernization and threats such as terrorism.[43] Most significant, for our purposes, is the notion of the folk devils. In moral panics scenarios, such as those that may come about as a result of high-profile terrorist attacks, there is a clearly identifiable group of "enemies" against whom social approbation and hatred are targeted. In the case of risks that are byproducts of modernity, that critical element is often (but again, not always) missing. As Sheldon Ungar notes, "[c]laims making on risk society issues is, in comparison with conventional moral panic issues, hedged in by... a comparative absence of distinguishable types of folk devils that evoke deep-seated hostility and fear."[44]

Moral panics create immense pressures on all three branches of government to "do something" about the threat. Violent crises bring about a broadening of the powers of the executive, in general, and law enforcement agencies in particular.[45] They also often result in a rush to legislate: if new offenses are added to the criminal code and the scope of existing offenses are broadened, and if the arsenal of law enforcement agencies is enhanced by putting at their disposal more sweeping powers, the country will be more secure and better able to face the emergency.[46] The need to respond quickly to future threats, as much as the need to assure the public that its government is acting with a vengeance against past and future terrorists, frequently results in legislation that is passed without much debate and at times forgoing normal legislative procedures. As moral panic erupts (facilitated by media exaggeration)[47] and as politicians and legislators engage increasingly in "symbolic alignments" (in which what counts is not the nature of the target, but rather being seen as taking a position against the devil and on the side of angels),[48] the focus is clearly put on a particular threat such as terrorism, caused by a clearly identifiable group of folk devils. Focus is put on it rather than on another type of threat: that is, infringement of civil liberties for "us." Moral panics identify "us" not merely as the good folk, but also as the "victims"[49] of the behavior of deviant "others." This leads to a "tough on crime" mentality among the public, the press, law enforcement agents, politicians, and the courts.[50] Infringements of due process rights and other civil liberties are unlikely to attract as much attention, and so to be as salient, in such an atmosphere—at least in the initial stages of the crisis.

The costs of infringements to civil liberties are not likely to be as salient as the costs of terrorist attacks for yet another reason. Individuals tend to undervalue future benefits and costs when comparing them with present benefits and costs. Whereas strong governmental responses against terrorism are perceived by the public as socially beneficial, the longer-term costs to individual rights and liberties tend to be overly discounted.[51] That such future costs seem mostly intangible and abstract (especially in comparison with the very tangible sense of fear for one's person and loved ones), coupled with a feeling of increased security as a result of governmental action and a sense that government's infringements on civil liberties target "others," only exacerbates this facet of risk assessment.[52] Terrorist attacks are concrete, imaginable events, whereas policies designed to curtail civil liberties seem much more remote, amorphous, and for many citizens, irrelevant to their daily lives.[53]

PROBABILITIES, POSSIBILITIES, AND EMOTIONS

Prospect theory and probability neglect suggest that individuals tend to give excessive weight to low-probability results when the stakes are high enough and the outcomes are particularly bad (or, for that matter, particularly good).[54] In cases of high-magnitude, low-probability risks, attention is directed almost exclusively to outcomes rather than to the likelihood of such outcomes materializing. Individuals perceive risks as more "serious," the more "dreaded" and "unknown" they are, and "as risks become increasingly dreaded and unknown, people demand that something be done about them regardless of the probability of their occurrence, the costs of avoiding the risk, or the benefits of declining to avoid the risk."[55] A risk is "dreaded" if people perceive it to be involuntary and potentially catastrophic, and one over which they lack control. It is "unknown" if it is new and not well understood, among other things. Terrorist attacks are "dreaded" risks and as such are considered to be of an especially serious nature.[56] At the same time, the range of "modern" terrorist threats creates what Kai Erikson calls a "new species of trouble" that makes analytical risk assessment extremely difficult and increases our reliance on affective assessment.[57]

Posner and Vermeule argue that "a standard view is that people ignore low-probability risks and that elected officials with short time horizons ignore remote ones; on this account, government will probably do too little to prevent terrorist threats, not too much."[58] Yet, in the context of high-magnitude, low-probability risks, individuals often demonstrate a diametrically opposite behavior, failing to assess at all the probability that a certain scenario will materialize. They instead focus exclusively on the worst-case scenario. Driven by a "powerful sense of cultural pessimism about society's ability to manage high-consequence risks to its security" a movement is underway away from thinking about risks in terms of probabilities toward a more "possibilistic" assessment of risks and threats. This movement is driven by institution and speculation rather than calculation.[59] Such possibilistic thinking, which is linked to a vulnerability-led attitude to contemporary crises, routinizes the expectation of worst possible outcomes, thus leading to the "occasional demand for a restrained and low-key response to the risk of terrorism [to be] overwhelmed by the alarmist narratives of worst-case scenario."[60] The sense that we may lack the information to calculate the likelihood of future (major) terrorist attacks thus leads to a worst-case analysis that, in turn, reinforces the narratives of fear of terrorism.[61] Probability neglect has been famously captured by former Vice President Dick Cheney's statement: "If there's a one percent chance that Pakistani scientists are helping Al Qaeda build or develop a nuclear weapon, we have to treat it as a certainty in terms of our response."[62] Such predictions are especially potent, and at the same time likely to be biased, when the expected outcome is "affect rich," as when it involves not merely a serious loss, but one that produces particularly strong emotions.[63]

The fact that violent crises breed very strong emotions, and that those emotions are particularly subject to emotional contagion (more on that below), increases the likelihood of distortions in another important way. Posner and Vermeule argue that strong emotions such as fear need not be construed as interfering with cognition and rational decision-making. Rather, fear may be seen to enhance the decision-maker's senses and provide motivation to act where such motivation is inappropriately lacking or is otherwise suboptimal, thus playing a constructive role in responding to crises.[64] They suggest that in emergencies fear may replace governmental complacency and stimulate public officials to action.[65]

The "dual process" theory of thinking, knowing, and information processing suggests that emotions are part of "System 1" (the "experiential system"), which is "fast, automatic, effortless, associative, and often emotionally charged," as contrasted with "System 2" (the "analytic system"), which is "slower, serial, effortful, and deliberately controlled."[66] As a general matter, System 1, which incorporates heuristic-based reasoning, is more error-prone than System 2,[67] and in cases where the outputs of the two systems conflict "people will often be better off if they can accomplish an analytic system override of the System 1-triggered output.... [I]n cases of response conflict, override is a statistically good bet."[68] Affective responses and the use of cognitive heuristics to deal with situations, actions, or other individuals (i.e., responses that belong in System 1) happen rapidly and automatically.[69] Such affective responses also guide, and frame, information processing and judgment by the analytic system and serve as an orienting mechanism for the deliberative processes that take place in System 2.[70] To the extent that violent crises invoke strong, even extreme, emotional responses that are likely to be amplified throughout society and groups of decision-makers, biases and errors that taint System 1 are likely to carry over and distort our long-term deliberative capacity working strongly against a possible, and statistically beneficial, override.[71] Once opinions about the risk of future terrorist attacks are formed, decision-makers and the public at large are likely to seek evidence that will further confirm their initial assessments and to reject and exclude relevant evidence that may contradict such assessments, leading to further entrenchment of mistakes.[72]

GROUP POLARIZATION AND ITS EFFECTS ON DECISION-MAKING DURING EMERGENCIES

Few situations can solidify broad national consensus behind the government. Violent crises are paradigmatic consensus-generating events. Moved by perceptions of substantial physical threat, motivated by growing personal fear of being the next victim, and frustrated by the continuance of terrorist activities, the public "rallies 'round the flag."[73] As James Madison observed, constitutions originated in the midst of great danger that led to "an enthusiastic confidence of the people in their patriotic leaders, which stifled the ordinary diversity of opinions on great national questions."[74] Significantly, such consensus is not merely about the nature of the threat facing the nation, but also about the identification of a particular group, the "devil folks," whose behavior and actions are deemed the causes for the threat and harm.[75] In addition, consensus may result in group polarization on both the level of the public at large and of distinct groups of experts: "When like-minded people deliberate with one another, they typically end up accepting a more extreme version of the views with which they began."[76] Such consensus and group polarization stifle robust debate about the responses to the crisis and help explain not only such phenomena as rushed legislation but also, more generally, the general acquiescence, indeed support, for the expansion, extension, and enhancement of governmental powers.

Of the various explanations for group polarization, four are of special significance in our context: namely, emotional contagion, social interactions, overconfidence, and "groupthink." Strong emotions such as anxiety, fear, hysteria, panic, outrage, and xenophobia are invoked by violent crises.

Such emotions carry a pronounced effect on people's perceptions of, and reactions to, risk becuase they act as multipliers of (perceived) likelihood of risk.[77] That effect is further amplified as a result of emotional contagion. Individuals are highly responsive to emotions expressed by others. Some emotions, such as fear, are particularly contagious.[78]

People also shape their opinions (particularly their expressed opinions) and adjust them so as to be in sync with the dominant position within the relevant reference group as they like to "belong" and to be favorably perceived and counted by others.[79] This is especially so the less people feel that they know about a certain issue; they would tend then to rely on the judgments of perceived experts who are "in the know." Decision-making that takes place under conditions of uncertainty is particularly prone to suffer from distortions that result from the interplay of informational and reputational influences and cascades. "In an informational cascade," writes Cass Sunstein, "people cease relying . . . on their private information or opinions. They decide instead on the basis of the signals conveyed by others. . . . It follows that the behavior of the first few people can, in theory, produce similar behavior from countless followers."[80] Matters of national security, in general, and counter-terrorism policies in particular, almost always present significant information asymmetries among the various branches of government and between the government and the public, and are thus especially prone to the effects of informational cascades. Informational cascades also partially explain why "civilians"—including not merely the public at large, but also the judicial and legislative branches of government, as well as individuals within the executive branch—tend to defer to the judgment of military experts in such matters.[81]

Informational and reputational cascades may be manipulated by availability entrepreneurs who have particular stake in the outcomes of the policymaking process and who seek to shape and influence public discourse so as to control the policy selection process.[82] Interest groups, seeking to influence national policy toward increased spending on defense and national security, and according greater weight to national security concerns in setting national priorities, enjoy the benefits of possessing and controlling specialized information and expertise about potential national security risks and of being highly organized. This may not only lead other organizations and institutions, including the courts, to accord a significant margin of appreciation and deference to the judgments of national security entrepreneurs, but it may also mold the general public's perception of the risks that terrorists, wars, or emergencies present to the nation.[83] If availability entrepreneurs acting in the area of national security present certain risks as highly likely to occur (or of special magnitude), their position will influence greatly decision-makers and the public at large.[84] The combination of emotional contagion and consensus, leading to the prioritization of a "dominant position," will increase the ability of availability entrepreneurs to shape and influence public opinion and policy-making through reputational cascades when "people think they know what is right, or what is likely to be right, but they nonetheless go along with the crowd in order to maintain the good opinion of others."[85] High-magnitude, low-probability threats are especially susceptible to governmental "probability inflation"[86] as they involve acute informational asymmetries between the executive and other government branches and the public, resulting in greater deference toward the former.[87]

At the same time, the more confident "trusted" officials are in the correctness of their own assessments, the likelier it is that more radical responses to perceived threats will emerge. As Sunstein suggests, "people with extreme views tend to have more confidence that they are right, and . . . as people gain confidence, they become more extreme in their beliefs."[88] The significant asymmetries in information between the experts and everyone else contribute to such confidence by the "experts" in the correctness of their positions. Overconfidence is often buttressed by notions of self-fulfilling prophecies and the observable tendency to prefer information that is consistent with one's previously held views, or to interpret information in ways that confirm those views.[89] This may also account for an attitude of suspicion and even disregard toward divergent positions that are advocated by "civilians." At the same time, the phenomenon of "Monday morning quarterbacking" (or "hindsight bias") means that people tend to believe that they knew and assessed correctly all along a particular risk and its probability, even though the risk was completely unanticipated.[90] The problem is that if people, in hindsight, believe that the risk was more foreseeable and still occurred, that might be interpreted to mean that not enough measures had been taken in order to prevent the harm from occurring in the first place. That may lead "experts" whose professional reputations depend on their ability to anticipate threats and foil them to claim that the only reason for the failure to prevent the threat from materializing must be that they (i.e., the nation) were forced to fight the threats "with one hand tied behind their back" and to put the blame for the failure to act on those who are castigated as "soft on terrorism."

Finally, group polarization is even more probable in circumstances that are likely to result in groupthink: a "mode of thinking that people engage in when they are deeply involved in a cohesive in-group, when the members' strivings for unanimity override their motivation to realistically appraise alternative courses of action."[91] In turn, groupthink is more likely when groups are insulated from outside influence, are relatively homogeneous, lack an impartial leader and systematic procedures for evaluating evidence, and make decisions in times of great stress.[92] Organizations such as the military and intelligence agencies with their insular organizational cultures and structural secrecy are particularly vulnerable to such pathologies.[93] The combination of the rallying around the flag, moral panic, and group polarization is likely to result in overemphasis given to the "security" interest as compared with "liberty," thus leading yet again to decision-making that is systematically biased.

MITIGATING COGNITIVE BIASES: THRESHOLDS

Cognitive theory of decision-making raises significant concerns about balancing tests and their outcomes, in general, and in the context of violent crises, in particular. After identifying and recognizing the biases and distortions noted above, three general inquiries ought to be followed in order to examine whether the effects of these biases might be moderated, mitigated, or prevented. The first inquiry pertains to institutional questions: whether some institutions (such as the courts, the legislature, or the executive branch of government) may be better suited than others to engage in balancing acts inasmuch as they are less prone to suffer from these cognitive biases.[94] The second is whether balancing should, and could, be disposed of in favor of some other mechanism. The third inquiry is whether, assuming balancing is here to stay, any changes could be made in the utilization of balancing tests in order to achieve results out of the balancing process that are less affected by the distortions discussed above. The remainder of this chapter turns to a brief discussion of this final inquiry by looking at the possibility of introducing certain corrective mechanisms into the balancing calculus. These mechanisms are aimed at curbing and moderating the pernicious effects of bias through the concept of doctrinal thresholds.[95] These thresholds are designed to operate as precommitments that are designed to limit, ex ante, our ability to engage in the cognitively fraught act of balancing of constitutional rights against overestimated possibilities of harm.[96]

One such mechanism that courts have been using in order to minimize the distortions that emerge when dealing with high-magnitude, low-probability risks are "probability thresholds" that enable the courts to focus on issues of likelihood and probability rather than on potential magnitude of harm.[97] Probability thresholds set a minimum boundary on how likely a potential harm must be in order for that harm to register in the constitutional calculus (i.e., be accounted for in any subsequent act of constitutional balancing, regardless of the harm's magnitude). The use of such thresholds prevents balancing from taking place unless the probability of the asserted harm crosses a certain threshold. Regardless of the projected magnitude of the particular harm, if its occurrence is so unlikely as to not clear the threshold, "courts [are directed] to refuse to weigh the expected harm from the event against the benefits that the speech in question is likely to produce."[98] As a result, low-probability harms are eliminated from consideration, and balancing will not take place, no matter how great their magnitude might be.

Even when a particular potential harm does cross the probability threshold, other mechanisms may be used to mitigate the harmful consequences of cognitive biases. Analyzing First Amendment jurisprudence through the prism of risk analysis,[99] it has been suggested that one major reason for the surprising fact that "in the United States, at least, the freedom of expression has gone largely untouched" by and during the war on terror is that "the First Amendment safeguards for political speech that may incite violence or impede war efforts have been ratcheted so high that a successful conviction for such speech is almost impossible to obtain."[100] The claim is that First Amendment case law has developed in that direction so as to recognize and guard "against the predictable shortcomings in our ability to perform accurate risk analysis."[101] A significant role in such developments has been played by another possible set of thresholds that focus not on the risk side of the equation (whether probability or magnitude of the risk), but rather on the nature of the values that are at stake. Such a "principled approach" that "relies upon the incorporation into domestic law of clearly enunciated rights, safeguarded through rules of procedure and evidence . . . ,"[102] seeks either to insulate certain rights against any possibility of balancing (for example, by pronouncing them to be non-derogable no matter the circumstances[103]) or by giving them a head start (by according them an extra weight) compared with other possible and competing values. This would make a balancing outcome that curtails or limits those rights more difficult and less likely. Indeed, in his contribution to this volume, Adrian Vermeule recognizes such mechanisms but argues that they do not detract from the overall validity of the trade-off thesis. He notes that the trade-off thesis does not exclude the possibility of "a deontological theory of rights according to which it is impermissible for society to choose policies such that liberty falls below the line K-K* . . . even if security and (perhaps) aggregate welfare would thereby be increased."[104]

In all but simple cases balancing tests undermine predictability and offer less by way of general guidance than bright-line rules.[105] The lack of objective criteria for valuing the relevant interests and for establishing the appropriate basis for comparing them results in decisions that are suffused with the decision-makers' own personal preferences while coated with a veneer of seemingly objective rhetoric.[106] Such subjective preferences and decisions are particularly vulnerable to cognitive biases when dealing with violent crises. Clear rules, either substantive or of the threshold variety, rather than standards may bring about similar benefits to those with formalized training, "match[ing] cultural and individual instincts that emerge in a crisis with commitments that flow from standard operating procedures and professional norms."[107]

CONCLUSION

Cognitive theory of decision-making under conditions of uncertainty suggests that balancing processes, in general, and those seeking to balance the interests of liberty and security, in particular, are likely to suffer from identifiable, systematic biases. Its insights indicate that the outcomes of such delicate and complex balancing acts are likely to be distorted and thus suboptimal. Although the theory does not necessarily make claims as to what the equilibrium between the competing interests ought to be in any given context (for example, it does not seek to determine what an acceptable level of risk from terrorist attacks ought to be), it does suggest that once such a decision is made, the analysis that decision-makers perform in particular cases and in adopting specific countermeasures is likely to be significantly flawed. Perhaps even more important, it suggests that such flaws are systematic and that they are going to be tilted in one direction—toward more security, rather than more liberty.

NOTES

* Irving Younger Professor of Law and Director, Institute for International Legal & Security Studies, University of Minnesota Law School; Thanks to Miri Gur-Arye and the participants in the conference on "The Long Decade: How 9/11 Has Changed the Law" for their helpful comments.

1. Adrian Vermeule, "Security and Liberty: Critiques of the Trade-Off Thesis," Chapter 2 in this volume; Eric Posner and Adrian Vermeule, *Terror in the Balance: Security, Liberty, and the Courts* (New York: Oxford University Press, 2007).
2. Jeremy Waldron, "Safety and Security" (2007) 85 *Nebraska L. Rev.* 454 at 455.
3. Posner and Vermeule, *supra* note 1 at 26–30.
4. Ibid. at 26–27.
5. Ibid. at 27.
6. Ibid. at 28.
7. Ibid. at 28.
8. Ibid. at 66.

9. Ibid. at 67.
10. Roger G. Noll and James E. Krier, "Some Implications of Cognitive Psychology for Risk Regulation" in Cass R. Sunstein, ed., *Behavioral Law & Economics* (Cambridge University, 2000) 325 at 327.
11. Herbert A. Simon, *Models of Man: Social and Rational*, 1st ed. (Wiley, 1957) at 198; Russell B. Korobkin and Thomas S. Ulen, "Law and Behavioral Science: Removing the Rationality Assumption from Law and Economics" (2000) 88 *California L. Rev.* 1051 at 1075–76.
12. See, for example, Melissa L. Finucane, et al., "The Affect Heuristic in Judgments of Risks and Benefits" (2000) 13 *Journal of Behavioral Decision Making* 1 at 5–8 (the effects of time pressure on the (inverse) relationship between perceived risks and perceived benefits of an activity).
13. Posner and Vermeule, *supra* note 1 at 66.
14. Scott Plous, *The Psychology of Judgment and Decision Making* (McGraw-Hill, 1993) at 109; Noll and Krier, *supra* note 10 at 327.
15. Susan T. Fiske and Shelley E. Taylor, *Social Cognition: From Brains to Culture*, 3d ed. (McGraw-Hill, 2007) at 13.
16. Plous, *supra* note 14 at 131–44.
17. Amos Tversky and Daniel Kahneman, "Availability: A Heuristic for Judging Frequency and Probability" (1973) 5 *Cognitive Psychology* 207; Amos Tversky and Daniel Kahneman, "Judgment under Uncertainty: Heuristics and Biases," in Daniel Kahneman, et al., eds. *Judgment under Uncertainty: Heuristics and Biases* (New York: Cambridge University Press, 1982) 3 at 11.
18. The flip side is that unavailability might lead to underestimation, and as a result also underreaction. This may have accounted for the intelligence failure in foiling the attacks of September 11 and comprehending the true nature of the risk. See, for example, Cass R. Sunstein, "On the Divergent American Reactions to Terrorism and Climate Change" (2007) 107 *Columbia L. Rev.* 503 at 535; Max H. Bazerman and Michael D. Watkins, *Predictable Surprises* (Boston: Harvard Business School Press, 2004) at 15–41; Noll and Krier, *supra* note 10 at 351. Another potential cause of underreaction is people's "belief that good things are more likely than average to happen to us and bad things are less likely than average to happen to us." Korobkin and Ulen, *supra* note 11 at 1091.
19. Plous, *supra* note 14 at 126.
20. George Loewenstein and Ted O'Donoghue, "'We Can Do This the Easy Way or the Hard Way': Negative Emotions, Self-Regulation, and the Law" (2006) 73 *U. Chicago L. Rev.* 183 at 201; Philip G. Zimbardo, "The Political Psychology of Terrorist Alarms" (2003), available online at, American Psychological Association, http://www.zimbardo.com/downloads/2002%20Political%20Psychology%20of%20Terrorist%20Alarms.pdf; J. N. Shapiro and D. K. Cohen, "Color blind: Lessons from the failed homeland security advisory system" (2007) 32 *International Security* 121; John Paul and Sangyoub Park, "With the Best of Intentions: The Color Coded Homeland Security Advisory System and the Law of Unintended Consequences" (2009) 4(2) *Research and Practice in Social Sciences* 1.
21. Paul Slovic, "What's Fear Got to Do with It? It's Affect We Need to Worry About" (2004) 69 *Missouri L. Rev.* 971 at 984–89.
22. Posner and Vermeule, *supra* note 1 at 67–68.
23. Ibid. at 67.
24. Sunstein, *supra* note 18 at 542–44.

25. Oren Gross, "Chaos and Rules: Should Responses to Violent Crises Always Be Constitutional?" (2003) 112 *Yale Law Journal* 1011 at 1082–85.
26. Ileana M. Porras, "On Terrorism: Reflections on Violence and the Outlaw" (1994) *Utah L. Rev.* 119 at 121–22. See also Deborah A. Small and George Loewenstein, "The Devil You Know: The Effects of Identifiability on Punishment" (2005) 18 *J. Behavioral Decision Making* 311 at 315–16.
27. David Cole, *Enemy Aliens: Double Standards and Constitutional Freedoms in the War on Terrorism* (New York: The New Press, 2003) 4–5. Compare with Sunstein, *supra* note 18 at 529–30.
28. Jeffrey J. Rachlinski, et al., "Inside the Bankruptcy Judge's Mind" (2006) 86 *Boston U. L. Rev.* 1227 at 1256. Rachlinski, Guthrie, and Wistrich suggest that mortality salience has more influence on an individual's decision-making when she is forced to contemplate her personal mortality rather than mortality in the abstract. Terrorist threats often lead to a strong sense of personal insecurity and fear of death or serious harm befalling oneself or loved ones.
29. Ibid. at 1250–52. See also Kenneth L. Karst, "Threats and Meanings: How the Facts Govern First Amendment Doctrine" (2006) 58 *Stanford L. Rev.* 1337 at 1342–43.
30. Linda Bosniak, "Citizenship Denationalized" (2000) 7 *Indiana J. Global Legal Stud.* 447; Christina E. Wells, "Fear and Loathing in Constitutional Decision-Making" (2005) *Wisconsin L. Rev.* 115.
31. See, for example, Rupert Brown, *Prejudice: Its Social Psychology* (Wiley-Blackwell, 1995).
32. Christina E. Wells, "Questioning Deference" (2004) 69 *Missouri L. Rev.* 903 at 909–21.
33. William M. Wiecek, "The Legal Foundations of Domestic Anti-Communism: The Background of *Dennis* v. *United States*" (2001) *Supreme Ct. Rev.* 375 at 381.
34. See, for example, David Berreby, *Us and Them: The Science of Identity*, 2d ed. (Chicago: Univ. of Chicago, 2008).
35. See Oren Gross and Fionnuala Ni Aolain, *Law in Times of Crisis: Emergency Powers in Theory and Practice* (Cambridge: Cambridge University Press, 2006) at 220–27.
36. Erich Goode and Nachman Ben-Yehuda, *Moral Panics: The Social Construction of Deviance*, 2d ed. (Wiley-Blackwell, 2009) at 37–38.
37. J. Glenn Gray, *The Warriors: Reflections on Men in Battle* (New York: Harper and Row, 1973) 157–202; Jon Hanson and David Yosifon, "The Situational Character: A Critical Realist Perspective on the Human Animal" (2004) 93 *Georgetown L.J.* 1 at 55–57.
38. Stanley Cohen, *Folk Devils and Moral Panics: The Creation of the Mods and Rockers* (London: MacGibbon and Kee, 1972) 11–12. See also David Livingstone Smith, *Less than Human: Why We Demean, Enslave, and Exterminate Others* (St. Martin's Press, 2011).
39. Goode and Ben-Yehuda, *supra* note 36 at 37–43; Daniel M. Filler, "Terrorism, Panic, and Pedophilia" (2003) 10 *Va. J. Soc. Pol'y & L.* 345 (discussing public anxiety post-9/11 in terms of moral panic and risk society panic).
40. Dawn Rothe and Stephen L. Muzzatti, "Enemies Everywhere: Terrorism, Moral Panic, and US Civil Society" (2004) 12 *Critical Criminology* 327.
41. Ulrich Beck, *Risk Society: Towards a New Modernity* (London: Sage, 1992).
42. Ibid. at 24.
43. See, for example, Sheldon Ungar, "Moral Panic versus the Risk Society: The Implications of the Changing Sites of Social Anxiety" (2001) 52(2) *British J. Sociology* 271.

44. Ibid. at 287; Goode and Ben-Yehuda, *supra* note 36 at 28.
45. Clinton L. Rossiter, *Constitutional Dictatorship: Crisis Government in the Modern Democracies* 15–28 (Princeton, N.J.: Princeton University Press, 1948).
46. Cohen, *supra* note 38 at 86–87; Kent Roach, "The Dangers of a Charter-Proof and Crime-Based Response to Terrorism," in *The Security of Freedom: Essays on Canada's Antiterrorism Bill,* ed. Ronald J. Daniels, Patrick Macklem, and Kent Roach (Toronto: University of Toronto Press, 2001), 131, 138–42; Gross, *supra* note 25 at 1031–34.
47. Goode and Ben-Yehuda, *supra* note 36 at 88–108.
48. Ibid. at 26.
49. Frank Furedi, "Fear and Security: A Vulnerability-led Policy Response" (2008) 42 *Social Pol'y & Administration* 645 at 651 ("A vulnerability-led analysis of contemporary times tends to regard society one-sidedely (*sic*) as a target and people as victims.... *Its defining feature is a powerful sense of vulnerability to risk and an inflated assessment of the threat it faces.*").
50. For the latter, see, for example, Joanna Cohn Weiss, "Tough on Crime: How Campaigns for State Judiciary Violate Criminal Defendants' Due Process Rights" (2006) 81 *N.Y.U. L. Rev.* 1101; see also Melissa Hamilton, "The Child Pornography Crusade and Its Net Widening Effect" (2012) 33 *Cardozo L. Rev.* 1679.
51. See also Sunstein, *supra* note 18 at 527–28, 531–32 (noting that "[w]hen the costs are placed squarely 'on screen,' people begin to weigh both costs and benefits, and their enthusiasm for regulatory expenditures diminishes," ibid. at 528); see also Richard H. McAdams, "Present Bias and Criminal Law," John M. Olin Law and Economics Working Paper No. 562, 2d Series, The University of Chicago Law School (2011), available online at Social Science Research Network, http://ssrn.com/abstract=1893008.
52. Sunstein, *supra* note 18 at 524–29.
53. The myopic perspective may seem, at first blush, to be counterbalanced by what is known as "optimism bias": people are often overly optimistic about the likelihood of positive outcomes of future actions and tend to underestimate the likelihood of negative effects of such actions. However, one notable exception to the optimism bias concerns terrorism threats, which make every member of the target community feel vulnerable. Slovic, *supra* note 11 at 986.
54. Daniel Kahneman and Amos Tversky, "Prospect Theory: An Analysis of Decision under Risk," in Daniel Kahneman and Amos Tversky, eds., *Choices, Values, and Frames* (Cambridge University Press, 2001) 17; Slovic, *supra* note 11 at 982–83.
55. Wells, *supra* note 32 at 925.
56. Paul Slovic, *The Perception of Risk* (London: Earthscan, 2000) 220–31; Slovic, *supra* note 11 at 985–86.
57. Kai Erikson, *A New Species of Trouble: Explorations in Disaster, Trauma, and Community* (Norton, 1994); Slovic, *supra* note 11 at 985.
58. Posner and Vermeule, *supra* note 1 at 65.
59. Furedi, *supra* note 49 at 653–54.
60. Ibid. at 654.
61. Ronnie D. Lipschultz, "Terror in the Suites: Narratives of Fear and the Political Economy of Danger" (1999) 13 *Global Society* 4 at 17; W. Kip Viscusi and Richard J. Zeckhauser, "Sacrificing Civil Liberties to Reduce Terrorism Risk" (2003) 26 *J. of Risk and Uncertainty* 99 at 101; The fact that such unknown risks create stronger emotional responses does not contradict the availability heuristic. As Masur observes, individuals "react most strongly to threats that have been much

discussed within the press but that are sufficiently complex or 'scientific' that the average layperson cannot comprehend them." Jonathan S. Masur, "Probability Thresholds" (2006–07) 92 *Iowa L. Rev.* 1293 at 1341–42.

62. Quoted in Ron Suskind, *The One Percent Doctrine: Deep Inside America's Pursuit of Its Enemies since 9/11* (New York: Simon and Schuster, 2006) at 61–62.
63. Cass R. Sunstein, "Probability Neglect: Emotions, Worst Cases, and Law" (2002) 112 *Yale L.J.* 61 at 66; Cass R. Sunstein, "The Laws of Fear" (2002) 115 *Harv. L. Rev.* 1119 at 1137–44; Cass R. Sunstein, *Laws of Fear: Beyond the Precautionary Principle* (New York: Cambridge University Press, 2005).
64. Posner and Vermeule, *supra* note 1 at 61–66.
65. Ibid. at 64.
66. Daniel Kahnman, "Maps of Bounded Rationality: Psychology for Behavioral Economics" (2003) 93 *Am. Econ. Rev.* 1449 at 1451; Paul Slovic, "What's Fear Got to Do with It? It's Affect We Need to Worry About" (2004) 69 *Missouri L. Rev.* 971 at 972. For discussion of the dual-process theory in the context of the rationality debate in cognitive science see, for example, Keith E. Stanovich, *The Robot's Rebellion: Finding Meaning in the Age of Darwin* (Chicago: University of Chicago Press, 2004).
67. Sunstein, *supra* note 18 at 522–23.
68. Keith E. Stanovich, "Distinguishing the reflective, algorithmic, and autonomous minds: Is it time for a tri-process theory?," in *In Two Minds: Dual Processes and Beyond*, ed. Jonathan Evans and Keith Frankish (New York: Oxford University Press, 2009) 55 at 55.
69. Slovic, *supra* note 11 at 971.
70. Ibid. at 974–75.
71. George F. Lowenstein, Elke U. Weber, Christopher K. Hsee and Ned Welch, "Risk as Feelings" (2001) 127 *Psychological Bulletin* 267 at 275–76.
72. Plous, *supra* note 14 at 233; Max Bazerman, *Judgment in Managerial Decision Making* (New York: Wiley, 1998) 35.
73. Bruce Russett, *Controlling the Sword: The Democratic Governance of National Security* (Cambridge, Mass.: Harvard University Press, 1990) at 34; Gad Barzilai, *A Democracy in Wartime: Conflict and Consensus in Israel* (Tel-Aviv: Sifriat Polaim, 1992) 248–60.
74. Jameas Madison, *The Federalist No. 49*, in *The Federalist Papers*, ed. Clinton Rossiter (New York: New American Library, 1961), 315; Karl R. Popper, *The Open Society and Its Enemies*, 5th ed., vol. 1 (1971) at 43, 198; E.L. Quarantelli and Russell R. Dynes, "Community Conflict: Its Absence and Its Presence in Natural Disasters" (1976) 1 *Mass Emergencies* 139 at 140, 145: Eugene V. Rostow, "The Japanese American Cases—A Disaster" (1945) 54 *Yale L.J.* 489, 490–91.
75. Goode and Ben-Yehuda, *supra* note 36 at 38–39.
76. Cass R. Sunstein, *Why Societies Need Dissent* (Cambridge, Mass.: Harvard University Press, 2003) 111–35. See also Cass R. Susnstein and Reid Hastie, "Four Failures of Deliberating Groups" (April 2008), available online at Social Science Research Network, http://ssrn.com/abstract=1121400).
77. Sunstein, *supra* note 18 at 544–45; Peter Sandman, "Hazard versus Outrage in the Public Perception of Risk," in Vincent T. Covello, et al., eds., *Effective Risk Communication: The Role and Responsibility of Government and Nongovernment Organizations* (New York: Plenum, 1989) 45 ("outrage model").
78. Elaine Hatfield, et al., *Emotional Contagion* (Cambridge: Cambridge University Press, 1993).
79. For discussion of "reputational cascade," see Sunstein, *supra* note 76 at 74–95.

80. Ibid. at 55.
81. Gross, *supra* note 25 at 1034.
82. Timur Kuran and Cass R. Sunstein, "Availability Cascades and Risk Regulation" (1999) 51 *Stanford Law Review* 683 at 727; Sunstein, *supra* note 18 at 539. See also Molly J. Walker Wilson and Megan P. Fuchs, "Publicity, Pressure, and Environmental Legislation: The Untold Story of Availability Campaigns" (2009) 30 *Cardozo L. Rev.* 2147.
83. Sunstein, *supra* note 76 at 54–95.
84. See also Oren Gross, "Words as Power: The Rhetoric of War" *J. Gender, Race and Justice* (forthcoming).
85. Sunstein and Hastie, *supra* note 76 at 15–17.
86. Masur, *supra* note 61 at 1325.
87. Ibid.at1329.Masurnotes,"High-magnitudeharmsarenational-security-implicating harms, and national-security-implicating harms are the province of the executive." Ibid. at 1330.
88. Sunstein, *Laws of Fear, supra* note 63 at 100; see also Jeffrey J. Rachlinski, "The Uncertain Psychological Case for Paternalism" (2003) 97 *Northwestern U. L. Rev.* 1165 at 1172–73.
89. Paul Horwitz, "Free Speech as Risk Analysis: Heuristics, Biases, and Institutions in the First Amendment" (2003) 76 *Temple L. Rev.* 1 at 17; Plous, *supra* note 14 at 231–34.
90. See, for example, Chris Guthrie, et al., "Inside the Judicial Mind" (2001) 86 *Cornell L. Rev.* 777 at 799-803.
91. Irving L. Janis, *Groupthink: Psychological Studies of Policy Decisions and Fiascoes* (New York: Houghton Mifflin, 1982) at 9.
92. Ibid. at 242–59; [Wells, *supra* note 32 at 927–28.
93. Deborah N. Pearlstein, "Form and Function in the National Security Constitution" (2009) 41 *Connecticut L. Rev.* 1549 at 1608–11.
94. On the significance of the "institutional" question see, for example, Cass Sunstein, "Behavioral Law and Economics: A Progress Report" (1999) 1 *Am. L. & Econ. Rev.* 115 at 146; Samuel Issacharoff, "Behavioral Decision Theory in the Court of Public Law" 87 *Cornell L. Rev.* (2002) 671 at 671–72.
95. For discussion of institutional, rather than doctrinal, mechanisms to mitigate the challenges of balancing, see Vincent Blasi, "The Pathological Perspective and the First Amendment" (1985) 85 *Columbia L. Rev.* 449. Blasi puts greater trust in the efficacy of "mechanistic measures" that confine the range of discretion that is left to future decision-makers over doctrinal standards that are more susceptible to distortions that would result in less speech protective outcomes under intense pressure. Ibid. at 474-80; see also John Hart Ely, Democracy and Distrust: A Theory of Judicial Review (Cambridge, Mass.: Harvard University Press, 1980) at 109-16.
96. Horwitz, *supra* note 89 at 66. See also Sanford Levinson, "'Precommitment' and 'Postcommitment': The Ban on Torture in the Wake of September 11" (2003) 81 *Texas L. Rev.* 2013; Steven R. Ratner, "Overcoming Temptations to Violate Human Dignity in Times of Crisis: On the Possibilities for Meaningful Self-Restraint" (2004) 5 *Theoretical Inquiries in Law* 81; Jon Elster, *Ulysses and the Sirens: Studies in Rationality and Irrationality*, rev. ed. (Cambridge: Cambridge University Press, 1984); Stephen Holmes, *Passions and Constraint: On the Theory of Liberal Democracy* (Chicago: University of Chicago Press, 1995); Note, "War, Schemas, and Legitimation: Analyzing the National Discourse about War" (2006) 119 *Harv. L. Rev.* 2099 at 2118–20.

97. Masur, *supra* note 61.
98. Ibid. at 1297.
99. Horwitz, *supra* note 89 at 27–49.
100. Ibid. at 2, 7.
101. Ibid. at 8.
102. Lucia Zedner, "Securing Liberty in the Face of Terror: Reflections from Criminal Justice" (2005) 32 *J. L. & Justice* 507 at 508.
103. Oren Gross, "'Once More unto the Breach': The Systemic Failure of Applying the European Convention on Human Rights to Entrenched Emergencies" (1998) 23 *Yale J. Int'l L.* 437 at 445–55.
104. Vermeule, *supra* note 1.
105. Antonin Scalia, "The Rule of Law as a Law of Rules" (1989) 56 *U. Chi. L. Rev.* 1175 at 1186.
106. T. Alexander Aleinikoff, "Constitutional Law in the Age of Balancing" (1987) 96 *Yale L. J.* 943 at 992–95; Aharon Barak, "The Supreme Court 2001 Term—Foreword: A Judge on Judging: The Role of a Supreme Court in a Democracy" (2002) 116 *Harvard L. Rev.* 16 at 95.
107. Pearlstein, *supra* note 93 at 1604.

CHAPTER 4

Preventing What? Post-9/11 Mission Amnesia and Mission Creep

KENT ROACH*

Much post-9/11 debate has assumed that the staggering amount of counter-terrorism measures pursued over the last decade have been taken in an attempt to prevent another 9/11. The debate has then proceeded along the lines of whether the appropriate balance or proportionality has been struck between the important objective of preventing terrorism and other values such as liberty and equality. In this volume, for example, Adrian Vermeule and Oren Gross argue over the nature of the security/liberty relationship.[1] This chapter does not address this trade-off directly, but focuses more on the question of whether counter-terrorism measures actually help to prevent terrorism or instead serve other objectives. It suggests that more critical attention needs to be given to assessing the objectives of various international and domestic measures taken in the name of countering terrorism.

The security objective is notoriously ambiguous and broad. Security, like beauty, is often in the eye of the beholder. Security can refer to judgments made by security professionals about risks to security and remote risks of terrorism.[2] The security objective becomes even broader when qualified by reference to "national security" because it then often includes national interests that may not be related to the prevention of terrorism. At the international level, more threats are falling under the rubric of threats to international peace and security and the Chapter VII jurisdiction of the U.N. Security Council.

A focus on terrorism is a bit more precise than a focus on security, but does not solve all the problems. The failure to reach international agreement on the definition of "terrorism" a decade after 9/11 underlines the ambiguity of the term. Terrorism can include non-violent dissent, and it can exclude state violence and violence committed in the name of liberation struggles.[3] Terrorist crimes in many countries include acts, such as financing, being a member of listed groups, collecting information, or receiving training, that are far removed from any specific act of terrorist violence.

The ambiguities of the objectives of counter-terrorism present dangers of both mission amnesia and mission creep. Mission amnesia means that measures that were originally or purportedly taken in an attempt to prevent violent terrorism become less connected to that objective and become ends in themselves. Mission amnesia is particularly dangerous because it could allow measures originally adopted or presented to the public as necessary to prevent terrorism to persist even though they may not be effective and even counterproductive in preventing terrorism. Some examples of mission amnesia examined in the first part of this chapter include terrorism financing measures, administrative and military detention, and the occupation of Afghanistan.

Mission creep refers to a different process where interventions taken for other objectives are presented as counter-terrorism measures. The second part of this chapter suggests that Security Council Resolution 1624 may be an example of mission creep. Although defended as a counter-terrorism measure enacted in the aftermath of the 2005 London bombings, it may have more to do with European concerns about militant democracy and the integration of Muslim minorities than the actual prevention of terrorism. The war in Iraq is another example of an intervention often seen as mission creep. Other examples of mission creep are the evolution of various security strategies that focused on terrorism into all-risk strategies and an increasing recognition that respect for human rights are an important component of security policies such as the U.N. General Assembly's Counter-Terrorism Strategy.

Although not specifically examined in this chapter, the US National Security Agency's (NSA) spying as revealed in 2013 by the Snowden leaks are suggestive of both mission amnesia and creeps. The collection of metadata originally done illegally in the wake of 9/11 seems to have become, consistent with mission amnesia, an end in itself without concrete connections to the prevention of terrorism. The NSA has also in an example of mission creep extended its spying to foreign allies in a manner that is not evenly remotely connected to the prevention of terrorism.

The third part of this chapter will explore political and legal strategies to evaluate and, when warranted, counter mission amnesia and mission creep. The main strategies fall into the categories of legal and political constitutionalism outlined by Mark Tushnet in his contribution to this volume:[4] namely, due process review and proportionality analysis as applied by the courts, and political reviews including legislative and watchdog review and sunsets of legislative counter-terrorism policies.

The concepts of mission amnesia and mission creep are presented here as analytical and descriptive concepts. In all cases, normative analysis will be necessary to suggest whether any particular example of mission amnesia and especially mission creep is justified. Mission amnesia may be a more intractable problem than mission creep because it is often less visible and less rational. It allows counter-terrorism measures to become self-sustaining regardless of their actual contribution to the prevention of terrorism. Although the phrase "mission creep" is often used in a pejorative manner, it can be politically and legally justified if the new mission is important in its own right and the measures are successful in achieving the added objective. There is a need for more precision and candour at both domestic and transnational levels about the objectives of various counter-terrorism measures. As Victor V. Ramraj suggests in his later chapter, the influence of various transnational actors in the counter-terrorism field makes it critically important not to focus simply on domestic policies. Domestic policies may be driven by transnational actors that are beset by mission amnesia and/or mission creep, particularly in the field of terrorism financing.[5] More candour about the precise objective of counter-terrorism policies can guard against mission amnesia, in which counter-terrorism strategies become self-sustaining regardless of their contribution to the prevention of terrorism, or mission creep, where objectives other than the prevention of violent terrorism are pursued without adequate justification.

MISSION AMNESIA

Terrorism Financing

In the immediate aftermath of 9/11, the Security Council enacted Resolution 1373 under its Chapter VII powers relating to international peace and security. It called on all states to ensure that terrorism and the financing of terrorism were treated as serious crimes. The Security Council's focus on terrorism financing was related to its past efforts under Resolution 1267 to place an asset freeze on Al Qaeda and the 1999 terrorism financing convention. It was also related to exaggerated views of bin Laden as a master financier of terrorism. With encouragement by the United Nations Counter-Terrorism Committee (CTC) created by 1373 and the Financial Action Task Force, terrorism financing has been added to money laundering laws despite important differences between the two phenomena. Compliance with these international mandates has become an end in itself, even while deadly acts of terrorism have been committed at low cost and by groups inspired, but not directly funded, by Al Qaeda. For example, Indonesia dutifully enacted a money laundering and terrorism financing law after 9/11 and before the October 2002 Bali bombings killed 202 people. The law did not attempt to define terrorism and wrongly grouped terrorism with organized crime as crimes that involved or produced large amounts of funds. Similar off-the-rack money laundering/terrorism financing laws were also enacted in Egypt and Syria, even while terrorism laws in both countries were abused to target non-violent dissent.[6] Suspicious transactions reports have increased dramatically in many countries, but this output should not be confused with the actual prevention of terrorism. Terrorism financing insiders are starting to question the efficacy of the costly reporting regimes.[7]

There have been increasing judicial challenges to the secretive intergovernmental listing regimes that are required to provide financial institutions with lists of blacklisted terrorists. The Security Council has responded with the use of redacted narrative summaries to explain listings, the creation of an Ombudsperson and in Resolution 1989, a significant reform of the listing process that gives the Ombudsperson's delisting recommendations presumptive but rebuttable force. As Martin Scheinin suggests later in this book,[8] there has been significant evolution in the Security Council's post-9/11 approach to security and an increasing recognition of the importance of human rights. The addition of human rights to security strategies may, as discussed in the next part, be a positive example of mission creep. Nevertheless, the point here is that the post-9/11 evolution of terrorist financing and listing regimes has been one of reaction to various due process challenges with very little examination, either in judicial or political forums, of whether terrorism financing regimes are actually effective. Given the evolution of Al Qaeda from a funder of terrorism to an ideology, there is a danger that terrorism financing regimes are an example of fighting the last war. To the extent that they are rightly or wrongly perceived as targeting Muslim charities and individuals with Arabic names, they might even be counterproductive by promoting an ideology that sees counter-terrorism measures as an attack on Islam and a defence of Israel.

Afghanistan

The invasion of Afghanistan, like Resolution 1373, was one of the first responses to 9/11. It responded to the sanctuary that bin Laden had received from the Taliban regime. The occupation has lasted more than a decade at great costs in terms of lives and money. Its success in preventing terrorist attacks is, however, unclear. Al Qaeda–inspired movements have migrated to other areas such as Yemen and the Taliban continues to engage in many acts of terrorism, including suicide bombing. Much debate about Afghanistan now reflects on matters such as democracy, development, and the treatment of women. Afghanistan is an example of mission amnesia in relation to its original counter-terrorism objective, combined with mission creep with relation to other objectives. As discussed below, mission creep may be justified on the basis of the added objective, but it cannot be justified as a counter-terrorism measure.

Military Detention

The facilities at Guantanamo Bay were first used for counter-terrorism purposes to hold captives from the American-led invasion of Afghanistan. The majority of those detainees have now been released with concerns about the detention of those not involved in terrorism and the release of detainees who may have returned to terrorism. Epic legal battles were fought over whether the detainees could seek habeas corpus. Despite his initial statement that he would close Guantanamo, President Obama has allowed it to remain open and Congress has placed restrictions on the ability to transfer Guantanamo detainees to the United States for trial in civilian courts and elsewhere.[9]

In its final report, the Guantanamo Review Task Force appointed by President Obama concluded that just under fifty of the detainees should be indefinitely detained without trial before either civilian courts or military commissions. This Task Force had access to secret information and, as such, its conclusions about the necessity of detention are not easily reviewed. Legal and political debates about Guantanamo have evolved in other directions. Congressional support of Guantanamo frequently seems related to dissatisfaction with the American criminal justice system: a desire to create a *Miranda*-free,[10] if not a law-free zone. There has, however, been some debate and concerns about whether Guantanamo has become counterproductive to the overall objective of preventing terrorism. This possibility is implicitly recognized in provisions that allow an executive waiver of military detention and trial, if necessary to ensure the transfer or extradition of a terrorist suspect or if military detention would otherwise impede counter-terrorism cooperation with other countries.[11] American law now recognizes that military detention may have outlived its usefulness at least in particular cases where it would hinder international co-operation.

Administrative Detention: Control Orders and Security Certificates

Control orders in the United Kingdom and security certificates in Canada remain the most controversial counter-terrorism measures in those countries. In late 2011, the U.K. government replaced control orders with a less strict scheme, terrorism prevention and investigation measures (TPIMs), that are not subject to annual reviews and renewals as were control orders. Control orders, like Guantanamo, were subject to important legal challenges, but ones that focused on disclosure and whether they were a deprivation of liberty under the European Convention on Human Rights.

In Canada, security certificates allow indeterminate detention of non-citizens declared by ministers to be a security threat. Like control orders, they have also been the subject of legal battles, including a ruling from the Supreme Court of Canada that led to the creation of special advocates to challenge the secret evidence.[12] Three of a total five alleged Al Qaeda–related security certificates remained in place in late 2013, but they have morphed into control orders as the three men have been released under conditions. The Canadian government has persisted with the cases even to the extent of claiming the ultimate right to deport the men to torture in their countries of citizenship.

Both the control order and security certificate debates demonstrate the danger of mission amnesia, as the measures have frequently been opposed and defended on their own terms with little attention to their ability to prevent acts of terrorism. Some control orders in the United Kingdom have been made in order to keep a person in a country. Such orders might help prevent terrorism abroad, but perhaps at the risk of terrorism at home. The Canadian government maintained that the three remaining detainees remain a security threat even though they had been subject to detention or restrictive conditions in the community for well over a decade. In both countries, security officials have gone to great (and frequently unsuccessful) lengths to defend the need for secrecy and the use of secret evidence.

Secrecy can aid and abet mission amnesia because intelligence agencies may view secrecy as an end in itself regardless of its actual contribution to the prevention of terrorism. Secrecy may prevent independent and fully informed judgments about whether control orders and security certificates have actually helped prevent terrorism.

Due process challenges may also have contributed to mission amnesia as governments have become entrenched in their positions. In Canada, the government responded to court challenges by introducing a special advocate regime, but not by rethinking the necessity of the scheme or the difficulties of ultimately deporting the detainees to their countries of citizenship. In the United Kingdom, a new Government abolished control orders in name, but new terrorism and investigation measures retained many of the same features of control orders. They still allow the use of secret evidence, and the government has simply relied upon court decisions to ensure that enough information is disclosed to the controlee.[13] Despite all the successful legal challenges to Guantanamo, security certificates, and control orders, all three measures persist in a modified form, even though their necessity in preventing terrorism is at best unclear.

MISSION CREEP

Resolution 1624

Shortly after the 2005 London bombings, the Security Council enacted Resolution 1624 calling for states to ensure that the incitement of terrorism was a crime. Another part of the resolution called for a dialogue between civilizations in a somewhat veiled reference to concerns about Islamic extremism. The resolution was championed by Prime Minister Blair who frequently expressed his determination to counter the extremist ideas that he believed motivated terrorism. He was able to win Security Council agreement more quickly for his proposal than that of his own Parliament, which resisted initial calls to criminalize speech that glorified terrorism.

Despite being presented as a counter-terrorism measure, Resolution 1624 constitutes mission creep that shifted focus from the prevention of terrorism to extremist speech and engagement with Islam. This shift in focus may or may not be justified, but it created a danger that measures taken for different objectives could be sold to international and domestic audiences under the counter-terrorism banner. Some non-democratic regimes in the Middle East and Asia reported back to the CTC that they had enacted laws prohibiting speech that incited terrorism, something that was difficult to refute given the absence of guidance in Resolution 1624 about the meaning of either incitement or terrorism. Mission creep in such regimes could shift to the repression of speech advocating peaceful dissent or separatism that might fall under overbroad definitions of terrorism. Both the United States and Canada resisted the mission creep towards speech regulation, telling the CTC that they would not enact new incitement offences, and with the United States relying on First Amendment jurisprudence. The anxieties that the United Kingdom and other European states have about their Muslim minorities may not apply in other states that have different histories. International mission creep promoted by one state will play out in different and perhaps unexpected ways in other countries, and this underlines the transnational complexities of global counter-terrorism policymaking.

The United Nations may be particularly susceptible to mission creep because of the Security Council's incentives to include a broad range of matters within the rubric of measures that are required to secure international peace and security and prevent terrorism. The packaging of Resolution 1624 as a counter-terrorism measure allowed the CTC to play a role in encouraging compliance with the resolution. There was, however, very little discussion about how 1624 would actually prevent terrorism. The importance of the public acts of incitement targeted by 1624 in the actual commission of terrorist acts is not known. It is also not known whether incitement prosecutions will persuade others not to engage in terrorism or perhaps have the opposite effect, if disaffected people conclude that the prosecutions demonstrate hostility to Islam or insensitivity to grievances that may promote extremism.

Iraq

Another example of mission creep is the American-led 2003 invasion of Iraq. Initial claims that the invasion was justified because of links between Iraq, weapons of mass destruction, and Al Qaeda have been refuted by subsequent inquiries in the United States and the United Kingdom. The Iraq war is a fairly crude and commonly accepted example of mission creep. The secret intelligence that originally was used to justify the invasion of Iraq as part of a global war against terrorism has now been closely examined by several commissions in both the United States and the United Kingdom and found to be faulty. The increasingly public nature of intelligence can help offset the danger that secrecy can protect both mission amnesia and mission creep. Leaks by Wikileaks and Edward Snowden have placed what are questions about mission amnesia and mission creep as well as privacy in relation to NSA spying on the public agenda. Conversely, secrecy remains one of the largest obstacles to detecting and countering either mission amnesia or mission creep.

Human Rights as Part of a Security Strategy

Another example of mission creep is the inclusion of human rights protection as part of security strategies. The U.N. General Assembly's 2006 Counter-Terrorism Strategy provides that the protection of human rights while countering terrorism is one of its four pillars. Human rights groups have also not been shy about appropriating the vague but weighty language of security and arguing that there can be no real security without human rights. It is also widely maintained that abuses of human rights may be counterproductive and inspire acts of terrorism. Mission creep that includes respect for human rights as part of a strategy to prevent terrorism may be justified because of the inherent importance of human rights. The point at this juncture is only to describe the significant post-9/11 evolution of security strategies and to identify this development as a form of mission creep.

All-Risks Security Strategies

Another example of mission creep is the growing prominence of all-risks security strategies. Canada adopted an all-risk strategy when, in 2004, it proclaimed its first national security strategy. The government took this approach because of a 2003 SARS outbreak in Toronto that killed over sixty people and to blunt some of the pressure of the Bush administration's single-minded focus on terrorism at that time. Reforms of emergency laws in the United Kingdom in 2004 also took an all-risks approach, and the United States and Australia have both moved towards an all-risks approach in the wake of Hurricane Katrina and other natural disasters. Philip Bobbitt has defended an all-risks approach and argued that the failure of governments effectively to govern after acts of terrorism or other disruptive events may cause more harm and panic than the initial disruptions.[14] Again, the point is not that this mission creep cannot be justified, but only that it underlines the multiple objectives of security strategies.

EVALUATING AND COUNTERING MISSION AMNESIA AND MISSION CREEP

So far, this chapter has articulated the concepts of mission amnesia and mission creep. It has suggested that the security field has been particularly vulnerable to both phenomena because of the vagueness of security and counter-terrorism objectives, as well as the secrecy that often accompanies them. Even if a reader is not persuaded by all the summary examples of mission amnesia and mission creep, there will hopefully be agreement about the existence or at least the potential of the phenomena. In what follows, the chapter next outlines some strategies for evaluating and, when justified, countering both mission amnesia and mission creep.

The courts will not be the primary institution to detect and counter either mission creep or mission amnesia. Courts decide relatively narrow questions and generally focus on the propriety and legality of impugned measures. They also do not routinely have access to secret information that may be required to evaluate the effectiveness of security measures. At the same time, there may be powerful incentives among elected branches of government not to reveal or respond to mission creep and mission amnesia. This means that the independent courts may be able to play some role, even if not ideally suited for the task. In addition, political and legal mechanisms may in some cases work together to counter mission creep and mission amnesia.

Distinguishing Good and Bad Mission Creep

Although mission creep is often used as a pejorative label, the intent here is not to suggest that it cannot be justified. What then distinguishes good mission creep from bad mission creep? One precondition seems to be candour about the added mission. The addition of human rights and all-risks to terrorism strategies are explicit for all the world to see, whereas the targeting of Islamic extremism or increasing the integration of Muslim minorities in European societies in Resolution 1624, or the advancement of American national interests in the invasion of Iraq, were less transparent. Transparency is a necessary, but not a sufficient condition for justifying mission creep.

The worthiness of the added mission is not enough to justify mission creep. The ability to achieve the added objective must be capable of evaluation to ensure that mission amnesia does not occur with respect to the added mission. It is one thing for the United Nations to say, as it increasingly does, that human rights are a key aspect of effective counter-terrorism, and it is another thing for it actually to achieve measurable success in achieving either goal. The CTC claims to be concerned with human rights in the implementation of Resolution 1624, but the lack of transparency in its work, aggravated by its decision to no longer publicly post reports from Member States, makes it difficult to assess how effective it is in ensuring greater respect for human rights.

Legal Constitutionalism and Mission Creep

Mission creep that acknowledges multiple objectives for a security measure may present challenges to courts in applying proportionality analysis. For example, laws against extremist speech that may incite terrorism can be defended on the basis that they help prevent terrorism, but also on the grounds that they help ensure that democratic freedoms are not abused in a militant democracy and/or that they counter hate speech. Courts that engage in proportionality analysis typically focus on whether there is a rational connection between one objective and the impugned law, and whether there are less drastic alternatives in achieving that one objective. A law that has multiple objectives presents challenges for proportionality analysis. There is a danger that multiple objectives will either be ignored in proportionality analysis or that they will be used as a form of tiebreaker in determining the overall balance between the good that a measure achieves and its adverse effects.

Political Constitutionalism and Mission Creep

Mission creep is not inherently bad, but it needs to be openly acknowledged and justified. It may be that various electorates have partially ratified the evolving mission in Afghanistan. President Bush was re-elected in 2004, but concerns about Iraq played a role in the election of President Obama in 2008. The electorate, however, is only in a position to make judgments about mission creep if it is aware that the creep has occurred and it is prepared to make judgments about the added mission. It is an interesting question whether President Obama would have been re-elected in 2012 if the public had the benefit of the Snowden leaks about NSA spying. The war on Iraq is now widely seen as an example of mission creep, but this recognition of mission creep may not have occurred had the underlying intelligence about weapons of mass destruction not been subject to critical and public evaluation. Political constitutionalism may actually be a more powerful control in the United States than in other countries, because of American restrictions on prior restraint of speech and the absence of any legislation resembling the U.K. Official Secrets Act, criminalizing the unauthorised release of classified information.[15]

Various forms of legislative and executive review and oversight may also play a role in countering mission creep. A review of how laws against the incitement of terrorism are connected to the actual prevention of terrorism might result in governments arguing that such a perspective is too limited and that incitement laws play a broader role with respect to community relations, immigration policy, hate speech, and other matters. Such an approach would make mission creep more explicit and allow for more rigorous and wide-ranging evaluation of incitement laws, as well as alternative measures to achieve the goals of those laws. At the same time, however, open acknowledgement of an expanded mission will make the task of political, as well as legal, evaluation more difficult. There may be a tendency to defend measures that may not be that effective in preventing terrorism on the basis of their contribution to other more broadly defined and less easily measured objectives, such as maintaining good community relations.

Countering Mission Amnesia

Mission amnesia involves an irrational ignorance and repression of the mission of the intended objective. As Nietzsche famously argued, to forget one's purpose is the commonest form of stupidity. There is always the possibility that what looks like mission amnesia about preventing terrorism may turn out to be mission creep, as some other objective has been added to the counter-terrorism mission. If this is the case, however, there should be candour and justification of the added mission. Much more so than mission creep, mission amnesia is irrational and almost always undesirable. It is also potentially dangerous because it encourages continued investment in security measures that may not be fit for purpose.

Legal Constitutionalism and Mission Amnesia

The traditional deference of courts when reviewing national security activities may prevent the courts from detecting and countering mission amnesia. That said, the courts have been more active in the post-9/11 era than many expected, and their use of proportionality review has the potential to reveal some forms of mission amnesia.

The landmark decision of the U.K. House of Lords in the *Belmarsh Case*[16] is a good example of how some forms of judicial review can counter mission amnesia by posing basic questions, such as whether the indeterminate detention of non-citizens suspected of terrorism is rationally connected to the object of preventing terrorism. In that case, the House of Lords concluded in 2004 that there was no rational connection given that the terrorist threat was not limited to non-citizens, something confirmed a year later in the deadly London bombings. Proportionality analysis requires clear articulation of the objective of the measure, whether the measure is rationally connected to that objective, and whether there are less rights-invasive means to achieve the objective. It is perhaps more concerned about the effectiveness of counter-terrorism measures than many of its proponents are willing to admit. For some, this will suggest that courts should continue to defer to the state's national security activities because they are incompetent to make determinations of effectiveness.[17] At the same time, judicial competence to make determinations about the effectiveness of various counter-terrorism measures should be compared to actual, not idealized, legislative and executive performance on such issues.[18]

The *Belmarsh Case* represents a departure from a prior pattern of judicial deference to the executive on security matters. The Newton Committee of Privy Counsellors had already laid much of the groundwork for the judgment by determining that indeterminate detention of non-citizens suspected of involvement in terrorism was not justified and that there were a wide range of less drastic alternatives to combat terrorism. The Newton Committee was composed of Privy Counsellors who had access to secret information. As Mark Tushnet has suggested in his contribution to this book, political and legal constitutionalism are not watertight compartments.[19] In the *Belmarsh Case*, a political review process helped the judges play a more robust role in countering mission amnesia.

Due process challenges will not always focus, as in the *Belmarsh Case*, on rational connection to the prevention of terrorism and whether the state has irrationally discriminated. Successful challenges to terrorist financing regimes, and to military and administrative detention, have focused more on due process than rational connection. Alas, such due process challenges have not been effective in countering the mission amnesia that besets these regimes. Even when governments have been forced to respond to these successful court challenges, they have not engaged in a fundamental examination of whether the measure is actually effective or required for preventing terrorism. For example, the U.N. Security Council has responded to an increasing number of judicial decisions that have criticized the 1267 terrorist listing process with a growing number of reforms, including the use of redacted narrative summaries to explain the listing, the creation of an Ombudsperson, and a restructuring of the listing process in Resolution 1989. These reforms have all been designed to respond to a due process deficit in listing on the basis of secret evidence and without access to a judicial remedy. None of them, however, have examined whether listing remains necessary to preventing terrorism in light of the evolution of Al Qaeda.

A similar story can be told about various legal challenges to military detention in the United States and administrative detention in the United Kingdom and Canada. Habeas corpus has been successfully asserted, but the Obama administration accepted indefinite military detention even before Congress started to restrict transfers from Guantanamo. Despite significant legal challenges to control orders and even a symbolic abolition of them as part of the Cameron/Clegg's government's self-proclaimed "correction in favour of liberty," the essence of control orders as preventive administrative measures that can use secret evidence persist in the United Kingdom in the form of TPIMs. In Canada, the government has lost some major security certificate cases and, in response, has introduced special advocates and changed the retention practices of intelligence agencies. Nevertheless, it soldiers on with the three remaining security certificates cases despite the costs of continued litigation and public criticism that the security certificate process is an unfair form of secret trial with the ultimate objective of deportation to torture.

In all these cases, successful due process challenges have not been an effective vehicle to counter mission amnesia. Unlike in the *Belmarsh Case*, the court cases have not engaged with the overall effectiveness of the scheme as a means of preventing terrorism. Rather, they have focused on narrower but real procedural deficiencies. Governments have not surprisingly responded to these due process challenges with new procedures, such as Ombudspersons and special advocates. It is possible that the success of the due process challenges has paradoxically caused governments to become even more committed to the impugned measure. Indeed, the need to respond to these due process challenges may have diverted limited resources away from fundamental challenges to the regimes. In short, the verdict on the ability of legal constitutionalism to counter mission amnesia is decidedly mixed, with proportionality analysis only emerging in the *Belmarsh Case* as a means to test the effectiveness of purported counter-terrorism measures and as an antidote to mission amnesia.

Political Constitutionalism and Mission Amnesia

If legal constitutionalism is not a reliable counter to mission amnesia, what about political constitutionalism? Executive watchdog review and audits can challenge mission amnesia by exploring whether particular counter-terrorism measures are contributing to the prevention of terrorism. Such reviews, however, face a number of challenges. There may not be appropriate review bodies in many jurisdictions. Many review bodies, such as the American Inspectors General, are still tied to particular agencies, even while many governments have taken a "whole-of-government" approach to terrorism issues.[20] A reviewer who only reviews one agency may fail to see the larger picture and become captured by the agency and its mission amnesia. Not all reviewers may have access to all the secret information that may be necessary to evaluate whether various counter-measures are effective. Even when legislators have access to secret information, they may not be able to make it public. Even successful executive or legislative review that identifies mission amnesia may be unable to convince the government actually to change a deficient policy. The Newton Committee in 2003 issued a scathing critique of indefinite detention of non-citizens without trial, but the Blair government did not take action until the scheme was declared inconsistent with rights by the House of Lords in the *Belmarsh Case* in late 2004.

Even a domestic government that concludes that a particular counter-terrorism measure is not fit for purpose may be unable to change that measure because of international pressure. Both the 9/11 Commission and Canada's Air India Flight 182 commission reached very pessimistic conclusions about the ability of terrorism financing laws to prevent acts of terrorism, but neither recommended that governments ramp down efforts to counter terrorism financing. The Canadian inquiry concluded that little could be done in the face of Canada's international obligations to counter terrorism financing.[21] Even if successfully discovered domestically, mission amnesia and mission creep may persist internationally, especially if the transnational organizations that support it, such as the Financial Action Task Force and the Security Council's Counter-Terrorism Committee, are not subject to effective review.

Over twelve years after 9/11, there is a need for review and sunset process for some counter-terrorism measures that may be the victim of mission amnesia. Such processes will have to be conducted at all levels of governance, including at the United Nations. One of the many dangers of the Security Council's counter-terrorism "legislation" is that it is permanent legislation that may no longer be fit for purpose. Sunsets alone are unlikely to work, and there is a danger that sunsets may facilitate a lack of deliberation before counter-terrorism measures are adopted. If they are to be effective, sunsets should be proceeded by a review process that evaluates the contribution that the measure is making to the prevention of terrorism. The review should have access to all relevant secret information, and it should place as much information about the effectiveness of the measure as possible into the public domain. Review and sunset process has not always worked well in the past.[22] Nevertheless, they may be one of the few mechanisms on the side of political constitutionalism that can counter mission amnesia.

The ultimate remedy from political constitutionalism may be a change of government. Although there is substantial continuity between the approach of the second Bush administration and the Obama administration, there has been some repudiation of some of the controversial approaches both with respect to Iraq and interrogation. In the United Kingdom, the Cameron/Clegg government promised a correction in favour of liberty. This was backed up by review mechanisms, most notably Lord Macdonald's inquiry. After reviewing secret information, it concluded that control orders hindered successful prosecutions.[23] The Cameron/Clegg government subsequently replaced control orders with TPIMS, which although less severe in their restrictions, resembled control orders in many ways.

CONCLUSION

More than 12 years after 9/11, it is appropriate to reflect on the evolving nature of counter-terrorism policies. Counter-terrorism policies are dynamic, as they respond to the evolving nature of terrorism and to the flexibility of the security objective. Mission creep should be expected, and it is not inherently bad. Nevertheless, it needs to be supplemented by open acknowledgment of the added mission. Such acknowledgment is a necessary precondition for political and legal debate about the necessity and wisdom of the added mission. It is also necessary to ensure that a policy does not obtain unwarranted legitimacy or staying power by being wrongly labelled as a counter-terrorism policy.

Although we should be vigilant about mission creep and subject it to debate and evaluation, mission amnesia is a more dangerous phenomena, because it allows counter-terrorism measures to persist without evaluating their effectiveness or necessity for their intended purpose. Mission amnesia may provide a false sense of security from terrorism. It may also allow controversial and rights-invasive measures to persist even if they do little to prevent terrorism or even are counterproductive to that purpose. Mission amnesia can only be countered by full political or legal evaluation of a particular measure, and in some cases this may require access to secret information.

All of the resources of both legal and political constitutionalism may be necessary to counter mission amnesia, and even then they may not be successful. Proportionality review has the potential to detect mission amnesia, but successful due process challenges may not always counter it. As in the case of military and administrative detention, such challenges may even entrench the commitment of governments to controversial measures. Even successful domestic checks on mission amnesia may be defeated by international and transnational demands for policies, such as terrorism financing laws that are themselves affected by mission amnesia.

NOTES

* Professor of Law and Prichard-Wilson Chair in Law and Public Policy, University of Toronto Faculty of Law.

1. Adrian Vermeule, "Security and Liberty: Critiques of the Tradeoff Thesis," Chapter 2 in this volume, and Oren Gross, "Security *vs.* Liberty: On Emotions and Cognition," Chapter 3 in this volume.
2. Lucia Zedner, *Security* (Abington: Routledge, 2009).
3. R. v. Gul [2013] UKSC 64.
4. Mark Tushnet, "Legal and Political Constitutionalism, and the Response to Terrorism," Chapter 8 in this volume.
5. Victor V. Ramraj, "Counter-terrorism's Engagement with Transnational Legality," Chapter 7 in this volume.
6. Kent Roach, *The 9/11 Effect: Comparative Counter-Terrorism* (Cambridge: Cambridge University Press, 2011) at 145–46 and ch. 3.
7. Richard Bartlett, "Time to Re-examine Regulation Designed to Counter the Financing of Terrorism" (2008) 41 *Case Western L. Rev.* 7.
8. Martin Scheinin, "Human Rights and Counter-Terrorism: Lessons from a Long Decade," the epilogue of this volume.
9. Fiona de Londras, "Guantanamo Bay, the Rise of Courts and the Revenge of Politics," Chapter 9 in this volume.
10. *Miranda* v. *Arizona*, 384 U.S. 436 (1966) (requiring detainees to be informed of the right to counsel).
11. National Defence Authorization Act for Fiscal Year 2012, H.R. 1540, 112th Cong. S. 1022.
12. *Charkaoui* v. *Canada*, [2007] 1 S.C.R.350.
13. See the decisions of the House of Lords in *Secretary of State for the Home Department v AF*, [2009] UKHL 28, and the European Court of Human Rights in *A and Others v United Kingdom*, [2009] ECHR 301.
14. Philip Bobbitt, *Terror and Consent* (New York: Anchor Books, 2008). See also Kent Roach, *September 11: Consequences for Canada* (Montreal: McGill-Queens University Press, 2003) at ch. 7 for a defence of an all-risks approach to security.

15. Jack Goldsmith *Power and Constraint: The Accountable Presidency after 9/11* (New York: Norton, 2012) at ch. 3.
16. *A and Others. v Secretary of State*, 2004 UKHL 56, aff'd by the European Court of Human Rights in *A and Others v United Kingdom*, [2009] ECHR 301.
17. Eric Posner and Adrian Vermeule, *Terror in the Balance* (New York: Oxford University Press, 2007).
18. Kent Roach, "Judicial Review of the State's Anti-terrorism Activities" (2009) 3 *Indian Journal of Constitutional Law* 138.
19. Tushnet, *supra* note 4.
20. Roach, *The 9/11 Effect, supra* note 6 at ch. 8.
21. *The 9/11 Commission Report* (New York: Norton, 2004) at 12.3; Commission of Inquiry into the Investigation of the Bombing of Air India Flight 182, *Air India Flight 182: A Canadian Tragedy* (Ottawa: Supply and Services, 2010) vol. 5.
22. Oren Gross and Fionnuala Ni Aolain, *Law in Times of Crisis: Emergency Powers in Theory and Practice* (Cambridge: Cambridge University Press, 2006). For slightly more optimistic accounts recognizing that sunset clauses can assist in review, see John Finn, "Sunset Clauses and Democratic Deliberation" (2009) 48 *Columbia J. of Transnational Law* 442; John Ip, "Sunset Clauses and Counter-Terrorism Legislation," [2013] *Public Law* 74.
23. U.K. Home Office, Review of Counter-Terrorism and Security Powers: A Report by Lord Macdonald of River Glaven, QC (Cm. 8003, January 2011).

PART TWO:

Terrorism in a Borderless World

CHAPTER 5

The War on Terrorism and International Law: Toward a Continental Divide

AMNON LEV*

Im Reich der Zwecke hat alles entweder einen Preis *oder eine* Würde.
Immanuel Kant, *Grundlegung zur Metaphysik der Sitten*

Having passed the tenth anniversary of the Al Qaeda attacks on September 11, 2001, we can begin to reflect not only on the legal and political changes that have accompanied the "war on terrorism," but also on our efforts to understand these changes. These efforts have for the most part focused on questions of boundary demarcation. Lawyers have been concerned either to extend the reach of law to those who have been deprived of its protection or to preserve constitutional order from being contaminated by what goes on beyond its boundary. The efforts to understand the way in which we have been affected by the war on terrorism can themselves be described in military terms, as a campaign to return law to a situation of normalcy. As in any war, the war on terrorism has seen both advances and setbacks. On the whole, however, legal scholarship has been unwavering in its belief that law and terror intersect only at the limit of legal order. It is no surprise then that the most widely read theory of the war on terrorism has been that of Agamben[1] which, in all its implausibility, scrupulously respects the format of boundary demarcation, only negating it.

This chapter looks at terror from a different angle. It explains how our reaction to terror reflects our conception of international legal order and of our place in it. To this end, it situates the advent of modern terror in relation to the Cold War. A mere twelve years separate the fall of the Berlin Wall from the attacks in New York. In that time, we have left behind a world which seemed to rest on firm foundations, a world united by a commitment to international law as an expression of the Western idea of human dignity. As we inquire into our reaction to terror, we shall find that although we in the West remain committed to the same basic values, our assessment of the threat that they have come under is not the same. To an increasing extent, the position of Europe within the international legal order reflects structures of our constitutional order that determine how we perceive terror and the war which we are fighting against it.

THE SYSTEM OF TOTAL DESTRUCTION

The balance of the Cold War revolved around the destructive capacity of the nuclear bomb. The state system which the Cold War system replaced had been organized around the idea of a relative equality between its parts. The dispersion of power between the states meant that the system was believed to be self-corrective. In the event of an act of aggression against a state which threatened its existence, the other states, whether they were directly affected by the aggression or not, would automatically restore the plurality of states, wherein lay the assurance of their own territorial integrity. Without fail, states would thus counter any imbalance within the system, preventing local pre-eminence from developing into global hegemony.[2] Although instability was inherent in the system, it was not seen to constitute a threat to its existence. On the contrary, it was seen as a safeguard of the territorial integrity of its parts. The near-tautological nature of this belief did not prevent it from becoming a maxim of public law in Europe from the sixteenth century, which explains the scandalized reaction of publicists to the dismemberment of Poland by Russia and Prussia in 1772 that showed this belief to be an illusion.

There was no place for such illusions in the Cold War. In a system based on the threat of mutual destruction, the parts present perfect mirror images of each other. They are formally identical as no criterion or measure exists to distinguish the opposing powers, which were both absolute insofar as the system of their interaction would not outlast the activation of either. If hegemony was theoretically impossible within the state system, the Cold War did not admit of victory. This had important consequences for the nexus between state and territory, which is theoretically weak because the concept of the state is territorially underdetermined. As Hobbes's analysis of the genesis of sovereign power reveals, the power of the state is not tied to any specific location. It can arise anywhere and can be undone in whatever position it occupies. Its only conceptually determinate border is the line which divides peace and war. Thus, only by opposing sovereign power to other sovereign powers can the commonwealth be stabilized as a specific state, occupying a determinate territory. This is why Hobbes, in chapter 13 of the *Leviathan*, is so quick to map the description of the state of nature onto the relations of sovereign persons, in which it is truly realized: "But though there had never been any time wherein particular men were in a condition of war one against another, yet in all times kings and persons of sovereign authority, because of their independency, are in continual jealousies and in the state and posture of gladiators, having their weapons pointing and their eyes fixed on one another."[3]

In a sense, this description of the international state of nature applied equally to the Cold War. Not only was the image of an arsenal of weapons pointed at the enemy prevalent during this period, but it also served the same purpose in our political imagination. However, the continuity between the oppositional logic of the state system and that of the Cold War should not blind us to the profound transformation of the status of the state that took place in the transition from the former to the latter. In the state system, it is the line which divides war from peace that situates the idea of the state. The capacity to uphold this line serves as the justification of the exorbitant power of the state that, by upholding the difference between battlefield and civilian territory, can claim to be the defender of the peace and a holder of determinate territory. This claim was compromised by the advent of nuclear weapons. By the scale of the destruction that they could bring about, they rendered meaningless the demarcation of a specific battlefield. In a system which revolves around the threat of total destruction, there is no separation between inner and outer, battlefield and civilian territory.

The passing away of this venerable line of demarcation is reflected in the confluence of the two legal regimes which have grown up around it. The affirmation by the International Court of Justice in the *Nuclear Weapons* case that international humanitarian law and human rights both apply on the battlefield accurately reflects the horizon of the Cold War, albeit in retrospect. Crucially, the Court, while stating that it should take account of the unique characteristics of nuclear weapons, in particular their destructive capacity, declined to consider whether their use could ever be proportional. This refusal entailed the implicit recognition that the calculus of military necessity, on which the legal regulation of war turns, gives out when applied to such destructive capacity.[4] The failure to engage with this question is mirrored by the Court's affirmation that the nature of the humanitarian law that would apply to nuclear warfare is itself not in doubt.[5] Two absolutes are thus juxtaposed in the reasoning of the Court: the capacity to inflict total destruction, which entails an indefinite extension of the ground of battle, and an unconditional need to protect that attaches not to the soldier, but to the human being, to which modern war reduces him. It is not without irony that the confluence of international humanitarian law and human rights, which Theodor Meron hailed as a humanization of the former that "driven to a large extent by . . . the principles of humanity" has its condition of possibility in our capacity to annihilate all of humanity.[6] If, as Meron points out, inroads have been made on the dominant role of reciprocity in international humanitarian law, it is because we cannot limit the exposure to the effects of modern war to those who have chosen to take part in it.

Reciprocity is therefore no longer an absolute imperative, because states are no longer seen to be the undisputed masters of war. In the nuclear age, territorial borders between states are not lines of scrimmage of a conflict that remains a matter of state. If the states of Europe, which had for centuries been organized around the idea of a balance of power between an irreducible plurality of sovereign states, could in a mere matter of years be stabilized in constellations that revolved around non-European hegemonial states, this was, in no small part, because the Iron Curtain, however arbitrary its trajectory, was the only territorially given border line which could serve as a symbol of the divide between order and chaos. The arms race, in which strength was measured in multiples of total destruction, was a surreal, yet rational function of this opposition, from which there was no exit—at least in theory. Opposition could only be resolved by military means which would bring about the destruction of all of mankind or through the admission of fault which would be tantamount to the auto-destruction of the penitent party.

A solution to this Cold War conundrum was not found. Instead, the implosion of the Soviet Union gave the lie to the existential investment in communism, leaving one ideology to represent the truth of the social existence of man. In a sense, Francis Fukuyama was simply stating the obvious when he affirmed that the demise of communism signified the global victory of liberal individualism. It could have no other meaning. Yet, triumphalism seems to have blinded him to the fact that his reading was self-evident only when seen within the context of an opposition of which one of the constituent moments had fallen away. Again, it is only a mere twelve years that separate the fall of the Berlin Wall from the terror attacks in New York which proved, if anything, that the opposition of individualism and class is not the only motive force of political history.

It would be unfair to demand foresight and perspicacity from those caught up in a history which we have ourselves not yet fully understood. If, in the following, this chapter draws attention to certain presuppositions of Fukuyama's triumphalism, it is not to take him to task for the inaccuracy of his predictions. They are of interest to us insofar as they reflect a failure to appreciate the specific nature of the state, as it has developed on the European continent. What appears as a heavy-handed reading of a philosophy which Fukuyama takes to be the blueprint of the state—the philosophy of Hegel—is perhaps better seen as an indication of the differences in the way in which popular sovereignty is reflected in the constitutional orders on both sides of the Atlantic. In the Cold War, such differences seemed inconsequential. By reintroducing into society the spectre of massive violence now perpetrated by individuals, terror has made them relevant.

THE END OF HISTORY REVISITED

History has come to an end because liberty, its chief motive force, has found perfect expression in the liberal state. This belief is at the heart of Fukuyama's thesis of the end of history. The liberal state is the realization of reason in history, in that it accommodates the dual aspects of liberty that correspond to the dimensions of human nature: the freedom to pursue one's self-interest (man as an economic agent) and the freedom to take part in government (man as a political being). Fukuyama articulates his thesis through a reading of Hegel's philosophy of right, but the tenor of his reading differs from that which resonates in Hegel's work. What we find there is not the self-assured assertion of a fact of history, but the acute intuition of a problem: the problem of how to ensure the social mediation of both aspects of liberty. Hegel, in this an heir to natural law, is painfully aware that economic freedom is not naturally directed at the common good; the *bourgeois* will not naturally coincide with the *citoyen*. The exercise of economic freedom will, if unchecked, unravel the fabric of society, transforming it into a disorganized plurality of individuals. Constitutional order, as envisioned by Hegel, revolves around the disenfranchisement of market society that is excluded from the mechanism of social mediation which he poses as the principle of modern society.

This breach of principle, to which the young Marx would draw attention, reflects the theoretical impossibility of an immediate translation of individual liberty into the constitutional order. It is by the intuition of this problem that Hegel prefigures the construction of the state as it has developed in Europe. He is the first to articulate the necessity of translating individual liberty into constitutional order and he is the last to believe this translation to be possible. After Hegel, the unity of state and individual disintegrates, leaving, on the one hand, a theory of civil society in which state and individual are dissolved in relations of recognition (Marx), and, on the other, a theory of monarchical power which is premised on the impossibility of reflecting individual liberty (Stahl).[7] In just a few decades, the notion of the individual as the source and foundation of civil authority ceased to have any pull within public law. In 1892, as Georg Jellinek sought to reintroduce individual will into public law, he could only do so by virtue of the recognition by the state that the individual will was directed at the common good.[8] Man as such had no originary legal standing; legal standing was seen to be a function of obligations that the state had imposed on itself in order to realize the common good. Seen in this perspective, the existence of the individual is constitutionally insignificant; it is nothing more than a formal requirement of the exercise of state power.

In Europe, the state has developed according to the pattern which Hegel intuited and of which he tried to inflect the trajectory. The state has entrenched its power through a form of auto-eclipse; instead of claiming full sovereign rights, it has allowed and even facilitated the expression of individualism as a means of social integration.[9] The self-expression of the individual has thus been used as a means to integrate her into the state, confirming the alienation of natural rights from subject to sovereign. As this chapter shows in more detail below, the movement towards closer integration among states in Europe has largely followed the same pattern; it has been driven by and in turn reinforced the primacy of executive power. Since 1975, executive power has been supplemented by a conscious strategy to develop a catalogue of individual rights—now fundamental rights—which are not, however, articulated from a notion of human liberty, but from the requirements of the community, especially as they relate to the workings of the internal market.

The excluded third between executive power and fundamental rights is the people as a political subject. What we have instead of a European demos is law without sovereignty, constitutionalism without politics. The absence of political community has been constant throughout, as the European Community added yet more constitutional dimensions in supplement of its basic economic constitution: the social, political, and security dimensions, of which Kaarlo Tuori speaks in his contribution to this volume.[10] The process of de-individualization, which he ties to the rise of the security constitution in response to terror, entails a movement beyond the individual, but it does not create any bond between them. The plurality is formal, unpolitical. Within the confines of the present work, we cannot undertake the analyses that would be needed to show why the absence of a robust political community has been a basic premise of the articulation of sovereign power in Europe, within and between states. However, it should be uncontroversial to assert that, for all its success, the European Union has not developed a political foundation in the strict sense. It is an open question whether its success does not depend on its lack of foundation.

This is a far cry from the universal and homogeneous state, the advent of which marks the end of history. Indeed, we shall not find this exemplary state in Europe. Fukuyama's belief that economic and political freedom can be mediated socially reflects a distinctly American experience. The pivot of this mediation is a specific nexus of popular sovereignty and constitutional order which is at the heart of the American political community. Taking the indication of Paul Kahn, we might say that, in the United States, the popular sovereign is manifested in and through the constitution in an act that affirms order.[11] The immediacy of popular sovereignty confers upon the constitution a political significance which it does not have in Europe, a difference perhaps best illustrated by the practice of constitutional review, as Kahn has showed so persuasively. This immediacy has its ground in an originary liberty which did not arise through sovereign concession, but attaches directly to the individual. Such has not been the format of European political thought. As we have seen, Hegel took from natural law the insight that individual liberty has no immediate political significance. Popular sovereignty may be the foundational principle of civil authority, but the alignment of economic and political freedom depends on the fact that individual liberty enters only into constitutional order as represented by the sovereign.

Even if one were to argue that this is in fact a liberal state, it is not a liberal state that rests on the twin pillars of economics and recognition, as Fukuyama tells us that it should. Representation—and only representation—is what makes us believe that it does. Not surprisingly, it is not to Hegel's theory of state, but to Tocqueville's analyses of American democracy that he looks to find examples of social practices in which economic freedom and recognition reinforce each other. If Fukuyama believes his vision of the liberal state to be the endpoint of the odyssey of reason through time and across the Atlantic divide, it is because he is certain that history has moved beyond Hegel's problem of how to reconcile economics and political community.[12] The hegemony of the United States does not solve the philosophical problem with which Hegel grappled. It only means that this problem is no longer perceived to be an acute problem that needs to be addressed. Fukuyama offers no argument to show why we no longer need to concern ourselves with the mediation of liberty, just an assertion that derives its persuasive pull from the historical context to which it is tied. His assurance reflects the moment of grace that followed the fall of the Berlin Wall, the moment of fusion with the world, in which the West could persuade itself that its hegemony was the perfect translation into history of liberty.

This moment of grace is reflected in the institutional developments of the European Community which followed in the wake of the fall of the Berlin Wall. In its 1993 review of the Maastricht treaty, the German Constitutional Court entertained the notion that a European-wide public domain could arise within the confines of the European Union to supplement national democracies.[13] Terror tore us away from this brief moment of grace. In doing so, it has brought to our attention differences between the constitutional orders on both sides of the Atlantic. It did not create those differences. The notion of an American exceptionalism which has replaced Fukuyama's universalism as the conventional wisdom on America's place in the international order revolves around the same constitutional structures. The disregard which the United States has demonstrated for international law in the war on terrorism is an aspect of the same political imagination which saw itself as being at one with the world. The most controversial elements of the U.S. policy on international law—the opting out of international legal regimes and the refusal to acknowledge the extraterritoriality of human rights—also refer back to the immediacy of popular sovereignty and to the felt need for its sanction.[14] Seen in this perspective, American exceptionalism is the other face of a triumphalism that we no longer quite understand. Equally, the development of Europe has been one of strong structural continuity. Ironically, the American stewardship of Europe proved to be a good incubator for the characteristics that now constitute the identity of the European legal order.

The impact of terror on the international legal order has thus been at the level of perception rather than at the level of structure. What has changed is not legal structure, but the sense that it carries. Terror has put into question the hegemony of the West. Is this an indication that hegemony of the West is on the wane? This has been the primary preoccupation of the United States since the attacks on September 11, 2001. If Americans have realized that their fusion with the world was but fleeting, they have attributed this fall from grace to the loss of a symbolic and military power that they once held. In Europe, the reflection on terror has taken a different course. It has not only made us aware that the unitary world order which emerged out of the Cold War is no more; it has also made us unable to understand that it ever was. As Europe stepped out of the binary format of the Cold

War, it found itself in a world that was new and yet strangely familiar. It found that it had caught up with itself, that it had developed into what it had, in a sense, been since its epoch ended: a domain in which law had taken the place of sovereignty, in which there were no peoples or nations, but only individuals with rights which attach to them by virtue of their humanity. In this world, boundaries do not really make sense, as reflected in the unease with which theorists of European integration have sought to square the universality of European ideals with their merely regional status.[15] This is not to suggest that the end of the Cold War brought about the passing away of the liberal states whose peaceful interaction would propel the history that would unfold beyond the end of history. Nevertheless, the world which the liberal states inhabit is no longer their world. It is the world of the individual, the subject of human rights. It may also be that of the terrorist.

TERROR AND CONSTITUTIONAL ORDER

A parallel might easily be suggested between individual and terrorist in that both have come to prominence in a time of crisis for the state, in a time where sovereignty has lost much of its explanatory power (even if it has lost none of its power of organization). The figure of the individual and that of the terrorist have taken up position within domains of power, which had hitherto been reserved for the state. However, is this parallel too easy? Does it extend beyond the surface? The perhaps most influential theory of terror of recent years is based on the assumption that it does. According to Philip Bobbitt, terrorism is a function of the constitutional order. All ages, or rather all constitutional orders, call forth a form of terrorism which is specific to them. The feudal order engendered the Crusades with their ideal of sacral violence and modern terrorism has arisen in response to the state's monopoly on legitimate violence. The terrorism of the twenty-first century is the product of a transformation of the state, which shifts the locus of its legitimacy from the nation to the individual or, more precisely, to the maximizing of individual welfare and the opening up of possibilities for individual self-expression. This transformation, which Bobbitt designates as a transition from welfare state to market state, is accomplished in and through the outsourcing of state functions that dissolves the edifice of the state into a global network of market relations. The terrorism of the twenty-first century has sprung from this network, gaining access to the information and technology that flow through the network, eventually, so Bobbitt prophesizes, getting hold of weapons of mass destruction. Modern terror, including the attacks of September 11, 2001, is an aspect of the same developments that have tied the legitimacy of the state to individual welfare. Hence Bobbitt's argument that the "same forces that are empowering the individual... are also empowering the forces of terror."[16]

These forces are affecting constitutional orders differently. As we have indicated, the development of sovereign power in Europe, both within and between states, has tended towards an ever more pronounced individualism. Europeans are at home in the world of modern terror which Bobbitt describes because they too are ultimate subjects. The United States, on the contrary, is removed from the world of terror by the presence of the popular sovereign. This difference conditions the manifestation of the terrorist. Whereas the terrorist appears as an individual in the eyes of Europeans, he appears as an alien to Americans, as an enemy of the state. The war on terrorism has made this difference relevant and, as David Jenkins has shown in his contribution to this volume,[17] it is no coincidence that the tension between the European human rights approach and the American insistence on the importance of the nation has been most palpable in the case law of the United Kingdom. Britain occupies at times an uncomfortable middle ground between the two extremes; it is geographically closer to Europe, to which it is tied by political history, but closer to the United States in the structure and spirit of its legal order. In the light of these differences, we might ask whether it is possible to write a comprehensive history of terror as a corollary to the history of constitutional order, as Bobbitt suggests. Does the belief that such a history can be written not repose upon the faith in the universality of one's perspective, as did the narrative of Fukuyama? If we consider the history which Bobbitt proposes, a number of observations come to mind, of which we shall mention two.

For one, the adoption of a unitary format commits Bobbitt to identifying forms of terror that correspond to premodern constitutional orders. Seeing such forms of organized violence as the Crusades, buccaneering, and the slave trade as instances of terror allows him to articulate an unbroken narrative, but it entails a loss of analytic precision. Although these practices share some of the characteristics of terror, they lack its political dimension. In the absence of this dimension, violence is best understood from the pragmatic end to which it is deployed: mere subsistence, economic gain or, as in the case of the Crusades, the conquest of a specific territory. More importantly, we should be warry of supposing, as Bobbitt does, that modern terror is a reaction to *our* constitutional order, a response to *our* categories of political thought and action. Such a belief is to be expected on the part of a victim who seeks to make sense of the attack which he has suffered. It also, however, reflects the world view of a power that may be beleaguered but which knows itself to have come under attack, as there is no one else to attack. The United States may only be the claviger and stweard, not the hegemon, of the system of transparent sovereignty that Bobbitt proposes as a replacement for the current system of international law. But this system revolves around the firm belief that the strategic interests of the United States will invariably coincide with those of all states which are not states of terror.[18] What is good for the United States is (still) good for the world.

It is not my aim to dispute the truth of this intuition, but simply to point out that it may miss the nature of the change of which terror is both a cause and a reflection. In the perspective that this chapter tries to outline, the significance of September 11, 2001, is that it opened our eyes to what had long been a fact: we are not living within the binary configuration of the Cold War that warranted the ideological hegemony of the United States. As the two world wars expanded the ambit of the state system to include two non-European states, so the end of the Cold War made new parts of the globe geopolitically relevant. Invariably, these new powers react against the dominance of the West, but we may be deluding ourselves if we think that the transformation of the global order can be understood simply as a reaction against us. In a sense, the bombs which terrorists set off across the Western world are obviously directed at us, but we may find that we do not enter into their strategic designs in anything but a formal capacity, as the token point of opposition. The terrorist who strikes at us may aim at something that we could neither give nor give up, as it is not subject to our control—the galvanization of a popular front on the Arab peninsula, to name but one possibility; thus, he may do violence not with a view to turn against us in some sort of crusade, which itself would only confirm that we still take centre stage, but in order to advance causes within contexts that remain closed to us.

This could be the novelty of the world into which terror has ushered us. We in the West will have to suffer the consequences of actions, whose strategic significance reveals itself only in contexts in which we are not present or are not in a privileged position to act. We will have to reconcile ourselves to the fact that cities in our part of the world will on occasion be used by others as a playground, in which they settle their differences, as we have on occasion used cities in other parts of the world to settle our differences. It remains to be seen whether we have at our disposal all the concepts needed to understand the consequences of this geopolitical reconfiguration for international law and politics. We will need to re-examine the primacy that we accord our own political order in the accounts we give of developments in international law and politics. We will have to come up with a new format to articulate these transformations that does not cast them simply as more or less successful reflections of our views in the West. If not exactly a new history, this would be a new format of historiography. Political history would, in a sense, begin again. Fukuyama may have been right after all, albeit in ways that he probably did not suspect and certainly did not intend.

CONCLUSION: TO ABSENT FRIENDS

If, as we have argued, the impact of terror on the international legal order has been at the level of perception rather than at the level of structure, we should expect this impact to pass under the radar of legal analysis. This has indeed been the case. There are, however, signs that the distance between the United States and Europe, which the war on terrorism has revealed and which terror has entrenched, is manifesting itself in what seems to be a dissipation of the cohesive force of the international legal order, a slackening of the ties that hold it together. Signs of this dissipation are, so one could would argue, evident in the recent *Kadi* judgment of the European Court of Justice (ECJ).[19] Asked to pronounce on Resolution 1267 of the U.N. Security Council that imposed measures to freeze funds of the Afghan Taliban, the ECJ reviewed the resolution for its compliance with the fundamental rights of the E.U. Charter, which incorporates the catalogue of human rights elaborated in the practice of the European Court of Human Rights. As a result of its review, the ECJ declined to give the resolution effect within the community, in contravention of article 103 of the U.N. Charter, which specifies that the obligations under the charter take precedence over all other international obligations of Member States. In doing so, the ECJ engaged in a bit of conceptual trickery, affirming that it did not in fact review the U.N. resolution, but the relevant E.U. Regulation, for its compliance with the E.U. Charter.

There is more than a whiff of bad faith about this argument, as the effect of this internal review is to subordinate international law to the fundamental rights and constitutional principles of E.U. law.[20] The question then arises how the decision situates the European legal order within the international legal order. The decision has sparked much discussion between those, on the one hand, who criticize the systemic inconsistencies that it creates within the structure of international law and those, on the other hand, who see the decision as a much-needed remedy against the inadequacies of the U.N. sanctions system. At the heart of this debate, however, lies another and more fundamental question: does the decision mark a rupture within international legal order, with the positing of an autonomous European legal order, or should it rather be seen as a natural stage in the development of the international legal order, a reflection of its ever-growing complexity and of the need for dialogue between competing legal orders?[21] If we put the question like this, there is only one right answer. As the decision does not establish a hierarchy of legal orders, we cannot assign a definite meaning to the notion of a rupture. Of the two perspectives, only the latter accommodates the complex reality of the international lawyer, for whom the existence of overlapping, competing legal orders is simply a fact of the workplace. Not surprisingly, legal scholars have overwhelmingly opted for a pluralist perspective in their attempts to unpack the meaning of the decision. An extensive and rapidly growing literature already exists to tell us how the triangulation of international law, E.U. law, and national law is likely to play out and how it might best be managed.

For our present purposes, the pluralist reading is not satisfactory. Its self-evidence rests upon an exclusion of the questions about the nature and direction of the motive forces that are affecting the configuration of the international legal order. If this chapter has tried to address these questions, it has not been with a view to criticizing the Court's decision. It is difficult to see how the Court could have held otherwise. Arguably, the implementation of Resolution 1267 in E.U. law would have been tantamount to negating the validity claims of the European legal order. Seen in this light, it seems excessive to speak of a foundational moment. One would have to say, rather, that this is a foundation *a minima*, that the ECJ posited only the foundation it needs to function, on par with its decisions in *Costa v. ENEL* and *Van Gend en Loos*.[22]

There would thus seem to be no reason to look for defining moments in the *Kadi* decision. However, the modest minimalism of the European foundation is perhaps the most telling sign of the structural change, the slackening of the international legal order, which we are trying to bring out. The reference by the ECJ to its own legal order mirrors the position of the U.S. courts; but unlike American exceptionalism, which for better or worse always holds within itself the possibility of being exemplary, the affirmation of European order does not carry a message for anybody. It could not, because it does not translate the will of a political subject. The decision to uphold the standards of the European Charter against a resolution of the U.N. Security Council was inevitable. It could not have been otherwise in a constitutional order, in which legitimacy hinges exclusively upon the protection of individual rights. However, the decision is also a sign that, unlike our allies and our enemies, we have no sense of urgency about the stakes of this war on terrorism. We are allied with the United States, but we are not fighting the same war. In fact, Europe is not fighting a war at all. The troops that European states have committed on the fronts of the war on terrorism are there as a matter of politics, not to avert an existential threat. Seen from Europe, there can be no existential threat, because there is no political subject whose existence could be threatened. We might regret this attitude of self-absorption which, at times, makes politics in Europe such a risible affair. The historical contingencies which it would take to change this attitude would, however, most likely give us even greater cause for regret. So what are the consequences for international law? There may be none, at least none that we can attribute exclusively to the advent of terror. This could simply yet be another moment in the incessant, but uneven process, by which international legal order is being shaped by the actions of its elements. Terror, thus understood, has brought out our implication in the shaping of the international legal order and the fact that we occupy a particular position within the international order. In this sense, terror has made us more of what we were. It depends on perspective whether this should give us cause for joy or regret.

NOTES

* Associate Professor, University of Copenhagen Faculty of Law.

1. See Giorgio Agamben, *State of Exception* (Chicago: University of Chicago Press, 2005).
2. For a full analysis, see Amnon Lev, "The Transformation of International Law in the 19th century" in Alexander Orakhelashvili, ed., *Research Handbook on Theory and History of International Law* (Cheltenham: Elgar Press, 2011) at 121–26.
3. Thomas Hobbes, *Leviathan*, ed. Edwin Curley (Indianapolis: Hackett, 1994 (1651)) at 78.
4. Legality of the Threat or Use of Nuclear Weapons, Advisory Opinion, 1996 ICJ Rep. 226, at para. 43, cf. para. 36.
5. Op.cit., para. 83.
6. Theodor Meron, "The Humanization of Humanitarian Law" (2000) 94 *American Journal of International Law* 2 at 239.
7. For an analysis of this bifurcation of the trajectory of political philosophy, see Amnon Lev, *Sovereignty and Liberty: A Study of the Foundations of Power* (Abingdon: Routledge, 2014) at 141–49, 151–58.
8. Georg Jellinek, *System der subjektiven öffentlichen Rechte* (Tübingen: J.C.B. Mohr, 1892) at 105.
9. G. W. F. Hegel, *Elements of the Philosophy of Right*, ed. Allen W. Wood (Cambridge: Cambridge University Press, 1991 (1821)) at § 270, 295–96.
10. Kaarlo Tuori, "A European Security Constitution," Chapter 6 in this volume.
11. Paul W. Kahn, *The Reign of Law:* Marbury *v.* Madison *and the Construction of America* (New Haven, Conn.: Yale University Press, 1997) at 69–74, 189–96, 219–29.
12. Francis Fukuyama, *The End of History and the Last Man* (London: Penguin Books, 1992) at 203–04.

13. BVerfGE 89, 155 of October 12, 1993: 2 BvR 2134, 2159/92 (98–99). The German Constitutional Court took a much less sanguine view in 2009, as it had to review the compatibility of the Lisbon treaty with the German constitution, this time emphasizing the pivotal role of national communities in the creation of a democratic public domain. See BVerfGE of June 29, 2009: 2 BvE 2/08 (251).
14. See Paul W. Kahn, "American Exceptionalism, Popular Sovereignty, and the Rule of Law" in Michael Ignatieff, ed., *American Exceptionalism and Human Rights* (Princeton N.J.: Princeton University Press, 2005) at 207–08, 217, 221.
15. See, for example, Mireille Delmas-Marty, *Pour un droit commun* (Paris: Éditions du Seuil, 1989) at 194–95, 224–26, and Joseph H.H. Weiler, *The Constitution of Europe* (Cambridge: Cambridge University Press, 1999) at 37–39, 90–94.
16. Philip Bobbitt, *Terror and Consent: The Wars for the Twenty-First Century*, 1st ed. (New York: Anchor Books, 2009) at 85.
17. David Jenkins, "Citizenship and the Limits of Due Process since 9/11," Chapter 10 in this volume.
18. Bobbitt, *supra* note 16 at 486–87.
19. *Kadi and Al Barakaat International Foundation* v, *Council and Commission* (C-402/05P & C-415/05P) (E.C.J.) at paras. 281, 282, and 285.
20. Ibid. at paras. 306–08.
21. I owe thanks to Professor Iain Cameron for explaining the stakes, both apparent and real, of the *Kadi* judgment.
22. ECR 585 (6/64), Judgment of 15 July 1964; ECR 1 (26/62), Judgment of 5 February 1963.

CHAPTER 6

A European Security Constitution?

KAARLO TUORI*

Is it warranted to speak of a security constitution, analogous to, for instance, an economic constitution or political constitution? In post-9/11 debates, the term "security constitution" or "national security constitution" has been used, but rather hesitantly. Indeed, modern constitutions have entertained an ambivalent relation with security. Security considerations have often—in a Hobbesian way, one could say—weighed heavily among the objectives of new political formation and its constitution (i.e., behind the constitutive functions of the constitution). However, constitutions fulfill not only constitutive or polity-building functions, but also restrictive ones: constitutions are expected to discipline the use of public power, primarily through fundamental rights, and democratic and judicial control. In the focus of the restrictive functions, closely related to the idea of a (democratic) *Rechtsstaat*, lie executive bodies and activities related to internal and external security, police and armed forces. From the perspective of restrictive functions, security is not something to be brought about by the constitution but something pre-existing it; security is a preceding reality to be submitted to constitutional forms, procedures, and limitations.

A typical ambiguity afflicts relationships between security and constitution: security seems to be unable to find a stable location in respect of the boundaries of the constitution, to establish itself either within or outside the constitution. This goes a long way in accounting for the hesitancy to develop the concept of a security constitution. Of course, it is always possible to point to individual constitutional provisions relating to security and to label their assemblage a "(national) security constitution," as, indeed, has been done in post-9/11 debates in the United States.[1]

As candidates for inclusion in such a "surface-level" security constitution, we can enlist, for instance, provisions on decisions about war and peace, on armed forces, and on states of emergency and emergency powers. In the context of the European Union, reference can be made to the fact that, ever since Maastricht, the treaties have included distinct titles or chapters not only on Common Foreign and Security Policy (CFSP) but on issues of internal security as well. However, if a "security constitution" is understood in more substantial terms than as a simply additive or enumerative category, a minimum degree of *coherence* uniting individual constitutional provisions should be required. Where do constitutions in general receive their coherence? Arguably, the main coherence-producing factors are, first, the object of constitutional regulation—the constitutional object—and, second, the constitutional culture animating the application and interpretation of individual constitutional provisions. Thus, talking of the European Union's security constitution could be warranted by reference to either security as a common object of regulation by individual treaty provisions or to a distinct "security culture" linking these provisions together and making them intelligible. A brief foray into general constitutional theory is needed to substantiate these premises.

DIMENSIONS AND LEVELS OF CONSTITUTION(ALISATION)

Even as a legal concept, "constitution" should be understood in relational terms. Through a constitution, the law relates to something else (or, in the case of the juridical constitution, to itself), to a *constitutional object* and, thus, establishes a *constitutional relation*. Insight into the relational nature of a constitution makes it possible to distinguish between diverse constitutional dimensions, all with their particular constitutional object. One can use the following taxonomy for discussing European, transnational constitution(s): economic constitution, juridical constitution, political constitution, social constitution, and security constitution.[2] Each of the fields appearing as constitutional objects has been discussed in constitutional terms; constitutional vocabulary, although perhaps not the very concept of a constitution, is employed in the object language with which a constitutional theorist at his/her slippery meta-level has to reckon.

The European constitution is not a standstill phenomenon but, rather, an ever-extending chain of constitutional speech acts. Instead of the revolutionary-tuned concepts of *constituent power, demos*, and *constitutional moment*, the key position in its examination is held by the evolutionary concept of *constitutionalisation*. Furthermore, European constitutionalisation has been a differentiated process: the European constitutions have not developed simultaneously or at the same pace but, rather, successively, in a distinct order. European constitutionalisation is susceptible to a periodisation where each stage receives its particular colouring from a particular constitution. Reflecting the temporal and functional primacy of economic integration, the first wave proceeded under the auspices of economic constitution. In the second phase, marked by the milestone decisions of the European Court of Justice (ECJ) in the 1960s, such as *van Gend en Loos* and *Costa v. Enel*,[3] the emphasis shifted to juridical constitution. During the third wave, with the 1993 Maastricht Treaty as the landmark, the focus was transferred to political constitution. Finally, in our contemporary age, say, since the Treaty of Amsterdam in 1998, the pacemaker role appears to have been taken by security constitution. The expansion of constitutionalisation from its original economic domicile to new fields appears to follow a particular constitutional logic: at the outset, constitutionalisation addresses requirements and/or consequences of the economic constitution but, subsequently, acquires a dynamic of its own. As discussed below, this has been the case with the security constitution, too.

Related to "constitutionalisation," even other process-oriented concepts are of particular relevance for Europe-level constitutional analysis. In important respects, constitutionalisation has equaled *transnationalisation*, superseding nation-state structures and detaching decision-making from Member State control. Transnationalisation has its corollary in *individualization*, establishing direct links between European institutions and individuals in their diverse roles.

The relational character of (constitutional) law leads us to discuss a general feature of legal concepts and doctrines—namely, the fact that they include at least an implicit or *hidden social theory*: that is, a conception of the particular social field under regulation. Property or contract law theories, for instance, involve a particular view of the basics of the economic system and its functioning. Constitutional concepts and theories are no exception. They, too, imply a conception of the constitutional object. This is an important observation for examining European constitutional discourse. Diverse constitutional concepts and conceptions may imply diverse social theoretical assumptions about the constitutional object. Accordingly, the decisive difference between two alternative views of the European economic constitution may lie in their respective interpretation of the functioning of the market economy and its interplay with political power.

With the idea of a "hidden social theory," implicit in constitutional doctrine(s), we have already arrived at the other issue of general constitutional theory, which is of particular relevance for discussing the European security constitution: the role of *constitutional culture*. Here the general starting point is the indispensable role legal culture plays in all law; it provides legal actors with the *Vorverständnis* through which they approach legal problems. Legal culture is not something external to law as legal order, as a symbolic-normative entity, but an integral element of it. The legal order cannot exist without its cultural underpinnings: the normative, conceptual, and methodological resources with which legal culture furnishes legal actors. Constitutional culture, which unfolds its impact through the *Vorverständnis* of constitutional actors, plays as important a role in constitutional law and discourse as does legal culture in general in law and legal discourse. A constitution should not be reduced to a "surface-level" normative phenomenon, consisting solely of explicit constitutional enactments and decisions. It should not be understood merely in terms of a formal constitution (i.e., as explicitly formulated norms). Rather, a formal constitution remains only signs on paper without the contribution of constitutional culture which imbues the signs with meaning. Constitutional law, as the normative pole of the constitutional relation, includes cultural layers, which add the flesh to the bones of explicit, "surface-level" normative material.

A crucial testing-stone in the search for a European security constitution is whether a unifying background concept(ion) of security exists which provides meaning for individual treaty provisions and informs the *Vorverständnis* of European security actors. The European security constitution can receive its coherence either from its regulatory object or from a distinct notion of security. It is important to notice that these two potential coherence-creating factors are not independent from each other but closely interrelated. Regulatory objects do not exist independently from the interpretative framework of the "hidden social theory," which is an integral part of the law's cultural level. This also goes for security as a constitutional object; there is no security as such, but only as seen through a distinct conceptual scheme.

FROM EMERGENCY TO SECURITY

At the treaty level—the "surface level" of E.U. constitutional law—we can observe an advancing constitutionalisation of the security dimension starting, from the declaration of listed security issues as "common interests" of the Member States in Maastricht, and ending up with the "communitarisation" of the entire Area of Freedom, Security and Justice (AFSJ) and the upgrading of security objectives in Lisbon. However, increased attention to security issues at the treaty level does not yet in itself corroborate the claim of a distinct European security constitution or—to use a somewhat less bold expression—a distinct security dimension of the European constitution, comparable to the European economic constitution. The necessary coherence can be brought about by the concept of security, which holds a key position in determining both the cultural level in and the regulatory object of the putative European security constitution.

This claim of the dependence of the regulatory object on the concept of security bears some resemblance to the constructivist approach of the Copenhagen School. What is called "security" or a "security problem" does not have any objective, independent existence but results from a naming or from a speech act by a securitizing actor: "by definition, something is a security problem when the elites declare it to be so."[4] This is neither an innocent declaration nor an innocent speech act, but implies the need of and, by the same token, a justification for extraordinary measures to maintain or restore security. Thus, "security is the move that takes politics beyond the established rules of the game and frames the issue either as a special kind of politics or as above politics."[5] In juridical terms, then, "politics beyond the established rules of the game" corresponds to a state of exception (state of emergency), and other extraordinary measures permitted during such a state.

While subscribing to the constructivist thesis, I would like to point to two related issues which are important to an exploration of the European security constitution. First, there are the wider cultural presuppositions of security-related speech acts and their success. These speech acts are not *Entscheidungen aus Nichts* but dependent on the cultural factors which inform the *Vorverständnis* of "securitizing actors." The speech acts also do not succeed in their justificatory intent if they do not find (cultural) resonance among the political and legal elites, as well as the public at large. Unlike Carl Schmitt, the Copenhagen School is aware of the importance of the cultural context of securitizing acts as speech acts.

What the Copenhagen School can be criticized for is holding—in Schmitt's wake—a sharp distinction between a state of exception and normal times. Constructivism under the Copenhagen School seems to be attached to a sharp distinction between exceptional and normal times. In this sense, it follows traditional constitutional doctrine, which has seen the state of exception and concomitant emergency powers as the main constitutional response to security concerns. However, as many observers have recently argued, the boundary separating exceptional from normal times has become increasingly blurred.[6] This is not to say that arguments centered around constitutional emergency powers exhausted all of their relevance,[7] nor does a strict demarcation correspond to the rationale of the European security constitution. It is true, though, that the Solidarity Clause in Art. 222 of the Treaty on the Functioning of the European Union (TFEU) evokes a pending emergency. However, this clause does not adhere to the continental European constitutional tradition, with its requirement of an explicit declaration of a state of emergency and the consequent (partial) suspension of such constitutional basics as fundamental rights, the rule of law, and the separation of powers. Tellingly, no emergency provision comparable to that of Art. 15 of the E.C.H.R. or Art. 4 of the U.N. Covenant on Civil and Political Rights was included in the E.U. Charter of Fundamental Rights.

What, then, has been the argumentative figure that has facilitated lowering the wall separating exceptional from normal times, and emergency measures from normal legislation? The concept of security has played a major part in this development. Under justification of security exigencies, normal legislation has in many countries acquired features that bring it close to the characteristic effects of a declaration of emergency or state of exception. Such features include limitations on fundamental rights, the rule of law, and the separation of powers, as well as increases in the powers of security authorities. For example, the typical nation-state reaction to 9/11 and the subsequent terrorist attacks in Europe did not consist of a declaration of emergency and time-limited emergency measures, but of rather far-reaching amendments to such normal legislation. Anti-terrorist legislation was adopted not only in the United States but in European countries as well. However, 9/11 only accelerated a long-term, post–World War II development. In the United States, for instance, the concept of national security has been invoked to warrant expanding presidential powers ever since the Truman presidency and the start of the Cold War.[8] "Security" or "national security" has become the main justification for a permanent state of exception in that country. E.U. constitutional law must be analysed in this general cultural framework, where a clear-cut concept of emergency or state of exception has increasingly yielded to a diffuse, expansionist, and boundary-breaking concept of security.

"Security" is a tricky concept, hard to pinpoint in an unambiguous definition. The most promising way to approach it is through the concept of risk—for many sociological observers a key concept in modern society—and to define "security" negatively, as connoting *fight against risks*.

Emergencies are temporarily and territorially limited and located, already realised risks, with identifiable appearances and sources. "Security" may cover already realised risks, too, but the emphasis is elsewhere, in *anticipation* and *prevention*. Security calls for continuous detection and assessment of risks and security threats. Hence the inherent *expansionism* of security; ever-new risks can be perceived and brought under the umbrella of "security," named as security threats, and, consequently, seen as calling for security measures. Such expansionism is also conspicuous in the development of the European Union's security dimension, say, from the modest start with anti-terrorist cooperation in the Trevi framework in the 1970s to the Internal Security Strategy for the European Union, approved by the European Council in March 2010. The strategy identifies the following security threats as "main challenges for the internal security of the EU": terrorism; serious and organised crime; cybercrime; cross-border crime; violence itself, such as youth violence or hooligan violence at sports events; as well as natural and man-made disasters, such as forest fires, earthquakes, floods and storms, droughts, energy shortages, and major information and communication technology breakdowns. A comprehensive concept of security is said to entail that "internal security must be seen as encompassing a wide range of measures with both horizontal and vertical dimensions"[9].

Related to its diffuse and expansionist character, "security" possesses an intrinsic boundary-breaking tendency. It tends to blur not only the distinction between exceptional and normal times, and extraordinary measures and normal legislation, but other important divisions of traditional Western constitutional doctrine as well, such as external and internal security, war and crime, or soldiering and policing. "Surface-level" E.U. constitutional law has still stuck to the dichotomy between external and internal security, the former—the previous first pillar—is still regulated by the TEU (Title V General Provisions on the Union's external action and specific provisions on the Common Foreign and Security Policy) and clearly dominated by intergovernmentalism. However, as responses to 9/11 clearly proved, the distinction is difficult to maintain, and AFSJ strategy documents make incursions into domains falling under Title V TEU.

The E.U. Internal Security Strategy also highlights the typical accent on prevention, calling for a "proactive, intelligence-led approach." A strategy of prevention and anticipation implies the need of continuous flows of *information* about potential risks. Indeed, data processing and exchange of information have been essential aspects of the European Union's security dimension. Since establishment of the SIS (Schengen Information System) through the Schengen Convention of 1990, Europe-wide information systems have abounded; E.U. agencies, such as Europol and Eurojust, as well as diverse networks of security professionals, have, to a significant extent, been sites for information sharing. The Hague AFSJ Programme of 2004 introduced the *principle of availability*, which was to epitomise "an innovative approach to the cross-border exchange of law-enforcement information."[10]

The crucial role of information sharing and data processing is not limited to law-enforcement, but extends to the whole field of security, defined in terms of risk management. Risks are something quantifiable, which can be calculated and assessed; such calculation requires information. Here we encounter a distinct feature of the modern mode of governance, which Michel Foucault discussed under the label of *dispositif de securité* and where the main object of power is not individuals, as they are for disciplinary mechanisms, but populations.

Since 9/11, terrorism has topped E.U. lists of security threats, although by no means was it a starting point for common anti-terrorist activities within the European Union. Terrorism exemplifies many of the typical features of the concept of security which lie behind E.U. legislation, as well as programmatic documents and practical activities. Terrorism has proved to be a phenomenon hard to capture in an unequivocal definition. Within the European Union, terrorism has not found a fixed location in relation to criminality. As the E.U. Framework Decision on Combating Terrorism makes clear, terrorism has been considered a criminal offence or, rather, a series of criminal offences. However, it seems not to be reducible to criminality, but instead goes beyond it. In E.U. legislation and programmes, terrorism is at times assimilated with "other" serious crimes and at others dealt with as a security threat separate from crime. The European Union retained a distance from the "war on terrorism" rhetoric of the Bush administration, but has not taken a firm position in favour of treating terrorism as a crime. It is as if defining terrorism "merely" as a crime would downplay the enormity of the threat to the universal values and principles invoked in the Preamble to the Framework Decision on Combating Terrorism.

Be that as it may, terrorism demonstrates how conceptual diffuseness and the breaking down of traditional constitutional distinctions go hand in hand; war and crime, external and internal security, soldiering and policing are hard to keep separate in combating terrorism. The fight against terrorism corroborates the connection among security, prevention, and information, too, as potential terrorists must be identified and terrorist plots unearthed before their realisation. There arises the never-saturated need for registering individuals and intercepting their communications. Terrorism is a *de-localised* and *de-individualised* security threat. It does not possess fixed headquarters, but operates through networks for which territorial boundaries pose no obstacles. Terrorists, in turn, are seen not so much as individual persons, but rather as replaceable cogs in an anonymous machine. The identity of a suicide-bomber is not important, and Al Qaeda is not in need of even Osama bin Laden. The difference in perceptions of criminal offenders and terrorists is conspicuous.[11]

SECURITY IN THE AREA OF FREEDOM, SECURITY AND JUSTICE

European Union treaty law puts (internal) security in the context of the Area of Freedom, Security and Justice (AFSJ). Much has been written about the "securitization" of the AFSJ, the subjection of freedom and justice to security, and the defining of freedom and justice by their relation to security. Indeed, such a tendency is easy to perceive, although it is perhaps not as unequivocal as critical observers are sometimes prone to claim. To begin with, the subordination of *freedom* to security is discernible in its depiction as the source of the security issues the AFSJ is expected to address. In this quality, freedom is defined, first of all, as freedom of movement within the European Union; abolishing internal border controls calls for "complementary" or "flanking" security measures. Art. 2 TEU-Amsterdam introduced the AFSJ objective in the following terms: "to maintain and develop the Union as an area of freedom, security and justice, in which the free movement of persons is assured in conjunction with appropriate measures with respect to external border controls, asylum, immigration and the prevention and combating of crime." The same connection between freedom and security, with an implicit reduction of freedom of movement, is still retained in Art. 3(2) TEU-Lisbon, and in the Preamble to the TEU, as well.

Yet, this is not the only way in which "freedom" has been defined through security. In the two first AFSJ programmes, adopted by the European Council in Tampere in 1999 and in The Hague in 2004, the envisaged policy measures were divided along the sub-areas of freedom, security, and justice. What fell under "freedom" was common policy in the field of asylum, migration, and borders, with a clear emphasis on security-related measures. In fact, the section "*Strengthening Freedom*" in The Hague Programme was mainly about strengthening security, about building up "Fortress Europe," as critics have put it.

However, from the very introduction of the AFSJ, a certain ambiguity in the definition of freedom can be depicted. Although "freedom" is primarily defined as freedom of movement within the European Union, the AFSJ programmes suggest that it can be assigned wider contents, too. The system of fundamental rights offers a natural point of reference for elaborating a more comprehensive notion that reaches beyond mere freedom of movement and, by the same token, detaches freedom from the rationale of the economic constitution. Indeed, all the AFSJ programmes adopted by the European Council have at least hinted at a link between the freedom dimension of the AFSJ and fundamental rights, although they have been rather indecisive as concerns the significance of this link for policy measures. The post-Lisbon Stockholm Programme of 2010 has taken the most far-reaching step—at least at the justificatory level—in the direction of disconnecting "freedom" from its narrow freedom-of-movement connotation and defining it in terms of fundamental rights and citizenship. Promoting citizenship and fundamental rights heads the list of political priorities in the introductory section of the programme: "European citizenship must become a tangible reality," and "the area of freedom, security and justice must, above all, be a single area in which fundamental rights and freedoms are protected."[12] The Stockholm Programme as a whole clearly aims to respond to criticism of the AFSJ, the main concerns of which have included its overall "securitization" and its lack of democratic and judicial accountability. Still, the AFSJ Title of the TFEU includes no mention of the E.U. Charter on Fundamental Rights, nor are there any mutual references between the AFSJ Title and the Citizenship Part of the TFEU.[13]

Finally, we have the concept of *justice*. How is it defined and what is its relation to security? Justice has not been discussed as a substantive value or principle but, rather, as a procedural and institutional issue. In all three AFSJ programmes, it has quite consistently been defined in terms of access to justice and judicial cooperation in cases with a cross-border dimension. In the Stockholm Programme, the principle of *mutual recognition*, already introduced in Tampere, is hailed as the cornerstone of judicial cooperation in both civil and criminal matters. Legislative harmonization is also enlisted as a means to achieve a European Area of Justice, but, as Art. 67(3) and 82(2) TFEU make clear, harmonization is secondary to mutual recognition.

Especially in judicial cooperation in criminal matters, justice maintains a close link with security. Measures that, according to Art. 67(3) TFEU, serve the objective of ensuring a high level of security include "coordination and cooperation between police and judicial authorities and other competent authorities, as well as . . . the mutual recognition of judgments in criminal matters and, if necessary, the approximation of criminal laws." The Tampere conclusions established an explicit connection between justice and security by, for instance, stating that "criminals must find no ways of exploiting differences in the judicial systems of Member States."[14]

Statements such as this lend credence to the claim that "security" is the main linking element in the conceptual cluster of freedom, security, and justice: "it is part of the rationale of the justice concept of the AFSJ and at the same time an essential condition of its concept of freedom."[15] Conceding this, as well as the primacy accorded to the fight against terrorism and other security concerns especially after 9/11, we should also at least register the programmatic efforts to conceive of freedom in terms of fundamental rights and citizenship. Furthermore, we should acknowledge the civil-law aspect of justice, which is not reducible to security, but rather addresses civil-law consequences of economic constitutionalisation.

THE INSECURE SECURITY CONSTITUTION

Treaty-level examination shows that there certainly is a constitutional aspect to the European Union's security dimension or—to put it in another way—that the security dimension can be approached from a constitutional perspective. Ever since the Maastricht Treaty, the security dimension has been regulated at the "surface level" of E.U. constitutional law. Moreover, security-related provisions have loosened their ties with the economic constitution; they no longer merely attend to the consequences of the economic constitution, but have acquired an independent constitutional rationale. It is also evident that the security dimension raises urgent questions of constitutional legitimacy: it touches on core areas of state sovereignty, as well as fundamental rights and liberties of individuals as objects of security measures.[16] Often enough, treaty provisions have merely ratified existing administrative and professional cooperation and thus bear witness to the legitimacy-enhancing function of constitutionalisation.

Still, to acknowledge the constitutional relevance of the security dimension or the concerns of constitutional legitimacy it raises is not equivalent to treating the security constitution as a relatively independent dimension of a European constitution. What is important is that a distinct constitutional regulatory object seems to emerge from our reflections in the preceding sections: *security as combating security risks or threats*. Arguably, such an understanding also imbues the constitutional *Vorverständnis* through which European security actors—including legislative and judicial institutions—tackle security issues as constitutional issues and interpret security-related provisions of constitutional law.

However, considering the diffuse and expansionist nature of "security," it is no wonder that tricky problems arise if we are asked to mark the exact boundaries of the security constitution. In the foregoing I have, without actually justifying my choice, identified the security dimension with internal security, regulated, first, by the third-pillar provisions of the Maastricht Treaty and, finally, after Lisbon, by the AFSJ provisions of Title V of Part Three TFEU. Nevertheless, one of the boundaries which the concept of security tends to break is that separating internal from external security. So, the choice here to focus on internal security could be questioned: should external security not also be included—that is, Common Foreign and Security Policy, the domain of the previous first pillar and now regulated by Title V of Chapter II TEU-Lisbon? Arguments both *pro* and *contra* could certainly be put forth. To take another boundary-drawing issue: should we, at the surface-level of treaty provisions, include in the security constitution the whole AFSJ or merely the security field, complemented with those issues subsumed under "freedom" or "justice," which are dominated by security considerations? To take a third example, should fundamental rights be conceived as constraints imposed on security measures from another constitutional dimension—from the political constitution—or should fundamental rights be included in the security constitution itself, at least rights with direct bearing on the security dimension, such as those enshrined in Chapters II (Freedom) and VI (Justice) of the E.U. Charter? Again, arguments in favour of both alternatives are available.

Such questions concerning the exact contours of the European security constitution are relevant, but can be left unanswered here; it is perhaps more important to take notice of them than to try to provide definite answers. What is vital is the fuzziness of the boundaries of the security constitution, at the poles of both constitutional law and constitutional object. If one assumes the existence of a specific security dimension in European constitutionalisation, one should also concede and explore the peculiarities that the security constitution displays, for example, when compared with the economic, juridical, or political ones. One of these peculiarities is that due to the diffuse, expansionist, and boundary-breaking character of "security," the security constitution does not possess clear-cut contours.

Another peculiarity is the *combination of transnationalism and intergovernmentalism*, which marks the institutional and procedural aspects of the security constitution. With regard to these aspects, constitutionalisation equals transnationalisation, and a central criterion of the advancing constitutionalisation of the security dimension is its advancing transnationalisation. However, intergovernmentalism has proven to be an ineradicable trait in this field. The Commission has obtained the power of initiative, but the TFEU still provides for a diluted form of Member State initiative, too (a quarter of Member States possess a legislative initiative parallel to that of the Commission in issues pertaining to police cooperation and judicial cooperation in criminal matters), and the special legislative procedure required in several AFSJ provisions include unanimity in the Council and a merely consultative role for the Parliament. Furthermore, E.U. agencies, such as Europol, Eurojust, or Frontex, do not have operational law-enforcement competences, nor do they wield public power in Member States. Their main function is to support Member-State authorities and to provide a site for professional cooperation, as well as for information sharing and data processing. Finally, regarding the justice dimension, establishing mutual recognition as the main option is an intergovernmental alternative to the transnationalism of legislative harmonization. All this lends credence to the claim[17] that *cooperation rather than integration* remains the prevailing principle and that this sets the AFSJ aside from domains falling under the economic constitution, such as competition policy or common commercial policy.

The reason for the lingering intergovernmentalism and the continuing dominance of the principle of cooperation should be evident. The security constitution touches on and is prone to collide with traditional core attributes of state sovereignty. These attributes are related to the Weberian characteristics of the modern state as possessor of a monopoly on legitimate violence, and, often enough, they are protected by basic constitutional principles which, according to the constitutional doctrine of Member States, pose insurmountable hurdles to additional competence transfers to transnational bodies. Transnational legislative or operational competence in criminal law, policing, and anti-terrorist measures are also prone to infringe on individual fundamental rights, and here too collisions with basic constitutional principles of Member States are possible. In this respect, the saga of the European Arrest Warrant and the constitutional assessment of its legislative implementation in Member States is instructive enough.[18]

Sovereign power is the main attribute in the traditional three-element concept of the state, the other two being population and territory. Member States have been quite jealous in guarding their control over their population and territory, too. Although transnationalisation has progressed further in the domain of migration, asylum, and borders than in criminal law and law-enforcement, Member States have retained their power to determine volumes of migration from third countries to their territory (Art. 79(5) TFEU) and the geographical demarcation of their borders (Art. 77(4) TFEU).

State sovereigntist concerns are more pronounced in some Member States than others, and national constitutional doctrines of core constitutional principles enjoying protection against transnational intrusion on the part of the European Union vary as well. This is a central backdrop to a further peculiarity of the security constitution: that is, its *mix of coherence and fragmentation*. The concept of security creates the necessary cultural and object-related coherence which in general justifies talking of a European security constitution. Moreover, the Lisbon Treaty has increased coherence at the constitutional "surface level" of treaty law by assembling AFSJ provisions under the same Title of the TFEU and by harmonizing available legislative instruments and procedures. At the same time, fragmentation is conspicuous; the security constitution does not earn very high marks in redeeming the constitutional promise of unity and order. Ever since its pre-Maastricht origins under the auspices of international law, the security dimension has been a model example of "variable geometry" and "enhanced cooperation": the Schengen system has never—neither before nor after incorporation of the Schengen *acquis* into the E.U. legal framework—covered all Member States, and the opt-outs of some Member States have been complemented by the opt-ins of non–Member State Schengen associates. If the AFSJ has managed to obtain some substantive coherence as a policy area, in geographical terms no unitary area of freedom, security, and justice exists.

The emphasis on cooperation instead of integration points to constitutionally relevant specificities in the operational *modus* of the security dimension. In transnational contexts, cooperation is the mode of operation predominately of the executive; of administrations, civil servants, and other government professionals. Indeed, a major part of AFSJ treaty provisions deal with such cooperation, and, as already pointed out, in many cases treaty provisions have merely added constitutional acknowledgement to developments already realized. The AFSJ is the promised land of networks of security officials and professionals, and even AFSJ agencies, some of them provided for in the Treaty (such as Europol and Eurojust), consist to a large extent of such networks. Associated with administrative and professional cooperation, *information exchange and data processing*, which are required for identifying and assessing security risks, are vital for the operational *modus* of the AFSJ. This raises constitutional concerns, especially in respect of data protection and the right to privacy.

Since its pre-Maastricht beginnings in Trevi and Schengen, the security dimension has been accused of *lack of transparency and democratic and judicial accountability*. The advancing constitutionalisation since Maastricht has not been able to quash the criticism. The post-Lisbon Stockholm Programme bears witness to its continuing pertinence. The European Council not only emphasises the link to fundamental rights, but also refers to "the increased role that the European Parliament and National

Parliaments will play following the entry into force of the *Lisbon Treaty* and to the greater opportunity Art. 11 TEU provides for citizens and associations to make known and publicly exchange their views in all areas of Union action."[19] Still it is more than doubtful that the Lisbon Treaty or the assurances of the Stockholm Programme will be able to efface concerns about transparency, democracy, and accountability. The emphasis on the executive instead of the legislative branch, the confidential nature of the data processed in the security dimension, and the scarcity of decisions with direct legal relevance pose formidable obstacles to realizing these values even in a nation-state context. In the AFSJ of the European Union, with its primacy of administrative and professional cooperation at the expense of legislative integration, the obstacles are still considerably higher. Exceptions to the ordinary legislative procedure, which confer even on the legislative process a character of executive intergovernmental cooperation and reduce the role of the European Parliament to mere consultations, or the curbing of the jurisdiction of the CJEU (former ECJ) in respect of Member-State security measures, do not exactly alleviate the situation.

CONCLUSION

This exploration of the peculiarities of the security constitution ought to conclude with some observations on the position of the individual. A democratic *Rechtsstaat*, as envisaged by such basic constitutional principles as fundamental rights, rule of law, and democracy, is premised on a conception of individuals as autonomous and responsible persons. European constitutionalisation has been a process of not only transnationalisation but also of individualization, of establishing links between transnational institutions and European individuals. In this respect, constitutionalization and its expansion to new dimensions have entailed a gradual enrichment of European citizenship. Here the security constitution makes an exception. Although both the security objective in Art. 3(2) TEU and the AFSJ programmes flirt with citizenship terminology, the security dimension does not furnish individuals with any new rights that would further enhance their European citizenship; as envisaged beneficiaries of security measures, individuals are passive recipients of collective goods rather than active citizens and bearers of rights.[20] Arguably, individuals enter the focus of security measures primarily, not as beneficiaries of increased security, but as potential security risks whose characteristics, propensities, and actions must be surveyed and recorded. As objects of surveillance and data processing individuals are treated as replaceable members of a group—a population, as Foucault would say—rather than as autonomous and responsible, both unique and equal persons, as an understanding of them as bearers of rights and freedoms and as citizens of a democratic polity would presuppose. In this sense, security is a domain of *de-individualisation*, rather than individualization.[21]

The security dimension comes up with new divisions and classifications of individuals that do not return to individuals their unique personhood, but do counteract the principle of equality. So, for example,[22] the ECJ's *ordre public* rulings in the 1970s gave birth to a "European individual," with a juridical locus in the grey zone between the law of nationals and the law of aliens. With the development of common policies on visas and migration, asylum and borders, new categories have abounded, such as third-country nationals and illegal immigrants, or refugees and asylum seekers. These groups have a legal status differing from that of full-blown citizens and, often enough, are objects of a diversified system of information and surveillance. The security constitution has not only de-individualizing, but also *unequalizing* consequences.

As argued in this chapter, "security" has largely replaced "emergency" and "state of exception" as the principal argumentative figure in the domain of the security constitution. European constitutional law hardly mentions emergencies; in institutional practice, though, emergency talk has retained at least part of its justificatory significance, as has recently been proven by the framing and handling of the sovereign debt crisis. At the national level, the security dimension is perhaps the primary *battlefield between constitutive and restrictive constitutional functions*. Within the European Union, too, the security constitution poses grave fundamental-rights problems, which are further aggravated by its de-individualizing and de-equalizing tendencies. In sum, even without the constitutional black or grey hole of a state of exception, the security constitution of the European Union displays conspicuous features of an *anti-constitution*. This is the ultimate paradox which afflicts it.

NOTES

* Professor of Jurisprudence, University of Helsinki Faculty of Law. The article has been written within the research programme of the Centre of Excellence in Foundations of European Law and Polity, financed by the Finnish Academy.

1. Jason Mazzone, "The Security Constitution" (2005) 53 *UCLA Law Review* 29.
2. Kaarlo Tuori, "The Many Constitutions of Europe" in Kaarlo Tuori and Suvi Sankari, eds., *The Many Constitutions of Europe* (Aldershot: Ashgate, 2010).
3. *Van Gend en Loos v. Netherlands Inland Revenue Administration* [1963] E.C.R. 1; *Costa v. Enel* [1964] E.C.R. 585.

4. Ole Waever, "Securitization and Desecuritization" in Ronnie D. Lipschutz, ed., *On Security* (New York: Columbia University Press, 1995) 46–86 at 54.
5. Harry Buzan, Ole Waever, and Jaap de Wilde, *Security: A New Framework for Analysis* (Boulder: Rinner, 1998) at 26.
6. Oren Gross, "Once More unto the Breach: The Systematic Failure of Applying the European Convention on Human Rights to Entrenched Emergencies" (1998) 23 *Yale Journal of International Law* 437; Oren Gross, "The Normless and Exceptionless Exception: Carl Schmitt's Theory of Emergency Powers and the 'Norm-Exception' Dichotomy" (2000) 21 *Cardozo Law Review* 1825; Oren Gross and Fionnuala Ni Aolain, "Emergency, War and International Law: Another Perspective" (2001) 70 *Nordic Journal of International Law* 29.
7. See, for example, Sandord Levinson and Jack M. Balkin, "Constitutional Dictatorship: Its Dangers and Its Design" (2010) 94 *Minnesota Law Review* 1789.
8. Kim Lane Scheppele, "Law in a Time of Emergency: States of Exception and the Temptations of 9/11" (2004) 6(5) *Journal of Constitutional Law* 1.
9. European Council *Internal Security Strategy for the European Union—Towards a European Security Model* (Luxembourg: Publications Office of the European Union, 2010).
10. European Council, *The Hague Programme—Strengthening Freedom, Security and Justice in the European Union*, 2005/C 53/01.
11. *Cf.* Oliver Lepsius, "Liberty, Security and Terrorism" (2004) 5 *German Law Journal* 436.
12. European Council, *The Stockholm Programme—an Open and Secure Europe Serving and Protecting Citizens*, 2010/C 115/01.
13. Jörg Monar, "The Area of Freedom, Security and Justice" in Armin von Bogdandy and Jürgen Bast, eds., *Principles of European Constitutional Law*, rev. 2d ed. (Oxford: Hart Publishing, 2010), 551–85 at 579–80.
14. Tampere European Council, "15 and 16 October 1999—Conclusions of the Presidency." *Bulletin of the European Union*, No. 10/1999.
15. Monar, *supra* note 13 at 562.
16. *Cf.* Neil Walker, "In Search of the Area of Freedom, Security and Justice: A Constitutional Odyssey" in Neil Walker, ed., *Europe's Area of Freedom, Security and Justice* (Oxford: Oxford University Press, 2004) 3–37.
17. Monar, *supra* note 13 at 573 ff.
18. Elsperth Guild, ed., *Constitutional Challenges to the European Arrest Warrant* (London: Wolf Legal Publishers, 2006); Jan Komárek, "European Constitutionalism and the European Arrest Warrant: In Search of the Limits of 'Contrapunctual Principles'" (2007) 44 *Common Market Law Review* 9 ff; Massimo Fichera, *The Implementation of the European Arrest Warrant in the European Union: Law, Policy and Practice* (Cambridge: Intersentia 2011).
19. European Council, *The Stockholm Programme—an Open and Secure Europe Serving and Protecting Citizens*, 2010/C 115/01.
20. *Cf.* Monar, *supra* note 13 at 579.
21. *Cf.* Oliver Lepsius, "Human Dignity and the Downing of Aircraft: The German Federal Constitutional Court Strikes Down a Prominent Anti-terrorism Provision in the New Air-Transport Security Act" (2006) 7 *German Law Journal* 761.
22. Samull Hurri, *The Birth of the European Individual*, academic dissertation, (Helsinki: 2011).

CHAPTER 7

Counter-Terrorism's Engagement with Transnational Legality

VICTOR V. RAMRAJ*

However much particular laws might have changed in the "long decade" since 9/11, there is something familiar about the tensions between security and liberty, between norm and exception, that resonates with historical experience. It is not surprising, then, that the literature on counter-terrorism, at least in Western liberal democracies, is increasingly looking to the past—from the dictatorship of the Roman Republic to the experiences of Weimar Germany and the Second World War—to see how these challenges have been addressed. Yet there is something distinctive about this particular "emergency" and the norms it has generated, at least in our modern context, for it has arisen at a time when transnational legal and institutional structures have also emerged, not solely or even primarily in response to terrorism, but rather as part of the steady rise of global governance structures and a resurgence of private power. As the United States and its allies have turned increasingly in their counter-terrorism policies to transnational organizations and to one another for assistance, the idea of *national* security law has become increasingly anachronistic.

To better appreciate how counter-terrorism law has developed in this supranational way, and to understand more fully the challenges it faces as it transcends state borders, we need to step back from content of the law and consider how counter-terrorism has engaged with the complex web of legal norms and institutions beyond the state. This chapter begins by situating counter-terrorism law within the broader context of transnational legal norms (understood, following Philip Jessup, as "law which regulates actions or events that transcend national frontiers" including "public and private international law... and all other rules that do not fit into such standard categories"[1]) and global governance (characterized by the "vast increase in the reach and forms of transnational regulation and administration designed to address the consequences of globalized interdependence"[2]). The second part considers the challenges of accountability that emerge from a counter-terrorism regime that is grafted onto global governance structures. The chapter concludes by asking how the quest for accountability beyond the state will be complicated by the disparate and asymmetrical impact of global counter-terrorism on local needs and priorities.

COUNTER-TERRORISM AND GLOBALISATION

Unlike the "home-grown" Oklahoma City bombing six years earlier, the 9/11 attacks were planned outside the United States and executed within it; whatever the failures of domestic intelligence and policing that enabled the attacks to succeed, the problem was conceived from its inception as an international one. A global "war on terror" was declared, with the United States deploying its considerable political, economic, military, and diplomatic power to strike back at Al Qaeda. There is a persuasive, critical body of literature in international law that seeks to show how important it was for the United States to portray the 9/11 attacks—contrary to the experience of other states, including many "Third World" ones—as "so radically different" as to "justify the retrenchment or severe weakening of certain fundamental, indeed constitutional, norms of international law, such as: the absolute ban on the practice of torture; the prohibition on the unilateral use of force by states... and the ban on pre-emptive strikes that do not conform to [article 51 of the U.N. *Charter*]."[3] The U.N. Security Council's novel response was remarkable in its attempt to "legislate" globally by way of Resolution 1373 (with state compliance monitored by its Counter-Terrorism Committee) and in the rigorous enforcement of targeted sanctions around the world, spearheaded by a sanctions committee previously established by Resolution 1267. That the United States would have sought the assistance of the Security Council was not entirely surprising; the pivotal role assumed by the Security Council was more surprising and, as seen below, is one of the most overtly controversial aspects of the international response to 9/11. However, the global response to 9/11 was also remarkable—though less visibly so—in its engagement with newly established structures and networks of global governance (such as the Financial Action Task Force (FATF)) and its revitilisation of older ones (wartime intelligence networks) to achieve its objectives, while sidestepping direct, formal accountability structures in the process.

One of the key changes in global governance well before 9/11 was the emergence of regulatory institutions that did not fit comfortably into formal international law structures. For example, some non-treaty bodies resemble their formal counterparts in their intergovernmental structure, but they do not have a formal status in international law and articulate "soft" law standards and guidelines that might gradually harden into formal law. One example is the Basel Committee on Banking Supervision, a group of central bank governors established in 1974. The Committee

> does not possess any formal supranational supervisory authority, and its conclusions do not, and were never intended to, have legal force. Rather, it formulates broad supervisory standards and guidelines and recommends statements of best practice in the expectation that individual authorities will take steps to implement them through detailed arrangements—statutory or otherwise—which are best suited to their own national systems. In this way, the Committee encourages convergence towards common approaches and common standards without attempting detailed harmonisation of member countries' supervisory techniques.[4]

Although the Basel Committee does not draft model legislation, it commands significant respect such that its recommendations on capital adequacy are regarded as minimum standards that, in time, find their way into hard law.[5]

As part of the architecture of a transnational counter-terrorism regime, the FATF emerged as a key institution in anti-terrorist financing. As with the Basel Committee, the FATF is a non-treaty-based, intergovernmental body, set up in this case by the G-7 Summit in Paris in 1989, with the responsibility of "examining money laundering techniques and trends, reviewing the action which had already been taken at a national or international level, and setting out the measures that still needed to be taken to combat money laundering."[6] In October 2001, its mandate was expanded to include the prevention of terrorist financing. The membership of the FATF consists of representatives of thirty-two governments of major international financial centres and two regional organizations, the European Commission and the Gulf Co-operation Council. The Committee has published forty recommendations and nine special recommendations, urging states, for example, to criminalize terrorist financing and money laundering, facilitate the freezing and confiscation of assets, ensure diligent record-keeping by financial institutions in relation to money transfer, regulate and monitor alternative forms of remittance, and provide legal assistance to other states in their anti-terrorist financing efforts.

Although the FATF's recommendations have no formal legal status, they nevertheless have significant practical force. The FATF monitors member and non–member states' compliance with its recommendations. A jurisdiction that fails to comply with the FATF's recommendations may, after a period of dialogue and engagement, face adverse reputational consequences. According to Ben Saul, "the FATF can publicly urge all States to advise their financial institutions to consider the additional risks posed by financial dealings with those States; this has the potential to affect adversely their reputation in the business and financial communities."[7] In February 2011, for example, the FATF published a list of "high-risk and non-cooperative jurisdictions."[8] In relation to the non-cooperative jurisdictions, it warns:

> The FATF is not yet satisfied that the following jurisdictions have made sufficient progress on their action plan agreed upon with the FATF. The most significant action plan items and/or the majority of their action plan items have not been addressed. If these jurisdictions do not take sufficient action to implement significant components of their action plan by June 2011, then the FATF will identify these jurisdictions as being out of compliance with their agreed action plans and will take the additional step of calling upon its members to consider the risks arising from the deficiencies associated with the jurisdiction.[9]

For Saul, the FATF has a powerful influence on the conduct of all states, because the consequences of non-compliance and exclusion are costly given that the FATF consists of the most powerful economies in the world, its provision of technical assistance makes compliance easier to achieve even when capacity is lacking, and its recommendations are intended to complement international legal norms.[10] The FATF works not only with states, but with the financial institutions themselves,[11] further enhancing its influence on the practices of financial institutions around the world.

Another important feature of global governance is the emergence of "horizontal" networks of national regulators and other authorities that formulate policies and strategies for dealing with issues of common concern. These "horizontal" networks of regulators include police, immigration officials, and, notably, security intelligence agencies. The security intelligence context demonstrates how extensively counter-terrorism policy has latched onto the global networks. It is increasingly clear, for instance, that the wartime military-intelligence model of spying, aimed at the collection of intelligence pertaining to other countries, has shifted its focus belatedly to the collection of intelligence relating to geographically dispersed non-state entities such as Al Qaeda. This shift gives the intelligence establishment in different states an even greater incentive, beyond their Security Council mandate,[12] to cooperate. One way to do so has been simply to expand pre-existing cooperation networks such as the post–World War II "Echelon" network (also known as "UKUSA" after the 1947 agreement that established it), which links the collection capacities of the American NSA, British GCHQ, and their counterparts in Australia, Canada, and New Zealand and assumes a shared responsibility for the surveillance of different parts of the world.[13] As seen below, the dark side of such cooperation can be noted in the way that individuals have been, at times on the basis of flawed intelligence-sharing between security intelligence agencies, "rendered" to other jurisdictions where they were tortured.

Even further removed from the treaty bodies of international law, some transnational institutions that have emerged in recent years are private, non-governmental organizations that have no formal standing in public international law, but nevertheless have a growing impact on the conduct of individuals and organizations.[14] One example is the Forestry Stewardship Council (FSC), a not-for-profit organization that "applies the directive of its membership to develop forest management and chain of custody standards, deliver trademark assurance and provide accreditation services to a global network of committed businesses, organizations and communities."[15] By setting standards for responsible forest management and certifying products accordingly, the FSC, through a "non-state market-driven"[16] form of regulation, has established a set of norms with a worldwide impact. Although not the focus of this chapter, in the context of counter-terrorism law, the privatization of counter-terrorism law and policy can be seen in the actors it seeks to control (that is, the terrorist organizations themselves, as the "non-state actors" of public international law), in the private military and security companies engaged by states to perform or support the state's security-enforcement functions in operations beyond its borders, and in the efforts of non-governmental organizations such as the International Commission of Jurists (which, through its Eminent Jurists Panel plays a significant role in monitoring counter-terrorism practices and exposing abuses).[17] Although there is much to be said about the "private" dimensions of the counter-terrorism regime, this chapter focuses on the ways in which the regime in its non-private dimensions has increasingly occupied a space of transnational legality situated beyond the state (though not always formally at the level of public international law), and the challenges for our understanding of legal order and accountability these bold new moves have generated.

GLOBAL COUNTER-TERRORISM AND ACCOUNTABILITY

When counter-terrorism is understood as a transnational enterprise that has latched on to the emerging structures of global governance, it becomes clear that one of the most profound questions about the transnational counter-terrorism regime post-9/11 concerns the mechanisms of accountability: that is, mechanisms to ensure that as power is transferred to global administrative bodies or networks, that power is not abused. Part of the solution lies, it seems, in the nascent field of global administrative law, in its attempt to map mechanisms of accountability at the supra-state level. Another part of the solution intersects with an important debate between global constitutionalists, who urge the consolidation of global legal structures modelled on domestic constitutional law, and legal pluralists who regard a multiplicity of legal orders, each competing to regulate a particular field of activity, as the best model to secure the accountability of global regulators. This part of the chapter explores the prospects for accountability of global administrative bodies at the domestic level, before considering the debate between global constitutionalists and legal pluralists over the structure of supranational accountability.

Domestic Accountability of Supra-State Bodies

As far as accountability of global administrative institutions is concerned, one possibility is domestic judicial review or legislative scrutiny. The idea that a formal international body such as the Security Council's Sanctions Committee might be subject to "domestic" judicial review is a contentious one that has attracted considerable attention, particularly since the European Court of Justice (ECJ) reviewed and declared invalid the European Commission's implementation of the U.N. sanctions regime in *Kadi and Al-Barakaat v. Council of the European Union*.[18] This case (which has counterparts in other jurisdictions, including Canada[19] and the United Kingdom[20]) has thrown into question the conceptual and normative foundations of the international legal order, and so is treated separately below. The question remains, however, whether the norms created by informal bodies such as the FATF or the activities of horizontal networks of national security intelligence agencies could be subject to domestic judicial review or legislative scrutiny.

For informal supranational bodies such as the FATF, it would be the rare case in which the norm-creating function could be subject to judicial review. The FATF's recommendations are voluntary, although non-compliance might be costly. Moreover, the willingness of the FATF to provide technical assistance to financial institutions enables it to bypass the state and exercise a direct regulatory impact on the practices of financial institutions, while eluding direct judicial review. Whether domestic courts could ever find a basis for reviewing the "soft law" recommendations of the FATF is an open question, although one might, by looking at other areas of law, imagine how domestic courts could respond. Here, sports law provides some useful insights.[21] Although disputes concerning international sports (e.g., between national and international governing bodies, or between those bodies and individual athletes) are increasingly resolved through arbitration before the Lausanne-based Court of Arbitration for Sport, some of these disputes continue to find their way into domestic courts. This might happen, for instance, when "international sports body agreements and rules are directly challenged in domestic courts as contrary to international law."[22] In these cases, domestic courts are divided. Some have ruled either that "international sports agreements and rules must comply with national law" while others have "adopted a deferential approach by refusing to apply national law to the challenged rules and agreements."[23]

A key issue is whether the courts regard the supranational body's decision as one that falls within the jurisdiction of the courts. For example, when the British Columbia Supreme Court was asked to find that the International Olympic Committee (IOC)'s decision not to include women's ski jumping as an event in the Vancouver Winter Olympic Games was contrary to the equality guarantee in the Canadian Charter of Rights and Freedoms, it refused to do so.[24] The court found that the Vancouver Organizing Committee (VANOC) was carrying out a governmental activity in staging the games[25] and that the IOC's decision not to include women's ski jumping as an event in the Vancouver Games discriminated against the women ski jumpers "in a substantive sense."[26] However, VANOC could not be found in breach of the Charter for implementing the decision of a private, "a Swiss-based organization"[27] that was not a party to the lawsuit. The Court of Appeal affirmed the result. In its view, the question of whether VANOC was engaged in a governmental activity and thus subject to the Charter did not have to be answered. It was "clear on the facts that neither government nor VANOC had any authority to make or alter the decision of the IOC not to include a women's ski jumping event in the 2010 Games" and so the IOC's decision was "not an activity to which the *Charter* applie[d]."[28]

Although the analogy between the IOC and the FATF is imperfect, the difficult jurisdictional choices facing domestic courts in these situations are evident. In the case of the FATF, the soft, indirect, and voluntary nature of its recommendations makes it even less likely that domestic courts would be inclined to intervene. In the absence of clear judicial checks, domestic legislative oversight could provide another potential source of accountability.[29] Nevertheless, there are difficulties here, too. For example, the "soft" or informal nature of the FATF's guidelines makes them less susceptible to legislative oversight. However, many governments do not participate in the standard-setting role of institutions such as the FATF; although governments might be invited by the FATF to comment on adverse findings,[30] they might nevertheless face considerable geopolitical or economic pressure to implement standards that they have had no formal role in creating.[31]

Judicial supervision of horizontal regulatory networks is also elusive, particularly in the context of national security, and specifically intelligence-collection and intelligence-sharing. From a state-centric perspective, the legal limits on intelligence-collection could be analysed in terms of the interception and collection of "human intelligence" or "signals intelligence" by one state in relation to another state, whether within the borders of the state seeking the information (e.g., intercepting signals intelligence from an embassy), within the borders of another state (obtaining state secrets from a source abroad), or transnationally (intercepting communications from one state to another).[32] Domestic and international law, including diplomatic and consular law, limit the conditions in which such information may be collected. It prohibits a state, for instance, from obtaining human intelligence by trespassing on another's property, by violating a diplomatic bag, or by torture.[33]

Problems arise in the context of intelligence-sharing, however, as the legal principles governing the sharing of intelligence within an intelligence "network" are thin and often governed as much by informal practice as by formal law. Moreover, there is a growing perception within the security establishment that the line between internal and external threats is blurring, leading to greater coordination and information-sharing by intelligence agencies.[34] As the post-9/11 experience has demonstrated, the opacity of the norms governing such practices has a dark side, allowing states to "outsource" their intelligence-collection to states that torture terrorist suspects. The experience of Maher Arar illustrates the depth of these problems and the challenges faced in trying to regulate transnational intelligence-sharing. Arar was a dual citizen of Canada and Syria who, on his way back to his home in Canada from a vacation in North Africa, flew into New York's John F. Kennedy airport in September 2002. Unknown to him, he was considered by the Canadian authorities to be a "person of interest" in their investigation of a suspected terrorist because his name appeared on the mortgage papers of a terrorist suspect. The Canadian authorities shared false or misleading information about Arar with their

U.S. counterparts and, during his transit through New York, he was detained in isolation and interrogated. Although resident in Canada, Arar was also a Syrian citizen; the United States, against his wishes, deported him to Syria, where he was tortured for several months until the Canadian authorities eventually arranged his repatriation to Canada.

The Canadian government launched an official commission of inquiry into these events, which completely vindicated Arar. The commission produced a lengthy report critical of the Canadian authorities' role in his ordeal.[35] The Canadian government eventually paid him CAN$10.5 million in compensation. The Arar Report resulted in a wave of reforms within the Canadian security establishment. In this respect, Arar was fortunate. However, domestic efforts to ensure accountability are often problematic given the need, stressed by domestic security agencies, to cooperate with other countries in intelligence gathering; if, for instance, Canada needs the help of other countries in its counter-terrorism operations and does not want to "[blind] its chief security intelligence agency,"[36] it would be under considerable pressure to cooperate with other agencies without imposing "unduly restrictive conditions" on the sharing of information.[37] Arar's attempt to find a remedy against the U.S. government for alleged abuses while in U.S. custody and for his rendition to torture in Syria have been unsuccessful, with the courts declaring that "in the context of extraordinary rendition, hesitation is warranted by special factors"[38] (for instance, when the matter concerns foreign policy or national security).[39] Although many countries, including Canada and the United States, have sophisticated oversight mechanisms that seek to hold their security intelligence agencies to account, the opaque supranational networks of intelligence agencies compound the problem, making it difficult to monitor the sharing of intelligence, and making it even more difficult for aggrieved individuals to secure a domestic remedy.[40]

Global Constitutionalism or Legal Pluralism?

What of the prospects for accountability beyond the state? As the previous analysis suggests, some forms of supranational governance and cooperation, such as intelligence-sharing, are not easily amenable to accountability at the domestic level and, at least in this field of informal intergovernmental activity, supranational accountability mechanisms are unlikely. At the other end of the spectrum of formality, an important debate has been about the prospects of accountability of institutions such as the U.N. Security Council and, in particular, its sanctions regime. This debate is, in some respects, an exploration of the consequences of the fragmentation of law at the supranational level, a problem that tracks Slaughter's observation that modern governments are no longer (if they ever were) unitary.[41] For example, in the early days of the Counter Terrorism Committee, the Committee regarded its role as monitoring compliance with Resolution 1373's counter-terrorism recommendations (by scrutinizing country reports) without inquiring into the compatibility of each country's counter-terrorism laws with its international human rights obligations.

Although there have been attempts to reconcile these competing international legal regimes, the problem of fragmentation endures. As Nico Krisch argues, in the context of counter-terrorism there are effectively two regimes. The first is a global security regime, one important aspect of which is the U.N. Security Council's efforts, initially through Resolution 1267, to maintain international peace and security by imposing sanctions (including the freezing of assets and imposition of a travel ban) on organizations and individuals associated with the Taliban and later Al Qaeda. At the same time, the second is a human rights regime (particularly in Europe) that has sought to impose substantive and procedural constraints on the global security regime.[42] The controversy that has emerged situates those who seek to remedy the problems of accountability through a coherent, hierarchical regime of international law (loosely associated with the idea of "global constitutionalism") in opposition to those who see a plurality of competing legal or normative regimes as the preferable approach ("legal pluralism"). The contrast between these views is best illustrated by the decision of the ECJ in *Kadi*.[43]

Kadi challenged the E.U. regulation that implemented the Sanctions Committee's decision to place him on its blacklist. Under the Committee's procedure, states could ask it to list an individual or organization. Unless a member of the committee objected, that person or entity would be placed on the list. Through this process, Kadi was listed by the Committee. The European Union adopted regulations to implement the Sanctions Committee's decisions. Because the Sanctions Committee did not permit individual petitions for delisting, Kadi challenged the European Union's implementing legislation. The Court of First Instance, citing the primacy of the U.N. Charter, decided that it could not review the Security Council's resolution (unless it violated jus cogens, which it found was not the case) and so it had no power to review the European Union's implementing legislation.

Reversing the Court of First Instance, the ECJ disagreed. By reviewing the European Union's implementing legislation, it was not thereby challenging the primacy of the Security Council Resolution: "[The] review by the Court of the validity of any Community measure in light of fundamental rights must be considered to be the expression, in a community based on the rule of law, of a constitutional guarantee stemming from the E.C. Treaty as an autonomous legal system which is not to be prejudiced by an international agreement."[44] The implementing regulation was inconsistent with fundamental rights insofar as it

> was adopted without any guarantee being given as to the communication of the inculpatory evidence against [the appellants] or as to their being heard in that connection, so that it must be found that the regulation was adopted according to a procedure in which the appellants' rights of defence were not observed, which has had the further consequence that the principle of effective judicial protection has been infringed.[45]

Moreover, by denying Kadi the ability to contest the regulation, the restrictions on his property rights could not be justified.[46] The Commission was given three months from the date of the judgment to remedy the infringement and provide Kadi with a summary of its allegations against him, but without disclosing the evidence in support; it subsequently renewed the sanctions against him. Kadi returned to the ECJ, which (in a case known as *Kadi II*[47]), applying the principles set out in *Kadi I*, held that his right to a fair hearing was infringed, and found in favour of Kadi.

The response to the *Kadi* case and its implications for supranational accountability have been mixed. For example, even while applauding "the specific outcome... from the short-term perspective of its insistence on minimum procedural-fairness requirements for those whose assets are to be indefinitely frozen pursuant to the implementation of a Security Council resolution," Gráinne de Búrca criticizes the decision for being "at odds with the conventional self-presentation of the E.U. as an organization which maintains particular fidelity to international law and institutions."[48] De Búrca self-consciously adopts a constitutionalist model of the international order which, in contrast with the ECJ's pluralist approach (which drew on the internal constitutional values of the European Union), would have challenged the sanctions regime by drawing on "customary international law as a basis for due process protection" as well as "the references to protection of human rights in the U.N. Charter itself [and] the general principles of international law and *jus cogens* principles which were invoked by the CFI."[49] The preferable approach, then, would have been to challenge *Kadi* from within the normative framework of international law, accepting its unity and coherence, even while contesting its hierarchical ordering of, in this case, security and human rights norms.

De Búrca distinguishes her position from legal pluralists, including Nico Krisch. For Krisch, the ECJ's decision in *Kadi* is a positive example of legal pluralism in operation. He regards it as part of an "overall pluralist structure, one that is characterized by the coexistence of different legal orders, all with their own foundational norms and substantive commitments."[50] The absence of a coherent, hierarchical international system does not concern Krisch, for he regards the "contest between legal orders" as positive, allowing space for contestation, resistance, and principled engagement. The tension he identifies between "a strong interest in effective security cooperation and the far-reaching disagreements among countries and institutions about the right balance between security concerns and the protection of fundamental rights" does not concern him:

> As we have seen, this tension has led to a *characteristic* process of approximation and distance between various layers of law and politics. The imperative of security cooperation has brought these layers closer together, creating an enmeshment of legal orders in the shaping and implementation of the sanctions regime. But the differences in values have also led to attempts to establish greater distance between the layers and thus a certain degree of political autonomy. The resulting maze is best characterized neither as monist or dualist but as pluralist—as deeply entangled yet not integrated into one coherent whole.[51]

So unlike de Búrca, who sees the ECJ's assertion of its autonomy in *Kadi* as a weakness in the international order, Krisch sees the coexistence of competing legal orders as a strength, one that makes that order more flexible and responsive to contestation and change, promotes the signalling of dissent, and provides a means of resistance in the face of asymmetrical distributions of political power.[52]

The distance between these positions is significant. The constitutionalist aspiration of a unified and coherent international order seems entirely inconsistent with a legal pluralist approach that welcomes the tension and contradictions between different, though enmeshed, legal orders that must be resolved through a principled political dialogue. Yet, in some ways, the distance between de Búrca's constitutionalist aspirations and Krisch's legal pluralism is not as great as it might first appear. De Búrca sees her position as a "soft" constitutionalist one that eschews absolute hierarchies and leaves room, within the international order, for tension and contestation.[53] Accordingly, de Búrca suggests, as an alternative to the ECJ's approach in *Kadi*, an approach akin to the *Solange* decisions in Germany, which sought to navigate the tension between internal constitutional norms and E.C. regulations through a "mutually disciplining relationship between the two legal systems."[54] De Búrca cites approvingly the German Constitutional Court's decision, in which it sees the invocation of a conflict between the two systems not as "a violation of the Treaty, but as [setting] in motion inside the European organs the Treaty mechanism which resolves the conflict on a political level."[55] To the extent that a global constitutional order seeks not to settle all controversies through a hierarchical order of norms, but to force a principled political dialogue against the background of competing legal principles, the distance between "soft" constitutionalism and legal pluralism begins to narrow. This all brings us back to *Kadi* and the opportunity it has generated (however it might eventually come to be framed) for a principled dialogue between the European judiciary and the members of the Security Council over the delisting procedure.

COUNTER-TERRORISM IN GLOBAL PERSPECTIVE

Counter-terrorism's engagement with the global legal order in all its complexity yields a mixed result in terms of accountability. With the emergence of bold new forms of governance—whether in the creation and enforcement of a sanctions regime by the Security Council, the emergence of informal financial regulation by intergovernmental bodies such as the FATF, the creation of information-sharing security intelligence networks—we are challenged to find creative new ways to hold supranational wielders of power to account. The FATF and security intelligence networks are at least indirectly under the control of states; we have not even begun to consider instances, where, for instance, private military and security companies are engaged by states in counter-terrorism operations beyond state borders, in which the problems of accountability are even more complex. As multi-layered counter-terrorism norms and institutions of a private and hybrid nature become increasingly common, traditional structures of accountability will increasingly prove unsatisfactory. As Clive Walker observes in his contribution to this volume, "governments and private sectors share basic interests in protective security" but "their accountability structures are very different. Corporate accountability to shareholders rather than customers affects modes of cooperation and transparency."[56] Finding solutions to the challenge of complex global counter-terrorism norms will force us to stretch our imagination beyond the confines of state law and inter-state law and think about law and accountability in novel ways.

As we do so, two further challenges will require our attention. The first is the challenge of creating fair and effective mechanisms of accountability against a backdrop of the asymmetric distribution of global power. Debates about the accountability of global regulators cannot easily be separated from the uneven distribution of power and resources at the supranational level.[57] The legitimacy of the U.N. Security Council remains deeply contested, with its anachronistic post–World War II permanent member system undermining its moral authority as a neutral enforcer of global peace and security. As Krisch observes, referring to *Kadi*, "it is not accidental that it was an attack from a court of the EU, one of the world's most influential players, that received the greatest attention in the UN."[58] So it remains to be seen whether, as Krisch suggests, less influential countries could make a difference at the global level within a pluralist legal order. Similarly, modern intelligence-sharing networks that facilitate the sharing of intelligence obtained through practices such as "rendition" to countries with a poor record on torture lends credence to the claim that post-9/11 changes to international law, including, presumably, changes governing intelligence-sharing, can usefully be analysed through a "third-world" lens that, according to Obiora Okafor, seeks "to expose, reform or even retrench those features of the international legal system that help to create or maintain the generally unequal, unfair, or unjust global order."[59] The same concerns could be raised about the FATF, an informal grouping of rich countries that have used soft law norms and tools to shape the practice of financial institutions around the world. Whether a poorer country could resist its influence without suffering adverse economic consequence is a question that deserves empirical analysis; however, the FATF seems to assume—along with the many countries that comply with its guidelines—that a poorer country would.

The second, related challenge concerns the demands that the global counter-terrorism regime and, in consequence, the *counter* counter-terrorism regime place on the resources and relative priorities of all states—but especially poorer states. Countering a threat of terrorism, including the threat of terrorist financing, requires a significant allocation of resources in response to pressure from supranational bodies such as the FATF. States may well find themselves under significant pressure, for instance, to reform their banking laws to ensure that suspicious transfers of funds can be tracked. However, the reform of these laws might in turn lead to pressure from other external (and internal) constituencies to constrain the abuse of counter-terrorism and counter-terrorism financing powers, requiring new laws and institutions concerning, say, data protection. Even when rich states or supranational agencies provide technical assistance to poorer states to help them meet their obligations, these multiple demands nevertheless siphon scarce resources from other areas of urgent need. The impact of "obligation overload" at the supranational level and its demands on developing countries is the subject of an important project by Kevin Davis and Benedict Kingsbury.[60] In some situations, it may well be that the most effective form of resistance is to do the minimum to comply formally with the obligations imposed by the transnational regime while diverting the state's scarce resources to more pressing problems.

CONCLUSION

Counter-terrorism's engagement with the transnational legal order in the long decade since September 11, 2001, has produced a host of complex legal problems that, with over ten years of hindsight, we are better able to see. Domestic constitutional checks, whether legal or political, will continue to play an important role in constraining state power.[61] However, inasmuch as the counter-terrorism regime "creeps" into transnational institutions and norms, and loses sight of its initial objectives,[62] these domestic checks will be considerably less effective. Whether constitutionalist or legal pluralist forms of accountability are better able to constrain supranational counter-terrorism powers remains to be investigated fully; in examining this important question, we should be mindful of the relative costs that the counter-terrorism regime imposes on states, whatever their immediate needs and priorities might be.

NOTES

* Associate Professor, National University of Singapore Faculty of Law.

1. Philip Jessup, *Transnational Law* (New Haven: Yale University Press, 1956) 136.
2. See Benedict Kingsbury, Nico Krisch, and Richard B. Stewart, "The Emergence of Global Administrative Law" (2004–2005) 68 *Law & Contemporary Problems* 15 at 16.
3. Obiora C. Okafor, "Newness, Imperialism, and International Legal Reform in Our Time: A TWAIL Perspective" (2005) 43 *Osgoode Hall Law Journal* 171 at 172.
4. This is the Committee's own description of its mandate, available online at Bank for International Settlements, www.bis.org/bcbs/history.htm.
5. Consider, for example, the reply by Singapore's Minister for Trade and Industry in Parliament in 2009 to a question concerning the government's response to the financial crisis of the previous year: "In December 2009, the Basel Committee on Banking Supervision released a package of proposals to strengthen global capital and liquidity regulations for consultation. These are targeted for adoption internationally by end-2012. Our relatively conservative regulatory framework and the strong capital and liquidity positions of our financial institutions mean that we are well placed to meet these new stringent international regulatory standards."
6. Available online at Financial Action Task Force, www.fatf-gafi.org/aboutfatf.
7. Ben Saul, "'Why Do They Hate Us?...They Hate Our Freedoms': The Globalisation of Terrorism and Counter-Terrorism" in Shawkat Alam, Natalie Klein and Juliette Overland, eds., *Globalisation and the Quest for International and Social Justice: The Relevance of International Law in an Evolving World Order* (New York: Routledge, 2011) 207–34 at 218.

8. Available online at Financial Action Task Force, http://www.fatf-gafi.org/topics/high-riskandnon-cooperativejurisdictions/documents/fatfpublicstatement-25february2011.html.
9. Available online at Financial Action Task Force, http://www.fatf-gafi.org/topics/high-riskandnon-cooperativejurisdictions/documents/improvingglobalamlcftcomplianceon-goingprocess-25february2011.html.
10. Saul, *supra* note 7.
11. Ibid.
12. Paragraph 2(f) of Resolution 1373 imposes an obligation on states to afford "one another the greatest measure of assistance in connection with criminal investigations or criminal proceedings relating to the financing or support of terrorist acts, including assistance in obtaining evidence in their possession necessary for the proceedings." See U.N. Security Council Resolution No. S/RES/1373 (2001).
13. Simon Chesterman, *One Nation under Surveillance* (Oxford: Oxford University Press, 2011) at 19.
14. *See* Steven Bernstein, "When Is Non-State Global Governance Really Governance?" (2010) 1 *Utah Law Review* 91.
15. Available online at Forestry Stewardship Council, www.fsc.org/about-fsc.html.
16. Bernstein, *supra* note 14 at 104.
17. See, for example, International Commission of Jurists, Eminent Jurists Panel, *Assessing Damage, Urging Action* (2009). The report was published following sixteen hearings, held over three years and involving forty countries.
18. (3 September 2008), C-402/05 P & 415/15 P (*Kadi I*).
19. *Abdelrazak* v. *Minister of Foreign Affairs (Canada)*, 2009 FC 580.
20. *H.M. Treasury* v. *Ahmed* [2010] UKSC 2.
21. Matthew J. Mitten and Hayden Opie, "'Sports Law': Implications for the Development of International, Comparative, and National Law, and Global Dispute Resolution" (2010) 85 *Tulane Law Review* 269.
22. Ibid. at 292–93.
23. Ibid. at 295.
24. *Sagen* v. *Vancouver Organizing Committee for the 2010 Olympic & Paralympic Winter Games* (2009), 2009 BCSC 942 (B.C. Supreme Court).
25. Ibid. at paras. 53–65.
26. Ibid. at para. 103.
27. Ibid. at para. 104 *et seq*.
28. 2009 BCCA 522, 313 D.L.R. (4th) 393 (B.C.C.A.), at paras. 49, 50.
29. Kingsbury, et al., *supra* note 2 at 33. Note that in the United States, "some federal regulatory officials afford notice and comment when participating in international standard-setting on certain topics" and the U.S. Congress "requires reports from U.S. regulatory agencies before agreeing to recommendations of financial regulatory groups such as the Basel Committee."
30. Ibid.
31. A. Claire Cutler, *Private Power and Global Authority: Transnational Merchant Law in the Global Political Economy* (Cambridge: Cambridge University Press, 2003) at 23.
32. See generally Craig Forcese, "Spies without Borders: International Law and Intelligence Collection" (2011) 5 *Journal of National Security Law and Policy* 179 at 182.
33. Ibid.
34. See generally Chesterman, *supra* note 13.

35. See Commission of Inquiry into the Actions of Canadian Officials in Relation to Maher Arar, *Report of the Events Relating to Maher Arar* (Ottawa: Public Works and Government Services Canada, 2006) ("Arar Report").
36. Forcese, *supra* note 32 at 210.
37. Ibid.
38. *Arar* v. *Ashcroft*, 585 F.3d 559 (2d Cir. 2009) (*en banc*).
39. Ibid. at 575.
40. See, in the Swedish context, Iain Cameron, "The Influence of 9/11 on Swedish Anti-terrorism Policy and Measures," Chapter 12 in this volume.
41. Anne-Marie Slaughter, *A New World Order* (Princeton, N.J.: Princeton University Press, 2004).
42. Nico Krisch, *Beyond Constitutionalism: The Pluralist Structure of Postnational Law* (Oxford: Oxford University Press, 2010) 153–88.
43. *Kadi and Al-Barakaat* v. *Council of the European Union* (3 September 2008), C-402/05 P & 415/15 P.
44. Ibid. at para. 316.
45. Ibid. at para. 352.
46. Ibid. at paras. 36–970.
47. *Kadi* v. *Commission* (30 September 2010), Case T 85/09.
48. Gráinne de Búrca, "The European Court of Justice and the International Legal Order after *Kadi*" (2010) 51 *Harvard International Law Journal* 1 at 41.
49. Ibid. at 42.
50. Krisch, *supra* note 42 at 172.
51. Ibid. at 188.
52. Ibid. at 183–87.
53. De Búrca, *supra* note 48 at 43.
54. Ibid. at 43.
55. Ibid.
56. Clive Walker, "'Protect' against Terrorism: In Service of State, Corporation, or the Citizen?," Chapter 11 in this volume.
57. In some ways, however, asymmetries in legal capacity and variations in the social importance of formal law make the global counter-terrorism regime less effective and so the potential for abuse less likely. See Victor V. Ramraj, "The Impossibility of Global Anti-Terrorism Law?" in Victor V. Ramraj, Michael Hor, Kent Roach, and George Williams, eds., *Global Anti-Terrorism Law and Policy* (Cambridge: Cambridge University Press, 2011).
58. Krisch, *supra* note 42 at 186.
59. Okafor, *supra* note 3 at 177.
60. Kevin Davis and Benedict Kingsbury, "Obligation Overload: Adjusting the Obligations of Fragile or Failed States," unpublished draft presented at the Hauser Globalization Colloquium, New York University School of Law, Fall 2010 (cited with permission of the authors).
61. Mark Tushnet, "Legal and Political Constitutionalism, and the Response to Terrorism," Chapter 8 in this volume.
62. Kent Roach, "Preventing What? Post 9/11 Mission Amnesia and Mission Creep," Chapter 4 in this volume.

PART THREE:

Constitutions under Stress

CHAPTER 8

Legal and Political Constitutionalism, and the Response to Terrorism

MARK TUSHNET*

The United States and the United Kingdom are sometimes said to exemplify two versions of constitutionalism. In the United States constitutionalism is primarily *legal* or, perhaps more precisely, *judicial* whereas in the United Kingdom it is primarily *political*. For the legal constitutionalist, most constitutional restraints on government power and constitutional provisions organizing government power are law in the ordinary sense. Those subject to the constitution's requirements are *legally* obligated to comply with those requirements, not merely morally required to do so or urged to comply as a matter of political prudence. Further, legal constitutionalism employs the usual way of enforcing legal obligations—a court order directing the actor to comply with the court's understanding of the constitution—to enforce compliance with the constitution's requirements. Most versions of legal constitutionalism take the court's understanding as definitive, if only to ensure that constitutional controversies have some conclusive resolution,[1] and for this reason, among others, it might have been better had the concept been labeled *judicial* constitutionalism.[2]

Politics plays some role in judicial constitutionalism, though not at its core. Normative constraints on politics may affect the selection of judges, for example, as when traditions develop strongly counseling the selection of higher-level judges from the existing pool of judges. Perhaps more important, some constitutional provisions may be nonjusticiable, implying that their normative content is to be enforced through political rather than judicial mechanisms. Yet, these political mechanisms of normative constraint must be small—as they are in the United States—for a system to remain one of legal/judicial constitutionalism.

Political constitutionalism takes constitutional requirements no less seriously, but insists that they be enforced primarily by political rather than legal mechanisms.[3] For political constitutionalists, actors subject to the constitution's requirements should comply with them because of political morality. However, political constitutionalism incorporates institutional mechanisms for enforcing compliance. It is not the courts, though, but ordinary political mechanisms—elections, pressure from interest groups, media exposure—that lead political actors to conform to a constitution's requirements. Respect for constitutional values is both a predicate of political constitutionalism and a phenomenon that has some causal effect on actors' compliance with constitutional requirements.

One feature of political constitutionalism is the Madisonian and Hamiltonian argument that separation of powers, by setting one power center against another, limits the actual exercise of prerogative powers unconstrained by law. In their separation-of-powers mode, political constitutionalists hope that politics will indirectly but securely guarantee individual rights. Yet, political constitutionalists cannot rely solely on the separation-of-powers argument. For one thing, the strongest academic defenders of political constitutionalism support parliamentary sovereignty, and indeed the term emerges out of discussions by scholars from the British Commonwealth defending parliamentary sovereignty against what they see as mistaken incursions from legal/judicial constitutionalism. So, political constitutionalists rely on, and seek institutional mechanisms that generate support for, widespread commitment in the public to constitutional values, with the primary institutional mechanism being civic education in varied forms. Such a commitment will induce politicians to defend and challenge policy proposals with constitutional arguments.

Notably, the choice between legal and political constitutionalism is itself a political one. Constitution designers and implementers respond to the circumstances they face by determining the extent to which they will embed legal or political constitutionalism in their systems. As circumstances change, so may the balance between legal and political constitutionalism. This is so, even though we can probably expect a fair amount of inertia in the face of those changing circumstances, because the existing institutional mechanisms are relatively robust and elaborate.

This chapter offers some speculations about the role of political and legal constitutionalism in structuring the response to terrorism since 2001, focusing primarily on the United States, but ending with some observations about the United Kingdom. It begins by sketching two claims about the legal regulation of anti-terrorism policy in the United States up to 2011. The first claim represents the conventional wisdom that the policies pursued by the Obama administration are not dramatically different from those pursued by the Bush administration after around 2006. The second claim is that, notwithstanding the Supreme Court's decisions that those detained but not criminally charged with terrorism offenses are entitled to writs of habeas corpus (and, necessarily, release when their continued detention cannot be lawfully justified), very few detainees—perhaps not a single one—have been released as a direct result of a final coercive judicial order. When suitably fleshed out, these claims are largely correct. The remainder of the chapter argues that political constitutionalism provides a better explanation for the state of affairs just described. A brief conclusion suggests that, perhaps ironically, in the United Kingdom, the home ground of political constitutionalism, legal/judicial constitutionalism has had a more substantial effect on anti-terrorism policy than it has had in the United States, the home ground of that form of constitutionalism.

ANTI-TERRORISM POLICY AND POLITICAL CONSTITUTIONALISM IN THE UNITED STATES

President George W. Bush's initial responses to terrorism after 2001 attracted a great deal of criticism. Many responses were, it was said, unconstitutional and illegal under international law. The Bush administration answered not by asserting that it was exercising power unregulated by law, but with legal arguments demonstrating (or so its lawyers asserted) that its actions were justified *by law*. In addition to invoking congressional approval for its actions in the broad language of the Authorization for Use of Military Force (AUMF) against those responsible for (and affiliated with) the attacks of September 11, 2001, the administration made more robust *legal* claims: the Constitution gave the president the power to act as commander in chief of the armed forces, which entailed that he had wide discretion in choosing methods for achieving victory in armed conflict, and Congress lacked power to impose statutory limits on that constitutionally granted power. Further, the president had a constitutional duty to preserve the nation, expressed only in part in the Constitution's language directed that he take care that the laws be faithfully executed, and, again, Congress lacked the power to impose statutory limits on his choices. The breadth of the Bush administration's claims should not obscure the fact that the administration operated within the framework of judicial constitutionalism: the administration's position was that courts should accept its claims, including claims about the limits the Constitution placed on the courts' role in anti-terrorist policy.

Over the next several years, the administration gradually altered many of the policies it had initially pursued, although generally without withdrawing from its original position that the policies were constitutional and lawful under international law. Importantly, the Bush administration obtained congressional approval of at least some versions of the policies it was then pursuing. The Obama administration continued most of what we can call the "late Bush" policies—dating from somewhere between 2005 to 2008.[4] The clearest departure from late-Bush policies is the reported closing of the so-called CIA "black sites" (facilities located in countries outside the United States at which persons held by U.S. officials were interrogated) while devising substitutes, such as prolonged detention at sea for interrogation purposes, that differed only on the margins from the abandoned policies.

It is sometimes said that the Obama administration repudiated the Bush policies involving waterboarding and at least some other methods of so-called "enhanced interrogation." This claim actually reveals where the difference between the late-Bush and Obama policies resides. The late-Bush policy was that the United States would not employ such techniques because they were no longer necessary (although some in the late Bush administration concluded that the techniques had been made unlawful by recently enacted statutes). The Obama administration's position was different, not in what actually occurred, but because its rejection of those techniques rested on a judgment that their use was indeed unlawful. The difference, that is, lies in the reasons for policy choices, not in the policy choices themselves. Another facet of that same phenomenon is that, although the Obama administration defended late-Bush policies that it continued to follow, it generally did so with more restrained legal arguments. Rather than relying on claims that the policies were lawful because they were within the scope of the president's powers under Article II of the Constitution, for example, the Obama administration typically relied on claims that the policies were lawful because authorized by Congress, whether in the AUMF dealing with those who supported the September 11 attacks or in later enacted statutes. This is not to say that the Obama administration completely abandoned Article II claims, but they held a much more subordinated place in the administration's arguments (appearing, for example, in footnotes or short concluding sections of administration legal briefs). As it was with the Bush administration, so it was with the Obama administration: both accepted judicial constitutionalism, though each took a different position on what courts operating within judicial constitutionalism were authorized to do.

A second domain of asserted continuity involves the policy and law relating to the detention of those associated with Al Qaeda at the facility at Guantanamo Bay Naval Base. For reasons of policy, the Bush administration began to release detainees from Guantanamo and the Obama administration continued that policy. As a result of Supreme Court decisions, the government now has to justify the continued detention of Guantanamo detainees in habeas corpus proceedings in federal court. Fiona de Londras in this volume suggests that the Supreme Court decisions "reassert[ed] important values" with significant symbolic importance. One might wonder, though, whether such decisions, when not followed up with substantial on-the-ground effects, *legitimate* the underlying policies more than they confer *legitimacy* on the constitutional system.

Indeed, on-the-ground effects of the Supreme Court decisions appear to have been relatively small. As the title of one article puts it, "What Good Is Habeas?"[5] Although the federal trial courts that heard the first cases from detainees ordered a nontrivial number released, the Circuit Court of Appeals gradually developed a quite government-friendly law of habeas corpus, making it easy for the government to offer legally acceptable justifications for continued detention.[6] Advocacy groups and interested observers have compiled "scorecards" of detainee/government wins and losses,[7] and the fairest interpretation of the scorecards is that not a single detainee has ever been released after a decision on habeas that his detention was unjustified. There are several reasons for this outcome. The most important practical reason is almost certainly that the population of detainees was so winnowed by "voluntary" releases that those remaining in detention were indeed highly likely to be properly subject to detention (if anyone was, in fact). So it is likely that some detainees were released under the shadow of habeas litigation (released, that is, in the sense that the government may have intensified its efforts to find somewhere else to relocate those detainees), because it was uncertain that it would ultimately prevail in habeas litigation. The most important legal reason may be that the Court of Appeals held that the federal courts lacked authority to order that detainees be released into the United States, even if the detainees had successfully shown that their detention was unjustified and the government conceded its inability to relocate them safely somewhere outside the United States. The most important groups of such irremovable detainees were a number of Uighurs, some of whom rejected relocation to specific venues outside the United States (and so who might be thought to have thereby waived their objections to continued detention), and an even larger number of citizens of Yemen, who have not been relocated to that country because conditions there are insufficient to guarantee (to an acceptable level of assurance) that they would not engage in terrorist activity.

In addition, the Obama administration's stated goal of prosecuting some detainees in federal court for criminal offenses was blocked by congressional opposition; consequently, it revived the military commission process for subjecting detainees who committed offenses cognizable under the ordinary laws of war to trials in military tribunals (the traditional forum for dealing with such offenders). The result was that a system of indefinite detention persisted under the Obama administration. Moreover, a substantial number of detainees did not have any available forum other than the federal court to challenge their continued detention. Indeed, by late 2012, the Obama administration had said that some detainees—the usual number cited was seventy-eight—faced indefinite detention without the prospect of a trial either in federal court for criminal offenses or in military tribunals for offenses against the laws of war.

Again, the Obama administration's legal rationale for its detention system differed from that offered by the early Bush administration. Under the main line of the Bush administration's legal rationale, detention was justified as an exercise of the president's power as commander in chief, supplemented to some extent by the congressional AUMF. In contrast, the Obama administration: (1) relied solely on the AUMF; (2) agreed, as the early Bush administration did not, that all detainees are entitled to review by a federal court of the justification for their continued detention; and (3) to some extent relied on a plea of necessity to excuse, if not justify (to use the language of the criminal law), the continued detention of a significant number of detainees.

The necessity excuse was as follows: improper practices, such as waterboarding, occurred under the Bush administration. These practices produced information that, if admissible into a civilian trial or military commission, would be sufficient to justify detention. The Obama administration believed that such information was accurate and that the detainees were in fact dangerous. It also believed that the information could not lawfully be admitted into evidence in either form of proceeding. Indefinite detention was appropriate nonetheless, because the detainees were in fact dangerous. This argument *might* place indefinite detention without trial in civilian court or military commission outside the domain of judicial constitutionalism. If the issue would ever come before the courts, they might accept the necessity excuse as legally sufficient. However, the Obama administration never indicated that it would reject any judicial determination that such detention was unconstitutional.

Overall, then, the pattern was this: there were dramatic differences between the policies pursued in the early Bush years and the later ones, similar though not identical policies pursued by the Bush administration in its late years and by the Obama administration, and substantial differences in the legal rationales offered by the late-Bush and Obama administrations for their policies. We can begin to account for this pattern by describing the primary difference in legal rationales. The early Bush administration relied heavily on claims that the president had authority flowing directly from the Constitution to take the actions he had, with that authority perhaps modestly supplemented by Congress in the AUMF and other statutes. However, according to the legal theories of the early-Bush period, congressional approval was not required, and the president had legal authority to act as he chose even in the face of clear statutes purporting to bar him from pursuing specific policies. The late-Bush administration and the Obama administration reversed the emphasis on Article II and congressional authorization, and the Obama administration never strongly asserted a "pure" Article II power. The late-Bush administration emphasized that Congress had authorized its actions, with that authority perhaps modestly supplemented by the president's Article II powers. The Obama administration went a bit further, reducing even more the secondary reliance on Article II.

The common ground for the changes and similarities is Congress. Members of Congress, supported of course by voices in the public, argued strenuously against the policy wisdom of the early-Bush policies, and argued as well that the early-Bush legal *justifications* were constitutionally suspect. The Bush administration responded by changing the policies it pursued, and by seeking congressional approval of much of what it had done and hoped to continue to do. Here, then, was political constitutionalism in operation in two ways. First, some political constitutionalists might argue that constitutionalism manifests itself in policy-choices rather than, or perhaps in addition to, legal rationales. Political pressure that leads an executive to change policy (on constitutionally relevant matters) is part of political constitutionalism, even if the executive's legal arguments do not change at all.[8] Second, Congress "enforces" its vision of what the Constitution requires by imposing political costs on an administration that has a different vision, and the administration responds by altering the view of the Constitution it is willing most forcefully to defend.[9]

Political constitutionalism operated during the Obama administration as well. The Obama administration's detention *policies* were substantially shaped—one might even say determined—by forceful opposition from Congress against many of its key features (such as closing the detention facility at Guantanamo Bay, transferring detainees to the mainland, and pursuing criminal charges against some detainees). Again, we must consider the relation between policies and the Constitution to determine whether this reflects political constitutionalism or, alternatively, ordinary politics without any interesting constitutional implications. More obviously constitutional are the legal rationales offered by the Obama administration to support its policies. Here what matters is the substantial difference between the early-Bush rationales and the late-Bush ones, and the substantial overlap between the late-Bush rationales and the Obama ones. As to the latter, there was the emergence of a consensus on what the Constitution requires and permits with respect to detention policies and on why the Constitution does so. Claims that Article II provides the president with power to pursue national-security goals through means inconsistent with those mandated by Congress eventually disappeared from serious political discussions. Of course, some scholars and commentators, unconstrained by politics, reject this consensus. These dissenters come primarily from the side of those defending unrestrained Article II power, but some come from the side urging even more substantial restrictions on presidential authority than are required under the consensus view.

Political constitutionalism gives no reason to think that any particular consensus (or equilibrium) is stable. Political circumstances can change and, as they do, the momentary political equilibrium will change. A caricatured sketch of the political constitutionalist account of post-September 11 anti-terrorism policy in the United States can bring out some relevant features: the early Bush administration was "conservative," as was Congress (though Congress was somewhat less conservative than the administration was); the late-Bush administration was "conservative," but it faced a more "liberal" Congress after the 2004 elections and even more so after the 2006 elections; the Obama administration was "liberal," facing a somewhat more "conservative" Congress from the outset and even more so after the 2010 elections. Political constitutionalism explains the change from early-Bush to late-Bush policies and justifications, and the similarity between late-Bush and Obama policies and justifications by identifying these arrays of political power. Of course, we do not know what policies and justifications would emerge were a "liberal" administration to be supported by a "liberal" Congress.

Political constitutionalism in practice has some connection to legal/judicial constitutionalism. As de Londras's contribution suggests, the rhetoric of law is inevitably a political resource within political constitutionalism, and it may be difficult to sustain such a rhetoric without some connection to legal constitutionalism and the courts. Otherwise, the rhetoric of rights can be countered by assertions that the rhetoric is "merely" a matter of partisan political preference. Judicial and political constitutionalism operate together, with judicial decisions providing arguments used in political contention. A rhetoric of *rights* is compatible with, and perhaps even required by, a vibrant political constitutionalism, but referring to rights that courts ignore may only demonstrate the rhetoric's emptiness. In the United States, the rhetoric of law and legally enforceable rights blurs the distinction between political and legal/judicial constitutionalism. Policymakers operating within a system of political constitutionalism worry about the possibility that other political actors will impose political costs, because they believe that the policies are inconsistent with fundamental ("constitutional") values. Within a system of judicial constitutionalism, they worry about the possibility that they will face judicial rather than, or in addition to, political sanctions for perceived violations of fundamental values. Facing even a small chance that judicial sanctions will be imposed, they devote more resources to assessing the lawfulness of their policies than they would in a purely political constitutionalist system.

De Londras offers another challenge to the argument that political constitutionalism accounts for—and can provide a defense of—the U.S. response to terrorism since 2001. She notes that in general Democratic politicians criticized President Bush when he was in office, and Republican politicians criticized President Obama. This suggests to her that *ordinary* quotidian politics rather than constitutional politics might be at work. There surely is something to that thought. Yet, overall Republicans appear to have accepted the broad contours of President Obama's modifications of late-Bush policies, and Democrats were among those who opposed some of President Obama's initiatives. At the least, ordinary politics were compounded with differences in risk-aversion between the executive and Congress, and, in my view, risk-aversion is a matter of constitutional politics.

David Jenkins's contribution to this volume suggests a final challenge. He discusses the differences between the constitutional treatment of citizens and noncitizens at common law and in modern British constitutionalism. The U.S. constitutional tradition has always distinguished between the protections afforded citizens and noncitizens, though all are entitled to basic due process protections within the United States. Beyond that, constitutional politics in the United States can export the costs of domestic policies to noncitizens, who by definition cannot participate directly in constitutional or indeed ordinary politics as expressed in elections. Perhaps such cost-exporting is constitutionally problematic.

That contention raises deep questions in political theory. To what extent do actors within a domestic constitutional order have some duty to consider the interests of noncitizens outside the domestic territory? International humanitarian law sets some limits, in its requirements of proportionality and discrimination, but—until the expansion of programs using drones to target specific individuals—few questions about the compatibility of U.S. policies with international humanitarian law arose.

Within the domestic territory, are there duties beyond those of basic fairness? Whatever the answer to that question, it bears noting that U.S. policies probably did not breach any such duties. The United States intensified its enforcement of its immigration laws after 2001. The intensification took the form of identifying people who had been admitted for lawful residence but who had violated some of the conditions placed on that admission, and then deporting them—"removal" was the term used in U.S. law—even though, prior to 2001, their violations would not have led to removal. Given the underlying law violations, I find it difficult to characterize the removals as problematic. In addition, for a period after 2001 the United States engaged in more surveillance of lawfully admitted noncitizens from some Moslem-majority nations than had occurred before, but that surveillance did not directly infringe any liberties (except to the extent that those subject to the surveillance were "chilled" in their exercise of their liberties by the knowledge that they were subject to surveillance).

In short, constitutional politics *might* lead to disregarding the interests of noncitizens, whether inside or outside the United States. Whether doing so is constitutionally problematic with respect to those outside the United States is a question of political theory about which there is serious disagreement. And, it is quite unclear that constitutional politics *did* lead to such a disregard with respect to those inside the United States.

I have been tempted to say that the U.S. system combines political with judicial constitutionalism, with the latter constraining the former. On reflection I think that doing so would be a mistake. In any constitutional polity, politics will determine the shape of policy, even policy bearing on fundamental values. Political constitutionalism holds that *only* politics does so, while judicial constitutionalism holds that enforceable law has a role in shaping policy. Political constitutionalists do not ignore law, of course. For them, politics shapes matters of basic institutional design, such as the balance to be struck between political and judicial constitutionalism. They see law in two ways. First, it is a political resource: political actors deploy legal arguments in the service of their political goals just as they deploy telephone banks to mobilize supporters. Second, law is *ultimately* though not proximately determined by politics: we have the judges we do, and so have the law we do, because of the way politics affects the selection and socialization of judges.[10] So, perhaps I should restate the point I made above. Political constitutionalism provides useful insights into the way in which politics constrains the development of policy affecting fundamental values by directing our attention away from the courts and by giving us some way to think about the implications of the fact that the courts have played a relatively small, perhaps even trivial, role in that process.

ANTI-TERRORISM POLICY AND CONSTITUTIONALISM IN THE UNITED KINGDOM

The contrast between political and judicial constitutionalism illuminates descriptive and normative issues, although few democratic nations today retain the strong tradition of complete parliamentary sovereignty that is political constitutionalism's hallmark. Perhaps the historical movement away from pure political constitutionalism reflects a normative judgment that, in the contemporary world, constitutionalism as such requires some mixture of political and judicial constitutionalism. The grounds for such a judgment are unclear, though they probably have to do with the complexity of contemporary society and the difficulty ordinary people have in comprehending and participating in the operation of the ordinary politics on which political constitutionalism rests. Much of the literature defending political constitutionalism should be read, then, as claiming that contemporary constitutionalists have a stronger commitment to pure or slightly diluted judicial constitutionalism than is justified by good accounts of constitutional democracy. Therefore, even if a normative commitment to pure political constitutionalism is ruled out by contemporary circumstances, the question of the appropriate mix of political and judicial constitutionalism remains open. Recent British experience may cast some light on that question.

The United Kingdom moved in the direction of judicial constitutionalism with the adoption of the Human Rights Act 1998. Even with such a short lineage, it has produced striking results, most notably in the *Belmarsh* decision.[11] In response to that decision, the government dropped its policy of detaining only foreign terrorist suspects in favor of a system of "control orders" (which people in the United States would describe as house arrest), applicable to both British citizens and noncitizens. Control orders allowed the former Belmarsh detainees and new controlees to live outside a jail, but subject to restrictions on their personal liberty.[12] It is probably relevant here that in early 2011 about a dozen people were subject to control orders, whereas around 170 were still detained at Guantanamo. After the Labour party lost the general election in May 2010, the new Tory-Liberal Democrat coalition government eventually replaced the control order legislation with a similar but less onerous system of "terrorism prevention and investigation measures" (or "TPIMS" as they are called), which came into force in early 2012.[13]

Considering government policies post-*Belmarsh*, I suggest that even a weak (because new) system of judicial constitutionalism in the United Kingdom has provided a set of anti-terrorism policies that is overall less restrictive of liberty than the policies being implemented in the United States. On the U.S. side of the comparison, as already argued above, despite the nation's nominal commitment to judicial constitutionalism, its anti-terrorism policies have been decisively shaped by political constitutionalism. Why the difference on the British side?

One possibility is that the British simply faced a smaller threat from terrorism than did the United States. It would take more argument than can be provided here to support fully the claim, which I think correct, that this statement is not accurate. To sketch the argument: the British have interrupted more terrorist operations at advanced planning stages than have American authorities—the planned attacks on British airports were more serious than the underpants bomber in Detroit, and farther along than whatever might have been planned by groups in New York and Virginia.[14] Decades of experience in the United Kingdom with terrorism associated with the conflict in Northern Ireland gave the British a better information base on which to build anti-terrorism policies that were both effective and liberty-protecting. Lacking that experience, the United States has chosen policies whose marginal contribution to protection against terrorism is small in comparison to the policies' marginal impairment of liberty.

Although I am inclined to think that experience with terrorism does improve anti-terrorism policy, I end this international comparison with another suggestion. The strong version is that the recent British experience shows the advantages of judicial over political constitutionalism. The weaker version is that a small amount of judicial constitutionalism layered onto a system of vigorous political constitutionalism produces overall better policies than a system in which political constitutionalism places substantial constraints on a previously vigorous judicial constitutionalism, even where judicial constitutionalism remains vigorous in other domains. I note, though, Jenkins's argument that adding judicial constitutionalism to political constitutionalism led to a weakening of the common law restraints on government policy, restraints that were themselves the product of pure political constitutionalism. If Jenkins is correct, he provides another, perhaps ironic argument in favor of political constitutionalism.

CONCLUSION

The idea of political constitutionalism provides insight into developments in anti-terrorism law since 2001. Judicial constitutionalism is the prevailing view in the United States, and U.S. commentators are likely to be skeptical about the ability of "mere" politics to constrain power. For some, the British experience since 2001 might seem somewhat more rights-protective than the U.S. experience and so vindicates judicial constitutionalism against political constitutionalism. In my view, the differences between the two experiences are relatively small and, perhaps more important, neither one is obviously "better" in terms of their jointly satisficing liberty and security. Even more important, we know that both political and judicial constitutionalism can misfire, as they did with Britain's sweeping detention schemes during World War II and in Northern Ireland, with the U.S. government's internment of Americans of Japanese origin during World War II, and perhaps in some respects even with certain anti-terrorism measures in both the United States and United Kingdom since 2001. Neither political nor judicial constitutionalism, that is, inevitably produces the "right" results from some external, normative point of view. Accordingly, the normative evaluation of them as alternative mechanisms for protecting rights (from whatever perspective) is exceedingly difficult.[15]

Finally, as this chapter has suggested, political and judicial constitutionalism are not sharply distinct from each other. For political constitutionalism to operate as an effective constraint on power, a nation's people must be ready and able to discipline politicians who adopt policies that depart from what the people regard as what those rights require. Also, in some political cultures (perhaps more so in the United States than in the United Kingdom) law enforced by courts is a source of information and education about fundamental rights.

NOTES

* William Nelson Cromwell Professor of Law, Harvard Law School; A somewhat different version of this essay appears in Clement Fatovic & Benjamin A. Kleinerman, *Extra-Legal Power and Legitimacy: Perspectives on Prerogative* (New York: Oxford University Press, 2013).

1. This is the "settlement" function that Alexander and Schauer emphasize. Larry Alexander and Frederick Schauer, "On Extrajudicial Constitutional Interpretation" (1997) 110 *Harv. L. Rev.* 1359.

2. Doing so, however, would have diverted attention from legal constitutionalism's place in decisions by nonjudicial actors.
3. For more detailed discussions of political constitutionalism, see Richard Bellamy, *Political Constitutionalism: A Republican Defence of the Constitutionality of Democracy* (New York: Cambridge University Press, 2007); Adam Tomkins, *Our Republican Constitution* (Portland, Ore.: Hart, 2005).
4. For a summary of what the author calls "substantive convergence" between the late-Bush and Obama policies, see Peter Margolies, "The Ivory Tower at Ground Zero: Conflict and Convergence in Legal Education's Responses to Terrorism" (2011) 60 *Journal of Legal Education* 373, 375–81.
5. Aziz Z. Huq, "What Good Is Habeas?" (2010) 26 *Constitutional Commentary* 385.
6. See, for example, *Al-Bihani* v. *Obama*, 590 F.3d 866 (D.C. Cir. 2010) ("support" for Al Qaeda defined broadly); *Salahi* v. *Obama*, 625 F.3d 745 (D.C. Cir. 2010) (being "part of" Al Qaeda broadly defined).
7. The figures have, of course, always been a moving target, but for an example, recent at the time of writing, see Benjamin Wittes, Updated Habeas Numbers, available online at http://www.lawfareblog.com/2011/08/updated-habeas-numbers-2/. Best described as a supporter of detention, Wittes reports zero wins and eleven (or thirteen) losses by detainees on the merits in the circuit court of appeals, as well as fourteen detainee victories at the district court level that the government accepted either by not appealing or withdrawing its appeals (usually, though not so stated by Wittes, because the detainess had been relocated to another country).
8. It is not clear to me that the effect of political pressure on policy should play this role in an account of political constitutionalism, although it is also not clear to me that it should not.
9. The refined vision then has some impact on the policies pursued: some of the early-Bush policies were more difficult to defend under the late-Bush legal rationale.
10. For an overview, see Mark Tushnet, *The Constitution of the United States: A Contextual Analysis* (Oxford: Hart, 2009) at 130–34.
11. *A and Others v Secretary of State*, [2004] UKHL 56.
12. Control orders ranged in severity from nearly twenty-four–hour house arrest, with stringent requirements to report when the person subject to the order leaves the house for any permitted reason, to quite mild monitoring through electronic bracelets without any restriction on movement.
13. See *Terrorism Prevention and Investigation Measures Act 2011*, c. 23.
14. However, it is possible that this difference may not result from some differential in the "intrinsic" seriousness of the plans, but in a greater British willingness to let the plans move forward before interrupting them.
15. The best exposition of the difficulties of which I am aware is Wojciech Sadurski, *Rights before Courts: A Study of Constitutional Courts in Postcommunist States of Central and Eastern Europe* (Dordrecht, The Netherlands: Springer, 2005) at ch. 2.

CHAPTER 9

Guantánamo Bay, the Rise of the Courts, and the Revenge of Politics

FIONA DE LONDRAS*

In the grand scheme of things, Guantánamo Bay is not the location or phenomenon of most concern in the "war on terrorism": it has housed a relatively small number of detainees, been under sustained attention from civil society institutions, and been the focus of considerable litigation in the American and British courts. As a result, we know a substantial amount about the prison and what has happened there, and its detainees have availed of the federal court system in trying to establish and enforce their rights. That notwithstanding, Guantánamo Bay remains the focus of substantial legal, scholarly, and political attention. This concentration on Guantánamo Bay has largely been because of its symbolism and the potency of the images that have emerged from it: orange jumpsuits and barbed wire have become deeply associated with injustice and arbitrariness in the popular imagination of the "war on terrorism." Guantánamo Bay has become "a semiotic for the extra-judicial 'war on terrorism,' a visceral expression of a nation that is troubled, not just by feelings of impotence and rage, but of guilt too."[1]

For some time Guantánamo Bay was (mis)characterised as a "legal black hole," but over the past ten years the U.S. Supreme Court has developed a jurisprudence to show that *at least some* law applies to what happens in Guantánamo Bay and that federal courts can exercise stronger-than-expected judicial review over activities there. Consequently, the Bush administration's original jurisdictional rationale for detaining suspected terrorists there has largely been undone. In spite of this, and in the face of President Obama's clear and high profile commitment to close the prison, Guantánamo Bay remains open. This chapter explores this paradox between the current legal position, in which Guantánamo Bay has lost much of the original rationale for its use, and a political reality in which Congress obstructed its closure throughout Obama's first term. The question is whether this congressional "push-back" represents what Mark Tushnet terms "political constitutionalism" in his contribution to this collection,[2] or whether it is mere *quotidian* politics, saturated in the hyperbolic and panic-ridden discourse of the "war on terrorism." This chapter argues the latter: that the refusal to close Guantánamo Bay was a matter of unvirtuous politics, rather than of political constitutionalism.

GUANTÁNAMO BAY AND THE CONSTRUCTION OF A "LEGAL BLACK HOLE"

Guantánamo Bay is a place that is fully bound up with law, in terms of both the arguments made by the Bush administration to justify the detention of suspected terrorists there and the degree to which those individuals are entitled to due process and other legal protections. Having decided to detain suspected terrorists as "enemy combatants" in the "war on terrorism," the Bush administration next had to decide where these people ought to be detained. The answer was multifaceted, seeming to depend on the prisoner's personal status and the place of capture. Thus, four different detention strategies developed in the course of the "war on terrorism": detention within the United States itself, detention on the "traditional" battlefields of Iraq and Afghanistan, detention in "black sites" operated by the CIA in other countries, and detention in Guantánamo Bay. When it comes to Guantánamo Bay, its unique territorial and jurisdictional status in American law was a primary consideration in its selection as a detention centre.

The Bush administration's jurisdictional reasoning went as follows: (1) Cuban law did not apply to Guantánamo Bay on the basis of the terms of the agreement leasing the property to the United States;[3] (2) U.S. federal courts had no jurisdiction and constitutional rights did not apply because it was de jure Cuban territory;[4] (3) U.S. statutes did not apply there unless they expressly provided for extraterritorial application; and (4) unincorporated international human rights law did not apply there because it had neither domestic nor extraterritorial effect. Although international humanitarian law (IHL) might have applied there (inasmuch as there was a qualifying armed conflict), the U.S. government claimed that IHL either allowed for the detentions in question or did not apply at all to the unconventional "war on terrorism." Law was therefore central to the construction of Guantánamo Bay as a place beyond law, and consequently "de-exceptionalised" Guantánamo Bay.[5] That is, it was law itself rather than power or politics alone that determined where and how the law would apply. According to the Bush administration's legal arguments, therefore, the law did not reach foreign enemy combatants detained at Guantánamo.

This jurisdictional reasoning accompanied an institutional concern with minimising judicial oversight. The perceived benefit of Guantánamo Bay, in the executive's mind, was its jurisdictional isolation so that the detainees there could not seek habeas corpus review of their treatment or detention. In his account of the aftermath of 9/11, John Yoo writes that a primary concern in relation to detention was to ensure that the federal courts would not have the capacity to "interfere" with detention policy.[6] This was to be achieved by arguing that not only was Guantánamo Bay beyond the geographical jurisdiction of the federal courts, but also it was beyond their institutional competence. Constructing the American response to the attacks as a "war" facilitated the argument that its management was an executive matter. The executive branch, it was argued, was authorised to detain individuals suspected of involvement in terrorist activity, under the Constitution, the Authorization for the Use of Military Force, and, in later years, various pieces of empowering legislation. Thus, the argument here was not that Guantánamo Bay was beyond law per se, but rather that the law itself placed the naval base beyond the courts' reach by means of elaborate jurisdictional rules. The government's legal argument might have lacked principle, but Guantánamo's territorial and jurisdictional status under it was nevertheless a legal construct.

Seen in this way, Guantánamo Bay was not a place wholly beyond law. However, this did not mean that it posed no challenge to law or, more specifically, to constitutionalism and liberal legalism. In fact, the challenge posed was a substantial one. In the first place, the attempted construction of Guantánamo Bay as a lawless space highlighted the capacity of fundamental legal rules to undermine the very rule-of-law principles they were designed and intended to protect. The paradoxical legal claim that law created lawlessness did not represent the radical Schmittian exception, but it did express the nihilistic potential of law when applied in an unprincipled manner, unshackled from a broader, liberal rule-of-law context. This nihilism was further highlighted by the Bush administration's sustained and deliberate attempts to ensure that the federal courts would not have any oversight of the Guantánamo prisons. To say that the mere location of governmental action ought to preclude all judicial review of executive decisions mounted a powerful challenge to law as a relevant and autonomous constitutionalist force.

THE RISE OF THE COURTS

The Bush administration's legal representation of Guantánamo Bay posed a challenge to liberal legal order and could for that reason be considered "counter-constitutionalist." However, the U.S. Supreme Court has resisted this counter-constitutionalism (at least to some extent) in a series of cases. Although those decisions do not appear to have resulted in effective and positive changes in the detainees' actual circumstances, they have sent an important constitutionalist message that the executive branch cannot so easily avoid judicial oversight. In this way, the Supreme Court has largely dismantled the legal rationale for detaining people at Guantánamo Bay. Although it still remains unclear exactly what rights those detained there are entitled to under the Constitution, it is now beyond question that the Constitution regulates government behaviour in Guantánamo Bay to at least some degree. This proposition is a considerably more constitutionalist one than that originally advanced by the Bush administration.

The first argument that the Supreme Court dismantled was the claim that the federal habeas statute did not extend to Guantánamo Bay. In *Rasul v. Bush*,[7] a number of Guantánamo detainees alleged that they had both statutory and constitutional rights of access to federal courts. Leaving the constitutional claim for future determination, the Supreme Court held that the habeas statute did apply to Guantánamo Bay, because it was under the complete and effective control of the U.S. government. Some members of Congress were outraged at this perceived judicial interference in Guantánamo Bay and national security affairs.[8] Within a very short period of time, the Detainee Treatment Act of 2005 (DTA) had been introduced, part of which was clearly directed towards undoing *Rasul*.[9] This act sought to strip the federal courts of their habeas jurisdiction over Guantánamo Bay. In *Hamdan v. Rumsfeld*,[10] the Supreme Court then interpreted the DTA in a way that frustrated Congress' intention. Because Hamdan had lodged his petition for habeas corpus before the passage of the DTA, the Court decided that the act had no retrospective effect in the case and that it could exercise jurisdiction based on *Rasul*. *Hamdan* then introduced some of the most significant procedural and rights-based changes to the detention and military commission regimes at Guantánamo Bay; through its interpretation of the Uniform Code of Military Justice (UCMJ), the Court found that the "war on terrorism" constituted a non-international armed conflict to which at least the minimum provisions of international humanitarian law, including Common Article 3 of the Geneva Conventions, applied.

As in *Rasul*, however, *Hamdan* based jurisdiction on statute, meaning that Congress could once again attempt to strip jurisdiction from the federal courts. Indeed, Congress tried to do this with the Military Commissions Act of 2006 (MCA), making it clear that the federal courts had no prospective or retrospective habeas jurisdiction over Guantánamo Bay.[11] By the time the case of *Boumediene* v. *Bush*[12] came before the Supreme Court, it was clear that the Court had two options: (1) either accept that it had no habeas jurisdiction because it had been stripped by the MCA and the constitutional habeas corpus provisions did not apply, or (2) find that, to at least some extent, detainees in Guantánamo Bay were constitutional rights bearers. The Court chose the latter course in *Boumediene*. Writing for the majority, Justice Kennedy repeated the reasoning of *Rasul*, explaining that Guantánamo Bay is to all intents and purposes a territory of the United States, giving it de facto sovereignty over the base. Consequently, as habeas corpus "must not be subject to manipulation by those whose power it is designed to restrain,"[13] at least some constitutional rights applied to those detained there. Although the exact scope of those rights was unclear, there was now no question that habeas corpus was among them. Congress could restrict that right only in conformity with the Constitution's suspension clause,[14] which it had not exercised in this instance.

These cases show a judicial resistance to the core claims of the U.S. government in relation to Guantánamo Bay. The first core claim—that Guantánamo Bay was beyond the reach of law—was categorically rejected in *Rasul*, but by means of what, it must be admitted, was a result-oriented reading of the existing authorities. It would have been just as easy, and more politically astute, of the Supreme Court to find that in fact the principle of extraterritoriality meant that statutory habeas corpus did not apply in Guantánamo Bay. Instead, the Court passed the baton back to Congress, which responded with express support for the executive preference for a legally unregulated space, or at least a space where the regulatory approach was a minimalistic one. The result was the Detainee Treatment Act, whereby Congress essentially handed full authority to the executive branch to operate Guantánamo Bay within the loosely defined, broad parameters of the Combatant Status Review Tribunals (CSRT) and military tribunals. Not only did Congress not succeed in closing off the petitions already lodged from Guantánamo Bay at the time of its enactment (due to *Hamdan*), but it also failed to deter the Supreme Court from finding in *Boumediene* that at least some of the Constitution applies in Guantánamo

Bay. This not only asserted beyond any doubt that Guantánamo Bay was governed by law, but also secured the judiciary's position as the final arbiter of constitutional meaning even there. Certainly, *Boumediene* can be criticised on a number of grounds, including the fact that it does little or nothing to relieve the deprivations of rights and liberty experienced by detainees. Nevertheless, if one views *Boumediene* from its constitutionalist perspective, it is an important reassertion of fundamental values: that is, that government action is subject to meaningful limits, including those laid down by the Constitution and that, no matter the exigencies of the situation, a counter-constitutionalist turn will be resisted by the Court.

Following these cases, it was clear that in the absence of a constitutional suspension of habeas corpus removing the federal courts' jurisdiction, the rationale for Guantánamo Bay's continued use as a detention centre for suspected terrorists had been badly wounded by the Supreme Court. This, perhaps, made it easier for Barack Obama to commit during the 2008 presidential campaign to closing Guantánamo Bay. Indeed, one of the first acts of his presidency was the signing of executive orders directed towards closing the Guantánamo prisons within a year of his inauguration.[15] Making the promise was relatively easy, but events over the first term of his presidency demonstrated that keeping that promise was almost insurmountably difficult.

THE REVENGE OF POLITICS

President Obama appointed a Task Force to review and report on the appropriate courses of action as regards the remaining detainees in Guantánamo Bay. That Task Force reported in 2010[16] outlining three primary categories of detainees: (1) those who were eligible for release or transfer, including those who could not be returned to their countries of origin for reasons of national security or their own personal safety; (2) those who were eligible for prosecution, although not necessarily before regularly constituted civilian courts; and (3) those who were not eligible for release or transfer, but who could not be tried and should therefore continue to be detained. In order to fulfil his ambition to close Guantánamo Bay, Obama had to put in place systems to manage detainees who fell into each of these categories. In each case, Congress acted to frustrate him.

The possibility of allowing individuals who were eligible for release or transfer to live freely (although under surveillance) in the United States was never seriously contemplated, or at least not in a public manner. This was so even in relation to those individuals who could not be repatriated to their countries of origin, because of the risk that they might be subjected to torture there or because the security position in that state made it unsafe to return them. The latter concern was largely connected with the fact that the Task Force did not consider that deeming someone eligible for release or transfer necessarily meant that the individual was not dangerous or did not pose a risk; still, any risk posed could be managed without the need for detention in Guantánamo Bay.[17] This then fed into the concern expressed both by politicians and, in some cases, by judges of "recidivism," or the "return to combat" dilemma.

The nature of this determination, together with the security expense, risk, and possible domestic unpopularity that a third country's government would have to take on in accepting a released detainee, already made the process of negotiating agreements with third countries difficult. Congress subsequently exacerbated that difficulty, however, by introducing a process of "proxy clearance." Under this system, Congress could restrict public expenditures for the transfer of detainees from Guantánamo Bay to third countries and subject them to a certification process at least thirty days prior to the transfer.[18] The secretary of defense, with the concurrence of the secretary of state, had to issue a certificate stating that the country to which the individual was to be transferred was: (1) not a designated state sponsor of terrorism, (2) maintained effective control over the detention facilities in which the individual is to be housed (if he is to be detained), (3) did not face a threat that was likely to have a substantial impact upon its capacity to exercise control over the transferee, (4) had agreed to take "effective steps" to make sure that the transferee could not undertake activities that would threaten the United States or its allies in the future, (5) had taken satisfactory steps to prevent the detainee's involvement in terrorist activities, and (6) had agreed to share certain information with the United States.[19] Thus, although transfers to third countries possible, it would be fair to say that Congress' certification process made them more difficult, on top of the already delicate political and diplomatic task of convincing a foreign state to accept former detainees.

The Task Force further identified forty-six detainees in relation to whom "prosecution in either federal court or a military commission was appropriate and potentially feasible."[20] If prosecution was feasible and appropriate it could take place either by normal criminal trial or by military commission; the Task Force did not prefer one over the other. Even before completion of the Task Force's final report, the Obama administration had shown a clear preference for prosecuting individuals in federal courts wherever possible. This was clear from the announcement in November 2009 that Khalid Sheikh Mohammed, the alleged "mastermind" of the 11 September 2001 attacks, and his alleged co-conspirators were to be prosecuted in New York City. That announcement immediately ignited controversy with a substantial number of commentators arguing that this would make the city vulnerable to further attack, although Attorney General Holder argued the decision had been based solely on prosecutorial rationality.[21] So great was the political and popular outcry against trying Mohammed and his alleged co-conspirators in New York City that this prosecutorial determination could withstand for only two months the political pressure to drop the prosecution.[22] After this executive retreat, any hopes for the swift prosecution of detainees, in order to facilitate the closure of Guantánamo Bay, seemed to dissipate as political resistance grew. That resistance culminated in Congress' passage of a legislative bar on transferring Guantánamo Bay detainees to the United States for *any* purpose, including trial.[23] President Obama was therefore placed in a position where he effectively had no option but to announce, in March 2011, that the military commissions suspended at the beginning of his term of office would be recommenced, albeit with more rights-based procedures than had previously been the case.[24]

The third category of detainees—those who were ineligible for release, transfer, or trial—posed a clear difficulty for any attempt to close Guantánamo Bay, as they would have to be detained *somewhere* if the recommendation of the Task Force was accepted. In 2009, President Obama expressed a desire to acquire the Thompson Correctional Center in Illinois, which could then be used as a dedicated facility exclusively for the detention of such individuals. It would be a maximum security facility, but its presence within the United States itself would mean that the detention in question was somewhat more regularised than that in Guantánamo Bay. Once again, however, Congress stepped in to prevent this, just as it had tried before to block prisoner transfers to the continental United States. Congress had previously made unsuccessful attempts to ensure that any proposed transfer of an individual from Guantánamo Bay to the mainland United States would be subject to a 120-day clearing period, during which Congress would be furnished with a report on the security risks of any transfer.[25] In 2009, after the administration's proposal to acquire the Illinois prison, provisions were inserted into four spending bills in order to prevent the acquisition of this prison or any expenditure required to close the base.[26] Although none of these early legislative attempts were successful, Congress finally passed the National Defense Authorization Act for Fiscal Year 2011, prohibiting the use of any federal monies for the transfer of Guantánamo detainees to the United States or for the acquisition or modification of detention facilities to hold them.[27]

On the whole, then, this congressional activity severely dented President Obama's capacity to close Guantánamo Bay, even though there remained clear pathways to doing so in a manner that would have likely satisfied security concerns. In late 2013 Congressional movements towards closure were finally taken, but the question remains: what did this congressional resistance mean in the broader context of judicial and political constitutionalism and, indeed, of politics more generally?

POLITICS OR CONSTITUTIONALISM?

The political reaction to the Supreme Court's systematic removal of the jurisdictional rationale for the Guantánamo Bay detentions displayed a "serial contempt for judicial propriety"[28] that is and ought to be of concern. This concern relates to constitutionalism and to the apparent political commitment to counter-constitutionalism. The cases about Guantánamo Bay might be presented and read as ones that implicate the long-standing inter-institutional tensions inherent in a system of separation of powers and checks and balances. However, they also point towards a rupture in the respective constitutionalist commitments of the American judicial and legislative branches. Although some commentators have criticised the Supreme Court majority for a perceived power grab in *Boumediene*,[29] that decision is better read as a reassertion not only of jurisdiction, but also of the values of judicialism in a system committed to constitutional supremacy: limited power, objective oversight, democratic values, the rule of law, and the limitation of liberty-sacrifice to that which is considered to be proportionate, justifiable, and equally experienced.

Congressional resistance to President Obama's attempts to close Guantánamo Bay contrasted starkly with Congress' approach to President Bush's determinations about Guantánamo Bay as a detention centre. In this and other matters, Congress originally supported President Bush, both before and after it became clear that American policy included controversial (if not illegal) processes, such as extraordinary rendition, waterboarding, and targeted killing. Even as time passed and concerns began to be voiced about Guantánamo Bay, rare attempts by legislators to shut Guantánamo Bay made little if any significant impact.[30] Instead, as noted above, Congress actually resisted federal court decisions that attempted to regularise Guantánamo Bay by exercising judicial review over it and extending constitutional rights to the detainees there. This pattern of resistance could be interpreted as *either* a manifestation of a principled political constitutionalism or crass politics simpliciter. Certainly, there was a hint of political constitutionalism here, with Congress signalling its view of the appropriate division of powers between courts and the executive branch in times of emergency, conflict, and war. Whether political constitutionalism emerged here or whether this legislative opposition to the courts was simply politics as usual is, however, best judged by developments with Guantánamo Bay since the beginning of the Obama presidency.

In a way, one would rather that congressional patterns could be explained by reference to principled political constitutionalism, for this at least would hint at some kind of grand constitutional vision informing the legislative processes there as they related to Guantánamo Bay, rather than political petulance. It is worth acknowledging here that the dividing line between political constitutionalism and ordinary politics is always blurred. This line arguably becomes more unclear in a crisis-ridden situation, where so much of so-called "everyday politics" is in fact constitutional politics; this is so, as "everyday politics" includes fundamental contestations about constitutional limitations and sometimes amendment of constitutional provisions to allow for action that is considered to be desirable or necessary.[31] In discussions at the Copenhagen symposium from which this volume emerged, Tushnet made the point that ordinary politics can be understood as the practice of political constitutionalism. This certainly seems to be right in at least some circumstances. However, the events outlined above show that this is not inevitably so (nor, by the way, do I wish to suggest that Tushnet claims that is the case). Rather, in my view, the political reaction to judicial attempts to legally regulate Guantánamo Bay and the executive attempts to close its prisons was simply politics and not principle.

The starting point for this view is that these developments are confounding when seen against the history of legislative relations with the executive in times of crisis generally, and in the "war on terrorism" more specifically. In such times, the long-observed pattern is of a facilitative legislature, bending to the executive's will. It seems certainly to be the case that congressional support for Bush-era policies regarding Guantánamo Bay was deferential. Such support can be read as having been politically constitutionalist, for it was truly about trying to arrange and scale out inter-institutional relations between the executive branch and the courts. However, the Obama-era politics of Guantánamo Bay has been different, primarily because of Congress' rejection of three epistemic factors to which legislatures will normally defer to one degree or another: judicial review, executive initiative, and political morality. It is no argument for political constitutionalism to say that the congressional position is simply a continuation of previous executive policy; after all, constitutionalism does not mean favouring a certain institutional weighting when one likes the persons populating the institution. That state of affairs is "just politics," which is precisely what we have here.

Politics writ bare like this are unprincipled and unwise. They lack virtue in the Aristotolean sense, and without virtue there is cowardice, rashness, and imprudence. From historical experience, we know that all of these things produce security-biased policies, as well as laws and actions that unnecessarily rupture society and constitutionalist principles. As Oren Gross argues in his contribution to this volume,[32] and as I have argued elsewhere,[33] what has transpired is law and policy affected by the panic and fear from which they emerge. What is particularly interesting about the Obama-era congressional engagement with Guantánamo Bay is that, unlike in the more immediate, panic-ridden aftermath of the 9/11 attacks, the discourse during Obama's first term was one that looked, felt, and operated much more like a classic manufactured moral panic.[34] In this panic, politicians told us of the risks of terrorism from those detained in Guantánamo Bay, from civilian trials and from the "quaintness" of due process. Such discourse, however, is quite in contradistinction to rational, expertise-led risk analyses that suggested that many detainees in Guantánamo Bay did not need (or deserve) to be detained from a security perspective, that policies such as Guantánamo Bay detention arguably festered anti-American sentiment that might itself lead to more rather than less terrorism, that civilian trials were possible and desirable, that constitutional principles applied in Guantánamo Bay, and so on. These kinds of expertise-led analyses informed the executive position in favour of closing Guantánamo Bay; indeed, Obama's Guantánamo policy was and remains distinctly expertise-led (if not even slightly technocratic), as it depends so heavily for its practical rationale on the security-based assessments of the Task Force. Congress' position up to late 2013, in contrast, seemed to disregard both the professional expertise and institutional preference that seemed to be held in such high political regard during the Bush administration.

CONCLUSION

Congress was on a solo run with its oppositionist turn in respect of Guantánamo Bay. Its obstructive course was not for constitutionalist reasons, but political ones, pure and simple. Being "strong on terrorism," protecting the country, "standing firm," and other machismo jargon are perceived by many politicians as playing well with the public. We may not feel as frightened, as vulnerable, and as insecure as we did in 2001, but people remember what that first panic felt like and some politicians are ready and willing to remind us, lest we would forget. To be sure, closing Guantánamo Bay would not necessarily solve anything. Indeed, it might even make things worse for some individual detainees, who could find themselves somewhere else with fewer legal protections, such as Bagram Airbase. That notwithstanding, keeping Guantánamo Bay open in the face of all the imperatives for its closure is a semiotic of the reluctance of politics to follow law and the refusal of politicians to give up a powerful political symbol a hundred or so miles off the Florida coast.

NOTES

* Professor of Law, Durham Law School.

1. Ian Ward, *Law, Text, Terror* (Cambridge: Cambridge University Press, 2009) at 148.
2. Mark Tushnet, "Legal and Political Constitutionalism, and the Response to Terrorism," Chapter 8 in this volume.
3. Lease of Lands for Coaling and Naval Stations, February 23, 1903, U.S.-Cuba, Article III, T.S. No. 418; Treaty Defining Relations with Cuba, May 29, 1934, U.S.-Cuba, Art. III, 48 Stat. 1683, T.S. No. 866.
4. *Johnson* v. *Eisentrager*, 339 U.S. 763 (1950).
5. Fleur Johns, "Guantánamo Bay and the Annihilation of the Exception" (2005) 16 *European Journal of International Law* 613.
6. John Yoo, *War by Other Means: An Insider's Account of the War on Terror* (New York: Atlantic Monthly Press, 2006).
7. *Rasul* v. *Bush*, 542 U.S. 466 (2004).
8. See, for example, the speech of Sen. Lindsey Graham in the U.S. Senate, 151 *Congressional Record* S12657 (10 Nov. 2005).
9. *Detainee Treatment Act of 2005*, Pub. L. No. 109-148, ss. 1001–1006 (2005).
10. *Hamdan* v. *Rumsfeld*, 548 U.S. 557 (2006).
11. *Military Commissions Act of 2006*, Pub. L. No. 109-366, 120 Stat. 2600 (2006).
12. *Boumediene* v. *Bush*, 553 U.S. 723 (2008).
13. Ibid. at 755–56 (2008).
14. Article 1(9)(2), U.S. Constitution: "The privilege of the writ of *habeas corpus* shall not be suspended, unless when in cases of rebellion or invasion the public safety may require it."
15. Review and Disposition of Individuals Detained at the Guantánamo Bay Naval Base and Closure of Detention Facilities, January 22, 2009, Executive Order No. 13,492, 74 Fed. 4897 Reg. (January 27, 2009); Review of Detention Policy Options, January 22, 2009, Executive Order No. 13,493, 74 Fed. Ref. 4901 (January 27, 2009).
16. Guantánamo Review Task Force, Final Report, January 22, 2010.
17. Ibid. at 17.
18. *National Defense Authorization Act for Fiscal Year 2011*, H.R. 6523, Pub.L. 111-383, § 1033(a)(1).
19. Ibid. at § 1033(b).
20. Guantánamo Review Task Force, *supra* note 16 at 19.
21. Eric Holder, Testimony to the Senate Judiciary Committee, 18 November 2009, available online at, U.S. Department of Justice, http://www.justice.gov/ag/testimony/2009/ag-testimony-091118.html (15 March 2011).

22. Scott Shane and Benjamin Wieser, "U.S. Drops Plan for a 9/11 Trial in New York City," *New York Times* (29 January 2010) A1.
23. See *supra* note 18, at § 1032.
24. Periodic Review of Individuals Detained at Guantánamo Bay Naval Station Pursuant to the Authorization for Use of Military Force, March 7, 2001, available online at The White House, http://www.whitehouse.gov/sites/default/files/Executive_Order_on_Periodic_Review.pdf (March 11, 2011).
25. H.R. 5136, § 1033, as placed on Senate Calendar; see discussion in Fiona de Londras, *Detention in the "War on Terror": Can Human Rights Fight Back?* (Cambridge: Cambridge University Press, 2011) at 125–26.
26. These provisions were inserted into spending and appropriations bills for the Departments of Homeland Security, Defense, State, Commerce, Justice and Science. See Walter Alarkon, "Congress Uses Spending Bills to Halt Closing of Guantánamo Bay" *The Hill* (4 October 2009).
27. *Supra* note 18 __ at § 1032.
28. Ward, *supra* note 1 at 155.
29. John Yoo, "The Supreme Court Goes to War," *Wall Street Journal* (17 June 2008) available online at Wall Street Journal, http://online.wsj.com/article/SB121366596327979497.html.
30. National *Defence Authorisation Act for Fiscal Year 2007*, S. 2766 (as originally introduced). See Manu Raju and Elana Schor, "Feinstein, Harkin aim to shut Guantánamo through Defence Authorisation Bill," *The Hill* (21 June 2007) available online at The Hill, http://thehill.com/leading-the-news/feinstein-harkin-aim-to-shut-guantnamo-through-defense-authorization-bill-process-2007-06-21.html; Editorial, "An Exit Strategy for Guantánamo," *The New York Times* (3 May 2007) available online at The New York Times, http://www.nytimes.com/2007/05/03/opinion/03thu2.html.
31. This is not limited to national security crises. Indeed, in the course of trying to manage the global financial crisis domestic politics in numerous states has become fundamentally constitutional. In Spain, for example, the Constitution was amended to put in place a constitutional limit on public debt. This was only the second amendment of the Spanish Constitution, which was introduced in 1978.
32. Oren Gross, "Security *vs.* Liberty: On Emotions and Cognition," Chapter 3 in this volume.
33. de Londras, *supra* note 25, ch 1.
34. Stanley Cohen, *Folk Devils and Moral Panics: The Creation of the Mods and Rockers* (London: MacGibbon and Kee, 1972).

CHAPTER 10

Citizenship and the Limits of Due Process since 9/11

DAVID JENKINS*

In a 2003 speech, Lord Steyn called the Guantanamo Bay prisons a "legal black hole," beyond the jurisdiction of the federal courts, free from the constraints of the rule of law, and governed at the sole discretion of the president of the United States.[1] This metaphor of the "black hole" quickly became symbolic of the Bush administration's global "war on terrorism," where the gloves had come off, the rules had changed, and national security trumped individual rights. In fighting this "war," the administration saw the world beyond American borders, including the U.S. Naval Station in Cuba, as a dangerous place where politics shaped policy with few or no legal restrictions. Moreover, although Lord Steyn did not draw attention to it, Guantanamo Bay was only one "black hole" among many. The Bush administration took care that extraordinary rendition, black sites, and enhanced interrogation techniques—euphemisms for kidnapping, secret prisons, and torture—occurred outside of the expected reach of the U.S. federal courts.

In *Boumediene* v. *Bush*,[2] the U.S. Supreme Court finally advanced the Constitution's fence-line, extending its writ of habeas corpus to Guantanamo Bay. In doing so, the Court constitutionally guaranteed the prisoners there some modicum of judicial process to review the legality of their ongoing detentions. *Boumediene*, however, was a conservative decision. The Supreme Court neither asserted a wide extraterritorial jurisdiction nor championed universal human rights. Rather, it exceptionally brought Guantanamo Bay and its detainees within the Constitution's delimited territorial boundaries, separating the American national community from the lawless, dangerous world beyond them. Within these boundaries and this national community, where a *citizen's* liberty or *national territory* is in question, the president's discretion rapidly wanes and the judges rule. Here the rule of law constrains the political decision. This contrasts with the position, so forcefully advanced by the Bush administration, that in foreign matters the president gets his way and aliens have few or no rights. Despite extending habeas, *Boumediene* itself reaffirmed a premise in American law that judicially enforceable rights (as opposed to abstract rights-principles) arise from membership in a national community, defined by territory and personal status. Members of this community are legally privileged over nonmembers and possess rights denied to others inhabiting the wider world. It was for this reason that the administration's military detention of two citizens and one resident alien as unlawful combatants, its secret program of illegal domestic wiretapping, and the Patriot Act's search and surveillance powers aroused especially strong controversies in the United States—probably even more so than those over Guantanamo Bay. Whatever the president and Congress might do to others in foreign lands, many Americans thought, those things do not happen *here* to *us*.

This boundaried world of rights, and the idea of a privileged nationhood to which it is connected, contrasts markedly to British attitudes in the post 9/11 decade. In the United Kingdom, government infringements on civil liberties have been directed against both citizens and aliens, with weak dividing lines between internal and external threats and responses. At the time of Lord Steyn's speech, British law expressly permitted twenty-eight days of detention without charge on suspicion of terrorism. Even this time-period was mild compared to the ninety days later sought unsuccessfully by the Blair government and to the forty-two days Prime Minister Brown failed to achieve. Parliament had also authorized the indefinite detention of aliens on national security grounds, when they could not be deported due to a risk of torture abroad—a measure so extreme that the government derogated from the right to personal liberty under Article 5 of the European Convention on Human Rights and Article 9 of the International Covenant on Civil and Political Rights. Moreover, Parliament denied these aliens important procedural rights in their immigration and detention hearings, such as knowledge of the factual allegations against them, access to secret government evidence, and full consultation with a lawyer. Britain did not have military commissions or Guantanamo Bay, but it did have detention without trial and Belmarsh Prison.

As in the United States, the courts in the United Kingdom have played an important role in reviewing the legality of such harsh anti-terrorism measures. Most famously, in the *Belmarsh Case*,[3] the House of Lords declared that the indefinite detention of aliens was incompatible with the European Convention, because it discriminated on the basis of national origin. Yet this decision is not quite the civil liberties victory it is often thought to be. In that decision, the Law Lords sacrificed the once-privileged status of citizenship to the Convention's non-discrimination and proportionality principles. Unlike *Boumediene*, the *Belmarsh Case* undermined the legal importance of citizenship and territory, and divorced rights from membership in the national community. In doing so, *Belmarsh* has possibly caused more harm than good to civil liberties in the United Kingdom. Its failure to articulate minimum due process standards did little to improve the lot of resident aliens. At the same time, it gave the government a legal excuse to pursue anti-terrorism measures that were more restrictive of the liberties of citizens.

A comparison of *Boumediene* and the *Belmarsh Case* reveals a divergence in American and British thinking about citizenship and rights. American law retains a conception of rights closely tied to nationhood, designed to protect "insiders" from both the hostile world beyond and tyranny at home. This is an old idea originating in English common law and political thought, which until recently also privileged the rights of citizens over aliens. In recent years, however, British law has gradually rejected the special duty of protection that the Crown once owed to citizens and the special commitment to due process that went with it. A more leveled notion of equality, but one lacking much rights-content, has taken its place. This doctrinal shift allows the government to justify restrictions of civil liberties more easily, based on generally applicable proportionality principles. Which country's approach is preferable is a normative choice, and one this chapter does not make; it focuses only on the problems inherent in each. Whereas American law still risks black holes, British law increasingly offers hollow promises to the citizens it is meant to protect. In both systems, then, the idea of "due process of law" has deep conceptual and doctrinal limitations, not easily corrected.

THE BORDERS OF AMERICAN DUE PROCESS

Very soon after the commencement of military operations in Afghanistan, President Bush ordered the internment of captured Taliban and Al Qaeda fighters in hastily constructed prisons at the Guantanamo Bay Naval Base. His military order denied captives prisoner of war status under the Third

Geneva Convention, classified them as "enemy combatants" exempt from many protections of humanitarian law, and provided for their trial by special military commissions.[4] The president's calculated decision to limit this order to aliens and to intern them at Guantanamo Bay was supported both by political and legal precedents. Some years before, President George H.W. Bush and President Clinton had detained Haitian "boat people" at Guantanamo Bay in order to prevent their entry into the United States. On one level, then, the second Bush administration mimicked its predecessors. It also invoked their legal rationale for using Guantanamo: because the naval base was on Cuban soil, federal courts arguably had no habeas corpus jurisdiction over aliens held there.

This legal argument primarily rested on the 1950 Supreme Court decision of *Johnson v. Eisentrager*.[5] In that case, the Court found no habeas jurisdiction over Germans captured in China, tried by American military commission, and imprisoned in occupied Germany. Jurisdiction hinged on the citizenship of the petitioners and the location of their detention. Writing for the Court, Justice Jackson explained the connection between rights and citizenship or territory:

> [E]ven by the most magnanimous view, our law does not abolish inherent distinctions recognized throughout the civilized world between citizens and aliens, nor between aliens of friendly and of enemy allegiance, . . . nor between resident enemy aliens who have submitted themselves to our laws and non-resident enemy aliens who at all times have remained with, and adhered to, enemy governments."[6]

The Court observed that, in the past, it had "been at pains to point out that it was the alien's presence within its territorial jurisdiction that gave the Judiciary power to act."[7] *Eisentrager* reaffirmed a long-held notion that aliens in foreign lands had no right to judicial access, unless Congress granted it by statute.

Even if courts did have jurisdiction, aliens still might not have substantive or procedural rights to enforce. In the 1990 case of *United States v. Verdugo-Urquidez*,[8] for example, the Supreme Court found that an alien on trial in federal court could not invoke Fourth Amendment rights against warrantless searches, where American law enforcement agents had seized evidence against the defendant outside of the country. Echoing *Eisentrager*, the Court emphasized that citizens enjoyed a privileged legal position, whereas an alien's rights depended on the nature of his relationship to the United States. As Chief Justice Rehnquist pointed out, reference to "the People" in the Bill of Rights "refers to a class of persons who are part of a national community or who have otherwise developed sufficient connection with this country to be considered part of that community."[9] Aliens residing wholly outside of U.S. territory were not part of this community, whatever any other personal attachments to the country they might have. Visiting and resident aliens were entitled to rights by virtue of their presence in the United States, but were not always due the same rights as citizens. Citizens, on the other hand, were always entitled to the full range of constitutional rights, wherever they were in the world.

The implications of the *Eisentrager* and *Verdugo-Urquidez* framework were ominous. According to it, the world beyond the Constitution's boundaries was a lawless one, where the political branches could do as they liked with little or no judicial interference. The good faith and common sense of the president was to be the U.S. government's guide and restraint in the world beyond American borders, checked only by Congress. Dissenting in *Eisentrager*, Justice Black drew attention to the dangers of such a view, particularly where individual liberty was at stake. He warned that "[t]he Court is fashioning wholly indefensible doctrine if it permits the executive branch, by deciding where its prisoners will be tried and imprisoned, to deprive all federal courts of their power to protect against a federal executive's illegal incarcerations."[10] The Bush administration hoped to exploit this very doctrine with the detentions at Guantanamo Bay. As Fiona de Londras points out in her contribution to this volume,[11] Guantanamo Bay was not so much an exception to law, as an anomalous legal construct: it was the law itself that determined it did not apply extraterritorially.

The Bush administration nevertheless lost three key cases before the Supreme Court. In the first, *Rasul* v. *Bush*,[12] the Court interpreted the federal habeas statute to permit extraterritorial petitions from Guantanamo Bay. It did so because the naval base was under the complete jurisdiction and control of the United States. De facto, rather than de jure, sovereignty determined the territorial reach of habeas corpus. Although Congress tried to restrict habeas in response to that decision, the Supreme Court interpreted that limitation to permit review of pending challenges to the military commission system. In one such case, *Hamdan* v. *Rumsfeld*,[13] the Court found that system to violate the Uniform Code of Military Justice,[14] which required greater procedural protections consistent with both the rules for courts-martial and the Third Geneva Convention. Indignant, Congress explicitly tried to strip the federal courts of habeas jurisdiction over all future or pending cases arising out of Guantanamo Bay. The attempt failed: in *Boumediene*, the Court constitutionally extended habeas to Guantanamo Bay, based on the same reasoning as *Rasul*. Because Guantanamo was de facto American territory, the Court held, it exceptionally fell within the jurisdictional boundaries of *Eisentrager*. Congress could strip the courts of habeas jurisdiction over Guantanamo only if it complied with the strict conditions of the Constitution's suspension clause.[15] Congress had not done so.

In light of *Verdugo-Urquidez, Boumediene* opened up the possibility that the Guantanamo detainees might possess Fifth Amendment due process rights. In the 2004 case of *Hamdi* v. *Rumsfeld*,[16] the Supreme Court had found that in some narrow circumstances the president might detain even a citizen as an unlawful combatant, but only if he was granted meaningful due process. At the minimum, Justice O'Connor suggested, a citizen disputing his designation as an unlawful combatant was entitled to know the factual basis for his classification and to rebut it before a neutral decision-maker. National security considerations, however, might allow some procedural shortcuts, particularly as these military detentions were technically administrative and not punitive. The Court did not say, but presumably aliens detained as unlawful combatants within the United States were entitled to similar, if not identical, due process protections as American detainees. Reading *Hamdi* together with *Boumediene* and *Verdugo-Urquidez*, it looked quite possible that the Guantanamo detainees had at least some constitutional rights to due process, enforceable upon a habeas petition.

Although one should not deny its importance, *Boumediene* has had only limited effects on law and government policy. The Supreme Court only extended habeas to Guantanamo Bay based on a functional test for de facto sovereignty. As such, *Boumediene* did not address habeas jurisdiction over other out-of-country detention sites. This was left for future, case-by-case litigation. In *Al Maqaleh* v. *Gates*,[17] for example, the D.C. Circuit Court of Appeals later refused to entertain habeas petitions from aliens detained at Bagram Airbase in Afghanistan, because it was not under the complete jurisdiction and control of the United States. President Obama could detain aliens there at his discretion, unless Congress conferred statutory habeas or other rights upon them. *Boumediene* therefore maintained the old territorial and personal distinctions of *Eisentrager*, tying rights to membership in the national community. Extraterritorial habeas jurisdiction constitutionally ran to rare territories where the United States had effectively assumed responsibility for governance. So far, this remains a category of one: Guantanamo Bay.

On the political front, Congress resisted giving practical effect to the *Boumediene* decision, limited though it was. It opposed President Obama's plans to close the Guantanamo Bay prisons by denying funding for the imprisonment or trial of detainees in the United States. The Obama administration itself successfully appealed a District Court order that individuals unlawfully detained at Guantanamo Bay were to be resettled in the United

States, when they were unable to be returned home or to other third countries.[18] Detentions at Bagram Airbase and on warships at sea continued, even if torture and secret black sites did not. Like administrations before it, the Obama one argued that—with the exception of Guantanamo Bay—aliens detained abroad remained beyond federal court jurisdiction. So, although the earlier types of abuses ended during President Obama's first term, political opposition to the spirit of *Boumediene* did not, as pointed out by de Londras.[19] Congressional opposition instead led to something of a "revenge of politics"—as she phrases it—on the courts for even moderate legal objections to government policies.[20]

The persistence of legal black holes is troubling. Yet they are symptomatic of doctrines that erect boundaries around rights, linking them to membership in the national community. The hooded prisoner in the orange jumpsuit and the mysterious ghost-plane are only particular, human manifestations of the immanent violence beyond the national Pale. Despite its result, *Boumediene* has reaffirmed the law of the frontier. This is not to say that Lord Steyn was wrong to criticize the abuses at Guantanamo Bay. The Bush administration unsuccessfully advanced radical constitutional theories of inherent executive power, immune from both judicial review and statutory limitations. In making policy, it flippantly disregarded "soft law" such as international human rights and humanitarian law. With hubris, that administration mistook the lack of judicially enforceable rules for legal, political, and moral impunity. Human rights violations at Guantanamo Bay or elsewhere resulted as much or even more from a failure of politics as from the limitations of law. As Mark Tushnet explains,[21] mounting political counter-pressures were just as responsible as adverse court decisions for moderating the policies of the late Bush administration. Yet, the Obama administration continued to defend executive prerogatives vigorously, even while abandoning the extreme claims of its predecessor.

The political resistance to *Boumediene*, and the decision's uncertain legal implications, suggest the constitutional instabilities that can result from even modest changes to entrenched legal doctrines linking rights to nationhood. These doctrines demarcate critical boundaries between the municipal rule of law and the realm of politics. To alter these boundaries risks judicial intrusion into delicate political matters and opens the door for politicians to tamper with the rights of citizens. Justice Scalia voiced this concern by strongly dissenting in *Hamdi* and the Guantanamo cases. In an ironic contrast to Justice Black's dissent in *Eisentrager*, for instance, Scalia condemned the *Boumediene* decision as dangerous constitutional doctrine. Extraterritorial habeas jurisdiction, he argued, would tie the hands of the political branches in protecting the national security. In *Hamdi*, in contrast, he took an uncompromising stand on the right of the citizen to be free from military detention of any sort, unless Congress suspended habeas corpus. The citizen suspected of terrorism was otherwise entitled to full criminal due process. According to Scalia, *Hamdi* endorsed an unprincipled, ad hoc balancing between a citizen's rights and the government's national security claims. This new approach, he feared, would dangerously increase state power at the expense of liberty.

Scalia's opinions in *Hamdi* and the Guantanamo cases at first appear inconsistent, but they are coherent in their reasoning. For Scalia, the Constitution establishes strong jurisdictional lines, which protect citizens and national territory from both foreign enemies and an overreaching government. In doing so, it grants few or no legal rights to those *not* belonging to the national community, beyond what Congress and the president might allow. The political branches have broad discretion to protect the country from security threats, considered to emanate mostly from aliens and the outside world. However, the law presumes the American citizen to be loyal and law-abiding, unless proven otherwise under criminal due process. Scalia exaggerated the extent to which *Boumediene* departed from this approach. Nevertheless, his basic argument is compelling: disconnecting rights from membership in the national community risks hampering the political branches in foreign matters of state, while inviting unwelcome government inroads on civil liberties at home.

BEING BRITISH: DETERMINING RIGHTS UNDER THE COMMON LAW

The *Belmarsh Case* represents the kind of ad hoc balancing approach that Scalia feared would open the door to more, not fewer, rights violations. Since 9/11, the British government's intrusions on both citizens' and aliens' rights have gradually increased. *Belmarsh* itself led to an onerous control orders regime and now permits other restrictions on citizens' rights that once might have been politically untenable. As such, the case represents an important shift in British attitudes toward citizenship and rights. This shift is from a rights jurisprudence premised on privileged nationhood to one of universal, but less robust, protection.

The *Eisentrager* and *Verdugo-Urquidez* framework is not a distinctly American legal doctrine. Rather, it is a classic, common-law approach to jurisdiction and rights, having close parallels in the United Kingdom. Historically, British law recognized that an individual's legal relationship to the national community fell along a continuum. Where a person fell on this continuum depended on his personal and territorial status. This analytical approach can be traced back to pre-1776 English decisions such as *Calvin's Case*[22] and *Somerset's Case*.[23] As the British Empire grew, the courts established that under the act of state doctrine the Crown had a discretionary power to dispose of the lives, liberty, and property of aliens outside of its dominions. *Buron v. Denman*[24] from 1848, for example, made clear that any actions taken by the Crown against a foreigner abroad were unreviewable acts of state, for which the Crown need not answer in a court of law.

The Crown did, however, have a protective duty toward aliens within the realm. The rights of these aliens depended on whether they were visitors or residents, and on the sovereign relationship between the United Kingdom and the alien's home country. In 1946, both *Netz v. Ede* and *Ex parte Kuechenmeister*[25] confirmed the ages-old proposition that the Crown could expel or intern an enemy alien—being a national of a state with which His Majesty was at war—under the prerogative without statutory authority. Presumed hostile, the enemy alien had rights neither to an individual hearing nor to release upon a writ of habeas corpus. In contrast, as seen in *Johnstone v. Pedlar*[26] from 1921, aliens from friendly nations were entitled to the Crown's protection while within the realm. They could be deprived of their liberty or property only with due process, even if they had broken the law, waged war against the Crown, or otherwise supported its enemies. All of these cases proceeded on the basis that an alien's personal or territorial connection to the nation, if there was any connection at all, determined the extent of his or her legal rights.

The British subject, in contrast, was legally privileged simply by reason of his nationality and presumed allegiance to the Crown. He carried his rights with him around the globe, whether he was located within the Crown's far-flung dominions (*Walker v. Baird*[27] from 1892) or somewhere without (*Attorney General v. Nissan*[28] from 1969). The Crown's officers had a duty to respect these rights wherever the citizen might be. Whereas an executive action against a foreigner abroad was an unreviewable act of state, the citizen always had recourse to the courts where sovereign immunity did not generally apply. In limited circumstances, the Crown might possibly act against the citizen under the prerogative. The courts, though, would limit such royal powers to exceptional situations such as martial law (recognized in Ireland in the 1920 case of *Re. Clifford and O'Sullivan*[29]); restrict them in favor of statute (as in *Attorney General v. De Keyser's Royal Hotel Ltd.*,[30] a World War I case decided in 1920); or attach conditions to their exercise (as happened in *Burmah Oil Co. v. Lord Advocate*,[31] a World War II case finally resolved in 1964). Of course, the sovereign Parliament was always free to limit the rights of the citizen. It could pass ex post facto laws or bills of attainder, authorize trials by special tribunals or courts-martial, authorize internment, or even outright suspend habeas corpus. In such rare instances, the courts were inclined to recognize wide ministerial discretion in exercising statutory powers, as it did in the World War II detention case of *Liversidge v. Anderson*.[32] Still, even the statutory detention power at issue in that case (arguably tantamount to a habeas suspension) required explicit parliamentary approval. Such exceptional, usually wartime legislative encroachments on citizens' liberties contrasted with the Crown's powers to detain enemy aliens under the prerogative or to act freely against aliens abroad under the act of state doctrine.

Accordingly, at 9/11, the United Kingdom and the United States shared a conceptually similar, common-law framework that based an individual's rights on his connections with the national community, as determined by personal status and territoriality. The law presumed citizens to be loyal and entitled to special protection, and they enjoyed stronger due process whenever that loyalty came into doubt. Aliens abroad, who were outside of the national community, had no rights other than what the political branches might grant them. Visiting and resident aliens, who were lawfully present in national territory but whose loyalty could be suspect, fell somewhere in between. This old rights approach was potentially discriminatory under Article 14 of the European Convention, incorporated unto British law under the Human Rights Act 1998. That article forbids the limitation of Convention rights on certain prohibited grounds such as national origin. Before the *Belmarsh Case*, however, no British judicial decision had as yet squarely dealt with this latent conflict.

Analyzed solely from the common-law perspective, then, what were the general rights-expectations of aliens who were in the United Kingdom and suspected of terrorist activities in 2001? First, unless their home country was in a formal state of war with the United Kingdom, they were entitled to a fair hearing and meaningful due process of law before they could be deprived of their personal liberty. This meant criminal indictment and trial or deportation under regular immigration procedures. Second, Parliament could nonetheless justify treating aliens differently from citizens in some situations. For example, it could toughen immigration law or perhaps even authorize preventive detention of some sort, in lieu of either deportation or prosecution. These two propositions, stated broadly, were in obvious tension. Yet they suggested a rough proportionality principle, requiring that the government justify any discriminatory infringements on aliens' rights and that the courts pay due attention to liberty concerns when interpreting such legislation. Nevertheless, even under this flexible common-law framework, the indefinite detention of aliens under Section 23 of the Anti-terrorism, Crime and Security Act 2001 (ATCSA) was an extreme legislative response that violated a serious constitutional principle: the right of everyone within the country, whether citizen or alien, to be free from a peacetime deprivation of liberty without due process of law.

BELMARSH AND THE HOLLOW PROMISES OF CITIZENSHIP

Section 23 of the ATCSA authorized the Home Secretary to detain aliens suspected of terrorism, but who could be neither deported nor released. The Labour government rushed the act through Parliament in the weeks following the September 11 attacks. Section 23, however, was a specific response to the 1996 judgment of the European Court of Human Rights in *Chahal v. United Kingdom*.[33] That decision forbade the return of an alien to a country where he risked torture. Because of this prohibition, Section 23 enabled the Home Secretary to detain an irremovable alien for a possibly indefinite time period. It was also preventive in purpose; it rested on a ministerial assessment of the alien's risk to national security, rather than on his commission of any criminal offense.

Indefinite detention was serious enough, but the ATCSA greatly restricted the ability of the individual to know and challenge the allegations against him. For example, the person could appeal the deportation and detention orders before the Special Immigration Appeals Commission (SIAC), but not a regular court of law. The government could withhold some or all of the evidence from the individual and his legal counsel, if it considered it to be too security-sensitive. Moreover, SIAC could hold closed hearings, excluding both the alien and his lawyer. In such instances, a special advocate would be appointed to represent the person in the closed hearing and view the withheld evidence. The individual had no right to confer with the special advocate after the latter had received the secret file. Accordingly, the discriminatory nature of Section 23 detention was the least constitutionally worrying of its problems. It permitted an extreme deprivation of the right to liberty, outside of wartime or insurrection, based on suspicion instead of actual wrongdoing, and without adequate due process of law.

In the *Belmarsh Case*, the House of Lords neglected this key issue, focusing instead on the discriminatory nature of Section 23. The Law Lords acknowledged that the Convention permitted some discrimination against aliens for the purposes of immigration control. They were also correct, however, to see Section 23 as something more than a normal immigration measure. Detention of an irremovable alien could not be for the purpose of effecting deportation, when it was prohibited by *Chahal*. Detention then became preventive to avoid the release of an allegedly dangerous person into the community. This risk assessment bore no relationship to the person's nationality. Nevertheless, Section 23 detention applied only to aliens, while similarly dangerous citizens roamed free. For these reasons, the Law Lords found that it unjustifiably violated the Convention's Article 5 right to liberty on the basis of national origin, prohibited by Article 14. Although the government had derogated from Article 5, this irrational discrimination exceeded Article 15's strict proportionality requirement for derogation. The House of Lords accordingly declared Section 23 incompatible with the Convention, pursuant to the Human Rights Act. The declaration did not invalidate the law, but it did put Parliament on notice that it had violated its Convention obligations. If it chose to authorize preventive detention, Parliament had to treat citizens and aliens equally.

The problem, however, was that the Law Lords did not say just what that equal treatment was. By not doing so, they missed the opportunity to impose minimum rights–standards on preventive detention generally. Following the reasoning in *Ex parte Singh*,[34] for example, the Law Lords might have read a time limit into Section 23 detention to reconcile it with Article 5. Alternatively, they could have declared that indefinite detention per se violated the Convention or some other unwritten constitutional principle. Several Law Lords suggested this in *obiter dicta*.[35] They might also have found that the procedures used to impose detention violated Article 5's own procedural requirements, which resembled Article 6 rights to a fair criminal trial (the European Court of Human Rights itself would later find this in *A and Others v. United Kingdom*).[36] Any of these alternatives might have avoided the serious conflict between the Convention's non-discrimination principle and the traditional common-law approach, which based rights on membership in the national community. Instead, in *Belmarsh*, the Law Lords failed to determine the minimum standards of treatment for alien detainees, while opening the door to more state intrusions on citizens' liberties. Lord Hoffman alone declared Section 23 incompatible on the alternative grounds that there was simply no Article 15 national emergency. In doing so, he refused to comment on the discrimination issue. He declined, because he "would not like to give the impression that all that was necessary was to extend the power [of detention] to United Kingdom citizens as well."[37] This was exactly the message his colleagues had sent.

A and Others backfired immediately. Soon after the decision, Parliament repealed Section 23 at the government's request, as neither was prepared to extend indefinite detention to British citizens. However, the government did not intend to abandon preventive measures altogether; alien terrorist suspects were not to see a sudden, scrupulous respect of their rights to liberty and due process. Instead, with the Prevention of Terrorism Act 2005, the government introduced a controversial system of preventive control orders targeted at aliens and citizens alike, forcing it through a now rebellious Parliament. Under this system, the Home Secretary could impose severe behavioral restrictions on anyone suspected of involvement in terrorism. In some cases, these restrictions could amount to house arrest. Aliens were arguably better off with control orders rather than with indefinite detention, but the big losers were undoubtedly British citizens. Unlike before, a citizen could now suffer a serious and long-term deprivation of liberty upon ministerial order without the benefit of criminal indictment and trial by jury. Orders were imposed pursuant to procedures based on those previously used before SIAC for Section 23 detention. Courts had a review power, but this was limited. The individual concerned had no right to know the whole of the government's case, to adduce evidence in her defense, or to communicate freely with the special advocate representing her in closed hearings. Control orders could be renewed indefinitely, so long as the Home Secretary believed the individual continued to present a terrorism risk.

Later, in the European version of the *Belmarsh Case*,[38] the European Court of Human Rights found the now-defunct Section 23 procedures to violate the procedural requirements for imposing detention under Convention Article 5. The House of Lords would eventually apply this holding to the similar control order procedures,[39] while a new Conservative-Liberal Democratic government would in turn replace control orders with a supposedly less onerous alternative of terrorism prevention and investigation measures, or TPIMs. Still, the *Belmarsh Case* and the control order regime had signaled an important shift in British legal thinking; unlike before, the citizen could no longer expect special rights to liberty and due process that were greater than those for aliens. This assault on citizens' liberties had begun earlier with restrictions on the right to silence, antisocial behavior orders, and extended detention without charge in anti-terrorism cases. Parliament would later go on to authorize peacetime trial without jury and to allow anonymous witness testimony in some felony trials, expressly overruling a House of Lords decision to do so. Measures such as these had last been used against citizens during the two world wars and to counter serious, violent unrest in Northern Ireland. Now they were to apply to citizens throughout the United Kingdom, in some circumstances having nothing to do with national security.

With *Belmarsh*, then, the Law Lords formally tore down the old firewall between citizens and aliens, officially severing rights from membership in the national community. The citizen's common-law entitlement to the special protection of the Crown—and the robust due process protections that once went with it—was gone. Under the Convention's non-discrimination and proportionality principles, the government could now do things to its own citizens once unthinkable outside of wartime or insurrection. Rights, divorced from membership in the national community, had wider application but suffered weaker protection against countervailing state interests. Justice Scalia's fears had become legal doctrine in the United Kingdom.

CONCLUSION: THE LIMITS OF DUE PROCESS

A comparison between *Boumediene* and the *Belmarsh Case* shows a significant divergence since 9/11 in American and British ideas about citizenship and rights. In the United States, *Boumediene* has retained an old common-law conception of rights premised upon an individual's membership in the national community. Under this approach, rights increase as one's relationship to that community deepens. American citizens therefore enjoy robust due process protections against state deprivations of liberty, even when national security is at stake. For the billions beyond the parapets, however, the municipal rule of law gives way to politics; the legislature and executive have wide discretion to act against aliens, in order to defend the nation and its citizens in a violent and uncertain world. By extending habeas corpus to Guantanamo Bay, as well as to any other detention sites under the de facto control of the U.S. government, *Boumediene* advanced the Constitution's ramparts. Nevertheless, in that case, the Supreme Court did not question the underlying link between rights and national belonging.

In the United Kingdom, a similar relationship between rights and nationhood long existed until the *Belmarsh Case* signaled a sea change in British law. With that decision, the House of Lords formally rejected the common law's old, discriminatory rights approach in favor of a universalist one under the Convention. Where the Convention applies, all individuals are now equal bearers of rights regardless of their personal status. This new approach also means that, unlike previously, citizens and aliens are equally susceptible to ever more state restrictions of their freedoms. The *Belmarsh Case* directly led to the control order regime, but it was symbolic of a worrying trend that had already begun some years earlier. Even before *Belmarsh* legally justified it, the British government was increasingly prepared to deprive citizens of their personal liberty, pursuant to less than criminal due process.

This chapter has not argued which of these approaches is best in normative terms. It has only sought to show how, during the decade since 9/11, the American and British legal systems have each attempted to balance judicial protections for rights with the political discretion needed for national security. *Boumediene's* old approach sharply divides law and politics along doctrinal lines of personal and territorial status. These lines expose aliens to greater government power, while simultaneously protecting citizens from it. In contrast, Britain's new Convention-based jurisprudence more equally and flexibly balances individual and state interests according to the circumstances. Citizenship will seldom be an appropriate consideration in this analysis. In choosing between these legal frameworks, one must therefore decide who should be the bearer of rights and why. To found rights on national belonging, as the common law does, is to temper reverence for nationhood with a fear of strong government. For the universalist, the equal dignity of all individuals is paramount, but with due consideration for government's communitarian concerns. Neither approach perfectly guarantees liberty and due process for all or ideally balances those rights with political discretion. So while American law admits the possibility of another Guantanamo Bay, British law accepts ever greater restrictions on once revered common-law rights. In each case, then, the choice is not only about whom the law should protect; it is also about whom the law should sacrifice.

NOTES

* Associate Professor of Comparative Constitutional Law, University of Copenhagen Faculty of Law.

1. Lord Steyn, "Guantanamo Bay: The Legal Black Hole" (2004) 53 *I.C.L.Q.* 1.
2. 552 U.S. 723 (2008).
3. *A and Others v. Secretary of State*, [2004] UKHL 56.
4. U.S. White House, Military Order: Detention, Treatment, and Trial of Certain Non-Citizens in the War Against Terrorism, 13 November 2001, Exec. Order No., 66 Fed. Reg. 57831 (16 November 2001).
5. 339 U.S. 763 (1950).
6. Ibid. at 769.
7. Ibid. at 771.
8. 494 U.S. 259 (1990).
9. Ibid. at 265.
10. 339 U.S. 763, 795.
11. Fiona de Londras, "Guantanamo Bay, the Rise of the Courts, and the Revenge of Politics," Chapter 9 in this volume.
12. 542 U.S. 466 (2004).
13. 548 U.S. 557 (2006).
14. Pub. L. No. 81-506, 64 Stat. 107 (1950), codified as amended at 10 U.S.C. §801 *et seq.* (2000).

15. Article 1(9)(2), U.S. Constitution: "The privilege of the writ of *habeas corpus* shall not be suspended, unless when in cases of rebellion or invasion the public safety may require it."
16. 542 U.S. 507 (2004).
17. 605 F.3d 84 (D.C. Cir. 2010).
18. *Kiyemba* v. *Obama*, 555 F.3d 1022 (D.C. Cir. 2009) (*Kiyemba I*), *vacated and remanded*, 130 S. Ct. 1235 (2010), *reinstated as modified*, 605 F.3d 1046 (2010) (*Kiyemba III*). See also *Kiyemba* v. *Obama*, 561 F.3d 509 (D.C. Cir. 2009) (*Kiyemba II*), *cert. denied*, 130 S. Ct. 1880 (2010).
19. De Londras, *supra* note 25 at 12 et seq.
20. See ibid. at 1, 8.
21. Mark Tushnet, "Legal and Political Constitutionalism, and the Response to Terrorism," Chapter 8 in this volume.
22. (1608) 7 Co. Rep. 1a.
23. 98 Eng. Rep. 499 (1772).
24. 154 ER 450 (1848).
25. *Netz v. Ede*, [1946] Ch. 224; *R. v. Bottrill, ex parte Kuechenmeister*, [1947] KB 41.
26. [1921] 2 AC 262 (H.L.).
27. [1892] AC 491 (P.C.).
28. [1970] AC 179 (H.L.).
29. [1921] 2 AC 570. (H.L.).
30. [1920] AC 508 (H.L.).
31. [1965] AC 75 (H.L.).
32. [1942] AC 206 (H.L.); See also *Ex parte Greene*, [1941] 3 All ER 104 (C.A.).
33. (1996) 23 EHRR 413.
34. [1984] 1 All ER 983 (Q.B.).
35. Nicholls, Hoffmann, and Scott all expressed serious reservations about indefinite detention, as cited in Jens Elo Rytter, "Terrorist Threats and Judicial Deference," Chapter 13 at 18, endnote 59 in this volume
36. (2009) 49 EHRR 29.
37. [2004] UKHL 56 at para. 97.
38. *A and Others* v. *United Kingdom*, [2009] ECHR 301.
39. *Secretary of State v. AF*, [2009] UKHL 28.

PART FOUR:

Risk Prevention

CHAPTER 11

"Protect" against Terrorism: In Service of the State, the Corporation, or the Citizen?

CLIVE WALKER*

For many legal observers, counter-terrorism conjures a continuum of either police and criminal justice interventions or exceptional executive powers. Thus, the most prominent legal disputes in jurisdictions such as the United Kingdom have revolved around either the length of post-arrest police detention or the merits or demerits of executive approaches such as detention without trial, and control orders.[1] Similar controversies continue to be just as hotly contested in the United States. President Obama undertook as his first major policy announcement the closure of Guantánamo Bay[2] in favour of prosecutions. The President was soon forced into retreat by doubts expressed by policy reviewers and then in 2011 by a Congressional refusal to appropriate funds for the closure of the Guantánamo Bay prisons.[3]

These individuated responses to terrorism are highly emblematic of the tolerance and values of a given society. Does it still trust in liberty and due process in the face of insecurity? Yet, the emblems may mask a deeper truth: contemporary counter-terrorism measures operate overwhelmingly on a collective basis and individuated treatment is highly exceptional. Some statistics from England and Wales underline this point. Between 19 February 2001 and 31 March 2011 there were just 1,963 arrests under the special powers of arrest specified by section 41 of the Terrorism Act 2000 (196 per annum on average) and merely 129 convictions for terrorism-related activities (13 per annum on average).[4] The same factors that complicate such individuated responses—the complexities of distinguishing friend from foe, security from insecurity, or even war from peace—stimulate a broader approach to counter-terrorism. This broader approach reflects the fact that terrorism appears to be an insidious, endemic, pervasive, and endless risk.

This embedded nature of terrorism therefore provokes "all-risks" security and policing measures, whereby the entire population—as opposed to just individuals—is treated as both risk engendering and risk running.[5] The application of these "all-risks" measures, which demand the collection of information about everyone, impose universal screening, or embed defensive regulations against all, owes more to a thematic, intelligence-led approach than to the collection of evidence against individual suspects. They reflect "a new and urgent emphasis on the need for security, the containment of danger, and the identification and management of any kind of risk."[6] The effect of these pervasive tactics is to treat anyone and everyone as a risk on the basis of data which is personally indistinct and unattached to any individual. The reason for impact on any given subject is not so much any grounded suspicion falling on that individual but the nature of a particular site, the belief in a generalised threat, or some common vulnerability. Thus, the risk calculation shifts from the personal to the situational or the collective. At the same time, "all-risks" policing is rarely applied evenly because of limited security resources and culturally embedded interpretations of enforcers. Although mathematical models of profiling might be used, their applications embody preconceptions or skewed application, both of which result in "targeted governance" directed at groups which are predetermined to be "risky."[7]

Once again, the statistics illustrate starkly "all risks" counter-terrorism. In 2009–2010 alone, there were 102,504 stops and searches in England and Wales under section 44 of the Terrorism Act 2000.[8] There were 65,684 "examinations" for longer than one hour under port controls in Schedule 7 of the Terrorism Act 2000 in 2009–2010 (2,288 lasting longer than one hour).[9] Figures for electronic surveillance are potentially infinite. Pursuant to Directive 2006/24/EC on the retention of data, the Data Retention (EC Directive) Regulations 2009[10] require that data about internet access, Internet email, and Internet telephony be retained for possible later investigative access for a standard retention period of twelve months. In strategic language, these "all risks" measures have been labelled "Protect" and "Prepare." The strategies and implementation of "Protect" within the United Kingdom form the core of this chapter.

The state's protection of individual rights to life, liberty, and property are rightly recognised as being amongst its most fundamental political duties.[11] As well as being recognised and implemented in domestic law, the protective duties also feature in international law, especially with regard to the right to life under Article 2 of the European Convention on Human Rights and Fundamental Freedoms of 1950. Activities around "Protect" are therefore to be welcomed in principle. At the same time, the assertion that there has occurred the transformation of a threatening national security state into a comforting "Protecting State"[12] should not seduce us away from harbouring suspicions about state powers. How a liberal democracy cohabits with the endemic terrorism risk created by late modern society is a challenge yet to be fully resolved. Amongst the critical issues to be addressed in this chapter are the instruments of implementation and whether they are appropriate, adequately coordinated, and suitably accountable. Second, implementation will heavily depend upon the involvement of the private sector, which gives rise to issues of ultimate control, information transfer, and accountability. Third, there are concerns about the displacement impacts of protective security. The fourth issue is the "securitization" of society—the pervasion and prominence of security agendas.

STRATEGIC SETTING

A comprehensive counter-terrorism strategy for the United Kingdom, "CONTEST," was first published by the government in 2006 and has been serially revised since then.[13] However, it has not wavered from its core vision:

> Our counter-terrorism strategy will continue to be organised around four workstreams, each comprising a number of key objectives:
> - Pursue: to stop terrorist attacks;
> - Prevent: to stop people becoming terrorists or supporting terrorism;
> - Protect: to strengthen our protection against a terrorist attack; and
> - Prepare: to mitigate the impact of a terrorist attack.[14]

"Protect" often becomes entangled with "Prepare," which takes the form of contingency planning for resilience and recovery. Both these workstreams are listed in the foregoing statement beneath "Pursue," which encompasses traditional policing and prosecutorial activities. They even follow the more innovative and controversial "Prevent" policy, in which the government has invested much faith.[15] As for "Protect," the focus of this chapter, the latest CONTEST iteration reveals that "current objectives will be to: strengthen U.K. border security; reduce the vulnerability of the transport network;

increase the resilience of the U.K.'s infrastructure; and improve protective security for crowded places."[16]

IMPLEMENTATION OF "PROTECT"

The "Protect" legal catalogue is hugely expansive. For the purposes of this short chapter, no more than a flavour can be offered.[17] A distinction will be made between measures of general application (affecting several or all targeted sectors) and those of specific application.

General Application

The most prominent legal measure of general application, already mentioned, has been the stop and search power in section 44 of the Terrorism Act 2000.[18] This form of intervention is claimed to be required to afford a chance to intercept munitions or to thwart plans.[19] Thus, objectives of prevention and protection through disruption, intelligence-gathering, and public reassurance are to the fore rather than "Pursue" though criminal justice, as reflected in the total absence of terrorism-related arrests following stops. The application of stop and search was almost halted for a time in 2010 following the adverse decision of the European Court of Human Rights in *Gillan and Quinton v United Kingdom*.[20] However, reforms have now been implemented, resulting in a replacement section 47A which is intended to be applied on a much reduced scale to "a specified area or place."[21] Commonplace usage has occurred at live security operations, railway stations, critical national infrastructure installations, and "postcard" sites in the centre of London.[22] It was further supposed that the stop power would also be sweepingly invoked during the London Olympics 2012. In fact, section 47A has not been invoked in Britain since its inception by any local police force, though by-laws and public order measures were heavily used in connection with the Olympics.[23]

The other general provisions which have already been mentioned are the port controls under Part V and Schedule 7 of the Terrorism Act 2000 which supplement for security purposes the regulation of entry under the Immigration Act 1971. Their purpose is to disrupt possible terrorist planning and logistics and also to gather low level intelligence about movements. The controls also deter attacks on the travel facilities themselves. Further controls were implemented by Section 118 of the Anti Terrorism, Crime and Security Act 2001 to travelers through any internal or external port.

Specific or Sectoral Application

Specialist protective applications include some of the tightest restrictions on firearms and explosives anywhere in Europe, if not the world. The Firearms Acts of 1968 and 1997 prohibit many types of weapons from private possession, including handguns.[24] The acquisition of firearms by terrorists has principally derived from foreign government suppliers (such as Libya), foreign dealers (especially in the United States), and latterly suppliers in Europe. The control of explosives is primarily a health and safety issue under the Manufacture and Storage of Explosives Regulations 2005.[25] The 1991 Montreal Convention on the Marking of Plastic Explosives for the Purpose of Detection is implemented by the Marking of Plastic Explosives for Detection Regulations 1996.[26] Advice and monitoring is also applied to suppliers and users (principally farmers) of nitrate materials in order to avoid illicit usage.[27] More specialist weapons of mass destruction (chemical, biological, radiological, and nuclear) have been the subject of copious legislation since 9/11, including in the Anti-Terrorism, Crime and Security Act 2001 and the Terrorism Act 2006. Many of the new criminal offences have never been prosecuted, but the regulation of laboratories for security purposes under the Anti Terrorism, Crime and Security Act 2001, Part VII, constitutes a significant advance.

Moving from weapons of offence to sites of vulnerability, Part VIII of the Anti-Terrorism, Crime and Security Act 2001 addresses the security of the nuclear industry. Its focus is on the security of organizations, installations, and information. The Terrorism Act 2006, Section 12, deals with trespass upon nuclear sites. Another prominent site of vulnerability to terrorism is considered to be the transportation sector, with predominant attention accorded to airports and air travel. Accordingly, Part IX of the Anti-Terrorism, Crime and Security Act 2001 supplements the substantial body of international laws relating to aviation security.[28] Protective measures for aircraft and aerodromes are required by a directive from the Secretary of State for Transport or the Director of the Transport Security and Contingencies Team (TRANSEC)[29] under Part II of the Aviation Security Act 1982. The processes by which protective security is applied locally have also been strengthened by the Policing and Crime Act 2009, Part VII. All relevant aerodromes must have a Police Services Agreement made between the manager of the aerodrome, the relevant police authority, and the local chief officer of police. Aviation security policy is overseen by the Department of Transport's Aviation Directorate.[30] The National Aviation Security Programme and Handbook[31] is applied at each airport by the processes already outlined.

Protective security for the Critical National Infrastructure (CNI) has also been the subject of enhanced attention since 9/11.[32] Two problems immediately arise, however. First, how is the CNI to be defined, and what does it comprise? Second, how can protective security be delivered effectively and fairly within a disparate set of highly complex enterprises, many of which are owned and operated for private profit rather than in the public interest? Neither point has received a convincing answer, especially as no comprehensive legislation has been passed. Instead, assorted legal offences, powers, regulations, and mechanisms afford protection to disparate elements within the CNI, whereas other aspects are left to the management of the market or the persuasion of government officials. The resultant large rag-bag of measures includes trespass offences,[33] the regulation of industrial sites,[34] and the maintenance of reserve stocks or facilities in power and fuel industries. Communications networks are treated as another CNI component, and various powers allow for emergency directions to be issued[35] and the suspension of telecommunications services to prevent overload in an emergency.[36] The resilience of the Internet features as another prominent facet of the CNI agenda. Threats are monitored by the Serious Organised Crime Agency's e-Crime Unit. The Office of Cyber Security and Information Assurance provides a strategic direction as a policy unit in the Cabinet Office, and the Cyber Security Operations Centre within the Government Communications Headquarters (GCHQ), the United Kingdom's centre for signals intelligence, oversees implementation.[37]

Finally, "crowded places" are mentioned as objects for protective security in the CONTEST documentation. However, aside from stop and search powers of general application, most delivery work has been comprised of practical advice about designs, systems, and processes. The emphasis has been placed on local partnerships, involvement of Counter Terrorism Security Advisers (CTSAs), consideration at planning processes, training for business, hotel, and retail staff under Project Argus,[38] and the issuance of guidelines by both the National Counter Terrorism Security Office (NaCTSO)[39] and by the Home Office.[40] These practice-based collusive processes have been most evident in the preparations for the Olympic Games in London in 2012, with funding for safety and security set at £600 million.[41] The London 2012 Olympic and Paralympic Security Strategy was concluded by the Home Office in 2009. The foremost organization is the Olympic and Paralympic Security Directorate within the Home Office. Head of operations is the National Olympic Security Co-ordinator, who works alongside the Assistant Commissioner for Specialist Operations in the Metropolitan Police. They are linked to the National Olympic Co-ordination Centre.

CRITICAL ISSUES

Implementation and Accountability

As rehearsed in the introduction to this chapter, several critical challenges remain to be resolved in the development and application of "Protect" so as to ensure that the responses under this workstream are appropriate, adequately coordinated, and accountable. However, these standards are not met. Implementation problems abound and are admittedly difficult to surmount because of the diffuse and often highly specialised nature of the workstream. As a result, the responses are not always pitched appropriately. For example, some arrangements for the CNI lack basic legality, in the technical sense that initiatives have been implemented either without proper legal basis or even in seeming contradiction of the legal basis.

As for adequate coordination, "Protect" has grown without the organisational structuring which has been evident for "Pursue" and even for "Prevent." As for "Pursue," policing policy development has been headed on a non-statutory basis by the Association of Chief Police Officer's Terrorism and Allied Matters business area (ACPO (TAM)), under which an impressive police counter-terrorism structure network has emerged. This structure is headed by the Counter-Terrorism Command (CTC) of the Metropolitan Police Service. The chief of the CTC acts nationally as the Senior National Coordinator, Counter-Terrorism, and there is also within CTC the National Co-ordinator of Terrorist Investigations. Outside London, there are four Counter-Terrorism Units (CTUs) located in the North East, North West, West Midlands, and Thames Valley, together with four Counter-Terrorism Intelligence Units (CTIUs) in Scotland, Wales, the South West, and East Midlands.[42] Provincial Special Branches are increasingly regionalized and concentrate on borders and special protective duties. The work of the counter-terrorism police network is coordinated by a Joint Counter Terrorism Oversight Group, overseen by a Police Counter Terrorism Board, chaired by the Home Secretary.[43]

As for "Prevent," governance is potentially just as tricky as for "Protect" because of its scattered impact. However, the strands of activity have been drawn together. Around three hundred specialist police officers within twenty-four forces work on the Prevent Strategy and Delivery Plan, launched in 2008.[44] The National Coordinator for Community Engagement, appointed by the ACPO, oversees the work. In addition, the government intends to establish a non-executive "Prevent" board to oversee the "Prevent" strategy and its local implementation.[45]

The structuring of the "Pursue" and "Prevent" workstreams contrasts with "Protect," where much less coordinated effort or oversight is apparent.

The task of implementing protective security in the CNI falls upon the Centre for the Protection of the National Infrastructure (CPNI), which was formed in 2007. The CPNI, based in the Security Service, provides security advice to relevant businesses and organisations, mainly disseminated via specialist police Counter-Terrorism Security Advisers (CTSAs) in each police force. The CPNI's key features include special access to intelligence and close working relationships with the private sectors and even with the public.[46] All aspects of the CPNI are said to operate under the Security Service Act 1989 and to be formally accountable to the Security Service. However, neither the establishment nor the operation of the CPNI has been explained in any consultation paper or debated in Parliament. The governance of the CNI poorly reflects constitutional normative standards.

The specialist policing oversight body of prime importance to protective security is the National Counter-Terrorism Security Office (NaCTSO), established in 2002 under the aegis of ACPO (TAM) and co-located in the CPNI. Its work, overseen by the Association of Chief Police Officers (ACPO) Director Protect and Prepare, involves the protection of vulnerable sites, delivered mainly through CTSAs. Several further specialist policing bodies are of relevance to protective security, including the Serious Organised Crime Agency, and the U.K. Border Agency. The Home Office announced in 2010 plans to incorporate these agencies into a National Crime Agency,[47] but the CPNI and CTUs remained outside the new institution pending the completion of the London Olympics. The Crime and Courts Act 2013, section 2(3) expressly allows for a transfer of functions, but no decision has yet been taken.

Other specialist bodies of importance to specific sectors include the British Transport Police (BTP), as constituted under the Railways and Transport Safety Act 2003, Part III.[48] The BTP's focus of operations is confined to railway property and purposes connected to the railways. There are around 2,800 officers, and their prime work arises from public order, assaults, and property offences, but terrorism has become a headline activity.

The Civil Nuclear Constabulary (CNC) is the lead protective force for the nuclear sector. As constituted by the Energy Act 2004, Section 52, the nine hundred CNC officers are tasked to provide physical protection at non-defence nuclear sites and at non-designated defence sites.[49] Thus, the CNC jurisdiction is confined to seventeen civil nuclear sites, a five kilometer radius around them, plus the transportation of nuclear materials. Aside from its remote system of accountability and the fact that it is funded by the industry, another notable feature of the CNC is that its officers are routinely armed.

"Protect" is further implemented by the Ministry of Defence Police (MDP) which subsists under the Ministry of Defence Police Act 1987. The MDP is a civilian (but armed) police force with around 3,500 officers. Its jurisdiction is formally confined to around two hundred Ministry of Defence establishments. However, the MDP regularly undertakes patrols in the Government Security Zone in Whitehall and Westminster under Metropolitan Police authority.[50] Similar assistance has also been given to the BTP and at demonstration sites, such as the U.S. installation at Menwith Hill. Another prominent aspect of MDP counter-terrorism deployment has included protective security for gas processing sites under Operation Vintage.[51] The MDP's national coverage and armed capability make it ideal for these purposes, and this role, which presumably falls within the Anti-Terrorism, Crime and Security Act 2001, Section 99, had become semi-permanent by 2008, even though Home Office guidelines state that assistance should not be "routinely requested."[52] This demand on MDP resources for CNI purposes was officially recognized by the Counter Terrorism Act 2008, Sections 85–90, but was not confined to terrorism risk.[53] The 2008 Act allows recovery from gas transporters of the costs of the "extra police services" incurred by the MDP or local forces at gas installations where, under Section 85(1), their deployment is considered by the Secretary of State to be: "(a) . . . necessary because of a risk of loss of or disruption to the supply of gas connected with it, and (b) that the loss or disruption would have a serious impact on the United Kingdom or any part of it." Seemingly, the MDP is stumbling towards the assumption of the mantle of CNI police. However, a comprehensive vision, encompassing consolidation with other specialist policing bodies and effective local and national accountability structures, is lacking. Consequently, the sundry "Protect" personnel, who also include ports police,[54] the U.K. Border Agency, and numerous private security guards, remain highly fragmented.[55]

As for accountability, the levels of engagement with localities are generally weak. Relationships are more evidently maintained between the relevant corporate sector and central government. Levels of transparency have improved in recent years, with many of the specialist police forces producing glossy annual reports, but some agencies, such as TRANSEC, have been guilty of "Spartan" reports[56] and unpublished reviews abound despite their policy importance.[57] Parliament has often performed feebly in maintaining oversight, while the Independent Reviewer of the Terrorism Legislation has no jurisdiction over much of this agenda.[58] As a result, the setting of priorities in terms of what is protected or how much public money is spent in a given sector remains hidden. A corporatist approach prevails, though the government has lately taken a lead by announcing measurements of success:

> Success in Protect will mean that:
> - We know where and how we are vulnerable to terrorist attack and have reduced those vulnerabilities to an acceptable and a proportionate level;
> - We share our priorities with the private sector and the international community and, wherever possible, we act together to address them; and
> - The disruptive effect and costs of our protective security work are proportionate to the risks we face.[59]

However, the calibration of these indicia and the responsible auditors are not specified.

Courts have not given as much attention to "Protect" as compared to "Pursue" and "Prevent," apparently because it seems a less menacing threat to human rights. Thus, the plaudits given to the judges for their condemnation of detention without trial in *A v. Secretary of State for the Home Department*,[60] often referred to as the *Belmarsh Case*, should be balanced against the dismissive treatment of rights to liberty and privacy in cases such as *Gillan*[61] and *Marper*,[62] a lax attitude later condemned by the European Court of Human Rights.[63] Consequently, there is a danger with "Protect" that even lawyers will lower their guard in the face of pervasive and routinised security impositions. Much implementation of the "Protect" framework lies in dreary regulatory processes within the private sector. Nevertheless, this low profile implementation should not be an excuse for the casual sacrifice of important rights for the convenience of the state and its favoured clients.

Private Sector Involvement

The majority of entities which are the subject of "Protect"—around 75 percent—operate under private ownership.[64] This private sector involvement entails issues of cooperation and control, information transfer and accountability, just as under the previous heading. The government has acknowledged the potential problems:

> [W]e…depend on close relationships with the private sector, who own much of the infrastructure and the systems that need to be protected. We will continue to be as transparent as we can in sharing our understanding of the threats we face and wherever possible will collaborate in the development of security solutions.[65]

As far as public policy is concerned, one impact tends to be that relations remain informal and insidious. Regulatory capture applies as much in counter-terrorism as in other fields. Two brief examples can be given of the complex relationships that sometimes result.

The first example concerns the data mining of financial information in order to detect terrorism. This technique is embodied in the U.S. Terrorist Finance Tracking Program,[66] which naturally impinges most on the private banking sector. In particular, U.S. investigators soon identified "SWIFT"—the Society for Worldwide Interbank Financial Telecommunication—as a key nodal point through which much data could be mined. SWIFT is based in Brussels and holds information for nearly nine thousand financial institutions about their daily electronic financial transactions. After September 11, the Office of Foreign Assets Control (OFAC) of the U.S. Department of the Treasury obtained by private negotiation unprecedented access to SWIFT data, probably in breach of European data protection laws.[67] It would seem that the financial institutions were content as they wanted to weed out potentially destabilising transactions but without any publicity which might undermine their customers' faith in client confidentiality. When details inevitably became public, there was pressure from E.U. institutions for greater transparency and safeguards. The response was a U.S.-E.U. compromise arrangement agreed in 2007, by which a set of "Representations" (unilateral assurances) about the processing, disclosure, and retention of personal data were given by the U.S. Treasury, all overseen by an "eminent European" monitor.[68] This arrangement proved to be unacceptable to the European Parliament and another agreement took its place in 2010,[69] though its safeguards are also criticised as lacking independent checks before transfer and an effective post-transfer complaints system. Another response has been realignment to the architecture of SWIFT, whereby U.S.-related data is partitioned. However, the European Union fears that this refinement diminishes the effectiveness of the project and so has called for a European equivalent system.[70]

The second example concerns government access to airline Passenger Name Records (PNRs)—the reservation and departure file for each passenger journey. Once again, the feature of surreptitious corporate collusion emerges. Some governments, especially the U.S. government, believe that PNRs might aid the tracking or disruption of terrorists. At the same time, airlines share a paramount interest in the safety of passengers. They were also in debt to governments in the aftermath of 9/11, when huge subsidies or other facilities were granted to the industry. In short, the U.S. government demanded in November 2001, pursuant to the Aviation and Transportation Security Act,[71] full disclosure of the PNRs from any airline operating in or to the United States. This automatic transfer of data triggered objections under the European Data Protection Directive 95/46/EC. Consequently, the bilateral E.U.-U.S. agreement for transfer in 2004 was condemned before the European Court of Justice.[72] A subsequent agreement was devised in 2006 but was disapproved by the European Parliament and is still being refined.[73] The idea of passenger data transfer for air travel between Europe and destinations other than the United States is now being advanced, first by a draft Framework Decision on the Use of Passenger Name Records for Law Enforcement Purposes in 2007[74] and latterly by a Proposal for a Directive of the European Parliament and of the Council on the use of Passenger Name Record data for the prevention, detection, investigation and prosecution of terrorist offences and serious crime.[75] The U.K. government has conversely criticized the draft for not applying to all travel formats (including rail) and to journeys inside the European Union.[76]

These examples illustrate how governments and private sectors share basic interests in protective security. However, their accountability structures are very different. Corporate accountability to shareholders rather than customers affects modes of cooperation and transparency. The feasibility of "partnership" in the co-production of security planning and delivery remains challenging, though the Pitt Review praised the work of the CPNI in this regard.[77] Since most relevant infrastructure resides within the hands of private sector responders, their willingness to share commercially sensitive information becomes crucial, as does the effectiveness of sector regulators.

Displacement

Displacement is a well-recognised hazard of protective crime prevention schemes. Displacement can be posited in terms of time, location, target, tactics, or crime type.[78] The same applies to counter-terrorism protective security. The assumptions with terrorism are that the main displacement impacts will fall in the geographical and targeting categories, and furthermore that terrorism is relatively inelastic, in the sense that highly motivated individuals will not be wholly deflected by extra security.[79] Thus, the main concerns about displacement arising from protective security are that adverse impacts may befall other locations, targets, or sectors, thereby nullifying the overall impact of protection. Two examples might be proffered. One is the geographical claim that the creation of a "Ring of Steel" around the City of London, following massive IRA truck bombs in 1992 and 1993, encouraged the deflection of economic bomb attacks to equally alluring but less defended targets within the striking distance, such as Heathrow or London Docklands (attacked in 1994 and 1996)[80] as well as to other cities such as Manchester (which suffered a shopping centre bombing in 1996).

The second example involves a partial sector shift. The stringency of air transportation security may have resulted in displacement to other civilian targets.[81] Sadly, other transportation systems and crowded places have been less secure, as evidenced by the Madrid bombings on March 11, 2004 and the London bombings on July 7, 2005. Most mass transit systems and public venues cannot feasibly operate if treated like air travel. A more insidious displacement is the transfer of the risk of terrorist attack to countries which accord a lower priority to security against terrorism, either because of their underlying cultures or because they view terrorism as the responsibility and consequence of the actions of others and consider themselves as absolved from risk. Alternatively, many states are simply less wealthy or technically capable than prime Western targets. As a result, terrorists have exploited the relative weaknesses in airport security in, say, Ghana (where Abdulmuttalab departed from en route to Detroit in 2009) or Yemen (where a series of bombs were loaded onto freight aircraft in 2010).[82]

Securitisation of Society

According to the latest version of the United Kingdom's National Security Strategy,[83] prime ("Tier 1") threats comprise not only international terrorism (along with hostile cyber attack, major accident or natural catastrophe, and international military crisis) but also, in Tiers 2 and 3, chemical, biological, radiological and nuclear attacks (CBRN), instabilities overseas which might be exploited by terrorists, organised crime, satellite disruption, and disruption to power or essential supplies. Treating rainfall (or the lack of it) as a threat to "security" somewhat strains the meaning of the term but reflects the view that "[t]oday, Britain faces a different and more complex range of threats from a myriad of sources."[84] This broad conception of national security creates the danger that the militaristic language and assertiveness of security agendas now permeate too many aspects of society and skew the attention and approaches to other social policies: "if every problem looks like a security issue then ministers will be conditioned to see the response in terms of seeking more security, through seeking military solutions overseas and threatening further restrictions domestically on individual liberty and privacy."[85]

Amongst the adverse consequences of such securitisation is the impact on individual rights, with many governments claiming that rights must be limited for the sake of delivering security against terrorism. Debates around impacts on individual rights have appeared mostly in relation to "Pursue" measures, with less attention given to individual rights affected by "Protect." The reasons for lower vigilance include the routinised and diffuse nature of the assault—in "all-risks" policing, no individual is unduly affected. In addition, many "Protect" measures are remote from ordinary lives and impact on corporate constituencies which are content with their treatment. A third, less excusable, reason for less debate about rights in "Protect" is that the threat to rights is more insidious. Thus, target-hardening through mass surveillance is imposed without individual discernment or judicial oversight but with consequent threat to privacy, expressive freedoms, and rights against discrimination.

While the discourse of rights may be less prominent within "Protect" than in other workstreams, the threats are real enough and occasionally surface in headlines. For instance, aviation security has posed multiple perils for individual privacy. The controversy over PNRs has already been mentioned. In addition, bodily searches at airports are the sole occasion when most of the population encounters counter-terrorism laws. Despite a remarkable degree of tolerance on the part of target populations to physically intrusive screening, their universal rights against privacy and discrimination are at risk. Disquiet was heightened by the summary introduction of body scanners in early 2010, in response to the failed attempt by Abdulmutallab to blow up a Detroit-bound aircraft.[86] Even so, the House of Commons Home Affairs Committee still estimated the privacy concerns as "overstated."[87]

Much of the debate about securitisation concerns its costs to individual rights, but other societal values are also affected. Thus, another conflict of values might involve international development versus security, with questions about whether aid to countries such as Pakistan should take the form of security assistance or humanitarian assistance. CONTEST tries to address this issue:

> 4.53 Specific counter-terrorist projects are principally funded by the cross-Government Counter-Terrorism Programme, which is managed by the Foreign & Commonwealth Office.... Spend is tightly aligned with addressing the highest risks to the UK and UK interests. Priority areas include: Pakistan, Somalia, Yemen and Afghanistan.
>
> 5.87 Tackling poverty and building a stable, prosperous and democratic Pakistan is a top priority for the UK Government. The UK's single largest development investment in Pakistan, which will also contribute to counter-radicalisation, will be through support to education reform.

> 5.88 DFID's poverty reduction work in Pakistan and in other fragile and conflict-affected States is consistent with CONTEST. As set out in the SDSR, the UK will use 30% of Official Development Assistance (ODA) by 2014/15 to support conflict-affected and fragile states, including countries such as Pakistan, Yemen and Somalia. This spending supports both poverty reduction and UK national security.[88]

In fairness, then, the United Kingdom government has recognized and engaged the values conflict between national security and international development.

However, another set of values and conflicts relates to public trust versus public security. Suspicions about terrorism must be reported to the police. This policy is enshrined in section 38B(2) of the Terrorism Act 2000, whereby a person commits an offence if, without reasonable excuse, his or she fails to disclose information about terrorism. Incitement to "snitching" reached new heights in 2010 with the following radio advertisement for the Anti-Terrorist Hotline:

> The following message is brought to you by Talk Sport and the Anti-Terrorist Hotline. The man at the end of the street doesn't talk to his neighbours much, because he likes to keep himself. He pays with cash because he doesn't have a bank card, and he keeps his curtains closed because his house is on a bus route. This may mean nothing, but together it could all add up to you having suspicions. We all have a role to play in combating terrorism. If you see anything suspicious, call the confidential, Anti-Terrorist Hotline on 0800 XXXXXX. If you suspect it, report it.[89]

The Advertising Standards Authority considered that the advertisement could equally describe, and thereby condemn as suspicious, entirely law-abiding behaviour. In that sense, the advertisement was in breach of the Broadcast Committee of Advertising Practice Radio Advertising Standards Code, Section 2 rule 9, as contrary to "Good Taste, Decency and Offence To Public Feeling."

The final aspect of the policy impact of securitisation is in relation to profiles of the security agencies themselves. As might be supposed, budgets for CTUs and the Security Service have increased substantially since 9/11.[90] As regards the police, this increase is continuing, with a rise in funding by £240 million (around a quarter) between 2007/2008 and 2010/2011.[91] The budget for counter-terrorism policing in England and Wales will exceed £560 million per annum for the following four years, with no hint of any cutback.[92] Terrorism has also grown in prominence as a police strategic priority. In the First National Policing Plan for 2003–06, terrorism was mentioned briefly as a matter for "Metropolitan Police and national agencies."[93] By the Second National Policing Plan 2004–07, counter-terrorism becomes an "underpinning theme" for all forces.[94] Under the successor statement, the Home Secretary's Strategic Policing Priorities 2009–10, one of four such priorities is: "Work with and through partners and local communities to tackle terrorism and violent extremism in line with the counter terrorism strategy. . . ."[95] Amplification in the security agencies is even more marked. The complement of 1,800 staff in the Security Service in 2001 grew to 3,000 by the end of 2007, with plans for 4,000 by the end of 2011. The budget for all security and intelligence work has more than doubled since September 11, 2001.[96]

These trends in counter-terrorism now contrast with the projected budgets for "normal" policing. According to a survey by HM Inspectorate of Constabulary,[97] police forces and authorities in England and Wales have responded to reduced financial targets set by the new government for 2010 to 2014. The total required reduction is £2.1 billion by 2014/2015, amounting to an average of 14 percent of police gross revenue expenditure. The practical impact will be a fall in frontline[98] numbers by 2 percent and in non-frontline numbers by 11 percent (translating into 16,200 police officers, 1,800 Police Community Support Officers, and 16,100 other staff). There has been no discussion as to whether this imbalance between counter-terrorism policing and local policing should be maintained or allowed to grow in time.

CONCLUSION

The ultimate objective of CONTEST is "to reduce the risk from international terrorism, so that people can go about their daily lives freely and with confidence."[99] Yet, one might question whether the real benefit accrues to the state and its corporate partners rather than to "people." Certainly, the experience of "Protect" contrasts with the grudging and sometimes miserly protection for direct individual victims of terrorism. Even amongst the three schemes of special state compensation, two have related to corporate victims—property owners or occupiers and airlines—rather than individuals. The latter has expired and so will not be discussed here.[100] The remaining corporate sector scheme is in the Reinsurance (Acts of Terrorism) Act 1993, which offers reinsurance against terrorism loss for commercial property. As for individuals, the standard Criminal Injuries Compensation Scheme, administered by the Criminal Injuries Compensation Authority under the Criminal Injuries Compensation Act 1995 is available to terrorism victims. The main complaints in Britain are that it is dilatory and ungenerous.[101] The other deficiency is that the scheme did not apply to terrorism inflicted overseas on British citizens. An accretion of tragic cases, such as arising from Bali in 2002, Sharm al-Sheikh in 2005, and Mumbai in 2008, eventually promoted a change in policy by way of "the Victims of Overseas Terrorism Compensation Scheme" which was added as an afterthought to the Crime and Security Act 2010. In conclusion, the energy, reflection, and resources which have been infused into the policy development and administration of "Protect" have been impressive. Nevertheless, the implementation remains incomplete and unravelled in some respects, so that the ultimate question remains: whose interests are truly served by the project?

NOTES

* Professor of Criminal Justice Studies, University of Leeds School of Law.

1. For a full discussion, see C. Walker, *Terrorism and the Law* (Oxford: Oxford University Press, 2011).
2. Executive Order 13491: Ensuring Lawful Interrogations; Executive Order 13492: Review and Disposition of Individuals Detained at the Guantanamo Bay Naval Base and Closure of Detention Facilities; Executive Order 13493.
3. Guantanamo Review Task Force, *Final Report* (Department of Justice, Washington DC, 2010); National Defense Authorization Act for Fiscal Year 2011, § 1032 ("Prohibition on the use of funds for the transfer or release of individuals detained at United States Naval Station, Guantanamo Bay, Cuba") (PL 111-383).
4. See Home Office, *Operation of police powers under the Terrorism Act 2000 and subsequent legislation, HOSB 15/11* (London: 2011) at Tables 1.01 and 1.09.
5. See C. Walker, "Neighbor terrorism and the all-risks policing of terrorism" (2009) 3 *Journal of National Security Law & Policy* 121.
6. D. Garland, *The Culture of Control* (Oxford: Oxford University Press, 2001) at 12.
7. See L. Amoore and M. de Goede, "Governance, risk and dataveillance in the war on terror" (2005) 43 *Crime, Law & Social Change* 149.
8. See Home Office, *HOSB 15/11, supra* note 4 at Table 2.01.
9. Ibid. at 43.
10. SI 2009/859. See Home Office, *Transposition of Directive 2006/24/EC* (London: 2008).
11. "In a world of startling change, the first duty of Government remains the security of our country." *The National Security Strategy—A Strong Britain in an Age of Uncertainty*, Cm.7953 (London: 2010) at 3.
12. See D. Omand, *Securing the State* (London: Hurst & Co., 2010) at 9.
13. Home Office, *Countering International Terrorism*, Cm.6888 (London: 2006), as developed by Cm.7547 (London: 2009), Cm.7833 (London: 2010), and Cm.8123 (London: 2011).

14. Home Office, *CONTEST: The United Kingdom's Strategy for Countering Terrorism*, Cm.8123 (London: 2011) para. 1.12.
15. See Home Office, *Prevent Strategy*, Cm.8092 (London: 2011).
16. Home Office, *Countering International Terrorism* Cm.8123, *supra* note 13 at para. 7.5.
17. *See* further C. Walker, *Terrorism and the Law* (Oxford University Press, Oxford, 2011) at ch. 10.
18. See ibid. at ch. 2.
19. *Inquiry into Legislation against Terrorism* Cm.3420, (London: 1996) at paras. 10.14 and 10.21.
20. App no 4158/05 (12 January 2010).
21. Terrorism Act 2000 (Remedial) Order 2011, SI 2011/631. The order was replaced by the Protection of Freedoms Act 2012 ss. 59-63.
22. See C. Walker, *Terrorism and the Law* (Oxford University Press, Oxford, 2011) at para. 2.137.
23. See Jones, C., *A "clean city": The Olympic Games and Civil Liberties* (London: Statewatch, 2012) available at http://www.statewatch.org/analyses/no-192-olympics.pdf.
24. See Lord Cullen, *The Public Inquiry into the Shootings at Dunblane Primary School on 13 March 1996* Cm 3386 (London: 1996).
25. SI 2005/1082.
26. SI 1996/890. In Northern Ireland, see SR 1996/262.
27. See online at U.K. National Counter Terrorism Security Office, http://www.secureyourfertiliser.gov.uk. See also Directive 76/769/EEC.
28. See P. Wilkinson, "Enhancing UK aviation security post 9/11" in P. Wilkinson, ed., *Homeland Security in the UK* (Abingdon: Routledge, 2007).
29. See online at http://www.dft.gov.uk/publications/transec-annual-report-2009-2010.
30. See Department for Transport, *Draft Civil Aviation Bill: An effective regulatory framework for UK aviation*, Cm 8234-I (London: 2011).
31. See Sir John Wheeler, *Report on Airport Security*, (London: Department for Transport, 2002) at paras. 1.3 and 3.28.
32. See C. Walker, "The governance of the Critical National Infrastructure" [2008] *Public Law* 323.
33. Railway Regulation Act 1840, § 16; Harbours, Docks and Piers Clauses Act 1847, § 83; Military Lands Act 1892, § 14; Civil Aviation Act 1982, § 39; Serious Organised Crime and Police Act 2005, § 128.
34. Control of Major Accident Hazards Regulations 1999 (COMAH), 1999 SI/743 as amended by 2005 SI/1088. See also Planning (Hazardous Substances) Act 1990; Dangerous Substances (Notification and Marking of Sites) Regulations 1990, SI 1990/304.
35. See Agreement Dated the 25th Day of January 1996 Between Her Majesty's Secretary of State for National Heritage and the British Broadcasting Corporation, at para. 8; Communications Act 2003, §§ 5, 132.
36. See Telecommunications Act 1984, § 94; Home Office, *Addressing Lessons from the Emergency Response to the 7 July 2005 London Bombings* (London: 2006) at paras. 55–62.
37. See Cabinet Office, *Cyber Security of the United Kingdom*, Cm7642 (London: 2009).
38. See online at: U.K. National Counter Terrorism Security Office, http://www.nactso.gov.uk/our-services.

39. See *Secure in the Knowledge; Expecting the Unexpected, Counter Terrorism Protective Security Advice for General Aviation; Security at General Aviation Aerodromes; Counter Terrorism Protective Security Advice for Bars, Pubs and Nightclubs; Counter Terrorism Protective Security Advice for Cinemas and Theatre; Counter Terrorism Protective Security Advice for Commercial Centres; Counter Terrorism Protective Security Advice for Higher and Further Education; Counter Terrorism Protective Security Advice for Major Events; Counter Terrorism Protective Security Advice for Health Counter Terrorism Protective Security Advice for Hotels and Restaurants; Counter Terrorism Protective Security Advice for Shopping Centres; Counter Terrorism Protective Security Advice for Stadia and Arenas; Counter Terrorism Protective Security Advice for Visitor Attractions* (London: Home Office, 2009). Note also CPNI, *Protecting against Terrorism*, 3d ed. (London: 2010).
40. *Working Together to Protect Crowded Places* (London: 2009 and 2010), *Safer Places* (London: 2009), *Crowded Places: The Planning System and Counter Terrorism* (London: 2010), *Protecting Crowded Places: Design and Technical Issues* (London: 2010).
41. See House of Commons Committee of Public Accounts, *The Budget for the London 2012 Olympic and Paralympic Games* (2007–08 HC 85).
42. See A. Staniforth, *Blackstone's Counter-Terrorism Handbook*, 2d ed. (Oxford: Oxford University Press, 2011) at ch.3.
43. See Home Office, *Pursue, Prevent, Protect, Prepare* Cm.7547, (London: 2009) at para. 14.30.
44. Home Office, *Prevent Strategy*, Cm.8092, *supra* note 15 at para. 9.16.
45. Ibid. at para. 11.8.
46. See online at U.K. Centre for the Protection of National Infrastructure, http://www.cpni.gov.uk/.
47. Home Office, *Policing in the 21st Century* (London: 2010) at paras. 4.32, 4.38.
48. See Department for Transport, *Modernising the British Transport Police* (London: 2001).
49. See Department for Trade and Industry, *Managing the Nuclear Legacy*, Cm5552 (London: 2002); J. Simpson, "The UK and the threat of nuclear terrorism" in P. Wilkinson, ed., *Homeland Security in the UK* (Abingdon: Routledge, 2007).
50. See Ministry of Defence Police and Guarding Agency, *Annual Report and Accounts 2007–2008* (2007–08 HC 699) at 29, 40.
51. See C. Walker, "The governance of the Critical National Infrastructure" [2008]) *Public Law* 323 at 338.
52. Home Office, *Circular 24/2002: A protocol between the Ministry of Defence Police and Home Office Police Forces*, (London: 2002) at para. 11.
53. Tony McNulty, Hansard HC Public Bill Committee on the Counter-Terrorism Bill (15 May 2008) at col.497.
54. Harbours, Docks and Piers Clauses Act 1847, §§ 79, 83, and the Port of London Act 1968, §§ss 154, 160, 170; Hansard HC 442 (7 June 2004) at col.72w.
55. Home Affairs Committee, *Policing in the 21st Century* (2007–08 HC 364) at para. 265.
56. House of Commons Transport Committee, *UK Transport Security* (2005–06 HC 637) at para. 37.
57. See Hansard HC 467 (14 November 2007) at col.44ws; Hansard HL 703 (22 July 2008) at col.153ws.
58. See Privy Counsellor Review Committee, *Anti-terrorism, Crime and Security Act 2001 Review Report* (2003-04 HC 100) at paras. 295, 311.

59. Home Office, *Countering International Terrorism*, Cm.8123, *supra* note 13 at para. 7.7.
60. [2004] UKHL 56. See also *A v United Kingdom*, App. no. 3455/05, 19 February 2009.
61. *R (Gillan) v Metropolitan Police Commissioner* [2006] UKHL 12. See also *Austin v Commissioner of Police of the Metropolis* [2009] UKHL 5.
62. *R v Chief Constable of South Yorkshire Police ex parte LS and Marper* [2004] UKHL 39.
63. *Gillan and Quinton v United Kingdom* App no 4158/05, 12 January 2010; *S and Marper v United Kingdom*, App nos. 30562/04, 30566/04, 4 December 2008.
64. Moteff, J., *Critical Infrastructure: The National Asset Database*, (Washington, DC: CRS Report for Congress, RL33648, 2007) at 3.
65. Home Office, *Countering International Terrorism*, Cm.8123, *supra* note 13 at para. 7.6.
66. The authority is Executive Order 13224 and the United Nations Participation Act of 1945 § 5 (22 USC 287c) available online at http://www.ustreas.gov/press/releases/reports/legalauthoritiesoftftp.pdf.
67. See Council of the EU, *Processing of EU Originating Personal Data by United States Treasury Department for Counter Terrorism Purposes–SWIFT*, 10741/2/07 Rev 2 (2007) at 2.
68. See Committee on Civil Liberties, Justice and Home Affairs, *First ECC report on the implementation of the EU-US SWIFT undertakings*,LIBE/6/73175 (16 February 2009).
69. Agreement between the European Union and the United States of America on the processing and transfer of Financial Messaging Data from the European Union to the US for the purposes of the Terrorist Finance Tracking Program (Brussels, 2010); European Commission, *Proposal for a Council Decision* (COM(2010) 316 final).
70. Communication from the Commission to the European Parliament and the Council, *A European terrorist finance tracking system: Available options* (COM(2011) 429 final).
71. 49 USC s 44909(c)(3); 8 CFR 231; 19 CFR 122.31.
72. See Council Decision 2004/496/EC of 17 May 2004, and Cases C-317/04 and C-318/04, European Parliament v Council of the European Union and European Parliament v Commission of the European Communities (2006).
73. Agreement between the European Union and the United States of America on the processing and transfer of passenger name record (PNR) data by air carriers to the United States Department of Homeland Security (13668/06) and Annexes (11304/07); Draft Agreement between the United States of America and the European Union on the use and transfer of Passenger Name Record data to the United States Department of Homeland Security (Council Document 10453111, 2011).
74. COM(2007) 654 final.
75. COM(2011) 32 final.
76. See House of Lords European Union Committee, *The Passenger Name Record (PNR) Framework Decision* (2007–08 HL 106) and *Government Reply*, Cm 7461 (London: 2008); House of Commons European Scrutiny Committee, *Seventh Report* (2007–08 HC 16-vii); Council Document 9941/11, 2011.
77. M. Pitt, *Learning Lessons from the 2007 Floods Final Report*, (London: Cabinet Office, 2008) at para. 99.

78. See T.A. Reppetto, "Crime Prevention and the Displacement Phenomenon" (1976) 22 *Crime & Delinquency* 166; M. Felson and R.V. Clarke, *Opportunity Makes the Thief*, Police Research Series Paper 98, (London: Home Office, 1998).
79. Compare R.V. Clarke and G.R. Newman, *Outsmarting the Terrorists*, (New York: Praeger, 2006).
80. See C. Walker, "Political violence and commercial risk" (2004) 56 *Current Legal Problems* 531; S. Graham, ed., *Cities, War and Terrorism* (Oxford: Blackwell, 2004); T. Craig, "Sabotage!" (2010) 25 *Intelligence and National Security* 309.
81. See W. Enders and T. Sandler, *The Political Economy of Terrorism* (Cambridge: Cambridge University Press, 2006), at chs. 3 and 5.
82. Ibid. at chs. 4 and 6.
83. *National Security Strategy — A Strong Britain in an Age of Uncertainty*, Cm.7953 (London: 2010). This paper was developed from *The National Security Strategy of the United Kingdom Security in an interdependent world*, Cm.7291 (London: 2008).
84. Ibid. at 3.
85. D. Omand, *Securing the State* (London: Hurst & Co., 2010) at 20.
86. Department for Transport, *Interim Code of Practice for the Acceptable Use of Advanced Imaging Technology (Body Scanners) in an Aviation Security Environment* (London: 2010).
87. House of Commons Home Affairs Committee, *Counter Terrorism Measures in British Airports* (2009–10 HC 311) at para. 30. Compare COM(2010) 311/4.
88. Home Office, *Countering International Terrorism*, Cm.8123, *supra* note 13. For DFID spend figures, see *Bilateral Aid Review* (London: 2010) at Annex F.
89. Complaint Ref: 122211, 2010.
90. Home Office, *Pursue, Prevent, Protect, Prepare*, Cm.7547, *supra* note 43 at para. 14.26.
91. Ibid. at para. 0.67.
92. Home Office, *Countering International Terrorism*, Cm.8123, *supra* note 13 at para. 11.30.
93. Home Office, *National Policing Plan 2003–2006* (London: 2002) at paras. 3.37, 4.37–4.40.
94. Home Office, *National Policing Plan 2004–2007* (London: 2003) at para. 3.3.
95. Jacqui Smith, Hansard HC 485(8 December 2008) at col.40WS.
96. Home Office, *Pursue, Prevent, Protect, Prepare*, Cm 7547 (London: 2009) at para. 13.08.
97. *Adapting to Austerity* (London: 2011).
98. For the definition of "frontline" in this sense, see HM Inspectorate of Constabulary, *Demanding Times* (London: Home Office, 2011).
99. Home Office, *Pursue, Prevent, Protect, Prepare*, Cm.7547, *supra* note 43 at para. 0.17.
100. For details of Troika (which expired in 2003), see C. Walker, "Political violence and commercial risk" (2004) 56 *Current Legal Problems* 531. A more ambitious U.S. scheme appeared in the Air Transportation Safety and System Stabilization Act 2001 (PL 107-42).
101. See Home Office, *Addressing Lessons from the Emergency Response to the 7 July 2005 London Bombings* (London: 2006) at paras. 30–35.

CHAPTER 12

The Influence of 9/11 on Swedish Anti-terrorism Policy and Measures

IAIN CAMERON*

The attacks of September 11, 2011, and the later ones in London on July 7, 2005, have had an undoubted influence on Swedish anti-terrorism policy and measures. Nevertheless, there has been no decisive shifting of the security/liberty border in Sweden. Rather, as is the case in many other countries, the changes which have been made reflect trends apparent long before 9/11. The dramatic visibility of the threat of international terrorism has, however, contributed to the acceptance of certain increases in security and police powers. These increased powers nonetheless appear to have been largely matched by improved safeguards. Although the changes made in police and security powers are justifiable (or at least acceptable), there are four areas which are potentially troublesome. Three of these concern Swedish implementation of international or European norms, which in two cases come indirectly from the influence of U.S. law.

This chapter begins with some background information to recent developments in Swedish anti-terrorism law, before discussing increased anti-terrorism powers. It distinguishes between measures, which the Swedish legislature has taken of its own motion, and measures which have been implemented in Swedish law as a result of E.U. initiatives. A word of explanation is necessary here for readers from non-E.U. states: the relationship between the European Union and E.U. Member States is complex. European Union law is, at least according to E.U. law itself, hierarchically superior to national law. However, the creation of most

E.U. law in the area of justice and home affairs has, until recently, only been possible with unanimous agreement. It is thus not a question of E.U. states having being legally "forced" to implement E.U. norms. However, smaller states still find it more difficult in practice to block the adoption of norms regarded as important by the bigger E.U. states. To put it another way, not all E.U. norms in justice and home affairs have been equally welcomed and supported by all E.U. states. After we look at the changes which have occurred in Sweden, this chapter then examines the legal and political safeguards which have been added to control increased state powers.

BACKGROUND: THE SWEDISH LEGAL SYSTEM

It is not the purpose of this chapter to give a detailed background on Swedish law and constitutional law, and the values underlying them, but something should be said about it. The Nordic countries have important similarities in legal culture, but there are some differences (e.g., regarding police powers). In Sweden, the main focus of rights protection is not the courts, but the legislative process. With the risk of too much simplification, the Swedish legislative process is meant to promote a reflective, rational response to a societal problem. There is often a significant academic and civil society input to the drafting process. In this vein, the courts in Sweden unreservedly accept the primacy of the principle of parliamentary democracy. Substantial judicial norm-creative power is difficult to reconcile with such a governing principle. This basic approach is reflected in the importance the courts place on the historical interpretative method, referring to the *travaux préparatoires* which contain detailed guidance. However, in substantive criminal law, the principle of legality enshrined in chapter 1, section 1 of *Regeringsformen*, the Instrument of Government (IG), means that the textual method (objective wording of the provision) has primacy. The courts often combine these two methods in practice. The process of recruitment and training of judges also tends to stress loyalty to the legislator. It is, however, too simplistic to say that the courts approach their task as pure "technicians." A precondition for the respect the courts show the legislature is the integrity of the lawmaking process and the quality of the final product. The higher courts will not be so inclined to place strong reliance on the *travaux préparatoires* where a law has not been properly prepared or is not well formulated.

Rights are set out in chapter 2 IG, as well as in the *Freedom of the Press* and *Freedom of Expression Acts*, all of which have constitutional status. In addition, the European Convention on Human Rights (ECHR) is incorporated by statute, although it has a quasi-constitutional status as a result of IG chapter 2 section 19. The ECHR provides only a minimum level of protection, and the constitutional rights of security of person and privacy (data protection, surveillance, et cetera) are relative rights which can be restricted. The ECHR does have an important feature, in that it requires positive legal support for state powers infringing rights and, if the state takes this seriously in the legislative process—which Sweden tends to do—it can have a preventive effect. Nevertheless, the ECHR is not the primary safeguard for rights. Instead, this lies in the legal culture in regard to police powers and the perception of how much insecurity or ineffectiveness one can or should tolerate (discussed further below).

An important part of rights protection is the concept of "legal security" (*rättssäkerhet*, from the German *Rechtssicherheit*). Foreseeability (legal certainty) is an important part of the concept, but does not encapsulate it fully. The concept tends to be used to evaluate critically the *lawful* exercise of authority, both when a bill proposes new powers or offences, and when the courts are applying the law (and two or more interpretations are possible). As regards criminal policy, at the risk of generalization, civil servants and politicians in Sweden have shown a (relatively speaking) high degree of respect for both the views of legal experts and criminological expertise in the area of crime control. Moreover, the government and political opposition in Sweden have often strived to obtain a consensus approach to criminal policy generally. The Swedish parliament, the Riksdag, has produced sensible principles for criminalization. Before behaviour is prohibited, it should give rise to concrete damage or danger, and a penal sanction is required by reference to the seriousness of the behaviour. Alternative measures to deal with the behaviour should be unavailable, would not be rational in the circumstances or would entail disproportionally high costs. A penal sanction should also be an effective means of countering the undesirable behaviour. Furthermore, the criminal justice system must have the resources necessary to deal with the extra burdens following from the criminalization.[1]

Nevertheless, these sensible principles have not always been adhered to in practice. Criminalization has certainly not always been treated as a "last resort." The views of criminal law and criminological experts have not always been followed. Examples of criminal legislation enacted for purposes of political point-scoring and which has had little or even negative effect on crime rates exist; it is fair to say that these examples have increased since the beginning of the 1990s. There are various explanations for this, amongst which are the role of the mass media in creating or strengthening public perceptions of insecurity and in proposing simple solutions (i.e., harder punishments) to complex social problems. I do not know if this mass-media tendency has become more pronounced since 9/11, but would suspect not. Indeed, I think the tendency for the Swedish press to be more critical of arguments promising a reduction in "insecurity" has been strengthened by post-9/11 events.

EXPANDED CRIMINALISATION AND INCREASED POLICE POWERS

Sweden lacks a number of the features considered important in criminal procedure in common-law states such as the United States and the United Kingdom. There is no jury trial (except in the few cases concerning freedom of expression). Swedish procedural law is based on the free admissibility and free evaluation of evidence. Unlawfully collected evidence is thus admissible (although under general principles, evidence obtained by torture would not be admitted, the issue has not arisen in either the ordinary or the administrative courts). Conviction rates are high in prosecutions of most categories of offence, apart from sexual offences.

Regarding the institutional division of competence and power in security, it should be noted that, like the other Nordic countries but unlike the situation in the United Kingdom, Germany, or the Netherlands, there is no civilian security service. Instead, the protection of internal security is a matter for the Security Police. At present, this is an autonomous part of the national police, but from 2015, it will be wholly separate from it. A significant part of the staff, however, now consists of civilian analysts. It has expanded considerably since the beginning of the 2000s and by 2012 was around one thousand people. There is, however, a civilian strategic intelligence service, *Försvarets radio anstalt* (FRA), which is the Swedish equivalent to the U.S. National Security Agency (NSA) and the U.K. Government Communications Headquarters (GCHQ), even though it is very small by comparison. In 2004, the Security Police established a Counter Terrorism Cooperation Council, in which representatives of all the other government agencies with relevant responsibilities participate. The Council inter alia produces threat assessments and the national action-plan against terrorism. In 2006 the police were also given the explicit power to call upon military assistance.[2]

As for changes in criminal procedure, the national police (from 2015 divided into seven regional authorities) and the security police were given new powers under the Act on Covert Eavesdropping.[3] This act allowed them to engage in electronic eavesdropping, which was not previously permissible. The procedural requirements for interception of letters and electronic communications have since 1952 been more relaxed for the security police compared to the ordinary police. Moreover, both the police and the security police were given powers to engage in *proactive* covert interception of telecommunications, covert telecommunications surveillance and data-retention, and covert camera surveillance for purposes of investigating certain serious crimes, including terrorist offences.[4] This is something which was permissible previously only to monitor the activities of foreign nationals in Sweden suspected of involvement in terrorism. Proactive surveillance is now allowed when, having regard to the circumstances, there is reason to believe that a person will perform criminal acts in the future, including certain listed offences (such as sabotage, arson, terrorist offences, and murder). This latter statute represents a clear divergence from the previously accepted view that the use of coercive measures, without a connection to a reasonable suspicion that a criminal offence has already been committed, can be justified only under exceptional circumstances. The parliament also passed a new law permitting police agents to use secret identities to infiltrate criminal groups.[5]

Sweden was also one of the states behind the European-wide initiative in 2006 to adopt the E.U. Data Retention Framework Decision, obliging states to require telecommunications providers to make telecommunications records available to the police (for a minimum period of six months) for the investigation of serious crime. Another change with an international dimension, discussed in more detail below, is that the FRA was permitted in 2008 to start intercepting cable traffic to and from Sweden for a number of purposes, including intelligence-gathering relating to international terrorism.[6] Swedish implementation of the E.U. framework decision on the European Arrest Warrant also means that extradition of Swedish citizens, previously permissible only to other Nordic states, is now possible to E.U. states, including for terrorist offences.[7]

As for the management of suspected individual security risks, no significant changes have been made in security screening. Screening for inter alia suspicion of involvement in international terrorism has for a long time been carried out in a large number of security-classed posts in public administration, critical transport infrastructure, et cetera. However, Sweden has had a variant of British-style "control orders" since 1989. These apply only against people against whom a deportation order had been issued, but where the order for humanitarian reasons cannot be carried out.[8] Such an order involves a restriction on freedom of movement, rather than a more serious deprivation of liberty, as it involves only a duty to report periodically (usually once a week) to a police station, which must not necessarily be in the subject's area of residence.

There have also been changes in substantive criminal law, many in line with international developments. The E.U. framework decision on terrorism has been implemented in Sweden by the Act on Criminal Responsibility for Terrorist Offences.[9] The Act increases considerably the penalty scales for a number of listed offences committed with a terrorist intent. As with Danish criminal procedure law, the use of search and seizure, surveillance, and other so-called "coercive measures" depends on the penalty scales for offences: more serious offences permit the use of more serious or long-term coercive measures. Thus, the 2003 Act has meant that the number of offences for which more serious coercive measures are permitted, and for longer periods, has expanded greatly.

Financing of terrorism was made an offence under the Act on Criminal Responsibility for the Financing of Particularly Serious Crime in Some Cases.[10] The 2005 Council of Europe Convention on the Prevention of Terrorism, along with an E.U. directive covering largely the same ground, have been implemented by the Act on Criminal Responsibility for Public Incitement, Recruitment and Training relating to Terrorist and Other Particularly Serious Crimes.[11] The E.U. directive on money laundering, which inter alia expands the categories of business subject to "due diligence" requirements and provides for duties of disclosure, has been implemented by the Act on Measures against Money Laundering and Financing of Terrorism.[12] All of the above changes appear to indicate that the events of 9/11 have exerted a very strong influence on Swedish criminal law, police powers, and criminal procedure, and that the Swedish government has since made considerable restrictions on various civil liberties in the name of security.

9/11 AND THE SECURITY/LIBERTY TRADE-OFF IN SWEDEN

Although the risk of terrorism was an important part of the motivation behind the new acts on proactive surveillance and bugging, the police and the security police had been requesting the powers to engage in such measures, in particular against organized crime, for many years before 9/11. Bugging had been up for discussion repeatedly during the 1980s and 1990s. It is undoubtedly difficult to obtain information on the activities of certain organized crime groups without resorting to bugging. The perception of the threat of transnational organized crime has increased, partly because of the freedom of movement within the European Union. It may well be that the actual threat is still not so great, but that politicians would eventually accept bugging was more or less inevitable. In terms of rights protection, what balances out this greater potential for infringement of privacy? Surveillance periods are rather short by international comparison, the same as for telecommunications interception warrants (i.e., four weeks), with the possibility for renewal. Certain categories of people are exempt. Surplus information which is generated relating to other offences committed may only be used if the offence in question is punishable by more than four years imprisonment. Notwithstanding the increase in penalties for terrorist offences, the normal penalty scales in Sweden are relatively low, meaning that it is mainly more serious offences which qualify.

Both the acts on bugging and on proactive surveillance were made time-limited to 2010, and subject to evaluation by a commission of inquiry. The acts were extended for another two years to 2012. While these acts can be criticized for having been inadequately prepared, the detailed evaluation subsequently made shows that bugging has not been used very frequently by the ordinary police: twenty-one times in a one year period (2009-2010), on ten occasions during the same period by the security police. Proactive surveillance was used in three cases by the ordinary police and in around fifty cases by the security police. According to the commission of inquiry, all cases of proactive surveillance were close to the threshold of initiation of an investigation (i.e., reasonable suspicion of a serious offence). The security police have complained about the requirements which have to be fulfilled before an intelligence-gathering operation can be launched under the Act and want freer hands.

However, the limited use of these powers is not any comfort for the people who have been targeted. The question here is how much room is there for abuse or overuse of power by the police in general, and the security police in particular? Here one should begin by noting the position of the Swedish prosecutor. The Swedish prosecutor can take charge of any investigation. Many investigations in practice are left to the police, but as regards more serious offences (such as terrorism), a prosecutor will invariably be in charge. The prosecutor is bound by the principle of objectivity; he or she shall gather all relevant evidence relating to an alleged crime, including both exculpatory evidence and evidence which implicates an accused. The prosecutor is also, from German legal traditions, bound by the principle of legality. Although this is subject to exceptions and the rules on multiplicity of offences must often be taken into account, important consequences nonetheless follow from it; this should be understood by readers from states with a discretionary system of prosecution (e.g., common law states and, for that matter, the Nordic states of Denmark and Norway).

Among other things, the principle of legality increases the need for care in formulating the offence, because less discretion is available to the prosecutor to prevent him or her from bringing inappropriate prosecutions. The pedagogical role of the principle can also be noted; instead of deciding freely who he or she should target, the prosecutor starts from the position that he or she is to go after everyone committing an offence. In these circumstances, it is more difficult (psychologically speaking) for the prosecutor and the police to take a preventive or "enemy-based" approach to the criminal law—something that is most pronounced in terrorism cases. In other words, by targeting all perpetrators more or less equally, it is harder for the prosecutor to take the attitude that he or she must protect "us" (the decent people) from "them" the criminals or terrorists, which he or she might more easily do with greater prosecutorial discretion.

During the Cold War, and up until the end of the 1980s, the security police were not strongly controlled by prosecutors. Moreover, in granting telecommunications interceptions warrants, the courts did not always take their job seriously. The best example of this is the telephone tapping of the Gothenburg Communist Party offices on suspicions of illegal paramilitary activity during the 1950s and 1960s. No evidence sufficient for a prosecution was produced during the seventeen years this surveillance went on, something which is all the more difficult to accept considering that authorization for it was renewed every four weeks. The security police were also left more or less on their own to decide which left-leaning political organizations were dangerous to the state, and on which members of these organizations personal files should be opened. The result was that intelligence was collected on a considerable number of people who were not in any way dangers to the state. An estimated fifty people suffered negative consequences to their careers as a result of failing security screening. It was the revelations of the 1980s which led to the modernization of the security police, in particular the broadening of its recruitment base. The increased recruitment of civilian analysts from a variety of different backgrounds has hopefully now led to a much more nuanced threat assessment in security cases. A specialist prosecutor chamber has now been created to concentrate expertise when investigating security crime.

An oversight body, the Register Board, was created in 1996 to provide a safeguard against over-collection of intelligence and overzealous security screening. This body, combined with tightened filing practices, greatly improved the level of privacy protection in this area. In 2007, this body was replaced by the Commission on Security and Integrity Protection (*Säkerhets- och integritetsskyddsnämnden*, or SIN) which was given an expanded oversight function over surveillance.[13] The main reason was the above-noted increased investigative powers, which were in the process of being granted to the police and the Security Police. There was also a realization that prosecutorial and judicial control only checked to ensure that there was reasonable cause to initiate surveillance; accordingly, there was no post hoc monitoring. SIN was thus given a follow-up function, namely to ensure that surveillance activities by the police, including the Security Police, are conducted in accordance with laws and other regulations. It retained the previous function of the Register Board to ensure that the Security Police filing of personal data is "conducted in accordance with laws and other regulations"[14] These laws include the limits set out on the filing of sensitive personal data by the constitution[15] and in the Police Data Act, as well as the Security Police's own regulations on initiating, adding to, correcting, and terminating personal files. Although SIN's mandate is only framed in terms of ensuring compliance with the law, a proportionality test is a fundamental part of this. Although much of the sensitive work of the Security Police falls within SIN's supervision, not all of it does. SIN has no overall mandate to supervise the work of the Security Police generally, to scrutinize its budget, management, or efficiency (except insofar as these matters overlap its specific mandate). SIN does not have a formal role to play in reviewing decisions to deport aliens or to deny citizenship and residence permits made on security grounds. Formally speaking, all of these decisions are appealable to the courts, but in practice the courts lack the competence to question the security assessment made.

Here it can be noted that one of the real black marks against Sweden in the "war against terror" was the decision made in December 2001 by the Swedish government to deport two Egyptian men to Egypt. The actual deportation was carried out by CIA officials on a CIA plane. It was an early example of the now notorious U.S. policy of extraordinary rendition of suspected terrorists. The Swedish government demanded and received a guarantee from the Egyptian government that the men would be treated according to the requirements of international law. However, very strong evidence indicates that the two men were tortured in Egypt. The diplomatic guarantee meant that the deportation decision was, technically, in accordance with the Swedish Aliens Act. However, both the decision and its implementation have been heavily criticized both in Sweden and in international fora.[16]

This decision to allow the rendition was clearly a grave error by the Swedish government. Still, although one should never be complacent, such decisions are unlikely in the future. The Swedish law has not been changed in substance, but, politically speaking, the government is now unlikely to authorize security deportations to regimes with dubious human rights records. The decision was made at a time when there were strong sympathies for the United States, but as the details have emerged of the nature of the U.S. rendition program, the decision has caused only embarrassment. The European Court of Human Rights has also clarified the extent of states' human rights obligations as regards extradition/deportation and made clear the limited value of diplomatic guarantees from non-democratic states in terrorist cases.[17] Moreover, there is now greater awareness of the need to evaluate more critically the reliability of data concerning the terrorist activities or intentions of aliens, when information has originated in other states. In this context, SIN has general competence to look at how the security police handle all personal data, including the personal data of aliens.

As for increased powers to retain telecommunications data, there is undoubtedly force in the argument that this involves a shift to a general monitoring of the population. This measure should be seen in the light of other ones, such as monitoring financial transactions (discussed below) and travel patterns. Monitoring where a person surfs on the Internet can reveal a great deal about his or her lifestyle. This is an infringement of privacy; when a person is aware that his or her telecommunications provider has a duty to make this data available to the police, this can affect what he or she chooses to look at. However, the infringement can be made acceptable by setting stringent standards which must be satisfied before allowing law enforcement or security access to this data. For example, this might only be permitted by a court, on application by a prosecutor, or where there is a reasonable suspicion that the person using the telecommunications address has already committed or is committing a serious offence.

The problem, of course, is that the Swedish police (like the police in other states) regard such standards as unworkable. They often want access to this data simply to help find out what is going on. They thus need it at an earlier stage in an investigation, where a reasonable suspicion might not yet exist. Moreover, they want to use this power to investigate even less-serious offences. However, what one can miss in this discussion is that the Swedish police use of this power has, up until now, been largely unrestricted. Investigators have simply contacted the telecommunications provider and requested the data, which was routinely delivered. SIN's mandate has now been extended to a follow-up supervision of police and Security Police access to teledata. This involves accepting the notion that such access is often an intelligence-gathering rather than an evidence-gathering tool. SIN's supervision would seem to constitute an improvement of the previous legal situation. The same can be said about proposals made (but not implemented) regarding police and Security Police use of infiltrators and informants, providing for statutory authority and a form of quasi-judicial authorization process for their use. This proposal has come about as a result of ECHR requirements for positive statutory authority.[18]

A similar point can be made about the change made allowing the FRA to monitor cable traffic. The FRA, during the Cold War, concentrated largely on military targets in line with the strategic threats against Sweden from the Warsaw Pact. Since the end of the Cold War, however, the targets have obviously shifted, as has the form telecommunications now take (the vast majority are now cable-borne). The choice was either to shut down the FRA or give it the power to look at cable-borne traffic. The latter option undoubtedly involves a considerable potential for expansion of surveillance of the population as a whole. The bill providing for this was prepared by the Defence Ministry, not the Ministry of Justice, and there was no discussion of the fact that strategic surveillance involved a restriction of personal integrity, and that there was a consequent need for safeguards, something which had been made clear some years before by the important ECHR case of *Weber and Saravia* v. *Germany*.[19] There was a very un-Swedish public outcry when the bill was introduced in the parliament. The government chose to push it through—which was very un-Swedish, too—but conceded that the protections for integrity were inadequate, and added in a subsequent bill a complicated battery of safeguards.[20]

The new law established a Defence Intelligence Court (*Försvarsunderrättelsedomstolen* or FUD) together with a control and monitoring body, the Defence Intelligence Inspection (*Statens inspektion för försvarsunderrättelseverksamheten* or SIUN).[21] Basically, the system is that the government, the Cabinet Office, and the defence forces may task FRA to produce foreign intelligence on a particular issue. FRA then requests a warrant from FUD, which sets out what search streams can be used and which signal bearers (i.e., which cables, going to which destinations) can be monitored. The raw intelligence is then delivered by telecom operators to a location physically under the control of SIUN, which monitors whether the conditions set by FUD have been complied with. Communications originating, transiting, or terminating in Sweden can be monitored, as well as communications having no connection with Sweden (e.g., satellites passing overhead). The raw intelligence is transferred for analysis to FRA, which then delivers the product to the body that requested it. Such strategic surveillance undoubtedly creates special dangers for privacy and other rights, but this is not a case of the FRA being let loose after 9/11. From World War II until 2008, the FRA was not really under any meaningful external control at all. Admittedly, one has to be particularly cautious in this area, as controls on paper may not work well in practice. With this having been said, the new Swedish act provides for a relatively tough control mechanism. It seems to be as strong as the German system, and much better than the minimal controls which exist in the United Kingdom. Time and experience will tell if the system actually works as well as it should.

If control over the police, the security police, and the FRA is in general better now than in the past, what areas of law and practice are more troublesome today? One is the above-mentioned implemention of the Council of Europe Convention on the Prevention of Terrorism and the E.U. Framework Decision on Combating Terrorism. This reflects and enhances a general tendency in the criminal law of today: namely, to upgrade the importance of prevention not only as a general justifying aim for the criminal law system, but also as a primary task for the system. This ultimately means that many basic principles that aim at legal security or securing liberty, but which might limit the efficiency of the system, are put under pressure. "Preventionism" is not new for security offences, as these have usually been regarded as "starting" early. A number of commentators have already discussed this tendency in detail,[22] but suffice it to say here that there is an increasing inclination to construct proscriptions in a way which allows for the imposition of criminal liability at a very early stage and on the basis of an evil intent on the part of the perpetrator. The ideal type for this kind of liability is the one imposed for preparatory conduct. The harm the government guards against can be very remote from the conduct of the accused, thereby increasing the risk for wrongful convictions. As the proscribed conduct will be more difficult to separate from lawful protest or other lawful forms of expression, which are the lifeblood of a democracy, then there is also a greater risk of unnecessary infringements of privacy and freedoms of expression and association.

Institutionally speaking, for states without a civilian security agency, the security police is supposed to investigate security *crime*. Admittedly, conspiracy and preparation to commit security offences are criminal offences in their own right. However, with these new types of offence now based largely on evil intent rather than overt actions, the Swedish Security Police is being asked and indeed wants to investigate "pre-crime." Moreover, it is finding itself at times stepping outside of its investigative role into a deterrence role, informing people or groups that it "has its eyes on them." With that having been said, from a law enforcement perspective, as Swedish law now stands, it has not been possible to get a conviction for conspiracy to commit terrorist acts. This is so even when it can be shown that a person has voluntarily received training at a training camp abroad and recordings exist of him declaring his willingness to take part in a mission involving an explosion and to become a martyr.[23] So, although there are undoubtedly dangers with this type of preventive legislation, it is at least clear that the

Swedish legislator is aware of these and has tried in the *travaux préparatoires* to minimize the problems.[24]

Another problem is that both the European Union and the United Nations have enabled the quasi-criminalization of groups in the form of blacklisting. This is a form of two-stage criminalization. First, a political body (the U.N. Security Council or the E.U. Council of Ministers) determines that an organisation is terrorist in nature. The assets of the organization are then frozen, and criminal penalties are imposed upon anyone who assists it economically. Although the prohibited conduct for the world at large under the relevant U.N. and E.U. norms is economic support for terrorism, one can also envisage support in the form of education or other forms of speech. I have written at length elsewhere about the different problems of blacklisting, so I will not repeat all of this criticism here.[25] I will content myself with saying that blacklisting has an uneasy coexistence with a criminal law approach to punishing the financing of terrorism. It elevates what is a standard for initiating an intelligence operation or, at most, justifying an interim measure (such as a freezing order) during the investigation of crime—namely *suspicion* of the commission of a security offence—to justify the imposition of a quasi-criminal *penalty* of unlimited duration. Even here, however, the Swedish position is relatively encouraging. Sweden is particularly sensitive to infringements in freedom of association. There has been a conviction in the Swedish courts for terrorist financing, but this was under the Financing of Particularly Serious Crime Act, where an intent to promote terrorism had to be and was shown. By contrast, the Swedish court of Appeal, unlike the approach of the U.S. Supreme Court, has rejected the view that financially assisting an organisation linked to Hamas is either automatically to be seen as assisting terrorism or a breach of E.U. sanctions issued against Hamas.[26]

Another unwelcome series of developments in my view is connected with U.S. desires to engage in data mining. The United States has a different approach to security and police access to data collected for other purposes, compared to the majority of E.U. states. The United States has put strong pressure on the European Union to accept inter alia automatic transfer of passenger name record (PNR) data and to allow scrutiny of financial transactions (the so-called Terrorist Finance Tracking System). Again, much can be said about this, but I will content myself with saying that I am sceptical about the value of these data-mining exercises: that is to say, whether the concrete benefits in terms of intelligence gains outweigh the potential risks of abuses, and the major infringements in privacy this general monitoring of the population entails. Sweden cannot wholly be blamed for all of these measures. They are more or less being imposed on Sweden (and probably several other E.U. states, too) by the United States.

The final potentially troublesome issue which I would highlight, which *is* under Swedish control, is changes in the law governing the tasking of the FRA. The power of the Security Police to task the FRA was removed in 2008. However, it is problematic not to allow the agency with exclusive responsibility for internal security to task the FRA directly. At the same time, the present battery of safeguards is constructed on the basis that it is only the government, the Cabinet Office, and the Ministry of Defence which can task the FRA. As regards terrorism, the FRA is focussed on strategic intelligence, and intelligence on the movement of technology potentially usable for the construction of weapons of mass destruction (a necessary responsibility for an export-based economy). The law was changed to allow the security police (and the ordinary police) to task FRA in 2012.[27] This is only meant to cover more "strategic" aspects of organised crime and terrorism. Nonetheless, permitting focus to shift to more law-enforcement concerns involves a paradigm shift, calls into question the coherence of the present system of controls, and gives rise to more problems when it comes to balancing the interests of investigation against those of integrity protection.

CONCLUSION

Obviously, the most important factor behind the balanced approach Sweden has tried to take in national law is that Swedes have not been the victims of many terrorist outrages. The failed suicide bombing in Stockholm in December 2010, although a shock, has not really put the much-vaunted Swedish tolerance to the test. Following the bombing, there was no rush to legislate to fill any perceived gaps in protection. Both the prime minister and the head of the Security Police made the measured, sensible point that an open society cannot guard itself fully against such acts, and that trying to secure total prevention would mean the end to the open society itself. Swedish political commentators took a similar approach after the bombing in Oslo and the Utøy massacre in July 2011, as did the Norwegian prime minister and other officials.

Of course, the moral high ground which Swedes like to see themselves as inhabiting may not be very secure. Still, it is also worth stating that the relative absence of terrorist threats in Swedish society is not the product of chance, but a combination of different factors. The first line of defence of Sweden itself is the welfare state and the inclusiveness of Swedish society. So far, this line of defence is largely holding, and terrorism is still seen largely as a problem for other states. At the same time, Swedish lawmakers, police, and prosecutors are aware that terrorists can both use Sweden as a base for gathering resources and as a relatively weakly defended place to attack foreign interests. And the events in Oslo and Utøy show that home-grown extremism can cause massive casualties in an unarmed and unsuspecting civilian population.

A future free from serious terrorism is certainly not guaranteed in Sweden. The more right-wing groups feel themselves to be threatened by multiculturalism, the more likely that their response will be violent. There are badly integrated immigrant communities in Sweden. The more extensive and more savage the conflicts which affect other states, the more likely that sections of these exile communities having origins in conflict-afflicted countries will be drawn into these, and that the effects of these conflicts will spill over into Sweden. This is illustrated by the already-mentioned Stockholm bombing, committed by a Swedish citizen of Iraqi origin in December 2010 (he was rumoured to have been influenced in his radicalization process by British caliphists). Sweden has also traditionally tried to maintain a neutral position, unlike the United States, in the Israeli-Palestinian conflict. The Swedish position—which I share—is that there are violent extremists on both sides of this conflict, and that both sorts of violence—terrorism and violations of international humanitarian law—should be equally condemned. On the other hand, the Swedish government has undoubtedly stepped away from a position of strict neutrality (and so gotten mired in certain unwinnable conflicts) as a result of its desire to show a commitment to peacekeeping and protection of the rights of the civilian population in Afghanistan.

It is nevertheless fair to say that there is a more widespread awareness among Swedish lawmakers, as compared to American lawmakers and those in some other European states, that criminalization of extraterritorial terrorism will not solve the underlying social or political problems in the states where terrorism is occurring. Terrorism is a crime with a political objective. International and European lawyers have been naïve or have shown hubris in thinking that they can solve what are essentially disputes over values and resources by applying a value-neutral, legal definition of terrorism.[28] If Sweden had more of a say in European and world anti-terrorism policy, it would probably take a more structural, preventive approach. This would focus less on legislating offences and more on doing something about the much more challenging causes of terrorism, together with the pragmatic approach of trying to minimize risks that terrorists get hold of very destructive bombs and weaponry.

In any case, the recurring theme of this chapter has been the problems that emerge when fundamental exercises of sovereignty and "one size fits all" solutions—particularly in regard to central concepts of criminal law and criminal procedure—become partly the domain of international organizations (such as the United Nations and the Council of Europe), and partly the domain of the European Union (something between an international organization and a proto-federal state). In this respect, I join the critics who have pointed out the risk that the E.U. fixation with terrorism can distort the E.U. criminal law agenda, leading to long-term loss in confidence for the European criminal lawmaking project.[29]

The United States has, historically speaking, helped Western Europe enormously—in World War II, in rebuilding it after the war, and in protecting it during the Cold War. Put in perspective, Sweden and other western European powers certainly have not suffered much from George W. Bush's "war on terrorism."[30] The direct victims have primarily been in Iraq and Afghanistan. The indirect victims have largely been in authoritarian states, which have been allowed to get on with "business as usual" in return for anti-terrorism cooperation, and more generally in the Third World as a whole, where the benevolent power and capacity of the United States to advance peace, and social, economic, and political development has suffered. However, if we move back to Swedish law, we see the Swedish parliament has accepted that criminalization of financing of terrorism and inchoate offences (such as preparation for acts of terrorism) is necessary, as are more extensive police or intelligence powers. Yet, it has also seen the risk for mistaken use and overuse of these powers, and has shown an awareness that increased criminalization and increased police powers should not contribute towards the very problem—alienation—they were designed to guard against.

NOTES

* Professor in Public International Law, Uppsala University Faculty of Law. The present chapter has been partly written within the framework of the multidisciplinary research programme "Impact of Religion: Challenges for Society, Law and Democracy," funded by the Swedish Research Council 2008–2018. See Uppsala University, Uppsala Religion and Society Research Centre, at www.impactofreligion.uu.se.

1. See Bill 1994/95:23 at 52–54.
2. Act on Defence Forces' Assistance to the Police in Combating Terrorism, 2006:343.
3. 2007:978.
4. Act on Measures to Prevent Certain Serious Crimes, 2007:979.
5. Act on Assumed Identities, 2006:939.
6. Act on Communications Interception for Defence Intelligence Purposes, 2008:717, § 1.
7. Act on Surrender from Sweden, 2003:1156, and the Ordinance on Surrender to Sweden according to the European Arrest Warrant, 2003:1178
8. Act on Special Controls over Aliens, 1991:572, § 11.

9. 2003:148.
10. 2002:444.
11. 2010:299.
12. 2009:62.
13. Act on Supervision of Certain Crime-Fighting Activities, 2007:980.
14. Ibid. at § 3.
15. Instrument of Government, ch. 2, § 6; European Convention on Human Rights, art. 8.
16. See Swedish ombudsman, JO Decision 2005-03-22, *Ahmed Hussein Mustafa Kamil Agiza* v. *Sweden*, Decision CAT/C/34/D/233/2003, UN Committee Against Torture (24 May 2005). Ex gratia compensation was later paid to the two victims.
17. See, in particular, *Saadi* v. *Italy*, [2008] ECHR 37201/06.
18. See Report of the Commission of Inquiry into Certain Police Methods, SOU 2010:103.
19. No. 54934/00 (29 June 2006).
20. Bill 2008/09:201.
21. See Security Protection Act 2009:966 and Ordinance 2009:969. SIUN also oversees the Military Intelligence Agency (MUST), which is limited to gathering of intelligence against external military threats. See the Defence Intelligence Activity Act 2000:130 and Ordinance 2000:131 as amended.
22. See, for example, N. Jareborg, "Vilken sorts straffrätt vill vi ha? Eller Om defensiv och offensiv straffrättspolitik, in Inkast i straffområdet" (Uppsala: Iustus, 2006); P. Asp and I. Cameron, "Terrorism and Legal Security—a Swedish and European perspective," in *De Lege Årsbook 2009* (Uppsala: Iustus, 2010).
23. Court of Appeal for Western Sweden, judgment B4645-10 (2009-03-02).
24. The person responsible for investigating how best to implement the norm, my university colleague Petter Asp, tried to minimize this risk by arguing that a court should always consider, before finding criminal responsibility, whether the risk that the public incitement or attempt would lead to a result was minimal. The legislator in the *travaux préparatoires* accepted this and in addition made clear that no criminal penalty should be imposed in "minor cases." Bill 2009/10:78 at 47–48.
25. See most recently, I. Cameron, "Blacklisting and Intelligence Accountability," in I. Leigh, H. Born, and A. Wills, eds., *International Intelligence Cooperation and Accountability* (Oxford: Routledge, 2011).
26. See, respectively, Court of Appeal (Svea hovrätt), 3 October 2005, B 3687-05, ILDC 280 SE (2005). Court of Appeal (Skåne and Blekinge) 9 November 2009, B 685-09. *Cf. Holder v. Humanitarian Law Project*, 130 S. Ct. 2705 (June 21, 2010). In the former Swedish case, money had been collected in Sweden by Swedish nationals and transferred out of the country to a foreign organization, which the court found was engaged in acts of terrorism in Iraq.
27. Bill 2011/12:179, Act 2012:801.
28. See, for example, T. Farer, *Confronting Global Terrorism and American Neo-conservatism* (Oxford: Oxford University Press, 2007).
29. See, for example, K. Nuotio, "Terrorism as a Catalyst for the Emergence, Harmonization and Reform of Criminal Law" (2006) 4 *J. Int'l. Crim. Justice* 998.
30. However, I can echo the point made by Amnon Lev, "The War on Terror and International Law: Towards a Continental Divide," Chapter 5 in this volume, that we should be puzzled as to why we so willingly embraced the "war on terrorism." Still, who knows? A day may come (of Chinese domination of world politics?) when Europeans remember fondly the *Pax Americana*.

PART FIVE:

Democratic Accountability, Human Rights, and the Rule of Law

CHAPTER 13

Terrorist Threats and Judicial Deference

JENS ELO RYTTER*

The increased terrorist threat since September 11, 2001, and the measures taken to counter it have accentuated the question of judicial deference in the field of national security. This chapter argues that, although there are indeed constitutional grounds for special judicial restraint in cases concerning national security and terrorism, those grounds do not justify the same degree of restraint on all questions, let alone an approach of general deference bordering on abstention. Accordingly, case law from European courts indicates that while judicial review in terrorism cases is carefully tailored to take into account the nature of terrorist threats and the expertise and responsibilities of the political branches, an essence of real judicial review remains even in emergencies. Generally speaking, European courts are not merely "rubber stamping" political counter-terrorism measures. Rather, since 9/11 the role of courts has become more prominent along with the increase in state counter-terrorism powers, which at times test the constitutional limits of political action.

GROUNDS FOR JUDICIAL RESTRAINT IN NATIONAL SECURITY CASES

In any democratic constitution based on the rule of law, courts are entrusted with interpreting and enforcing the law. This judicial function of courts extends to the protection of constitutional rights and liberties (as well as international human rights). While political branches have a democratic mandate and are thus in general pre-eminently responsible for balancing security and liberty (as they are with regard to balancing other basic societal interests), this does not hold true whenever the balancing encroaches upon constitutional and international human rights.[1] Behind the basic constitutional principles of human rights, the rule of law and the separation of powers lies the suspicion—based on historical experience—that unlimited and unchecked powers of government may lead to abuse and unwarranted encroachments on individual rights.

Therefore, the legal starting point for any discussion of judicial deference is the presumed competence of courts to review acts of the political branches for their conformity with constitutional and international rights. Any judicial deference must be justified on constitutional and institutional grounds. This also holds true whenever the executive or legislature encroaches upon individual rights and liberties in order to protect national security even in emergencies (e.g., by anti-terrorism measures). A government might suspend or derogate from rights in some circumstances, but even then courts may review the legality of such declarations. Thus, even in the field of national security, the burden of justification is on those in favour of deference, not on those favouring unrestricted judicial review.[2] This burden becomes only heavier as the degree of deference sought increases. Although some advocates of deference[3] would place the burden of justification on those seeking judicial review of national security decisions—thus reversing the institutional presumption—this opinion simply does not reflect the law as pronounced by European courts at either the national or supranational levels. Accordingly, such deference arguments are descriptively, as well as normatively, flawed.

A Strong Theory of Judicial Deference?

Some argue in favour of general judicial deference—at times bordering on abstention—in matters relating to national security and terrorism. For instance, American scholars Posner and Vermeule claim that "Government is better than courts or legislators at striking the correct balance between security and liberty during emergencies" and find that, consequently, "[during emergencies] the executive branch, not Congress or the judicial branch, should make the tradeoff between security and liberty."[4] Although they explicitly refer to emergencies only, their supportive argumentation would seem to have more general relevance to all cases concerning national security and terorrism.[5] Such a position is simply incompatible with the core position of individual rights in European constitutional thinking and human rights law. First, this argument of deference seems to presuppose that a straightforward cost-benefit trade-off between security and liberty is the decisive legal analysis.[6] It is not. Human rights are not based on this kind of utilitarian cost-benefit rationality, which has only a limited place in legal analysis. Rights are also based on morality and values, which are to be upheld as far as possible even when they collide with national security interests. That is why there is such a thing as absolute rights (e.g., the prohibition against torture).

More important, such a sweeping call for judicial deference contradicts the wisdom on which our constitutions are built: that is, acknowledging the risk of abuse inherent in unfettered powers. That is why independent courts of law have been entrusted with the protection of constitutional rights. While the executive and legislature together have the preeminent political responsibility for the common good (including providing security) and must decide delicate political questions, the judiciary has the preeminent constitutional role of protecting individual rights against encroachment by the political branches. The courts' legal responsibility not only ensures the place of moral values in public decision-making, but institutionally limits the power of the political branches, especially the executive. However, rejecting the deference argument in its broad form does not mean that the executive may not in terrorism matters sometimes be better suited than courts to assess the situation and take appropriate action. It does mean, however, that executive power can never be limitless or arbitrary, even at times when the legislature might seem to acquiesce.

Grounds for Special Judicial Restraint in Terrorism Cases

Leaving such sweeping claims of judicial deference aside, there might be more specific grounds for judicial restraint in national security and terrorism cases, which can be reconciled with our constitutional order, the protection of individual rights, and the separation of powers. It is one thing that judicial deference may be called for in any field of law, if only because some legal notions are so vague or political in nature that they are not easily enforceable in a court of law. Beyond this, we must look for other characteristics of measures relating to national security, including anti-terrorism measures, that might justify *special* judicial restraint in this field, having regard to the respective constitutional responsibilities and competences of the political branches and courts—what has been labelled "demarcation of functions" or "relative institutional competence."[7]

Judicial restraint is generally described as an approach by which courts allow the political branches some "leeway," a "margin of appreciation," or a "scope of discretion." Such language needs qualification. Judicial deference is not only a matter of how much; it is also a matter of what kind. Notably, judicial restraint may be exercised with regard to both legal questions based on fact (such as evidence, threat, or necessity) and legal questions based on norms (such as interpretation or proportionality). Furthermore, judicial restraint may relate to both procedural and substantive legal issues or rights. So the question is, what arguments might justify just what kind of judicial deference in terrorism cases? There are several grounds for varying degrees of deference:

1) *The stakes are high*: In emergency terrorism cases the stakes are extraordinarily high, so that the cost of failure may be serious, perhaps even disastrous.[8] This is a general argument for judicial restraint, which also forms the background to the other grounds for restraint mentioned below. The strength of this argument will vary with the level and urgency of the terrorist threat, and it will be relevant regardless of whether an emergency has been declared or could be said to exist.[9] Overall, the post-9/11 situation in the West could probably best be characterised as one of a heightened threat of terrorist attacks, at times and in certain states rising to a "mild" emergency. In Europe, the United Kingdom is the only state to have declared a state of emergency after 9/11, pursuant to Article 15 of the European Convention on Human Rights.

2) *Government's first responsibility:* The executive and the legislature have primary responsibility for national security and protecting the life of the nation. Although the political branches have many primary responsibilities in political matters, protecting the state and the security of its people is arguably the very first responsibility of government, and an original *raison d'etre* of state power and legitimacy. Thus, this argument seems especially relevant in the face of serious threats to national security and emergencies.[10] By its nature, it is a general argument for judicial deference.

3) *Government's expertise:* The executive with its expertise is better equipped than courts to assess national security risks and decide on what steps are necessary to counter it.[11] No doubt, this claim is credible. It is primarily an argument for some judicial restraint when it comes to reviewing substantial legal requirements based on fact (including predictions), which allows the executive and legislative branches a certain margin of appreciation as to assessment of the evidence, the nature of the threat, and the necessity and degree of rights restrictions. In contrast, subsequent

proportionality review should not be seriously affected by this argument, as proportionality analysis in the narrow sense is essentially a normative exercise subject to judicial evaluation.

4) *Secrecy of intelligence*: In protecting national security, secrecy is often of the essence, and so to ensure the effectiveness of intelligence work, the confidentiality of intelligence methods and sources must be protected. This is primarily an argument for the necessity of adjusting ordinary due process requirements in order to protect the essential secrecy of intelligence.

JUDICIAL RESTRAINT IN TERRORISM CASE LAW

Examples from European case law show how and to what extent European courts are actually deferring to the political branches in terrorist cases. Attention here will be on case law from the European Court of Human Rights (ECtHR) in Strasbourg, the European Court of Justice (ECJ) in Luxembourg, and national courts in Denmark, the United Kingdom, Norway, and Germany.

Accommodating Secrecy

Many different courts generally accept that the secrecy of intelligence is essential to the protection of national security. Accordingly, courts have in terrorism cases been willing to adjust the ordinary requirements of due process and relax judicial review of detention to the extent necessary to protect sensitive information. Judicial deference here takes the form of flexibility in interpreting rights and legal requirements, but does not entail abstention from review. Accordingly, courts have insisted on finding ways to preserve the essence of due process in terrorism cases. They have insisted on exercising independent and effective review, and have required some form of adversarial proceedings by which the authorities must establish or substantiate the factual basis for their assessment that a terrorist threat exists. Courts also evaluate the necessity of the government measures chosen to counter that threat, and have required that the government convincingly demonstrate the necessity of any temporary derogations from rights on account of a declared national security emergency.

The ECtHR recognises that in terrorist cases some restrictions of ordinary due process may be necessary to protect the secrecy of information relating to national security. Nonetheless, the essence of due process must be respected.[12] Whenever human rights are restricted, there must be access to effective and meaningful judicial review bearing on the factual basis, the legal classification, and the proportionality of the measure. The court has defined four minimum requirements:

- the court or other independent tribunal must be informed of reasons and factual basis for the restriction;
- the court or independent authority must be competent to reject the executive's assertion that there is a threat to national security if it finds it arbitrary or unreasonable;
- there must be some form of adversarial proceedings, if need be using a security-cleared special advocate, and the person affected must be able effectively to challenge the authorities' allegations against him or her on the basis of the open evidence; and
- the court or independent authority must be able to assess whether a fair balance has been struck between the individual's rights and national security.[13]

Secret surveillance presents a special problem, however, as the person affected cannot be informed; immediate due process with adversarial proceedings is therefore excluded. The ECtHR nevertheless recognises that secret surveillance can be necessary in a democracy. The requirement, then, is to make due process "as effective as can be" under the circumstances inherent in a system of secret surveillance (i.e., some system of a priori external control and ex post facto judicial review).[14]

The ECtHR has also accepted that judicial review of detention may be delayed in a situation of serious terrorist threat, but even so has upheld prompt review as of the essence, finding detention on remand of a terrorist suspect for little more than four days to be a violation of article 5(3) of the ECHR.[15] Even in case of an emergency where ordinary due process may be suspended to the extent strictly required, pursuant to Article 15, the Court has upheld due process requirements when the government could provide no justification as to why the immediate situation rendered judicial review of detention impossible.[16]

The ECtHR in the *Kadi* case[17] held that the principle of effective judicial protection applies in the field of counter-terrorism, albeit with restrictions necessary to ensure the efficiency of the measures and the secrecy of intelligence sources. The case concerned the freezing of assets belonging to suspected terrorist individuals and organisations, without those affected being informed of the reasons for the suspicion. The Court held that the rights of defence, in particular the right to be heard, had not been respected.[18]

The Danish Supreme Court has also upheld the European Convention requirements of due process in terrorism cases, despite post-9/11 legislative attempts by the Danish government to limit judicial review. The Danish parliament enacted legislation in 2002 empowering the executive to detain and deport aliens whom the intelligence service considered a danger to national security, without providing access for the courts to investigate the factual basis for this danger assessment. This was an apparent violation of Articles 5(4) and 13 of the ECHR. The Danish Supreme Court, in a decision from 2008,[19] reviewed the authorities' decision to detain a Tunisian terrorist suspect with a view to deporting him on the grounds that he posed a danger to national security. Based on secret surveillance, the intelligence service suspected the Muslim alien of having taken part in plans to kill the Danish cartoonist responsible for one of the infamous "Mohammad cartoons" in a Danish newspaper. The Court held that the authorities were required to provide some substantiation (to a standard of reasonable probability) that the assessment of the alien's danger to national security had a factual basis. The authorities were required to present the evidence necessary for such substantiation in an adversarial process, so as to preclude arbitrary detention, prohibited by Article 5(4) of ECHR. The Court unanimously held that the authorities had not fulfilled this requirement. In a subsequent proceeding, the intelligence service did reveal more information, but not enough to satisfy the Court, which therefore held the detention to be unlawful.[20] In another case involving a co-suspect, the demands were fulfilled, as the intelligence service had provided material evidence from searches and specific surveillance information, while the suspect had been fully able to counter the allegations in adversarial proceedings.[21]

In light of the 2002 legislation's incompatibility with the European Convention and the ECtHR's guidelines in *A and Others v United Kingdom*,[22] Parliament introduced in 2009 a special judicial process with partially closed proceedings and special advocates, which sought to ensure due process while at the same time protecting the confidentiality of secret intelligence information withheld from the person to be detained. On this basis, the Danish Supreme Court reviewed for a second time the decision to expel the above-mentioned Tunisian terrorist suspect, who by then had been ordered removed pursuant to the new process. The Court unanimously invalidated the decision once again on due process grounds, holding that the suspect had not been able to challenge effectively the allegations against him even with the special advocate. It did so because the open material released to the deportee did not specify the factual basis for the allegations (such as to time, place, and circumstances), but contained merely general allegations that did not permit the individual to know the case against him and adequately defend himself, despite the presence of the special advocate.[23]

The tough line of the Danish Supreme Court is not unique in Scandinavia. For example, the Norwegian Supreme Court, in a case concerning the expulsion of an Iraqi resident considered to be a terrorist threat, held that it was also competent to review the factual evidence on which the decision to expel was based. It could also determine whether the executive's assessment of the facts had been defensible, The fact that national security was involved justified only some limited judicial restraint in this respect.[24]

Deferential Review of Requirements for Restricting Substantive Rights

Most substantive rights under the ECHR are relative in that they may on certain conditions be restricted on, inter alia, national security grounds. It is perhaps this fact, in particular, that supports deference arguments in the European context.[25] Clearly, courts will and must not substitute their own assessment for that of the political authorities as to what is the best security policy.[26] The question is to what extent courts will review in terrorism cases the assessment of the political branches as to whether the legal requirements for restriction have been fulfilled (i.e., the categorisation of the facts as a threat, danger, or emergency, as well the rationality, necessity, and proportionality of the specific measures taken to counter it).

Categorisation: Threat, Danger, Emergency

A first condition of restricting rights in terrorism cases is that the individual suspect poses a personal threat or danger to national security, or, when a derogation of rights is called for, that the terrorist threat has created a general emergency under Article 15 of the ECHR. Although courts consider themselves competent to review this legal categorisation, it seems they will generally defer to the security assessment of the authorities, unless on the facts it appears arbitrary or indefensible. Regarding the existence of an "emergency," deference is almost complete, judicial intervention being reserved for outright abuses. The ECtHR has held that in reviewing terrorism cases, national courts must be competent to reject the executive's assertion that there is a threat to national security, if it finds it arbitrary or unreasonable.[27] When assessing the reasonable suspicion of terrorist activity, the Court has acknowledged the need for caution. However, this does not mean that the executive has a free hand to detain anyone at will; there must be judicial review of whether there is a plausible and objective basis for the suspicion.[28]

National courts have followed this approach. The U.K. House of Lords has held that while considerable deference is owed to the expertise of the executive, the notion of national security remains a legal construction subject to review.[29] The Norwegian Supreme Court, in the 2007 expulsion case mentioned above, held that courts should show restraint when considering the question of whether the evidence merits the conclusion that a person poses a threat to national security. Nevertheless, courts must still review whether that evidence supports that view.[30] The Danish Supreme Court, in the 2008 case already discussed,[31] examined on its own whether a person planning to kill the Mohammad cartoonist could rightly be considered a danger to national security. In this instance, the Court upheld the authorities' assessment in this respect, finding that killing a person for the reason that he had made a controversial cartoon of Mohammad could be considered an attempt to scare and intimidate the public and thereby undermine freedom of speech and public debate.

As for the existence of an emergency, the ECtHR allows a very wide margin of appreciation to national governments.[32] Thus, the Court has so far never overruled a government's claim that an emergency existed.[33] After 9/11, a similar deferential approach was taken by the House of Lords majority in the *Belmarsh Case*. Lord Bingham stated that great weight must be attached to the government's assessment that an emergency exists, as it is "a pre-eminently political judgment," where predictions of future events are uncertain. He recognized that "it would have been irresponsible not to err, if at all, on the side of safety."[34] Although several Law Lords were sceptical about the government's assessment, they allowed the government the benefit of the doubt.[35] Baroness Hale defined the outer limit of judicial deference as to the existence of an emergency as the situation where there is a manifest abuse of the emergency declaration.[36] Only Lord Hoffmann went so far as to reject outright the government's claim that there was a national emergency qualifying for derogation under Article 15.[37]

Rationality

Restrictive measures chosen by the authorities to counter terrorist threats must at least be rational,[38] useful in principle, and non-discriminatory. Generally, courts will strictly enforce these requirements in terrorist cases, even during declared emergencies pursuant to ECHR Article 15. The question of rationality came to the fore in the *Belmarsh Case*. The British Parliament had enacted legislation allowing indefinite detention of alien terrorist suspects, but not of British citizens posing a similar threat. The House of Lords (and subsequently the ECtHR) held this detention to be discriminatory on grounds of national origins, as there was no justification for the difference in treatment between aliens and citizens. The indefinite detention measure was therefore incompatible with Articles 5 and 14 of the ECHR. By excluding British terrorist suspects who posed just as much of a threat, the measure was not rationally tailored to its purpose of preventing terrorism. Accordingly, the discrimination against alien suspects was unnecessary, a conclusion that Lord Bingham found to be "irresistible."[39] The ECtHR agreed.[40] The insistence on treating aliens and citizens alike may be at odds with some constitutional law traditions.[41] In human rights terms, however, such equality is an inescapable result of the principle of non-discrimination. Indeed, the equality requirement should be a sobering exercise for governments contemplating new security measures, as they must recognise that any drastic measures must be applied to citizens, too.

Necessity

Whether a rational measure is necessary depends on factual assessments of the terrorist threat and the effectiveness of less intrusive alternatives. Generally, courts considerably defer to the executive in this regard. They allow the executive the benefit of the doubt, unless there appears prima facie to be less intrusive alternatives. Accordingly, in many terrorism cases, courts have applied a presumption of necessity, reversing the burden of proof by requiring the individual subject to counter-terrorism measures to prove that they are not necessary. Lord Slynn of the House of Lords, in *Rehman*, justified this cautious approach, remarking that the government "is undoubtedly in the best position to judge what national security requires even if his decision is open to review. The assessment of what is needed... is primarily for him."[42] The ECtHR has applied a similar approach with regard to secret surveillance[43] and when considering whether an emergency measure was "strictly required" under the derogation requirements of Article 15 of the ECHR.[44]

In Scandinavia, the Norwegian Supreme Court in the 2007 case mentioned above upheld the immigration authorities' decision to expel an Iraqi citizen from Norway on the grounds that this was necessary for the sake of national security. The Court held that the courts must generally leave the necessity of expulsion to the final decision of the executive in national security cases, intervening only in case of an outright abuse of authority.[45] Occasionally, when there appears prima facie to be less intrusive alternatives to a government's chosen measures, the necessity requirement has been more strictly enforced. In such cases, a court would require the executive to prove that less intrusive measures would be insufficient to meet the security threat. The House of Lords did this, for example, in the *Belmarsh Case*.[46] Accordingly, even emergency measures are subject to necessity review, as the ECtHR has confirmed.[47] However, so far the Court has only struck down emergency measures that have unduly restricted access to the judicial review of detention, or were irrational or discriminatory.

Proportionality

Courts will review anti-terrorism measures restricting individual rights as to their proportionality. Presumably, however, courts will not strike down on proportionality grounds measures which they accept as a rational and necessary response to a serious threat, unless they deem the measure to be manifestly excessive or disproportionate to the aim.

Proportionality is a normative question for which there is ultimately no rational balancing exercise. Proportionality depends in each case on the relative weight attached to the colliding interests and values involved. In terrorism cases, while the normative weight of rights remains constant, the weight of the colliding security interest increases with the seriousness and urgency of the threat. It follows from the proportionality principle that the more weighty the national security interest, the more likely it will outweigh the individual rights in question. This analytical exercise has nothing to do with judicial restraint. Rather, judicial restraint in proportionality review presupposes that the courts will relax their ordinary standard of balancing interests so as to allow the political branches some extra margin of discretion by only striking down those counter-terorrism measures which the courts deem to be manifestly excessive and disproportionate. The grounds for such restraint would be the national stakes involved and the government's responsibility for public safety, but not its expertise. In any case, courts generally deem themselves competent to review proportionality even in terrorism cases, including emergencies. The ECtHR in *A and Others* joined the House of Lords in the *Belmarsh Case* by underlining that "the question of proportionality is ultimately a judicial decision."[48]

The ECtHR has accordingly held that for there to be due process in terrorism cases, national courts must be able to assess whether the government has struck a fair balance between the individual's rights and national security.[49] The Court will, of course, independently review the proportionality of anti-terrorism measures. In *Gillan and Quinton* the Court held the British stop-and-search scheme introduced by the Terrorism Act 2000 violated rule-of-law requirements in Article 8 of the ECHR due to the risk of arbitrariness; the act in question conferred too broad of a discretion on the police. This might seem a very intrusive judgment to some, considering the relative harmlessness of stop-and-searches compared to other anti-terrorism measures. However, the Court was also impressed by statistical information showing that out of hundreds of thousands of searches undertaken (the number increasing by the year), not one had exposed a terrorist offence. The measure had simply had no effect.[50] Thus, the measure was useless and therefore manifestly disproportionate. Presumably, targeted measures of surveillance will generally be more effective and less arbitrary, and thus easier to justify. Targeted measures will also more easily be approved by the courts. Presented with requests for warrants to make secret surveillance or searches, courts will almost always approve, whether because of judicial deference or because such measures are only requested on reasonable grounds.[51] It would seem likely that proportionality review will be less strict when the stakes are high, but manifest excesses are still unlikely to pass. There were indications in the *Belmarsh Case* that even in the post-9/11 emergency, the House of Lords would not have accepted indefinite detention without trial even if it had been applied to all without discrimination.

In Denmark, the 2008 Act providing for tightened control orders—obligations of reporting and residence, to be imposed on aliens who are subject to deportation, but cannot be forced to leave the country on *non-refoulement* grounds—similarly appears to be overbroad. It serves purposes beyond security; in reality, it arguably aims to make the life of these aliens so hard that they eventually choose to leave the country, regardless of any risks to their personal safety abroad. The Act may not be irrational in that it does control aliens thought to be a security risk, but it would seem manifestly disproportionate for those aliens who are in fact not a security threat, yet fall under the Act. Harsh restrictions on movement and residence (similar to control orders in the United Kingdom) may not amount to a deprivation of liberty under Article 5 of ECHR, but they still seriously restrict the liberty of movement. Such a restriction requires substantial justification under Article 2 of Additional Protocol 4 to the ECHR. Accordingly, a recent Danish Supreme Court ruling struck down as disproportionate a specific control order based on the Danish 2008 Act. The order was served on an Iranian citizen convicted of drug dealing in Denmark, who could not be deported to Iran due to a risk of torture in his country of origin. The order obliged the Iranian to reside in a specific holding center and to report to the police three times a week, for the purpose of knowing his whereabouts should expulsion eventually become possible. The order had been in force for some five years, while the terms had been tightened after the coming into force of the 2008 Act—the residence requirement had been upheld throughout, while in 2009 the reporting requirement had been extended from one to three times a week. The Supreme Court considered the order to be a substantial restriction on the alien's freedom of movement under Article 2 of Additional Protocol 4 to the ECHR. According to the Court, there was no indication that the Iranian might want to hide from the police, or that he was likely to commit another crime; furthermore, there was—after five years—still no prospect of executing the expulsion order against him. On this background, the Court unanimously held that the control order imposed on the Iranian was (or had at least after five years become) a disproportionate interference with his freedom of movement, incompatible with Article 2 of Additional Protocol 4 to the ECHR.[52]

Absolute Rights

There are core basic rights from which no derogation is allowed under either the ECHR or international law, even in times of a public emergency. European courts strictly uphold these prohibitions even in cases related to terrorism. These include rights not to be tortured or deported to a risk of torture, right not to be indefinitely detained without trial, and a right to life.

Torture

The ECtHR has consistently affirmed the absolute nature of the prohibition of torture in Article 3 of the ECHR and other international conventions. This prohibition allows no exceptions even in times of emergency, and applies regardless of the conduct of the person or the need to combat terrorism.[53] The absolute prohibition of torture also has an extraterritorial effect that precludes the deportation of persons who run a real risk of being subjected to torture in the receiving state. This prohibition on deportation applies regardless of whether the person is considered dangerous, even though the ECtHR recognises "the immense difficulties faced by states in protecting their communities from terrorist violence."[54] As these and many more cases show, the Court strictly enforces the absolute prohibition of torture, regardless of the weight and urgency of the competing interest in preventing terrorism and saving lives.[55]

Indefinite Detention without Trial

During normal times, preventive detention without trial in the fight against terrorism is incompatible with the right to liberty under international law;[56] it is not entirely clear whether an emergency short of war might justify indefinite detention without trial in extraordinary circumstances. This would, however, be clearly problematic in a state based on the rule of law.[57] When the *Belmarsh Case* came before the House of Lords, the alien terrorist suspects had been detained for some three years and were unlikely to be released anytime soon. As noted earlier, the House of Lords held the act to be discriminatory in contravention of the ECHR and thus had no need to take a definitive stand on indefinite detention without trial as an emergency measure. However, several of the Law Lords expressed serious reservations in *obiter dicta* as to the justifiability of such measures in general, implying that they might not have approved such a detention scheme, even if it had been applied to aliens and citizens alike.[58]

The Right to Life

In a much debated decision from 2006, the German Constitutional Court struck down parts of the new Aviation Security Act, which the parliament had passed in 2005 as a response to 9/11 and a 2003 German incident where a mentally disturbed man had hijacked a small airplane, threatening to fly it into the European Central Bank in Frankfurt. The Act authorised the German military to shoot down a civilian airplane if it had been hijacked for the purpose of being used as a terrorist bomb and to destroy it would save lives on the ground. The Constitutional Court struck down the Act, holding it to be incompatible with the protection of human dignity under the German constitution. Human dignity is the supreme value of the German constitutional order, which according to the Court rules out any possibility of using the individual as an object of the state. In the Court's view, this was exactly what the Aviation Security Act allowed. By authorising state officials to kill innocent and helpless passengers wilfully in order to save the lives of others, the Act disregarded the worth and human dignity of the passengers. This could not be constitutionally justified under any circumstances, regardless of how certain a terrorist attack might seem and of the number of lives that would likely be saved by shooting down a hijacked plane. This highly moral decision is as far as one can get from a cost-benefit analysis of rationality, as it prioritizes a fundamental, absolute principle over any balancing exercise.[59]

CONCLUSION

A constitution calls upon courts to review the acts of the political branches to ensure their compatibility with constitutional and international human rights norms. This power of judicial review also encompasses counter-terrorism measures. Consequently, a sweeping doctrine of judicial deference in terrorism cases is incompatible with constitutional government. Nevertheless, there are constitutional grounds which may justify some special judicial restraint in terrorism cases. Governments (and legislatures) have primary responsibility for the protection of national security; the consequences of inaction can be disastrous. The expertise as to what is necessary in this respect mostly lies with the executive, which moreover has a legitimate need of secrecy to protect national security. However, the increased terrorist threat since 9/11 has not, it seems, paralysed European courts in their constitutional role as protectors of individual liberties and rights. The case law highlighted in this chapter indicates that, generally, European courts exercise real judicial review of anti-terrorism measures, albeit in a tailored fashion. They will flexibly enforce basic due process (including access to independent review, adversarial proceedings, and the right to know the factual basis of a charge), strictly enforce absolute rights, and ensure the rationality of rights restrictions. They will, however, exercise more restraint when reviewing questions relating to the existence of a threat and the necessity of the measures taken to counter it. Finally, European courts do generally uphold proportionality review even in times of emergency, to avert government excesses.

In the decade since 9/11 the power of the executive to counter terrorism has naturally increased. This has been to some extent at the expense of individual liberty and legal certainty. At the same time, however, and for that very reason, the role of the judiciary has also increased, as the political branches have tested the constitutional limits of their power. Accordingly, in European cases, judicial review in terrorist cases is more than mere window dressing. It sometimes leads courts to overrule executive measures or legislative schemes adopted in the fight against terrorism, even during a declared emergency. For instance, the ECtHR has made it clear that states may not subject or expel terrorist suspects to torture, the German Constitutional Court has forbidden the authorities from shooting down a hijacked civilian airplane to avert a terrorist attack, the British House of Lords has denounced the discriminatory detention of alien terrorist suspects, and the Danish courts will not allow the government to detain and deport alien terrorist suspects on the basis of secret evidence. As these examples show, it is crucial that judicial review be effective, even if it must be cautious. Too much judicial restraint might be as dangerous as too little, because it might reduce the constitutional function of courts into rubber-stamping political action, thereby providing the latter with a legal legitimacy it may not deserve.[60]

Some will argue that the cost to national security flowing from judicial intervention is too high compared to the gains in individual liberty and legal certainty which is furthered by such intervention. However, this is a normative assertion that simply misses the mark. This is because the European constitutions of today, as well as the international human rights commitments undertaken by European states, are simply not based on the mere utilitarian calculations proposed by some supporters of judicial deference and strong executive power. These constitutions are instead built on values, which inform the contents of domestic constitutional rights and human rights law. In accordance with the principle of separation of powers, the courts are ultimately entrusted to protect those values against even weighty government interests. Counterarguments in favour of deference, especially where it leads to judicial abstention, simply do not reflect the prevailing European legal order. In establishing that order, constructed in the aftermath of the Second World War, we Europeans have accepted that there is a price to be paid for upholding our values and liberties—even in the face of terrorism and other threats to our common security.

NOTES

* Professor of Constitutional Law, University of Copenhagen Faculty of Law.

1. This point was strongly emphasised by Lord Bingham on behalf of the House of Lords in *A and Others* v. *Secretary of State* [2004] UKHL 56 at para. 42.
2. For a different view, see Eric Posner and Adrian Vermeule, *Terror in the Balance: Security, Liberty, and the Courts* (Oxford: Oxford University Press, 2007) at 29. They argue that because, during emergencies, U.S. courts have deferred heavily to the executive branch, critics should have the burden of justification. Whether or not this is a reasonable line of argument in the American context, European courts have not deferred to this extent, even during emergencies.
3. Ibid.
4. Ibid. at 6 and 5, respectively. See also ibid. at 43 and 53–54.
5. Ibid. at 31, 56, 115 and especially 256.

6. Ibid. at 12, 28, and 40; see also Adrian Vermeule, "Security and Liberty: Critiques of the Trade-Off Thesis," Chapter 2 in this volume.
7. See David Dyzenhaus, "Deference, Security and Human Rights," in B.J. Goold and L. Lazarus, eds., *Security and Human Rights* (Oxford: Hart, 2007) at 125–39; see also *A and Others, supra* note 1 at para. 29 (*per* Lord Bingham).
8. See Posner and Vermeule, *supra* note 2 at 119; see also *Secretary of State v. Rehman* [2001] UKHL 47, para. 62 (*per* Lord Hoffmann); *A and Others, supra* note 1 at paras. 29 (*per* Lord Bingham), 79–80 (*per* Lord Nicholls), 112 and 116 (*per* Lord Hope), 154 (*per* Lord Scott), and 226 (*per* Baroness Hale).
9. See *Brogan and Others v. United Kingdom* (29 November 1988) App. no. 11209/84, 11 EHRR 117 at para. 48; *A and Others v. United Kingdom* (19 February 2009) App. no. 3455/05, 49 EHRR 29 at para. 216.
10. See *Ireland v. United Kingdom* (18 January 1978) App. no. 5310/71, 2 EHRR 25 at para. 207.
11. See, for example, *Rehman, supra* note 8 at paras. 26 (*per* Lord Slynn), 57, and 62 (*per* Lord Hoffmann).
12. See, for example, *Chahal v. United Kingdom* (15 November 1996) App. no. 22414/93, 23 EHRR 413 at para. 131 (violation); *Al-Nashif v. Bulgaria* (20 June 2002) App. no. 50963/99, 36 EHRR 655 at paras. 136–37 (violation); *A and Others, supra* note 9 at para. 205.
13. See, for example, *Al-Nashif, supra* note 12 at para. 137; *A and Others, supra* note 9 at paras. 218 and 220.
14. *Klass and Others v. Germany* (6 September 1978) App. no. 5029/71, 2 EHRR 214 at para. 69; *Association for European Integration and Human Rights v. Bulgaria* (28 June 2007) Appl. no. 62540/00, ECHR 533 at para. 99.
15. *Brogan, supra* note 9 at paras. 61–62.
16. *Aksoy v. Turkey* (26 November 1996) App. no. 21987/93, 23 EHRR 553; *Demir and Others v. Turkey* (23 September 1998) App. nos. 21380/93, 21381/93 and 21383/93, 33 EHRR 43; *Nuray Sen v. Turkey* (17 June 2003) App. no. 41478/98, ECHR 297.
17. *Kadi & Al Barakaat International Foundation v. Council and Commission* (C-402/05 and C-415/05), [2008] ECR I-6351.
18. Ibid. at paras. 335–53.
19. Danish Supreme Court, 2 July 2008, in *Ugeskrift for Retsvæsen* 2008, 2394 *et seq.*
20. Danish Supreme Court, 19 November 2008, in *Ugeskrift for Retsvæsen* 2009, 426 *et seq.*
21. Ibid. at 420 *et seq.*
22. *A and Others v. United Kingdom, supra* note 9.
23. Danish Supreme Court (24 June 2011) *Ugeskrift for Retsvæsen* 2011, 2695 *et seq.*
24. Norwegian Supreme Court (8 November 2007) in *Norsk Retstidende* 2007, 1573 at para. 49. See also *Rehman, supra* note 8 at para. 54 (*per* Lord Hoffmann).
25. See *Murray v. United Kingdom* (28 October 1994) App. no. 14310/88, 19 EHRR 193 at paras. 90–91; *Al-Nashif, supra* note 12 at para. 137; See also *Rehman, supra* note 8 at paras. 26 (*per* Lord Slynn), 28 (*per* Lord Steyn), 50–54, 57, and 62 (per Lord Hoffmann).
26. See *Klass, supra* note 14 at para. 47; *Murray, supra* note 24 at para. 90–91; *A and Others, supra* note 9 at para. 202.
27. See *Al-Nashif, supra* note 12 at para. 137; *A and Others, supra* note 9 at paras. 218 and 220.
28. *Murray, supra* note 24 at paras. 58 and 63.

29. *Rehman, supra* note 8 at para. 29 (*per* Lord Slynn), 50, 53, and 56 (*per* Lord Hoffmann).
30. Norwegian Supreme Court, *supra* note 23 at 1573, paras. 51–58.
31. Danish Supreme Court, *supra* note 18 at 2394.
32. *Ireland, supra* note 10 at para. 207; *Brannigan and McBride v. United Kingdom* (25 May 1993) App. no. 14553/89 and 14554/89, 17 EHRR 539 at para. 43; *A and Others, supra* note 9 at para. 173.
33. See A. Mokhtar, "Human Rights Obligations v. Derogations: Article 15 of the European Convention on Human Rights" (2004) 8 *International Journal of Human Rights* 65 at 69; D.J. Harris, M. O'Boyle, E.P. Bates, and C.M. Buckley, *Harris, O'Boyle & Warbrick: Law of the European Convention on Human Rights*, 2d ed. (Oxford: Oxford University Press, 2009) 625; *A and Others, supra* note 1 at paras. 28 (*per* Lord Bingham), 165 (*per* Lord Rodger).
34. *A and Others* (HL), *supra* note 1. at para. 29 (*per* Lord Bingham), 79–80 (*per* Lord Nicholls), 112, 116 (*per* Lord Hope), 154 (*per* Lord Scott), 166 (*per* Lord Rodger), and 226 (*per* Lord Hale).
35. Ibid. at paras. 26 (*per* Lord Bingham), 154 (*per* Lord Scott), 165 (*per* Lord Rodger).
36. Ibid. at para. 226 (*per* Lord Hale).
37. Ibid. at para. 96.
38. See, for example, ibid. at para. 30 (*per* Lord Bingham) and even Posner and Vermeule, *supra* note 2 at para. 17.
39. *A and Others* (HL), *supra* note 1 at paras. 35, 43, and 68 (*per* Lord Bingham), 76–77 (*per* Lord Nicholls), 97 (*per* Lord Hoffmann), 129–32 (*per* Lord Hope), 155–56 (*per* Lord Scott), 188–89 (*per* Lord Rodger), 228, and 231 (*per* Lord Hale).
40. *A and Others* (E.Ct.H.R.), *supra* note 9 at para. 186.
41. For a critical account, see Posner and Vermeule, *supra* note 2 at 121 and 123–27. See also David Jenkins, "Citizenship and the Limits of Process since 9/11," Chapter 10 in this volume.
42. *Rehman, supra* note 8 at para. 26 (*per* Lord Slynn).
43. *Klass, supra* note 14 at para. 59.
44. *Ireland, supra* note 10 at para. 214. See also *Brannigan, supra* note 31 at para. 51.
45. Norwegian Supreme Court, *supra* note 23 at 1573, paras. 56–58.
46. *A and Others, supra* note 1 at paras. 35, 44 (*per* Lord Bingham), 76–77 (*per* Lord Nicholls), 121, 126 (*per* Lord Hope), 155 (*per* Lord Scott) 167 (*per* Lord Rodger), and 228 (*per* Lord Hale).
47. *A and Others, supra* note 9 at para. 184.
48. Ibid.
49. See, for example, *Al-Nashif, supra* note 12 at para. 137; *A and Others, supra* note 9 at paras. 218 and 220.
50. *Gillan and Quinton* (12 January 2010) App. no. 4158/05, 50 EHRR 45 at para. 84.
51. In Denmark, there is evidence suggesting that during the Cold War the courts almost invariably approved requests by the National Security and Intelligence Service for a court warrant to perform telephone tapping. See *PET-kommissionens beretning, Bind 4: PET's virkemidler* (Copenhagen, 2009) at 191–96. The situation is unlikely to have changed much since. The situation in other countries is not likely to be much different.
52. Danish Supreme Court judgment (1 June 2012) Case 10/2011.
53. See *Ireland, supra* note 10 at para. 163; *A and Others, supra* note 9 at para. 126.
54. See *Chahal, supra* note 12 at paras. 79–80; *Saadi v. Italy* (28 February 2008) App. no. 37201/06, 49 EHRR 30 at paras. 125–27.

55. On kidnapping, see also *Gäfgen v. Germany* (1 June 2010) App. no. 22978/05, 52 EHRR 1.
56. See *A and Others, supra* note 9 at para. 172.
57. See *Siracusa Principles on the Limitation and Derogation Provision in the International Covenant on Civil and Political Rights* (1984) at para. 70b.
58. *A and Others, supra* note 1 at para. 76 (*per* Lord Nicholls), 97 (*per* Lord Hoffmann), and 155 (*per* Lord Scott).
59. German Constitutional Court (15 February 2006) Case 1, BvR 357/05 at paras. 118–39.
60. See, for example, Dyzenhaus, *supra* note 7; See also *A and Others, supra* note 1 at para. 41 (*per* Lord Bingham).

CHAPTER 14

Open Secrets in U.S. Counter-Terrorism Policy

AMANDA JACOBSEN*

Over the past decade, following the September 11, 2001, terrorist attacks on the United States of America, there has been a proliferation of open secrets concerning U.S. counter-terrorism policy. The concept of "open secrets" refers to information that is officially secret and, therefore, not publicly acknowledged by government officials, but that is, nonetheless, widely acknowledged in the public by unofficial sources. The rise of open secrets concerning U.S. counter-terrorism activity stems from the convergence of two major trends. On the one hand, due to new security threats brought to light by the terrorist attacks of September 11, a new imperative has grown within the United States for government control over information related to terrorist threats. On the other hand, due to changing social norms and developments in technology, information has become more widely accessible, broadly sourced, and rapidly and cheaply distributed than ever before, leading to a decline in government authority over information. Thus, while the U.S. government increasingly asserts a national security interest in keeping information under official seal, the ability for that information to be confirmed by unofficial or nongovernmental sources is also increasing. As a result, when it comes to counter-terrorism, open secrets have become commonplace.

To date, what little attention that has been paid to this phenomenon has focused principally on how to prevent the release of secret information into the public domain. The focus of this chapter, however, is on the decision to maintain official secrecy over information that is open to the public. Although open secrets are not a new legal phenomenon, the prevalence of open secrets in U.S. counter-terrorism policy raises questions regarding what ends are being served by this decision, how effectively, and at what costs. Several explanations may be provided for the decision by the U.S. government to maintain official secrecy concerning its counter-terrorism activity after that information has become public, including domestic politics, international diplomacy, and legal accountability. However, the explanation that is repeatedly provided by U.S. government officials, namely, that withholding official acknowledgment of this information is important for the prevention of future terrorist attacks and the security of the nation is far from evident. To the contrary, maintaining open secrets appears to have many negative consequences—not only for national security, but also for democracy and the rule of law.

THE POST-9/11 IMPERATIVE FOR GOVERNMENT CONTROL OVER MORE INFORMATION

Whereas the U.S. government previously responded to terrorist threats principally under a crime and punishment paradigm, relying on the public sanction of wrongful acts to deter future wrongful conduct, in the aftermath of 9/11, a new imperative has been placed upon the prevention of future terrorist attacks. In light of the sheer magnitude of destruction that can be wrought by an individual act of terrorism, a widespread consensus has emerged that society can no longer afford to absorb the "first blow," especially at the hands of suicide bombers, for whom the threat of retributive punishment is likely to have little deterrent effect. Instead, government officials are increasingly being called upon to predict where terrorist threats will arise and to intervene before those threats can materialize, thus placing a premium on government control of information related to terrorist threats.

The scope of the information that the government seeks to control has also become more expansive, not only as a result of the government's increased focus on inchoate activity, but also because the threats themselves are more diverse and more widespread. The threat of terrorism is not bound by the confines of a nation-state or territory, and its targets are often civilian, or even pedestrian. Indeed, today, everything is a potential target: airports, railways, shopping malls, sporting events, monuments, water supplies. The list of potential targets is endless.

In addition, the need to protect information related to these targets is heightened by the unprecedented capacity for terrorists to obtain, analyze, and disseminate huge amounts of information related to their mission. According to former Secretary of Defense Donald Rumsfeld, an Al Qaeda training manual recovered in Afghanistan instructed its trainees that by "[u]sing public sources openly and without resorting to illegal means, it is possible to gather at least 80 percent of all information required" for terrorist operations.[1] An incredible amount of information is available via the Internet with little to no monetary or temporal investment, making the threat of terrorist use of information both instantaneous and perpetual.

In response to these new threats, the U.S. government has taken several steps to increase its control over information related to terrorist activity. Foremost, government agencies have wielded their classification authority more broadly,[2] classifying more information, declassifying less, and increasing the use of Freedom of Information Act (FOIA) exemptions, including by the creation of a new category of exemption for "critical infrastructure information."[3] Moreover, for the first time in history, classification authority was given to various organizations not typically considered within the security sector, including the Department of Agriculture, the Environmental Protection Agency, and the Department of Health and Human Services.[4] The government also engaged in a massive reclassification project, in which tens of thousands of documents, previously declassified and released to the public, were reclassified and removed from the National Archives, presidential libraries, and other public record collections.[5] Beyond classification, government agencies have identified dozens of new categories of "sensitive but unclassified" information, deemed too sensitive for public disclosure.[6] In addition, government agencies have increasingly invoked the "mosaic theory," arguing that even trivial or innocuous information must be withheld from the public, if it might be used in combination with other information to create a dangerous picture.[7]

While information-sharing between executive agencies became a major priority in the aftermath of 9/11,[8] outside the confines of this interagency exchange, examples of government secrecy in the aftermath of 9/11 abound: the U.S. government held hundreds of unidentified "ghost prisoners" in unacknowledged "black sites" around the globe,[9] covertly transferred hundreds more by extraordinary rendition,[10] conducted secret surveillance of American citizens without warrant,[11] restricted public access to court proceedings,[12] sealed entire dockets,[13] expanded the use of the state secrets privilege,[14] withheld information from Congress,[15] denied access to investigative bodies,[16] compelled companies to secretly hand over client records,[17] and refused to disclose legal and policy standards governing its conduct in the "war on terrorism."[18] Although some of these practices may have since been abandoned, what remains over ten years later is a heightened emphasis on government secrecy in counter-terrorism efforts.

Of course, secrecy is by no means new to U.S. national security policy.[19] However, in the post-9/11 period, secrecy has become an enormous part of the establishment. As *The Washington Post* reported in 2010, the number of buildings that have been constructed for top secret intelligence work in Washington, DC, and the surrounding area since September 2001 "occupy the equivalent of almost three Pentagons or 22 U.S. Capitol buildings."[20] Moreover, according to the *Post*, an estimated 854,000 people, nearly 1.5 times as many people as live in Washington DC, hold top secret security clearances. Notably, the *Post*'s investigation focused solely on "top secret" government activity, because the amount of activity classified at the "secret" or "confidential" level was simply too large to track accurately.

THE INFORMATION REVOLUTION AND TRANSPARENCY MOVEMENT

At the same time as the government's initiative to control information related to terrorist threats has expanded, other developments have meant that information has become more open and accessible than ever before. At the global level, the overarching trend both in law and policy has been toward greater public access to information. Beginning in the years before 9/11 and continuing in the years thereafter, a powerful transparency movement has been making its way across the globe. Truth commissions have been established to expose human rights abuses in dozens of countries,[21] the United Nations and other international human rights bodies have provided formal recognition of the right to information as a fundamental right,[22] and a new liberal consensus has emerged making freedom of information a threshold requirement for any government to be considered a democracy. Whereas, in 1990, only thirteen countries had adopted access to information laws, today, over ninety countries now recognize a right to government-held information, with eighty of those countries recognizing it as a constitutional right.[23] Moreover, the majority of these laws have been adopted in the last ten years (i.e., in the post-9/11 period).[24]

In the United States, although the FOIA has an established history, government transparency has recently become a popular topic, backed by widespread bipartisan support. Poll data shows that about 80 percent of Americans think making the federal government more open and accountable is an important priority.[25] Even President George W. Bush, who some have dubbed the "Secrecy President,"[26] took several steps to enhance government transparency before he left office[27] and President Obama came into office at least promising an "unprecedented era of openness."[28]

In addition to a political transparency movement, however, major technological developments are also promoting the openness of information. Today, information can be shared instantaneously between vast networks of people at almost zero economic cost and with virtually unlimited space available for each subject. Indeed, the amount of information that exists in the digital universe today is approximately thirty-million times the amount of information in all of the books that have ever been written.[29] Moreover, digital information is growing exponentially: in the past five years alone, the digital universe has grown ten times in size and, in the decade ahead,[30] it is estimated that the information in the digital universe will grow by a factor of forty-four.[31] Perhaps more important, however, the ability to search for and find information has also improved tremendously. With such a vast wealth of information, instantaneously available to anyone with a good broadband connection, it is hard not to believe that we are living in an unprecedented era of openness.

What is unique about the information revolution, however, is not merely the amount of information that is now publicly accessible, or even how easily this information can be sorted or found; rather, it is the way people participate in the creation of information. With over two-billion people worldwide now engaged as routine Internet users,[32] the Internet has changed not only the ability of information to spread instantaneously and inexpensively across borders, but also served to empower people in terms of giving meaning to that information. Thus, Google prioritization and network newsworthiness are not decided merely by editors-in-chief, but by the number of people interacting with or linking to that information. As an example of how information is being developed from the bottom up and by piecemeal collaboration, one need only look at Wikipedia, the free, Web-based multilingual encyclopedia, written and edited collaboratively by individual volunteer contributors. Although people have always shared information with each other on a self-organized basis, it is only recently that this sector of society has become powerful enough to be able to have a national or even global impact on a widespread number of issues.[33]

One result of this development is that governments no longer control the bulk of information. More than 70 percent of the information available in the digital universe is created by individual Internet users.[34] Moreover, a globalized information commons means that information no longer has to appear in one country's press to affect that country's politics, undermining the "my country 'tis of thee" objection to the publication of sensitive information. This development, combined with how cheaply, easily, quickly, and widely information can be spread, has meant that it is exceedingly difficult, if not impossible, to stop the spread of information once it has entered the information commons.

This is not to say, however, that nations or other institutions can no longer constrain the flow of information. To be sure, the Internet has not become the borderless open space, where information moves free of geographic, economic, or governmental constraints, that many envisioned it to be in its earlier days.[35] Despite reports to the contrary, even WikiLeaks has not been engaging in "radical transparency," but rather has redacted names and other sensitive information from its disclosures.[36] Real-world considerations undoubtedly continue to compromise the free flow of information. Nonetheless, the impact of the Internet on access to and exchange of information has proved revolutionary. Blogs, wikis, and other Web 2.0 programs are changing the social order, multiplying the number of people who command authority and undermining the authority once afforded to government information. Moreover, although governments may still be able to assert their power to affect the spread of information, tight control over information may be inimical to economic productivity. As information has become more readily available, a culture has developed in which people have come to expect access to information, and society has come to depend on interconnected networks of communication, meaning that real-world costs also make openness imperative.

THE CLASH BETWEEN GOVERNMENT CONTROL OVER INFORMATION AND THE OPENNESS OF THE INFORMATION REVOLUTION

Deference for National Security Concerns

Over the past decade, where national security imperatives have come into conflict with openness initiatives, the national security imperatives have largely prevailed. Despite broad-based changes in the way information is being shared, the national security sector stands as an exception that belies the general trend of the transparency movement.[37] Notably, every right-to-information law recognizes a vast (and largely undefined) "national security" exception to its disclosure requirements, the use of truth commissions has been limited to collapsed regimes and "transitional justice," and, in the legal and political arenas, widespread deference continues to be provided when national security is at stake. This deference is reflected in public opinion polls conducted in December 2010, which found that 75 percent of Americans agree that the public should not be given access to information that "might affect" national security,[38] and almost 80 percent disapproved of even the limited number of U.S. diplomatic and military documents released by WikiLeaks.[39] Moreover, despite President Obama's pledge for an unprecedented era of openness and steps made in that direction by his administration,[40] when it comes in practice to protecting national security information, there is significant continuity between the Obama and Bush administrations.[41] Although openness agendas are prominently displayed on all of the U.S. intelligence community websites, the disclosures made by the intelligence community are, at best, records of historical relevance.[42]

The Rise of Open Secrets in the Name of National Security

Nonetheless, despite the political and legal deference to secrecy in the national security sector, this sector is being impacted by the newfound openness of information. As a result of this countervailing trend, more and more information that the government agencies in this sector seek to classify is not under their exclusive ownership or authority, and, therefore, there has been a marked rise in the number of open secrets.

Several factors contribute to the rise in open secrets. Foremost, in the last ten years, the intelligence community has itself begun to realize that open source information often surpasses covertly obtained information in terms of quality, quantity, usability, speed, and costs.[43] As former director of the National Security Agency and former director of the Central Intelligence Agency Michael Hayden has stated, these days "secret information isn't always the brass ring" of the intelligence community.[44] As a result, the intelligence community incorporates more open source material into their classified materials, and overt and covert streams of intelligence become increasingly mingled. As Hayden explains: "The information is unclassified. Our interest in it is not."[45] A gray area has thus developed at the intersection of open source information and open source intelligence.

Second, with the rise in the number of different agencies with authority to classify or seal information, there has also been a rise of inconsistency in the classification and sealing processes. Claims of ownership over information may be made by multiple agencies in regard to the same substantive information, and what is a secret to one agency may not be to another.[46] Without a clear standard or agreement on what is secret, startling discrepancies in the classification and declassification practices of the various government agencies arise. Notably, the National Security Archive—an independent nongovernmental research institute and library located at George Washington University, which collects and publishes declassified documents obtained through the U.S. Freedom of Information Act—houses dozens of documents that have been marked both classified and unclassified by the government at the same time.[47]

Third, open secrets occur because the widespread disclosure of information does not automatically compel a change in the designation of information as classified.[48] Thus, information may remain classified long after it has been disseminated broadly to the public. For example, even though the Pentagon Papers were leaked forty-four years ago, and have been cited and circulated by academics and politicians repeatedly (including in open congressional hearings), it was only in June 2011 that the government officially declassified them.[49]

In addition, open secrets also result because some information is considered to be "born classified,"[50] even though it is not under the exclusive control of the government. For example, the U.S. government often claims secrecy over scientific information that is independently discoverable. Likewise, the firsthand experiences of individuals, who are not employed by the government, but who encounter government secret activity, are not under government control or ownership. As the world becomes more connected and information moves around the globe more freely, the old policies of containment have become increasingly difficult to enforce. As a result, in the last decade, open secrets have proliferated.

Notably, open secrets, as such, are not new. In the United States, the legal basis for open secrets was well-established before 9/11;[51] however, this precedent has been strengthened tremendously in the last ten years, as the government has asserted secrecy claims more broadly and the public has gained easier and wider access to information. Indeed, it is estimated that approximately 90 percent of government "secrets" are obtainable through open sources.[52]

The clearest example of open secrecy in post-9/11 America is probably seen in the government's treatment of the WikiLeaks disclosures. Even after these disclosures have been published and garnered tremendous international media attention, the U.S. government has continued to protect their potentially classified status, instructing government employees not to view these documents from home or at work.[53] Even though publicly available, the documents remain officially secret.[54] At the same time, however, the government refuses to confirm or deny that any individual document disclosed by WikiLeaks is in fact an official government document.[55] In addition, while government officials trumpet the danger created by the disclosures,[56] others note that many of the documents simply confirm what was already widely believed by the public.[57]

In the past ten years, rather than being the subject of one leaky source, many open secrets have been the product of gradual and repeated substantiation of this nature. In September 2006, for example, President Bush acknowledged that the United States had been operating "secret prisons" overseas since 2001.[58] However, the fact that the United States operated these prisons could, at that time, hardly have been considered a secret. *The Washington Post* had done a major "exposé" on these "secret prisons" almost one year prior to the President's admission[59] and, even before that, the existence of these facilities had been an open secret for years. In March 2002, President Bush himself announced that the United States had captured suspected terrorist abu Zubaydah and that he was being held in an undisclosed location.[60] Moreover, in 2002, 2003, and 2004, in the United States alone, the *New York Times*, *Washington Post*, *U.S. News & World Report*, and Human Rights Watch all reported on the existence of secret overseas detention centers being used for suspected terrorists.[61]

Likewise, a claim of secrecy has persisted in regard to extraordinary renditions and so-called "enhanced interrogation techniques" (such as waterboarding), despite repeated exposés and reports over the years. Moreover, even now—after the government has released a list of enhanced interrogation techniques that were authorized for use,[62] the Red Cross has released its interviews with "high value detainees" regarding their interrogations,[63] and many released detainees have published their own accounts of their experiences[64]—the only authorized interrogation technique that the government has officially acknowledged using is waterboarding: a technique the government says it used only on three detainees.[65] Nonetheless, in the habeas cases of these three detainees, as well as for the remaining detainees, the government argues against the detainees' ability to provide their own account of their experiences because, according to the government, this would give the imprimatur of official acknowledgment.[66] Likewise, in civil suits regarding the use of renditions—despite flight logs, eyewitnesses, and forensic evidence in the public domain to support these claims—the government has successfully argued for dismissal on grounds of state secrets.[67]

EVALUATING THE IMPACT OF OPEN SECRETS

The prevalence of open secrets concerning U.S. counter-terrorism policy raises two major questions: first, how effectively does the maintenance of official secrecy of open information serve national security interests, and, second, what costs are associated with the creation of open secrets?

Effectiveness

In court proceedings, as well as in the media, government officials routinely argue that the government must not be expected to provide official acknowledgment of its counter-terrorism policies because terrorists could use this information to carry out attacks and evade detection. It is not clear, however, that government refusal to acknowledge information officially is an effective means of preventing access to, or deterring reliance on, that information by potential terrorists.

Government officials often provide three main arguments in support of their position. First, they point out that government disclosure may heighten accessibility of information to terrorists, making attacks more likely. According to this argument, just because information exists in the public domain, does not mean that the government should point it out for terrorists. To the contrary, government restraint may help to insure that any attention brought to this information is isolated. As an example, during World War II, the *Chicago Tribune* published the fact that the United States had broken the Japanese code. As it happened, Japanese officials did not read the *Tribune* that day; however, had they been aware that their code had been broken, the United States would not have been able to use the code to its advantage in the Battle of Midway. Accordingly, even if it is not possible to prevent public disclosure of sensitive information, there may still be a security benefit to limiting accessibility. This argument is bolstered by the sheer volume of information that is available in the public domain these days. With so much information available, if attention is not drawn to dangerous information, its significance may easily be missed. Moreover, even in the age of the Internet, there is not instantaneous and complete revelation of the facts. Despite claims of "breaking news" and "exposés," these stories often build upon prior reports of the same information and tell a story that has developed gradually, or even been repeatedly conveyed.

This first argument loses credibility, however, when the information has already gained the attention of the world community, as clearly has been the case in regard to many of the open secrets pertaining to counter-terrorism that the United States maintains. Moreover, as news feeds become increasingly tailored to the individual based upon his or her interests, the accessibility of information becomes less and less a matter of mainstream attention. It bears questioning, therefore, from *whom* exactly the government is keeping the information secret. In the case of detainee abuse, for example, the United States obviously does not keep these methods a secret from the detainees who experienced the techniques firsthand. The Doonesbury cartoon at the start of this chapter makes this point: for the people who experience U.S. policies firsthand (as well as for anyone these people may tell about their experiences), American policies are not a secret. A key difference between the 1970s, when the "secret bombings" of Cambodia depicted in this Doonesbury cartoon took place, and today, however, is the connectivity of information. As Steven Aftergood of the Project on Government Secrecy has stated: "It would not be possible to conduct a secret war in Cambodia, as took place in the Nixon administration."[68] Indeed, it was literally within hours of the first not–officially acknowledged missile strikes in Yemen that amateur video appeared on YouTube, labeling the strikes as American.[69]

The second major argument that government officials raise is that there is a distinction between loose bits of information (such as an individual YouTube clip) and collected information. According to this argument, when information is collected together, it becomes more understandable and actionable. The government made this argument successfully in the *Progressive* case of 1979, in which the District Court for the Western District of Wisconsin enjoined the publication of an article purporting to reveal the "secret" of the hydrogen bomb; it did so, even though all of the information in the article was available in and had originated in the public domain.[70] Even at that time, however, the government eventually dropped its case, calling it moot after another author collected and independently published the information. Although it is true that information becomes more understandable and actionable when it is distilled, it is also true that the tendency of information is not to exist loosely and chaotically until the government chooses to analyze it. To the contrary, information wants to be organized and analyzed and cross-referenced. Accordingly, this government argument reduces to a question of delaying the collection of information, and, notably, as a result of advances in technology, the ability for people to connect and cross-reference information has only become more efficient.

Third, government officials argue that official disclosure bestows significance on information that unofficial reports cannot. As the D.C. Circuit Court of Appeals has stated: "It is one thing [for someone] to say that [a thing] is so, it is quite another for one in a position to know of it officially to say that it is so."[71] The official version of information undoubtedly still maintains special value. It is important, however, not to overestimate the deference afforded to the official version. Outside of the court system, a standard of proof that says that one cannot know something is a fact until a person in authority explicitly acknowledges it to be so, is not a standard to which the public generally adheres. In this generation, the official version of information is no longer the only, nor even the most, authoritative source. Belief in the supreme value of the official version ignores the flood of information reaching people, and assumes that greater heed will be paid to nuggets from the government than broadly based, publicly generated sources of information. To the contrary, even though the government has neither confirmed nor denied that any particular individual report appearing on the WikiLeaks website is an official government document, no one really doubts that the WikiLeaks documents are real. It is not clear, therefore, that withholding official acknowledgment of information in the public domain is an effective means of deterring terrorist reliance on that information.

Costs/Consequences

Even if a policy of government nondisclosure were effective, the second major question is what costs are attendant upon the maintenance of open secrets. At the outset, the existence of open secrets threatens to devalue the bright-line concept of a secret. As it becomes more common for officials, who are charged with safeguarding secrets, to encounter this "secret" information in the public domain, these officials face an increasing risk of becoming desensitized to the idea that secrets do not need to be tightly held. Indeed, the capacity to isolate sensitive information from non-sensitive information is a key precondition to the legitimacy of the government secrecy system. Loose classification standards undermine the integrity of the entire classification process, making it more difficult to ensure that vital secrets are maintained. In this way, excessive secrecy is self-defeating. The only effective way to curb leaks is to disgorge most of the information being held. The private sector is also learning this lesson: according to a February 2011 issue of *The Economist*, "[i]n the digital era of exploding quantities of data that are increasingly hard to contain, more companies are likely to become more transparent."[72] Attempts to keep such vast and fluid information secret by holding it more tightly are proving futile.

In addition, it seems clear that not acknowledging information may actually deprive government officials of the ability to obtain the best information. By refusing to acknowledge information, debate and dissent may be muted, important facts may be overlooked, and preexisting biases may be amplified. Although government officials are still able to collect information from uncleared scholars or experts, they cannot engage in an exchange of information. However, it is precisely this dialogue, facilitated by open, networked communication, which increases creativity and improves innovation. Thus, in regard to computer technology, it has become common practice for companies to make their source code visible for the world to see, so the community as a whole can help spot and solve problems.[73] Making information visible also creates the possibility of unforeseen synergies. For example, after eighteen years of his evading detection in the United States, what ultimately led to the capture of the so-called "Unabomber" was that a copy of his manuscript was widely distributed to the public; as a result, his brother, recognizing the writings, came forward and led the authorities to him.[74]

According to the U.S. government, the reason for creating new categories of "sensitive but unclassified" information was to allow information to be shared more freely and not be limited to people with security clearances. However, the use of the "sensitive but unclassified" categorization still relies on the concept of a "need to know," in which dissemination of information is triggered by the identification of people to whom the information should be given. A centrally controlled system of this nature continues to miss the importance of participatory involvement in the information revolution. Although openly secret information may be available, such that the public can approach the government with feedback, efforts to make the information less accessible and usable for terrorists may also have the cost of discouraging societal engagement with this information for beneficial uses. While those who have a distinct interest in the information may nonetheless seek it out, many who are not already interested may not take the time to look. Likewise, by not encouraging open exchange with and participatory involvement from the public, the government may lose the public's engagement and trust: a result that not only stifles communication, but also creates a problem for democracy.

Another major consequence of the U.S. government not having to acknowledge open secrets is a lack of democratic accountability. Account is taken only when it is a boon for the government, and as such, finding solutions to problems may be disincentivized. Without accountability, there is also greater susceptibility for government abuse of power. It is important to recognize, therefore, that there is not a simple one-to-one correlation between secrecy and security; several other factors weigh in the balance. Foremost, government officials often promote secrecy as a tool to obtain and maintain bureaucratic power.[75] From the viewpoint of secret-keepers, one of the main virtues of secrecy is the ability to deflect or dismiss criticism by pretending to possess more complete and more accurate information. According to Rodley B. McDaniel, the former Executive Secretary of the National Security Counsel, "[a]s a practitioner in the real world, it's about 90% bureaucratic turf, 10% legitimate protection of secrets, as far as I am concerned."[76] Thus, even before 9/11, the Bush administration had already started taking noticeable steps to increase secrecy within the executive branch,[77] and national security became a justification only after the fact. Moreover, the Obama administration readily acknowledges its role in the killing of Osama bin Laden, but refuses to acknowledge less popular covert operations, a pattern that has caused his administration to be accused of selective leaking for political gain.[78]

CONCLUSION

According to a surprisingly candid editorial written by former CIA officer Joseph Weisberg, the significance of official acknowledgment is largely a matter of political and legal accountability:

> Even if every foreign government in the world knows about our cover arrangements, countless diplomatic and legal problems would be created if we officially admitted that we use them... If the government openly admitted various C.I.A. activities, even those that are already well-known, it could also precipitate a great deal of negative news coverage in the foreign press. (It would create yet another public perception problem to admit we classify information because of public perception, which is one of the reasons the fiction is maintained that information is classified because it is secret.) In the end, then, the classification system serves a perfectly valid purpose. It draws a distinction between the information

> that the government does, and does not, want to discuss. What ends up classified may seem a bit perverse at times, such as when information in the public domain is ruled off limits for publication. But that's troubling only if you make the mistake of thinking that classified information is supposed to be secret.[79]

The troubling aspect of this explanation, of course, is that it has no roots in the rule of law. "[W]hat the government does and does not want to discuss" is not a valid legal distinction when it comes to classification,[80] for the reason that such unfettered discretion would undermine the rule of law. Government secrecy has many virtues, but in a rule-of-law society avoiding accountability cannot be one of them.

To be sure, the impact of official disclosure on foreign relations is a valid consideration and may, at times, warrant the government's classification of information. However, this is permissible only when official acknowledgment of public information could reasonably be expected to cause harm to the nation's security, a situation far more rare than the current number of open secrets would suggest. As Secretary of Defense Robert Gates admitted concerning the WikiLeaks disclosures: "Is this embarrassing? Yes. Is it awkward? Yes. Consequences for U.S. foreign policy? I think fairly modest."[81] All in all, too much deference is currently afforded to the government claim that withholding official acknowledgment of publicly available information is necessary for national security. Maintaining official secrecy of publicly available information does not only seem ineffective at deterring terrorist access to, understanding of, or reliance on that information; the maintenance of open secrets also comes with high costs, not only for democracy and for the rule of law, but even for national security itself.

Moreover, the U.S. government's refusal to acknowledge open information officially not only has political and diplomatic consequences, but also has an impact upon individual legal cases. For example, the officially classified status of the documents disclosed on WikiLeaks means that, although anyone in the public can view them online, the remaining Guantanamo detainees to whose cases they are relevant are not permitted to see them or even discuss them with their lawyers.[82] Likewise, with civil actions such as the *El Masri* or *Jeppesen* cases,[83] despite a plethora of information in the public domain to support these plaintiffs' claims, their cases are being dismissed outright, because the government says that the truth or falsity of this information is officially secret.[84] Access to justice is, therefore, denied to them. The greatest cost of open secrets, therefore, may be that of justice for individuals whose rights have been infringed by U.S. counter-terrorism measures. For this reason, if for no other, it is worth pushing back on the government's claimed need for open secrets.

NOTES

* Amanda Jacobsen is a Research Fellow at the University of Copenhagen Faculty of Law.

1. Donald Rumsfeld, "Memorandum from Secretary of Defense Rumsfeld to the Pentagon" (15 January 2003), online at http://www.fas.org/sgp/news/2003/01/dodweb.html.
2. See, for example, "[Annual] Secrecy Report Card," OpentheGovernment.org (2004–2010); see also "[Annual] Report to the President," Information Security Oversight Office (2001–2010).
3. Critical Infrastructure Information Act of 2002, 6 U.S.C. §§ 131–134 (25 November 2002).
4. Designation Under Executive Order 12958, Order of Sept. 26, 2002, Fed. Register, 67: 189 (Dep't of Agr.); Order of May 6, 2002, Fed. Register, 67: 90 (EPA); Order of Dec. 12, 2001, Fed. Register 66:239 (DHHS).
5. See, for example, Information Security Oversight Office, "Audit of the Withdrawal of Records from Public Access at the National Archives and Records Administration for Classification Purposes" (26 April 2006), online at http://www.archives.gov/isoo/reports/2006-audit-report.html.
6. See, for example, Government Accountability Office, "Report on Information Sharing," GAO-06-385 (17 March 2006), online at http://www.gao.gov/assets/250/249607.html.
7. See, for example, David Pozen, "The Mosaic Theory, National Security, and the FOIA" (2005) 115 *Yale L.J.* 628.
8. See, for example, "U.S. Intelligence Community, Information Sharing Strategy" (22 February 2008), online at http://www.fas.org/irp/dni/iss.pdf.
9. See, for example, Jason Burke, "Secret world of U.S. jails" *The Observer* (12 June 12 2004).
10. See, for example, Frontline, "Extraordinary Rendition" PBS (4 November 2007).
11. See, for example, James Risen and Eric Lichtblau, "Bush Lets U.S. Spy on Callers without Courts" N.Y. Times (16 December 2005).
12. See, for example, Michael Creppy, "Memorandum: Cases requiring special procedures" (21 September 2001), online at http://fl1.findlaw.com/news.findlaw.com/wp/docs/aclu/creppy092101memo.pdf.
13. See, for example, Michael J. Sniffen and John Solomon, "Thousands of Federal Trials Kept Secret" USA Today (5 March 2006).
14. See, for example, Steven D. Schwinn, "The State Secrets Privilege in the Post 9/11 Era" (2010) 30 *Pace L R.* 778.
15. See, for example, Kathleen Clark, "'A New Era of Openness?' Disclosing Intelligence to Congress under Obama" (2010) 26 *Constitutional Commentary* 3.
16. See, for example, U.S. Department of Justice, Office of the Inspector General, "A Review of the FBI's Involvement in and Observations of Detainee Interrogations in Guantanamo Bay, Afghanistan, and Iraq" (May 2008).
17. See, for example, U.S. Department of Justice, Office of Inspector General, "Review of the FBI's Use of National Security Letters" (9 March 2007).
18. See, for example, Senator Russ Feinberg, "Secret Laws" L.A. Times (8 May 2008).
19. See, for example, Report of the Commission on Protecting and Reducing Government Secrecy (3 March 1997) (finding a vast system of secrecy had developed within the American government over the eighty years prior).

20. Dana Priest and William M. Arkin, "Top Secret America" Washington Post (19 July 2010).
21. See, for example, Priscilla B. Hayner, "Truth Commissions: A Schematic Overview" (June 2006) 88 *ICRC* 862; Geoff Dancy, Hunjoon Kim, and Eric Wiebelhaus-Brahm, "The Turn to Truth: Trends in Truth Commission Experimentation" (1 January 2010), online at Social Science Research Network, http://ssrn.com/abstract=1611740.
22. See, for example, Joint Declaration of the UN Special Rappporteur on Freedom of Opinion and Expression, the OAS Special Rapporteur on Freedom of Expression and the OSCE Representative on Freedom of the Media, Nov. 26, 1999; 2nd Joint Declaration of 2004; European Convention on Human Rights, art. 10; *TASZ v. Hungary* (14 April 2009), App. No. 37374/05; *Kenedi v. Hungary* (26 May 2009), App. No. 31475/05; American Convention on Human Rights, art. 13; *Claude Reyes and others v. Chile* (19 September 2006) IACHR no. 151; Declaration of Principles on Freedom of Expression in Africa (October 2002).
23. Article 19, "Five Billion Now Have Right to Information" (28 September 2010).
24. Ibid.; see also Roger Vleugels, "Overview of all FOIA laws" (20 September 2010).
25. Cary Coglianese, "The Transparency President? The Obama Administration and Open Government," University of Pennsylvania Public Law and Legal Theory Research Paper Series, Paper No. 09-18, online at Social Science Research Network, http://papers.ssrn.com/sol3/papers.cfm?abstract_id=1433815.
26. See, for example, United States House of Representatives Committee on Government Reform—Minority Staff Special Investigations Division, "Secrecy in the Bush Administration" (14 September 2004).
27. See, for example, E-Government Act of 2002, Pub. L. 107-347 (17 December 2002); see also OPEN Government Act of 2007.
28. President Barack Obama, "Transparency and Open Government," Memorandum for Heads of Executive Departments and Agencies (12 January 2009).
29. International Data Corporation, "The Diverse and Exploding Digital Universe: An Updated Forecast of Worldwide Information Growth through 2011" (March 2008). See also International Data Corporation, "The Expanding Digital Universe: A Forecast of Worldwide Information Growth through 2010" (March 2007).
30. See ibid. (regarding growth of the digital universe in the five years between 2006 and 2011).
31. International Data Corporation, "The Digital Universe Decade—Are You Ready?" (May 2010) (projecting growth of the digitial universe by 2020).
32. International Telecommunication Union, "The World in 2010: Facts and Figures" (10 October 2010).
33. See Micah L. Sifry, *WikiLeaks and the Age of Transparency* (New Haven, Conn.: Yale University Press, 2011).
34. International Data Corporation, *supra* note 29.
35. *See* Jack Goldsmith and Tim Wu, *Who Controls the Internet? Illusions of a Borderless World* (Oxford: Oxford University Press, 2006).
36. See, for example, "Debunked: 'Wikileaks Did Not Redact the Afghanistan War Logs'" WL Central (28 November 2010), online at http://wlcentral.org/node/379.
37. *See* Alasdair Roberts, *Blacked Out: Government Secrecy in the Information Age* (Cambridge: Cambridge University Press, 2006).
38. Stephanie Condon, "Poll: Americans Concerned WikiLeaks Dump Will Hurt the U.S." CBS News (3 December 2010).

39. CNN Political Unit, "Poll: WikiLeaks Has Few Fans in U.S." CNN (30 December 2010).
40. Compare, for example, Executive Order 13292 with Executive Order 13526.
41. For example, Obama has continued to assert the state secrets privilege in extraordinary rendition and warrantless wiretapping cases, intervened to prevent the court-ordered disclosure of pictures of detainee torture, and threatened to veto a bill expanding the intelligence community disclosure obligations to Congress beyond the "gang of eight."
42. For example, as of August 2011, a search for "Guantanamo" among the CIA's post-9/11 document disclosures produces only one hit: a one-page memorandum, encouraging officers not to be sidetracked from the importance of the mission by controversy in the news, see online at http://www.foia.cia.gov/docs/DOC_0001480623/DOC_0001480623.pdf.
43. See, for example, Director of National Intelligence, "Vision 2015: A Globally Networked and Integrated Intelligence Enterprise" (22 July 22 2008) ("No aspect of collection... holds more promise than open source information").
44. See, for example, June Crowe and Thomas S. Davidson, "The 'Grey' Intersection of Open Source Information and Intelligence," GL10 Conference in Amsterdam (8 December 2008).
45. See Noah Shactman, "Open Source Intel Rocks—Sorry, It's Classified" Wired (17 September 2008).
46. See, for example, Scott Shane, "Secrets in Plain Sight" New York Times (17 September 2010) (describing the Dep't of Defense decision to buy and destroy the entire first printing of Anthony Schaffer's *Operation Dark Heart*, even after the Army approved its publication, because the DIA believed classified information remained).
47. Thomas Blanton, Statement to the Committee on the Judiciary, U.S. House of Representatives, Hearing on the Espionage Act and the Legal and Constitutional Implications of Wikileaks (16 December 2010).
48. See Executive Order 13526, § 1.1(b)(d), Classified National Security Information (29 December 2009).
49. Tamara Keith, "Pentagon Papers Declassified after 40 Years" NPR (13 June 2011).
50. See, for example, Howard Morland, *Born Secret*, 26 *Cardozo L. Rev.* 1401 (2005).
51. See, for example, *Fitzgibbon v. CIA*, 911 F.2d 755 (D.C. Cir. 1990) ("official acknowledgment" doctrine); *CIA v. Sims*, 471 U.S. 159 (1985) (mosaic theory); *United States v. Progressive*, 467 F. Supp. 990 (W.D. Wisc. 1979).
52. See Arnaud De Borchgrave, "The High Cost of Intelligence Secrecy" Newsmax (16 January 2008).
53. "U.S. agencies warn unauthorized employees not to look at WikiLeaks" CNN (3 December 2010).
54. See, for example, *ACLU v. Dep't of State*, Memorandum Opinion, Civ. No. 11-01072, D.D.C. (23 July 2012).
55. See, for example, "Respondents' Response to Petitioner's Emergency Application for Immediate Access to All Publicly Available WikiLeaks Documents Relevant to Petitioner's Case" *Paracha v. Obama*, Civ. No. 04-2002 (15 June 2011).
56. See, for example, Hilary Clinton, "Remarks to the Press on Release of Purportedly Confidential Documents by WikiLeaks" (29 November 2010), online at http://www.state.gov/secretary/rm/2010/11/152078.htm.
57. See, for example, Matt Apuzzo, "U.S., Canada Are Close Allies. That's Classified?" Associated Press (9 December 2010); Slavoj Zizek, "Good Manners in the Age of

WikiLeaks" (20 January 2011) 33 *London Review of Books* 2 ("The only surprising thing about the WikiLeaks revelations is that they contain no surprises.").

58. See, for example, "Bush Admits to CIA Secret Prisons" BBC (7 September 2006).
59. Dana Priest, "CIA Holds Terror Suspects in Secret Prisons" Washington Post (2 November 2005).
60. President George W. Bush, "Remarks by the President at Connecticut Republican Committee Luncheon" (9 April 2002), online at http://georgewbush-whitehouse.archives.gov/news/releases/2002/04/20020409-8.html.
61. See Alasdair Roberts, "Open Secrets and Dirty Hands" in Austin Sarat, Lawrence Douglas, and Martha Umphrey, ed., *The Secrets of Law* (Palo Alto, Cal.: Stanford University Press, 2011).
62. See, for example, Jay S. Bybee "Standards of Conduct for Interrogation under 18 U.S.C. §§ 2340–2340A," Memorandum for John Rizzo, Acting General Counsel of the Central Intelligence Agency, from Jay S. Bybee, Assistant Attorney General. U.S. Department of Justice, Office of Legal Counsel (1 August 2002); see also CIA Inspector General, "Special Review, Counterterrorism Detention and Interrogation Activities" (7 May 2004).
63. International Committee for the Red Cross, "Report on the Treatment of Fourteen 'High Value Detainees' in CIA Custody" (14 February 2007), online at: www.nybooks.com/ic -report.pdf.
64. See, for example, Andy Worthington, "Seven Years of Torture: Binyam Mohamed Tells His Story" (8 March 2009); Center for Human Rights and Global Justice, "Surviving the Darkness: Testimony from the Secret 'Black Sites'" (2007); Craig S. Smith and Souad Mekhennet, "Algerian Tells of Dark Term in U.S. Hands" New York Times (7 July 2006) A1.8.
65. Brian Ross and Richard Esposito, "Exclusive: Only Three Have Been Waterboarded by CIA," ABC News (2 November 2007).
66. See, for example, *Husayn v. Gates*, Petitioner's Memorandum in Support of Motion for Relief from Improper Classification, 08-cv-1360, D.D.C. (11 May 2009) at 24; *Khan v. Gates*, Respondent's Opposition to the Motion of the New York Times Company, the Associated Press, and USA Today to Unseal Classified Documents, 07-cv-1324, D.C. Cir. (28 March 2008) at 18–19.
67. See, for example, *El-Masri v. Tenet*, 437 F. Supp. 2d 530 (E.D. Va. 2006), aff'd 479 F.3d 296 (4th Cir. 2007), cert. denied 552 U.S. 947 (2007); *Mohamed v. Jeppesen Dataplan, Inc.*, 614 F.3d 1070 (9th Cir. 2010), cert. denied 131 S. Ct. 2442 (2011).
68. Scott Shane, "Keeping Secrets WikiSafe" New York Times (11 December 2010).
69. See Full video of alleged air strike aftermath in Yemen (Dec. 16, 2009), online at http://www.youtube.com/watch?v=aWuY6UOzEH4; see also Wikileaks cable corroborates evidence of US airstrikes in Yemen, Amnesty International (Dec. 1, 2010).
70. See *United States v. Progressive, supra* note 51.
71. *ACLU v. U.S. Dep't of Defense*, 628 F.3d 612, 621–22 (D.C. Cir. 2011).
72. "The leaky corportation: Digital information is easy not only to store but also to leak. Companies must decide what they really need to keep secret, and how best to do so," The Economist (26 February 2011).
73. See, for example, Bruce Perens, "Why Security through Obscurity Won't Work" Slashdot (20 July 1998); Chad Perrin, "Security through visibility: the secrets of open source security" TechRepublic (25 April 2006).
74. William Claiborne, "FBI Gives Reward to Unabomber's Brother" Washington Post (21 August 1998).

75. See, for example, Max Weber, *Essays in Sociology*, H.H. Gerth and C. Wright Mills, eds. (New York: Oxford University Press, 1946).
76. See Robert Steele, *On Intelligence: Spies and Secrecy in an Open World* (Fairfax, Va.: AFCEA International Press, 2000).
77. See generally U.S. House of Representatives Committee on Government Reform Minority Staff, "Secrecy in the Bush Administration" (14 September 2004).
78. See, for example, Greg McNeal, "Obama's Self-Serving Leaks, His Selective Outrage and the Need for a Special Counsel" Forbes (8 June 2012).
79. Joseph Weisberg, "The CIA's Open Secrets" New York Times (27 August 2007).
80. Executive Order 13526, § 1.7, Classification Prohibitions and Limitations
81. Jack Goldsmith, "Realism 101 on Wikileaks" Lawfare (1 December 2010) ("Every other government in the world knows the U.S. government leaks like a sieve and it has for a long time... Governments deal with the United States because it is in their interest... not because they believe we can keep secrets.").
82. See, for example, *Abd al Hakim Ghalib Ahmad v. Obama* (refusing to grant counsel access to WikiLeaks documents for use in merits hearing); see also Protective Order.
83. *Supra* note 66.
84. More recently, the U.S. government has applied the same "state secrets" argument to call for the dismissal of a claim that the U.S. government is engaging in racial and religious discrimination against its own citizens in carrying out its counter-terrorism policies on U.S. soil. Declaration of Eric H. Holder, *Fazaga v. FBI*, 8:11-cv-00301-CJC –VBK, C.D. Ca. (1 August 2010).

CHAPTER 15

Views from Mars, Views from Venus: Minding the Gap between What We Say and What We Do on Terrorism

GABOR RONA*

The "war on terror" is over. The United States has turned the page, reinstituting respect for applicable international law.[1]

Or so the Obama administration would like us to believe, in order to distance itself from the legacy of illegality, abuse, and rank incompetence reflected in the policies and practices of its predecessor. To many observers, especially those reared on American visions of the scope of application and content of international humanitarian and human rights law, the claims of a new, post-Bush dawn ring true. After all, has President Obama not ended torture, CIA detention, and extraordinary rendition; begun presiding over a "reformed" military commission system; pledged to close Guantanamo; and most important, rejected the view that the United States is "at war" against terrorism per se, in favor of a more restricted view of the conflict? However, for those observers whose perspectives on applicable law come from other countries, especially European ones, the distinctions between Bush and Obama pale in comparison with the divergence of American policy, under both Bush and Obama, from applicable principles and rules of international law.

This chapter first examines the differences between Americans' and others' perspectives on international law relevant to terrorism, in order to explain why the Obama administration can assert a clean break from the Bush era, while those reared in international law traditions outside the United States see a continuum between the two administrations, and a continued disconnect between U.S. counter-terrorism policies and applicable international law. Second, this chapter details aspects of targeting, detention, treatment, and trial of terrorism suspects, as well as of accountability mechanisms, where the U.S. claims to abide by international law but manifestly does not. Third, the chapter briefly considers why the contrasts between American and other visions of applicable law—and between what the United States says and what the United States does-matter.

IS THE UNITED STATES FROM MARS?

The peculiarly American perspective on international law and the fora constructed to enforce it is a good place to start: "Our strength as a nation state will continue to be challenged by those who employ a strategy of the weak using international fora, judicial processes and terrorism," states the 2005 National Defense Strategy of the United States of America.[2] In other words, international law, like terrorism, is for weaklings. Although this Bush-era vision is not repeated in Obama-era doctrine, it indicates the long-standing, and continuing prickly relationship between the United States and international law.

A more benign explanation for this apparent hostility to international law might be couched in terms of "American exceptionalism." To some, these words conjure images of a global understanding, if not consensus, that the United States bears a unique leadership role in international relations and sets the bar for others to follow. This vision applies particularly to the history, and claimed necessity, of American leadership in the promotion of human rights. Former State Department Legal Advisor Harold Koh, for example, is fond of noting that in matters of human rights, the United States is an "indispensable" force.[3] To others, "American exceptionalism" represents a self-issued license for hypocrisy—preaching standards to others that America itself disregards; to be exceptional means to take exception. Louis Henkin, often called the father of human rights law, famously characterized the United States as a flying buttress outside the cathedral of human rights, rather than a pillar within it.[4] American interpretations of international law have long provided fuel for detractors who take the less generous of these views.

Policies implemented after 9/11 have drastically widened the gulf between Americans' and others' understandings of both the scope of application, and the requirements, of the international laws of armed conflict and human rights. Reconciliation of these differences would likely mean a return toward interpretations, policies, and practices that better serve the complementary interests of security and liberty than the policies and practices we have witnessed and experienced since 9/11.

IHL on Mars, IHL on Venus

Among a plurality of nations where the field has developed significant jurisprudence, the law of armed conflict is chiefly referred to as International Humanitarian Law (IHL). In the United States, it has traditionally been called the Law of War (LoW). These discrepant terms reflect the substantive differences between two branches of this body of law. One branch, primarily codified in the Geneva Conventions and their Additional Protocols, covers protection of persons in the power of the enemy: persons "*hors de combat*," including in detention and under occupation. The other branch, primarily codified in the Hague Conventions, covers conduct of hostilities: the means and methods of warfare.

Beyond American shores, the effects of wars in living memory have been felt equally by combatants and the civilian population. Thus, in Europe, there is more or less equal emphasis on Geneva law and Hague law. In addition, the Geneva Conventions' requirement that the content of humanitarian law be taught and widely disseminated among the civilian population, as well as within the armed forces, is better respected in Europe than in the United States, largely owing to the work of the Geneva-based International Committee of the Red Cross and various national Red Cross societies.

American civilians, for the last century and a half, have largely been spared the effects of war. An American law student is lucky to find IHL taught in her school, let alone generally disseminated among the civilian population. In the United States, the "laws of war" are largely seen as the province of the armed forces. Military academies and manuals place greater emphasis on Hague concepts than on those of Geneva; this may reflect an expectation that "our wars" threaten the safety of soldiers, not of our civilians. Consequently, American soldiers have at times been instructed that in the conduct of hostilities, the goal is to "have chalk on your shoes" or, in other words, come as close as possible to the boundaries of permissible conduct. More traditional European visions of the law of armed conflict counsel otherwise. For example, the First Additional Protocol to the Geneva Conventions instructs that if there is doubt about whether someone is a combatant subject to attack or civilian immune from attack, he or she should be presumed to be a civilian.[5]

The Bush administration made two early and incorrect determinations, consistent with the greater historical U.S. emphasis on conduct of hostilities rules (Hague law) rather than on rules designed for the protection of civilians (Geneva law). One, Bush asserted a virtually unlimited scope of application of the laws of war: thus, the global "war on terrorism." Two, Bush denied Geneva Convention protections to both the objects and subjects of that "war."[6] The U.S. Supreme Court has required a recalibration of some of the exceptionalist Bush policies derived from these visions, most notably in *Hamdan* v. *Rumsfeld*, which applies the Geneva Conventions' Common Article 3 and its requirements of humane treatment and fair trials of detainees.[7] Matters of detainee treatment aside, as discussed below, the Bush legacy still remains largely intact in the scope and content of Obama administration policies on targeting, detention powers, and trial of terrorism suspects.

IHRL on Mars, IHRL on Venus

In Europe, it is no longer doubted that in armed conflict, where IHL is the primarily applicable legal framework, International Human Rights Law (IHRL) also applies. Thus, parties to armed conflict are bound by their European Convention on Human Rights (ECHR) obligations in circumstances of armed conflict both within their borders, and beyond their borders when and where they exercise effective control.[8]

This does not mean that all rules of the ECHR, the law of general application, or *lex generalis*, are enforceable in armed conflict; rather, it means that only those human rights law rules not supplanted by the *lex specialis* in war, IHL, continue to apply. For example, human rights law generally prohibits detention absent judicial process. However, that requirement does not apply in wars between "High Contracting Parties" to the Geneva Conventions, under which members of the enemy armed forces may be detained as Prisoners of War (POWs) without a right of judicial review. This is because the *lex specialis* that is the Third Geneva Convention on Prisoners of War contains alternative procedures for determining whether a person is detainable as a POW.[9]

The United States is party to the major international human rights instruments, such as the International Covenant on Civil and Political Rights (ICCPR) and the Convention against Torture (CAT). The United States has signed, but not ratified, the American Convention on Human Rights (ACHR). Nevertheless, the United States has taken exception to the claimed application of human rights law to both armed conflict and to its extraterritorial conduct.

The United States has, at times, claimed that IHL is the exclusive legal framework applicable in armed conflict. The rejection of IHRL's application is based on a different reading of the *lex specialis* choice-of-law rule than that which prevails in Europe. As noted, IHL is the *lex specialis* in armed conflict and IHRL a *lex generalis*. The United States has taken a "framework exclusion" view: where IHL applies, IHRL does not. Europe takes a "rule exclusion" view: where IHL applies but fails to address an issue, the relevant IHRL rule applies. The "rule exclusion" view is more favorable to human rights and is the better view for two reasons.

One, IHL treaty law does not address certain questions, such as detention powers in non-international armed conflict. This is not an oversight. There are excellent reasons, explained later in this chapter, why IHL must govern detention in armed conflicts between states, but not armed conflicts involving nonstate armed groups. Two, IHL instruments make explicit and implicit reference to the continued application of human rights law, especially in non-international armed conflict. For example, the Preamble to the Second Additional Protocol to the Geneva Conventions recalls that "international instruments relating to human rights offer a basic protection to the human person."[10] The Geneva Conventions' Common Article 3 speaks of "judicial guarantees recognized as indispensible by civilized peoples," applicable in non-international armed conflicts.[11] As Common Article 3 does not itemize those rights, unlike other provisions of the Conventions that apply to international armed conflict, rights are found in IHRL. A second example of IHRL applicable in armed conflict is the prohibition against torture. The Convention against Torture is explicit in the application of the prohibition in wartime.[12]

The United States also asserts that even if IHRL were applicable in armed conflict, it would not apply to the country's extraterritorial conduct.[13] This understanding is rejected by the Human Rights Committee, a body created by the ICCPR to monitor ICCPR compliance, and by the jurisprudence of the International Court of Justice, the International Criminal Tribunals for Rwanda and for the former Yugoslavia, and the organs of the Inter-American human rights system. The U.S. position rejecting extraterritorial application of the ICCPR rests on some exquisite wordsmithing: whether the word "and" is disjunctive or conjunctive in the ICCPR's scope of application provision, Article 2.1, obligating a State Party to respect and ensure respect for the provisions of the Convention as "to all individuals within its territory and subject to its jurisdiction."[14]

The historic rejection by the United States of IHRL to both armed conflict and to its extraterritorial conduct is perfected by two phenomena. One, the U.S. courts present substantial barriers to the assertion of international law: the act-of-state and political question doctrines; principles of non–self-execution of treaty obligations that have not been statutorily implemented into domestic law; limitations based on reservations, understandings, and declarations (RUDs) attached to treaties; interposition of "state secrets" claims by the government (which are increasingly being utilized to bar entire claims, rather than discrete pieces of evidence); and statutes explicitly prohibiting assertion and application of international law.[15] Two, and perhaps enabling all these barriers, the United States answers to no higher authority than itself in the interpretation and application of its human rights and humanitarian law obligations. In contrast, Council of Europe members must answer to the European Court of Human Rights.

Why IHRL?

Most armed conflicts in the world today are between states and nonstate armed groups or involve such armed groups against each other. The differences between Europe and the United States on IHRL application are particularly significant in these armed conflicts. This is because IHL—a specialized body of law applicable only in armed conflict—is rather detailed for armed conflicts between "high contracting parties to the Geneva Conventions" (otherwise known as international armed conflict, or IAC), but not for other types of armed conflict, where at least one party, such as the Taliban or Al Qaeda, is not a party to the Conventions (otherwise known as non-international armed conflict, or NIAC). On the matter of detention powers, for example, the difference between the breadth of IHL in IAC and in NIAC, and therefore, the importance of human rights law in NIAC, is especially great. In NIAC, where one finds no guidance on questions of detention authority in IHL treaty law, it is necessary to turn to IHRL, the body of law that is of general application in both wartime and peacetime.

It may be tempting to claim that IHL's failure to address detention powers in NIAC is emblematic of its failure to keep pace with the vagaries of modern conflicts. This claim is wrong; there are powerful reasons for IHL to maintain silence on the question. The reason IHL addresses detention at all, instead of leaving it to applicable domestic and human rights law, has to do with the rights of combatants in IAC. These so-called "privileged belligerents," usually members of a state's armed forces, have a limited license to kill in war. Their hostile acts against legitimate military objectives (as distinct from their war crimes) are not subject to the normal application of domestic criminal law. They may not be detained under such law. Yet, the humanitarian purposes of IHL are served by requiring detention (rather than killing) of enemy forces who are "*hors de combat*." Therefore, a specific

IHL regime—namely, the Third Geneva Convention on Prisoners of War—was developed to govern such detention.

In contrast, in NIAC there is no "privilege of belligerency" for rebels. Their hostile acts against legitimate military objectives may not be prohibited by IHL, but unlike combatants in IAC, NIAC fighters enjoy no immunity under IHL from domestic criminal law charges, such as assault and murder. Consequently, IHL does not need to address matters of their detention, which is covered by domestic law as tempered by human rights law obligations (such as the American right to habeas corpus or other mechanisms for the judicial review of detentions). However, the Bush administration soon after 9/11 denied even the "humane treatment" provisions of the Geneva Conventions.[16] Because the United States maintains a willful blindness to the application of human rights law in armed conflict, it was able to claim that where IHL is lacking, there simply is no law.

IHL: "Quaint" on Mars, Not on Venus

Complaints that gaps in IHL must be remedied by reforms to IHL stem in part from rejection of the application of IHRL in armed conflict. However, not all conflict is war and so it is correct that the laws of war do not apply to, let alone resolve, all contingencies presented in modern conflicts. That distinction tends to be lost on those who believe that the laws of armed conflict should apply to everything for which domestic law authorizes the use of military force or everything we label "war." In fact, there are excellent reasons the law of armed conflict does not, and should not, have such broad application. There are also excellent reasons that even where IHL applies, it is complemented by human rights law.

Early after 9/11, then U.S. attorney general Alberto Gonzales infamously defended the Bush administration's departure from accepted interpretations of the Geneva Conventions, which he labeled "quaint."[17] Since then, many defenders and critics alike of the legal interpretations, policies, and practices of the Bush and now Obama administrations relating to targeting, detention, treatment, and trial of terrorism suspects have complained that the laws of armed conflict have not kept pace with the changing nature of war. Therefore, they argue, those laws are in need of revision. Their premise is partially correct but their conclusion is entirely wrong. Specifically, the argument fails to appreciate the relative benefits of generality over specificity in the rules of IHL, and of the significant role of IHRL. Their interpretation, essentially "if it's not prohibited, then it's permitted," again belies the historic American emphasis on protecting "our" combatants rather than "their" civilians. Beyond the United States, prevalent interpretations look more to IHL's humanitarian purposes, as well as the applicability of IHRL. This latter view encourages the reader to interpret, rather than to dismiss, the Conventions' application to nonstate armed actors.

It should be noted that, as of this writing, the Obama administration has not stated a position on these questions of IHRL scope of application and may yet part from its predecessors. Still, the positions the Obama administration has taken in "war on terrorism" litigation remain consistent with previous U.S. positions on these IHRL scope-of-application issues.

Why Not IHL?

Europe and the United States not only differ on the scope of application of human rights law extraterritorially and in armed conflict, but also on the very scope of application of humanitarian law. Europe takes the more restrained view. The United States construes the concept of armed conflict, and thus, its powers under IHL, more broadly.

IHL applies to armed hostilities both between nations and between nations and certain nonstate armed groups. In the latter case, IHL applies only if two criteria are met. First, the nonstate armed group must be sufficiently organized so as to be identifiable as a party to armed conflict (under the law of armed conflict, rights and obligations manifest only through "parties"). Second, hostilities must be sufficiently frequent or severe so as to rise above a level characterized by "sporadic acts of violence" or "occasional riots." In other words, IHL does not apply to levels of violence that are properly and exclusively the province of domestic and human rights law. The boundaries between the presence and absence of armed conflict—between the conditions in which IHL does or does not apply—matter. In war, killing is lawful. IHL also dispenses with certain due process protections of human rights law and domestic law in detention and trials.

There is one more indicator of how the minimalist American approach to considerations of international law leads the United States astray. After 9/11, Congress passed the Authorization for Use of Military Force (AUMF), which provided legislative approval for U.S. war in Afghanistan.[18] Because the AUMF is so closely tied to the concept of "war," little thought is given to the fact that the use of military force is not necessarily armed conflict and therefore, does not necessarily trigger application of IHL. In other words, the U.S. approach overlooks internationally recognized conditions that do trigger application of IHL: a threshold of hostilities attributable to identifiable parties. This weakness is especially troublesome, in light of pending congressional efforts to expand the post-9/11 AUMF to entities with increasingly tenuous links to the 9/11 attacks.[19] Likewise, the oversight is important to any discussion of the legal basis for targeted killings in, for example, Somalia and Yemen. Were the United States more attentive to the conditions that trigger application of IHL in international law, and less inclined to presume that domestic authorizations for the use of force serve the same function, there would be more alignment across the Atlantic.

From the non-American, majority view of applicable international law, the U.S. experience presents three identifiable phenomena:

1) overly broad assertion of armed conflict, and thus, of IHL;
2) overly narrow application of the protections of IHL, in situations that are properly the subject of that body of law; and
3) improper rejection of the application of IHRL a) to U.S. conduct abroad, and b) in situations where IHL also applies.

Each of these phenomena reflects the "personal history" of the United States, a nation that knows little of the consequences of war to its own civilian population. Likewise, each contributes to the erroneous position that existing law cannot adequately address contingencies of modern conflicts and, thus, that these omissions necessitate revisions to the laws of war.

In fact, a less expansive assertion of the scope of armed conflict, a more generous application of the laws of armed conflict designed to protect civilians and others in the power of the enemy, and a more realistic application of international human rights law in situations of both war and peace will go a long way toward reducing conflicting views between the United States and its allies, decreasing resentment of the United States by its existing and potential enemies, and increasing security and liberty in the face of modern challenges to both.

WHERE THE UNITED STATES STILL FALLS SHORT

The Obama administration has done much to bring the United States back from "the dark side" of counter-terrorism, but how the administration's practices stack up against what it preaches is another question. The answers to that question reveal a good deal about which aspects of applicable international law are being respected and which are merely receiving lip service.

To understand the current state of U.S. counter-terrorism policy, begin with the first and most significant of the Torture Memos, the Bush

Memorandum of February 7, 2002,[20] in which executive branch attorneys radically refashioned interpretations of international law. The United States could affirm "the *principles*" of the Geneva Conventions—the phrase "the principles of Geneva" appears four times in the two-page memo—to assert American righteousness amid a sea of foreign enemy barbarians. In fact, what they meant and what the United States did was just the opposite: the United States rejected the most fundamental principle of the Geneva Conventions, namely, the requirement of humane treatment of detainees. Thus, the Department of Defense directed military commanders to apply Geneva principles but not Geneva rules. At the time, no one knew what that meant. In retrospect, we understand what it wrought: the atrocities of Abu Ghraib, Guantanamo, and rendition to torture.

Torture

The Obama administration carried forward the emphasis on principles, rather than rules. Having renounced CIA secret detention, extraordinary rendition, and "enhanced interrogation techniques,"[21] the administration noted in a report to the U.N. Human Rights Council that President Obama recently "unequivocally reaffirm[ed] U.S. support for [the Convention Against Torture's] principles."[22] This prevarication suggests that government lawyers know their law. They know that the United States has absolutely failed to honor its Convention obligations to bring its torturers to justice. They also know that their success in blocking lawsuits by torture victims on "state secrets" grounds—whereby courts have disallowed lawsuits that might reveal evidence potentially harmful to national security—means they cannot claim that the United States abides by its Convention obligation to provide an enforceable remedy to torture victims.

The statement in the U.N. submission that the United States "takes vigilant action to prevent such conduct and to hold those who commit acts of official cruelty accountable for their wrongful acts"[23] is a further example of the administration's prevarication. First, "vigilant action" sounds forceful but amounts to no particular undertaking. By contrast, the Convention Against Torture obligates each party to do something quite specific: prosecute torturers. Second—and this is a subtle but significant point—the Convention requires prosecution not only for "official cruelty," in the sense of "authorized by the State," but also for cruelty under the broader rubric that in the United States is called "under the color of law." This latter phrase refers to actions done while wielding the power of the state, whether or not the particular act of torture is authorized by law.

Likewise, the U.S. reference to "wrongful acts" rather than to "torture" allows the administration to give a pass to those who commit authorized torture (which therefore, may be defended as not "wrongful," even if it is illegal).

Such hairsplitting is clearly prohibited under the Convention Against Torture; yet, it remains the articulated policy of the Obama administration, which has concluded that there will be no consideration of accountability for acts of torture and abuse unless they went beyond the bounds authorized by Department of Justice legal opinions: the infamous torture memos.[24] This might sound acceptable (the defense of "superior orders" does have its place[25]), until one recalls that the memos can be read as having authorized virtually any form of mistreatment short of that resulting in pain associated with organ failure and death.[26]

In addition to failures in the realm of accountability, present interrogation policies still permit coercive interrogation techniques, such as sleep deprivation, prolonged isolation, sensory deprivation, and inducing fear and humiliation of prisoners. Pursuant to the Army Field Manual, such tactics may be used alone or in combination.[27] Such treatment may or may not amount to torture, but is certainly within the Torture Convention's prohibition against acts of cruel, inhuman, or degrading treatment or punishment that do not amount to torture[28] and Common Article 3 of the Geneva Conventions, which requires that detainees "in all circumstances shall be treated humanely."[29]

In the broader scheme of things, the administration's exquisite wordsmithing suggests that its counter-terrorism policies and practices are entirely in keeping with applicable international law. As State Department Legal Advisor Harold Koh explained to the American Society of International Law in March 2011: "Let there be no doubt: the Obama administration is firmly committed to complying with all applicable law, including the laws of war, in all aspects of these ongoing armed conflicts."[30] Note, however, that "being committed to" is not quite the same as "complying with."

Targeting

The laws of war permit targeting of enemy armed forces, of civilians while they take direct part in hostilities (DPH), and those civilians who, although not directly participating in hostilities, perform a continuous combat function (CCF).[31] As members of Al Qaeda and the Taliban are not soldiers belonging to a state's army, they fall within the more limited criteria applicable to targeting civilians: DPH or CCF. The United States does not publicize its targeting rules, but there is some evidence that they are significantly broader than what international law permits. For example, the 2001 congressional Authorization for the Use of Military Force says, "the President is authorized to use all necessary and appropriate force against those nations, organizations, or persons he determines planned, authorized, committed, or aided the terrorist attacks that occurred on September 11, 2001, or harbored such organizations or persons . . ."[32] This net is obviously wider than DPH/CCF. Administration officials have also been known to suggest that Afghan drug lords who financially support the enemy may be targeted, even though that conduct, while criminal, is no more "direct participation in hostilities" under international law than is paying taxes that fund a war. According to a Senate Foreign Relations Committee Report produced in 2009, American generals serving in Afghanistan authorized the targeting of fifty drug traffickers with links to the Taliban insurgency.[33] More recently, Pentagon legal counsel reportedly approved the targeting of "combatants" associated with rebel groups "affiliated" with Al Qaeda, but operating beyond Afghanistan and Iraq, even if those groups present no imminent threat to the United States.[34]

Although it may just be loose talk, there are also indications that conduct sufficient to merit the label "terrorist" is, itself, sufficient grounds for targeting in U.S. practice, even if it violates international law. Discussing Anwar al-Awlaki, the American Al Qaeda propagandist who was killed in a U.S. drone strike in Yemen, CIA Chief Leon Panetta said that al-Awlaki was "first and foremost a terrorist and we're going to treat him like a terrorist."[35] Likewise, State Department official Daniel Benjamin said that Awlaki is a lawful target because he "has been personally involved in planning terrorist operations against the U.S."[36] In 2010, Director of National Intelligence Dennis Blair declared that persons involved in terrorist activities may be targeted for "taking action that threatens Americans."[37]

Whether al-Awlaki's conduct amounts to "direct participation in hostilities" is unclear. However, it is clear that being a suspected terrorist does not, ipso facto, permit extrajudicial killing, that the government has never indicated the limits of its claimed license to kill, and that these comments from high government officials do not reflect, and damage the public view of, applicable international law. CIA spokesperson Marie Harf was emphatic, stating: "This agency acts in strict accord with American law." Note that Harf said American law, not international law. Does this mean that the CIA complies with both, as international law is presumed to be part of U.S. law? This is a difficult question to answer and is yet another example of a representation that satisfies only so long as one does not scratch the surface.

Detention Powers

While, in mid-2011, the population of Guantanamo was 171, the Obama administration imprisoned approximately 3,200 people at Bagram Air Force Base in Afghanistan.[38] Bagram detainees have fought in the U.S. federal courts for the same habeas corpus rights that are available to Guantanamo detainees, but the Obama administration has opposed them and so far has prevailed. The procedures at Bagram, known as Detainee Review Boards (DRBs), do not permit the detainees to have a lawyer, do permit the use of secret evidence, and are not before a neutral and independent decision-maker.[39] These procedures offer less protection against arbitrary detention than did the Guantanamo Combatant Status Review Tribunals (CSRTs), which were ruled inadequate by the U.S. Supreme Court.[40]

Military Commissions

Military commissions are ad hoc proceedings that purport to prosecute war criminals. However, many of the crimes that have been charged do not constitute traditional violations of the laws of war. They are crimes that were created and defined after the acts were committed. This violates the most fundamental principle of international criminal law, the principle of legality: one cannot be tried or punished for conduct that was not illegal at the time it was committed. Ironically, many other acts charged in military commissions were already violations of U.S. law applicable in the regular civilian federal criminal courts. Indeed, hundreds of terrorism cases have been successfully prosecuted there since 9/11.[41] There is strong circumstantial evidence that American officials and legislators know or suspect that military commissions are illegal, even while they claim the contrary. Why else, when passing the Military Commissions Act, would they have amended the U.S. War Crimes Act to remove the war crime of subjecting persons to trials that fail to provide "judicial guarantees recognized as indispensible by civilized peoples?"[42]

SO WHAT?

One might ask why U.S. practice on targeting, on treatment of and due process for terrorism suspects, and on accountability for those who violate international law in the name of counter-terrorism needs to be harmonized with either European visions of applicable law or, for that matter, with

U.S. rhetoric about respect for international law. One reason is specific to the fight against international terrorism. International cooperation is key to effective counter-terrorism, as suggested by the many compass points implicated in the execution of the 9/11 attacks. In sharing intelligence with, or in transferring suspects to, the United States, other states must consider whether their cooperation amounts to complicity in American violations of IHL and IHRL. If so, those states may be challenged and held to account in the various human rights enforcement fora to which they are subject.

This concern is not merely theoretical. In 2004, NATO forces fighting alongside U.S. forces in Afghanistan stopped transferring Al Qaeda and Taliban suspects to American custody after news broke of torture at Abu Ghraib prison in Iraq. Obviously, not even U.S. coalition partners believed the "few bad apples" meme pushed by the Bush administration.[43] Still, the Obama administration has come a long way from the illegal practices of the early post-9/11 Bush administration in matters of detainee treatment. So why is the NATO policy still in place? Maybe it has something to do with continued U.S. detentions in Afghanistan, where detainees are denied the right to see or challenge the evidence against them, let alone to have a lawyer. Perhaps it is that the United States continues to insist on the right to transfer suspects to countries with records of detainee abuse under a veneer of "diplomatic assurances" that they will not be tortured, without giving the detainee a right to challenge the decision.[44]

Allies of the United States have shown reluctance to cooperate in other ways, as well. In early 2011, Germany stopped providing intelligence to the United States on terrorist activity in Pakistan due to concerns about the legality of the U.S. targeted killing policy there.[45] Also, a Canadian appeals court rejected the U.S. request to extradite the brother of former Guantanamo detainee Omar Khadr, on grounds that the evidence against him was procured through torture, for which the United States was partly responsible and because such evidence might be used against him in a U.S. judicial proceeding.[46] There have also been instances in which European governments have declined to transfer suspects to the United States for fear they would be sent to Guantanamo or subjected to military commission trials. This is not idle speculation. Congress has clearly expressed its preference for Guantanamo detention and military commission trials for terrorism suspects, rather than federal court trials.[47]

Other impediments to cooperation with the United States include fear that suspects will be subjected to "enhanced interrogation" or to inhumane treatment and conditions in the U.S. Supermax prisons, that evidence obtained through torture would be used against them, or that they might be subjected to the death penalty.[48] In Europe, for example, several extraditions to the

United States were temporarily blocked pending a decision by the European Court of Human Rights (ECtHR), on the grounds that the possible criminal sanctions in the United States might exceed those deemed legitimate under the European Convention on Human Rights.[49] The United States has also entered agreements with several nations, as well as with the European Union, which would permit extradition to the Unites States by removing the possibility of capital punishment.[50] Regardless of what the United States thinks of the legality of these policies and practices, it must harmonize its conduct with the sensibilities of its allies in order to earn their cooperation.

The second reason that the United States should work to close the divide goes beyond counter-terrorism. For better and worse, the United States sets the bar for compliance with IHL and IHRL. There have been countless instances in which U.S. complaints about human rights violations by other, despotic regimes are met with responses of "Guantanamo," "CIA torture," and "Abu Ghraib."[51] These and other aspects of the American experience diminish the value of U.S. diplomacy on human rights, as human rights violators rightly accuse the United States of a double standard.[52]

CONCLUSION

This chapter has evaluated dissimilar notions of international law prevalent in the United States and Europe. It aims neither to vilify the United States nor to exalt Europe. As mentioned, the Obama administration has done much that is right and different from earlier policies and practices. Meanwhile, Europe is not without flaws, including but not limited to its complicity with the worst "extraordinary rendition" abuses of the CIA. Nevertheless, it is significant that the difference between Europe and the United States is not merely quantitative, as in the scope of abuses, but also qualitative. Unlike Europe, which has sometimes admitted and at other times denied its involvement in questionable practices without defending their legality, the United States has both admitted and at times defended broad targeting authority, extraordinary rendition, torture, arbitrary detention, trials that fail to meet minimum international law requirements of due process, and impunity for the authors of the worst of these abuses. This is reflected in the president's "belief that we need to look forward as opposed to looking backwards."[53] The inconsistency between the president's views on accountability for Americans and for others is made clear by his 2010 remarks on Indonesia: "We have to acknowledge that those past human rights abuses existed. We can't go forward without looking backwards."[54]

Marking 9/11 at the Pentagon, President Obama said of those responsible for the attacks: "They may seek to exploit our freedoms, but we will not sacrifice the liberties we cherish. . . ."[55] Optimists may recall Winston Churchill's wry observation that the United States always does the right thing—after it has exhausted all the other possibilities. The world is still waiting.

NOTES

* International Legal Director of Human Rights First and former legal advisor in the legal division of the International Committee of the Red Cross; Thanks to Robert McGuire for his helpful comments; The views expressed here are the author's and do not necessarily reflect the positions of the ICRC, Human Rights First or any other organization.

1. See Juliette Kayyem, former Asst. Secretary, Dept. Homeland Security under Obama, Op-Ed., "The War on Terror is Over," Boston Globe (10 September 2011), available online at http://articles.boston.com/2011-09-10/bostonglobe/30139939_1_terror-war-homeland-security-adviser.
2. U.S. Dep't of Defense, The National Defense Strategy of the United States of America 6 (2005), available online at http://www.au.af.mil/au/awc/awcgate/nds/nds2005.pdf.
3. See Harold Hongju Koh, "On American Exceptionalism," (2003) 55 *Stan. L. Rev.* 1479 at 1491.
4. William Grimes, "Louis Henkin, Leader in Field of Human Rights Law, Dies at 92," N.Y. Times (17 October 2010) A28.
5. See Protocol Additional to The Geneva Conventions of 1949 relating to the Protection of Victims of International Armed Conflict, art. 50(1) (8 June 1977) 1125 U.N.T.S. 3.
6. Memorandum from George W. Bush, President to Richard B. Cheney, Vice President et al., "Humane Treatment of al Qaeda and Taliban Detainees" (7 February 2002), available online at http://www.dia.mil/publicaffairs/foia/pdf/detainee/Humane Treatment of al Qaeda and Taliban Detainees.pdf [hereinafter "Bush memo"].
7. 548 U.S. 557, 631–32 (2006).
8. See, e.g., Al Skeini & Others v. United Kingdom, [2011] ECHR, App. No. 55271/07, available online at http://cmiskp.echr.coe.int/tkp197/view.asp?item=3&portal=hbkm&action=prof&highlight=&sessionid=78863859&skin=hudoc-en; *Al Jedda* v. *United Kingdom*, [2011] ECHR, App. No. 27021/08, available online at http://cmiskp.echr.coe.int/tkp197/view.asp?item=4&portal=hbkm&action=prof&highlight=&sessionid=78863859&skin=hudoc-en.
9. Geneva Convention (III) Relative to the Treatment of Prisoners of War, arts. 5,118 (12 August 1949), 6 U.S.T. 3316, 75 U.N.T.S. [hereinafter "Geneva III"].
10. See, e.g., Protocol Additional to the Geneva Conventions of 12 August 1949 and relating to the Protection of Victims of Non-International Armed Conflicts, preamble, 1125 UN Treaty Ser 609 (1978).
11. Geneva III, *supra* note 9, art. 3. See also Gabor Rona, Remarks at the Eminent Jurists Panel on Terrorism, Counter-Terrorism and Human Rights (19 September 2006), available online at http://www.humanrightsfirst.org/wp-content/uploads/pdf/06922-usls-icj-ej-panel-hrf-pres.pdf.

12. See Art. 2.2, Convention Against Torture and Other Cruel, Inhuman or Degrading Treatment or Punishment, opened for signature Dec. 10, 1984, S. Treaty Doc. No. 100-20 (1988), 1465 U.N.T.S. 85 [hereinafter "CAT"].
13. Matthew Waxman, Opening Statement of Matthew Waxman, Head of U.S. Delegation before the UN Human Rights Committee (17 July 2006), available online at http://2001-2009.state.gov/g/drl/rls/70392.htm, cited in Marko Milanovic, *Extraterritorial Application of Human Rights Treaties: Law, Principles, and Policy* (Oxford: Oxford University Press, 2011) at 58, n.11.
14. G.A. res. 2200A (XXI), 21 U.N. GAOR Supp. (No. 16) at 52, U.N. Doc. A/6316 (1966), 999 U.N.T.S. 171 (entered into force 23 March 1976).
15. See Military Commissions Act of 2009, Pub. L. No. 111-84, § 123 Stat. 2190 (to be codified at 10 U.S.C. § 47A (2006)); Military Commissions Act of 2006, Pub. L. No. 109-366, 120 Stat. 2600: § 5(a). See also Aaron Fellmeth, American Society of International Law, "International Law and Foreign Laws in the U.S. State Legislatures" (26 May 2011), *available at* http://www.asil.org/insights110526.cfm (last visited Sept. 22, 2011) (detailing state law initiatives).
16. Bush memo, *supra* note 6.
17. Draft Memorandum from Alberto R. Gonzales, to the president, "Decision Re Application of the Geneva Convention on Prisoners of War to the Conflict with Al-Qaeda and the Taliban" (25 January 2002), available online at http://news.lp.findlaw.com/hdocs/docs/torture/gnzls12502mem2gwb2.html.
18. Authorization for Use of Military Force, Pub. L. No. 107-40, 115 Stat. 224 (2001) (codified at 50 U.S.C. §1541 (2006)) [hereinafter "A.U.M.F."].
19. Compare AUMF with National Defense Authorization Act for Fiscal Year 2012, H.R. 1540, 112th Congress ¶ 1034 (2011).
20. Bush memo, *supra* note 6.
21. Exec. Order No. 13,491, Ensuring Lawful Interrogations, 74 Fed. Reg. 4893 (27 January 2009).
22. U.S. Dep't of State, Report of the United States of America: Submitted to the U.N. High Commissioner for Human Rights in Conjunction with the Universal Periodic Review 21, available online at http://www.state.gov/documents/organization/146379.pdf.
23. Ibid.
24. See Karen J. Greenberg and Joshua L. Dratel, eds., *The Torture Papers: The Road to Abu Ghraib* (Cambridge: Cambridge University Press, 2005) [hereinafter "Torture Papers"].
25. Rome Statute of the International Criminal Court (1998) art. 33, U.N. Doc. A/Conf. 183/9th (opened for signature 17 July 17 1998), available online at http://untreaty.un.org/cod/icc/statute/romefra.htm (last visited Sept. 27, 2011).
26. Anthony Lewis, Introduction to Torture Papers, *supra* note 24 at xiii (quoting Jay S. Bybee, "Standards of Conduct for Interrogation under 18 U.S.C. §§ 2340–2340A," Memorandum for Alberto R. Gonzales, Counsel to the President, from Jay S. Bybee, Asst. Atty. General (1 August 2002)).
27. See U.S. Dep't of Army, Field Manual FM 2-22.3, Human Intelligence Collector Operations, Appendix M (September 2006). For a discussion of Appendix M, see Human Rights First, *The U.S. Army Field Manual on Interrogation: A Strong Document in Need of Careful Revision*, available online at http://www.humanrightsfirst.org/wp-content/uploads/pdf/Army_Field_Manual.pdf.
28. *See* CAT, art. 16(1), *supra* note 12.
29. Geneva III, art. 3, *supra* note 9.

30. Harold Hongju Koh, U.S. Dep't of State, "Remarks at Annual Meeting of the American Society of International Law" (25 March 2010), available online at http://www.state.gov/s/l/releases/remarks/139119.htm (last visited Sept. 25, 2011).
31. Int'l Comm. of the Red Cross, *Interpretive Guidance on the Notion of Direct Participation in Hostilities under International Humanitarian Law* (May 2009) (prepared by Nils Melzer), available online at http://www.icrc.org/eng/assets/files/other/icrc-002-0990.pdf.
32. A.U.M.F., *supra* note 18.
33. Staff of S. Comm. on Foreign Rel., 111th Cong., Afghanistan's Narco-War: Breaking the Link between Drug Traffickers and Insurgents (Comm. Print 2009), available online at http://frwebgate.access.gpo.gov/cgi-bin/getdoc.cgi?dbname=111_cong_senate_committee_prints&docid=f:51521.pdf.
34. See Daphne Eviatar, "High Stakes for an Administration Battle: A National Security Nightmare" (16 September 2011), available online at Human Rights First Blog, http://www.humanrightsfirst.org/2011/09/16/high-stakes-for-an-administration-battle-a-national-security-nightmare/.
35. ABC, "This Week: Jake Tapper Interviews CIA Director Leon Panetta" (27 June 2010), Transcript of Television Broadcast, available online at ABC News, http://abcnews.go.com/ThisWeek/week-transcript-panetta/story?id=11025299&page=4.
36. Daniel Benjamin, U.S. Dep't of State, "U.S. Counterterrorism Strategy in Yemen: Remarks to the U.S. Institute of Peace, Washington D.C." (8 September 2010), available online at http://www.state.gov/s/ct/rls/rm/2010/147296.htm.
37. Dennis C. Blair, Director of National Intelligence, Statement for the Record (2 February 2010) Hearing Before House Permanent Select Committee on Intelligence, 111th Congress at 74.
38. See Andrei Scheinkman et al., "The Guantánamo Docket" N.Y. Times, available online at http://projects.nytimes.com/guantanamo (last visited November 4, 2013); see also U.S. Senator Lindsey Graham, "Comments at Carnegie Endowment for International Peace" (15 June 2011), available online at http://carnegieendowment.org/files/0615carnegie-graham.pdf (at 00:46:07 of transcript) (last visited November 4, 2013).
39. Human Rights First, *Detained and Denied in Afghanistan: How to Make U.S. Detention Comply with the Law* (2011) at 15–17, available online at http://www.humanrightsfirst.org/wp-content/uploads/pdf/Detained-Denied-in-Afghanistan.pdf.
40. *Boumediene v. Bush*, 128 S. Ct. 2229, 2270 (2008).
41. See Richard B. Zabel & James J. Benjamin Jr., "In Pursuit of Justice: Prosecuting Terrorism Cases in the Federal Courts: 2009 Update and Recent Developments," Human Rights First (2009), available online at http://www.humanrightsfirst.org/wp-content/uploads/pdf/090723-LS-in-pursuit-justice-09-update.pdf.
42. Geneva III, art 3, *supra* note 9.
43. *See* Paul Gallis, "NATO in Afghanistan: A Test of the Transatlantic Alliance," Congressional Research Service, RL33627 (2006) at 9 (some allies reportedly against transfer of prisoners to United States).
44. *See* Michael John Garcia, et al., "Closing the Guantanamo Detention Center: Legal Issues," Congressional Research Service, R40139, (2011) at 11. See also Human Rights First, "Assessing the Obama Administration's Record of Compliance with the Rule of Law and Human Rights in National Security Policy" (2011) at 3, *available at* http://www.humanrightsfirst.org/wp-content/uploads/HRF-Natl-Sec-Rep-Card.pdf.

45. Holger Stark, "Germany Limits Information Exchange with US Intelligence," Der Spiegel (17 May 2011) (Christopher Sultan, trans.), available online at http://www.spiegel.de/international/germany/0,1518,druck-762873,00.html.
46. *United States v. Khadr*, [2011] O.N.C.A. 358. See also "Canada Court Denies Khadr Terror Extradition Appeal" BBC (6 May 2011) at 10:19 PM, available online at http://www.bbc.co.uk/news/world-us-canada-13319957.
47. National Defense Authorization Act for Fiscal Year 2012, H.R. 1540, 112th Congress ¶ 1032 (2011).
48. See *Soering v. United Kingdom*, 161 ECHR (ser. A) (1989), 98 I.L.R. 270 (1989); *Babar Ahmad & Others v. United Kingdom* (7 July 2010) App. No. 24027/07, available online at http://cmiskp.echr.coe.int/tkp197/view.asp?action=html&documentId=871046&portal=hbkm&source=externalbydocnumber&table=F69A27FD8FB86142BF01C1166DEA398649.
49. European Court of Human Rights, Press Unit, "Factsheet—Expulsions and Extraditions" (June 2011), available online at http://www.echr.coe.int/NR/rdonlyres/211A6F9C-A4EC-4CF7-AB2E 42E9D49FB2EF/0/FICHES_Expulsions_and_extradition_EN.pdf.
50. Michael John Garcia & Charles Doyle, "Extradition To and From the United States: Overview of the Law and Recent Treaties," Congressional Research Service (2010), available online at http://www.fas.org/sgp/crs/misc/98-958.pdf (listing similar treaties with nations including Jordan, Argentina, Paraguay, and Bolivia).
51. For a most recent example, see CNN Wire Staff, "Freed hikers recount 2 years of 'lies and false hope'"(25 September 2011), available online at CNN http://articles.cnn.com/2011-09-25/us/us_us-iran-hikers_1_sarah-shourd-iranian-authorities-iranian-prison?_s=PM:US.
52. See Jimmy Carter, Op-ed, "Obama's Human Rights Opportunity," The Washington Post (10 December 2008), available online at http://www.cartercenter.org/news/editorials_speeches/obamas_human_rights_opportunity.html. See also "US 'erodes' global human rights" BBC (13 January 2005) at 11:54 PM, available online at http://news.bbc.co.uk/2/hi/americas/4171177.stm (summarizing Human Rights Watch, World Report (2005) at 6). *Accord* Pope John Paul II, "Address of Pope John Paul II to the Honorable George W. Bush President of the United States of America (4 June 2004)," Insegnamenti di Giovanni Paolo II, XXVII at 747–49, available online at http://www.vatican.va/holy_father/john_paul_ii/speeches/2004/june/documents/hf_jp-ii_spe_20040604_president-usa_en.html.
53. "Obama Reluctant to Look Into Bush Programs," New York Times (12 January 2009), available online at http://www.nytimes.com/2009/01/12/us/politics/12inquire.html?pagewanted=all.
54. See Glenn Greenwald, "When Presidential Sermons Collide" (25 March 2010), available online at http://www.salon.com/news/opinion/glenn_greenwald/2010/03/25/obama.
55. President Barack Obama, "Remarks by the President at the Pentagon Memorial" (11 September 2010), available online at http://www.whitehouse.gov/the-press-office/2010/09/11/remarks-president-pentagon-memorial.

CHAPTER 16

Epilogue

Human Rights and Counter-Terrorism: Lessons from a Long Decade

MARTIN SCHEININ*

The attacks of 9/11 and state responses in their aftermath were a major blow to the international protection of human rights. The achievements of the post–World War II human rights movement—the ideas that human rights (some even absolute, allowing no restrictions of any sort) limit the power of the state to impair human freedom and dignity—appeared to be forgotten in the subsequent desperate rush to take strong counter-terrorism measures. Some Western governments, once thought by human rights defenders to be allies, were now suddenly on the other side of the barricade. Governments pulled from their pool of legal expertise a whole arsenal of revisionist legal arguments for limiting the application and scope of human rights law when countering terrorism, suggesting that their earlier pro-human rights positions had been mere rhetoric. These negative trends were real: I witnessed them in the course of my work with the United Nations, first as a member of the Human Rights Committee until the end of 2004, then as the first Special Rapporteur on Human Rights and Counter-Terrorism (hereinafter "Special Rapporteur") in 2005–2011.

However, although there was indeed a backlash against human rights protections during the early part of the "long decade," I also saw important, positive developments over time. Together with the lessons from the negative trends, these positive features have enabled the emergence of a new and stronger discourse on human rights. This discourse is cautiously optimistic and realistic without losing sight of the legally binding nature of international human rights law. Reflecting on the difficult years after 9/11, I have identified ten positive trends that gradually emerged after the initial panic of 9/11, in response to the human rights challenges that followed it.

TREND 1: FROM UNFOCUSED CONCERNS TO A FOCUSED DEBATE

In the immediate aftermath of 9/11, human rights groups and scholars were unprepared for the coming backlash. They were alarmed by the sudden marginalization of human rights in quickly enacted state counter-terrorism measures, seeing them as a partly rational but panicked response to the terrorist attacks of 9/11. With these counter-measures, policymakers in many countries made a radical shift towards national security considerations, giving them absolute priority. They also introduced many such measures in a desperate attempt to do (and to be seen by a frightened public as doing) "something," whatever that might be. For some time, the concerns voiced by those within human rights circles remained abstract, negatively formulated (i.e., restrictive of state power), and unfocused in response to these developments. They offered few positively framed suggestions for protecting rights while responding to the new terrorism threat. Instead, human rights advocates often appeared to object reflexively to any counter-terrorism measures, as if the threat was not real and no special response was necessary. This perception, by many politicians and much of the public, had the effect that human rights defenders lost more and more ground in their cause due to the evaporation of popular support.

The lack of focus within the human rights community perhaps stemmed from its staunch reliance on pre-9/11 human rights models and resources that (naturally) did not comprehend a terrorism emergency of such a scale. For example, less than two months before 9/11, the Human Rights Committee had concluded its work on General Comment Number 29 on States of Emergency.[1] Although very few states had actually ever declared a state of emergency because of terrorism,[2] and although terrorism was not prominent in the scenarios of emergencies that the Committee members had in mind when drafting the General Comment, this document was to become highly important in structuring the human rights response to new counter-terrorism laws and other measures resorted to by states. The General Comment's significance was partly because: (1) no better guidance with a focus on counter-terrorism was readily available, and (2) there was a broad understanding that the whole post-9/11 world was going through a de facto emergency, even without de jure declarations to that effect. Among the basic propositions of the General Comment were the defence of absolute and non-derogable rights (such as the prohibition against torture), the idea that even derogable rights contain an inviolable core, and the tests of necessity and proportionality in assessing any measures taken pursuant to a state of emergency.[3] These abstract principles remained important, but—at least as contained in the General Comment—they were not adequately focused on the new terrorism emergency at hand. Although the Comment was therefore a useful starting point in the human rights response to new counter-terrorism measures, its abstracted approach typified the lack of focus that would undermine more effective human rights criticisms of those measures.

The lack of a more robust, terrorism-specific legal framework for human rights was only further compounded by the swift (and often harsh) actions not only by states, but the United Nations itself. In dismay, the human rights world saw the Counter-Terrorism Committee (CTC) of the Security Council, established in 2001 through U.N. Security Council Resolution 1373, take an approach that was insensitive or even hostile to the need to secure state compliance with human rights when introducing counter-terrorism measures. Resolution 1373 contained only one passing—and problematic—reference to human rights[4] and, under its first Chairman, [5] the CTC took an approach that emphasized Charter obligations, including those dictated in the form of a Chapter VII resolution. This approach pushed aside other normative commitments of Member States, such as human rights. The CTC's "Guidance"[6] to states on the implementation of Resolution 1373 accordingly ignored human rights. Already in early November 2001, Mary Robinson, as High Commissioner for Human Rights, approached the CTC with a proposal that was intended as "Further Guidance"[7] by the CTC itself, in order to encourage states to incorporate a human rights dimension in their implementation of Resolution 1373. This document was largely based on the aforementioned General Comment 29 by the Human Rights Committee.[8] The CTC did not adopt the proposal. This beginning marked an early disjunction between the political responses to terrorism (which were generally dismissive of human rights concerns) and the efforts of the human rights community (itself challenged in making arguments that seemed relevant to what much of the public perceived as a great crisis).

Today, there is an agenda for framing the so-called "security versus rights" debate in a more focused, effectual way. That agenda is represented by a fairly long list of substantive topics through which the discussion on the promotion and protection of human rights while countering terrorism can be framed and pursued in its proper context. If one were to identify only one area where the mandate of the Special Rapporteur has made a difference, it would be in shaping the agenda for a structured and substantive discourse on the relationship between counter-terrorism and human rights. During the six years I served as Special Rapporteur, my annual reports to the Human Rights Council and the General Assembly covered many topics that focused greater human rights attention on this special context of counter-terrorism in the post-9/11 period. These topics included best practices in countering terrorism,[9] the human rights obligations of intelligence agencies,[10] rights to privacy and association,[11] freedom from discrimination,[12] and fair trials[13] (among other things).[14] The impact of these reports—which were not written in an ivory tower, but instead benefited from attention to what non-governmental organizations (NGOs) and human rights expert bodies[15] were simultaneously developing "on the ground"—is seen in the gradual accumulation of substantive topics covered in the annual resolutions on human rights and counter-terrorism by the U.N. Human Rights Council and the General Assembly.[16] As a result of efforts such as these, the human rights response to counter-terrorism measures—and terrorism itself—gradually gained greater clarity, positive vision, and focus over the course of the long decade. Over time, human rights have therefore slowly regained some of the ground lost in the initial post-9/11 backlash.

TREND 2: THE HUMAN RIGHTS CONSEQUENCES OF COUNTER-TERRORISM MEASURES: FROM SEEING THE TIP OF THE ICEBERG TO ASSESSING THE TOTAL PHENOMENON

Initially, when confronted with the drastic post-9/11 backlash against human rights, and shocked by the gravity of human rights violations by the United States and some other Western states, the human rights community focused on deeply intrusive counter-terrorism measures that targeted real terrorists or those wrongly suspected of being terrorists, such as torture. It was certainly true that the human rights community retained a principled approach, including in defining the absolute nature of the prohibition against torture. However, a less fortunate side effect of how the human rights debate was framed was that human rights activists, NGOs, and lawyers appeared to be defending the human rights of "terrorists" at the expense of both public security and the victims of terrorism. The seemingly endless debate on the justification of torture in the fallacious "ticking time-bomb" scenario is just one example of how the human rights debate was distracted and derailed. At a time when policymakers and much of the general public were focusing on security, the tone of this debate resulted in an increased level of confrontation between human rights activists and policymakers. It also alienated major segments of the public.

Over the years, the human rights community has gradually learned how to remain uncompromising on principles, while at the same time to appreciate and address the whole scope of human rights concerns that arise from both terrorism and counter-terrorism. Torture and other serious abuses, done in the name of countering terrorism, are now seen as just the visible tip of the iceberg. Broader agendas of human rights and counter-terrorism must also be explored and addressed, so that the human rights of everyone—including victims of terrorism and the general public—receive attention. Gradually, a better informed discussion on the whole spectrum of human rights and intrusive counter-terrorism measures has developed. For instance, counter-terrorism measures that interfere with the right to privacy and data protection affect the mainstream population, not just individuals targeted as suspected terrorists. Even if many people are willing to compromise some of their privacy in exchange for better security—an understandable concern that human rights advocates must now take into account—they should nevertheless appreciate that human rights activists care about them and safeguarding their privacy rights from government abuse, just as they also care about keeping them safe from terrorism.

TREND 3: FROM FOCUSING ON THE HUMAN RIGHTS OF "TERRORISTS" TO CARING FOR THE HUMAN RIGHTS OF EVERYONE

As Trend 2 indicated, an increasing appreciation of the wider human rights context to countering terrorism quickly leads to a greater recognition of the care due to the general public, not just individual terrorist suspects. The gradual shift to discussing how counter-terrorism measures affect everyone's right to privacy, for example, is indicative of this greater trend of broadening not only the scope of issues examined, but also the categories of people whose human rights are addressed. In addition to the rights of the public, the rights of the victims of terrorism have received new emphasis in human rights discourse. However, sincere respect for terrorism's victims also means recognizing their rights as one equally valuable but constituent part of the complex human rights context surrounding terrorism. That is to say, attention to victims' rights are important for better realizing everyone's human rights in a system of mutually reinforcing dignity, rather than seeing any one group's rights as irreconcilably opposed to anyone else's rights.

In fact, one of the lessons learned over the long decade is that governments tend to use the human rights of terrorism's victims as an excuse for violating the rights of suspected individuals or groups; this cynical, simplistic invocation of victims' rights reduces those victims to mere means in the state's justification of controversial policies. Human rights groups need to do (and have done) better, by bringing a broader human rights approach to the situation of victims of terrorism. With such an approach, victims are not simply excuses for bad government behavior, but real objects of concern, whose well-being is inextricably linked to a larger, shared notion of human dignity. Everyone's dignity is therefore debased—including that of the victims of terrorism—when anyone's rights are used as an excuse to perpetuate a cycle of human rights abuses. Notably, Mr. Ben Emmerson, the new Special Rapporteur, who succeeded me in August of 2011, has in this way sought to bring greater attention to the rights of terrorism's victims.[17] This issue is also as much of a security matter as it is a human rights one. Real protection for human rights, as for public security, can only be achieved by recognizing injustices wherever they occur and regardless of the actor—a point revisited below.

TREND 4: FROM A "WAR PARADIGM" (OR ITS DENIAL) TO A NUANCED ASSESSMENT OF APPLICABLE LAW

From the early days after 9/11, the human rights community was consistent in insisting that terrorism is a form of serious crime and should be fought within a law enforcement paradigm that includes full respect for human rights law. Even if this position was and is correct, it was insufficient in the sense that, in the minds of many people, the U.S. government presented a compelling case when asserting that its fight against Al Qaeda was an armed conflict that triggered the laws of war. In the distorted rhetoric of the Bush administration, however, this (wrongly) meant putting aside human rights law altogether. Gradually, human rights academics and advocates have become more willing to admit that, despite the general strategic and policy preference of a law enforcement paradigm, there is a need to address the question of whether the law of armed conflict is relevant in certain defined periods of time, in certain geographical areas, and in respect of certain identifiable parties to an armed conflict. Human rights law would not be displaced, as the Bush administration argued, but it would apply within the special context of its overlap with the *lex specialis* of humanitarian law.

By earnestly engaging in this discourse, the human rights community has become stronger; it can now effectively assess the combined effect of human rights law and humanitarian law in these limited situations, rather than just denying any relevance of the latter. In most practical cases, it will still be possible to demonstrate that human rights law remains the proper legal framework, without any need to apply humanitarian law. By strengthening its expertise in issues of humanitarian law, the human rights community has therefore become more persuasive, notably to lawyers and other professionals in the military, who generally work under a law-of-war paradigm.

TREND 5: FROM A SEPARATION BETWEEN COUNTER-TERRORISM AND HUMAN RIGHTS TOWARDS COORDINATION BETWEEN THE TWO

Through Resolution 1373, the U.N. Security Council established its Counter-Terrorism Committee. In its early years, the CTC and its Executive Directorate (CTED) were ignorant, even hostile, to any effort to sensitize them to the human rights consequences of counter-terrorism measures. As mentioned above, the CTC advocated counter-terrorism measures that disregarded or even undermined human rights. As a result, human rights bodies had to fight an uphill battle in telling the same states reporting to the CTC that they should comply with human rights while countering terrorism. Gradually, the CTC started to accept briefings about human rights, while the Security Council approved statements that states (in Resolutions 1456[18] and 1624) and even the Security Council itself (in Resolutions 1822[19] and 1905) needed to comply with human rights while countering terrorism. Gradually, in line with the General Assembly's 2006 Global Counter-Terrorism Strategy,[20] the CTC and CTED started to acknowledge the benefits of human rights sensitivity, even compliance, in an effective and sustainable fight against terrorism. In 2006, the CTC adopted its own policy guidance on human rights.[21] In this way, lines of communication and institutional links were developed between what, early on, had seemed to be different or even opposing counter-terrorism and human rights worlds. The work of the U.N.-level inter-agency Counter-Terrorism Implementation Task Force (CTITF) has been important in this respect.[22] The slow reconciliation of human rights and counter-terrorism concerns has therefore progressed through increasing cooperation between the institutions and professional circles of both the human rights and security communities.

TREND 6: FROM SEEING HUMAN RIGHTS AS AN OBSTACLE TO UNDERSTANDING THEIR POSITIVE ROLE IN SUSTAINABLE COUNTER-TERRORISM STRATEGY

In the 2006 Global Strategy, the promotion and protection of human rights is itself one of the four pillars,[23] as well an ingredient in the other pillars. The strategy acknowledges that deeply embedded structural human rights violations, such as economic and social exclusion coupled with discrimination and political marginalization, amount to "conditions conducive"[24] to the spread of terrorism (these contributing factors are for that reason, referred to as "structural causes"). It also recognizes that the promotion of human rights for all (including economic, social, and cultural rights) is a cornerstone in building societies free from terrorism.

Furthermore, counter-terrorism professionals have by now learned to understand that vague, broad, and politically motivated national definitions of terrorism are not only ineffective when casting a wide net, but are in fact counterproductive by diverting national attention and resources from the actual international terrorism to actors that are of no concern to the international community. Notably, in their engagement with individual countries, the CTC and CTED have been using the work of the Special Rapporteur on definitions of terrorism to teach countries to focus on real terrorism, instead of using the stigma of terrorism for other, often politically motivated purposes. Such awareness helps to prevent costly mistakes caused by overreactions, prejudices, or distractions by other political agendas.

TREND 7: FROM TREATING HUMAN RIGHTS AS (INCONVENIENT) MINIMUM STANDARDS TO EXPANDING THEIR SCOPE AS BEST PRACTICE

As seen by Trend 6, a commitment to human rights in countering terrorism actually improves the quality, effectiveness, and sustainability of security efforts. Contrary to much of the dominant rhetoric after 9/11, human rights are therefore a facilitator or aid to counter-terrorism measures, rather than an inhibitor. This positive role of human rights was often overlooked by both politicians and human rights advocates alike in the early years of the long decade, when human rights were usually characterized—by both sides—as only restrictions or limitations on state behaviour, rather than a proactive tool for achieving security itself.

This misstep in discourse was perhaps understandable as human rights are so often expressed in negative terms and the human rights community had difficulty focusing their criticisms in a way sensitive to the complex post-9/11 terrorism context. In the form of treaty law or customary international law, human rights represent legally binding obligations on states. When confronted by national security threats, states often tend to emphasize their sovereignty and freedom to act, and seek to minimize the effect of their international obligations. Hence, states may exploit all possibilities to introduce exceptions to international law and to fashion legal doctrines that justify unilateral actions. The efforts by many states to reduce the effect of human rights law while countering terrorism was therefore, in many ways, a typical (if particularly stark) example of this type of legal maneuvering by states.[25] As mentioned earlier, the invocation of a war paradigm, and with it humanitarian law, was the major strategy for attempting just this sort of escape from international human rights obligations, seen by many politicians and much of the public as obstructive—not constructive—to counter-terrorism efforts.

However, towards the end of the long decade, there was increasing support for an opposite trend, growing out of the one towards a positive role for human rights in countering terrorism. This new trend saw human rights compliance not only as a legal obligation, but as a form of best practice: that is, as a strategy for getting things right at home and for showing a good example to other countries. Both aspects of best practices expand and strengthen effective international political and legal fronts against terrorism. The approach of the Special Rapporteur in prioritizing countries with experience of real terrorism in his programme of country visits, and in producing a compilation of best practices in human rights compliance while countering terrorism, is one example of this trend.[26] Once again, this development shows how counter-terrorism efforts and human rights are mutually reinforcing, rather than opposed.

TREND 8: FROM BAD FAITH "COPY-CATTING" ACROSS BORDERS TO LESSONS LEARNED

The trend towards best practices shows that the experience of countries confronted with terrorism (in its different forms) is invaluable for other nations. In many cases, a "lessons learned" approach—leading to the identification of best practices—has demonstrated how success in countering terrorism has been achieved not only through a sensitivity to human rights concerns, but also attention to the counterproductive effects of counter-terrorism measures that violate human rights. This critical approach has, at least in part, replaced an earlier selective approach of "pick-and-choose," where elements of the counter-terrorism laws of other countries were taken out of context and applied in an opportunistic fashion to justify whatever new measures a government was introducing.

The end result of such opportunism was to "copy-cat" other countries' counter-terrorism measures. This often led not only to a "lowest common-denominator" standard of human rights protection, but even to poorly crafted, ineffectual security measures. In contrast, through a "lessons learned" approach, states learn from others' bad (and good) experiences, so as to improve their own counter-terrorism measures. They do this not through blind imitation, but by avoiding others' mistakes and continually working towards an evolving best practice.

TREND 9: A "BETTER LAW" APPROACH: FROM ABSTRACT "BALANCING" TO A "PERMISSIBLE LIMITATIONS" TEST

One dimension of the post-9/11 backlash against human rights was the reduction of human rights law to a mere argument in an overall process of "balancing" between liberty and security. This unanalytical framework was itself partly a symptom of the discursive disjunction between security proponents and human rights advocates in the early period after 9/11, a time when the human rights community was poorly focused and too often ineffectual in persuading both politicians and the general public of the continuing value of human rights. The abstract metaphor of "balancing" between security and human rights was widely used to push aside the effect of human rights as legal norms and to reduce their effect to just one policy consideration among others. For rights nihilists and "realists," 9/11 opened an opportunity to reduce law to represent just one "view" of many, which could be overruled by opinions from other fields of expertise. Such an approach to "balancing" resulted in the undermining of absolute (non-derogable) human rights, in accepting intrusions into the essential core of other human rights, and in a reordering of values, so that security would *always* trump human rights. Even some of the finest judicial institutions in the world bowed under pressure and engaged in rhetoric about the application of human rights law ultimately being a question of balancing.[27]

This debate may not be over, but there is gradual recognition that law is not one weight to be balanced against other considerations. Rather, law is the balance; it is the framework within which the necessity and proportionality of permissible limitations upon human rights can be assessed without sacrificing the normative force of human rights, as such. As many of these trends show, there is now a growing realization that security and human rights are closely intertwined in many complex ways. As such, they cannot conceptually be opposed or balanced against one another in such a way that human rights are overridden. Instead, for resolving hard cases, human rights law provides an analytically rigorous test of permissible limitations on human rights, providing for a carefully designed space for a proportionality assessment as the final step.[28] Proportionate measures continue to protect the human rights of everyone, as seen within the full context of the fight against terrorism, allowing for specific counter-terrorism measures that are properly focused, carefully made, and more effective in doing their job over the long-term.

TREND 10: FROM STATE-CENTERED TO TRANSNATIONAL HUMAN RIGHTS PROTECTIONS

In many ways, the human rights challenges of the long decade have required a more fundamental, introspective look at human rights law itself. As states have challenged human rights principles of equality and universality, human rights advocates have had to re-examine these principles in light of the political pressures. State efforts to evade their human rights obligations in the fight against terrorism have often included arguments to deny human rights to "outsiders" on the basis of either their personal status or geographical location. For example, in the latter part of the long decade, there has been the emergence of a meaningful debate on the complicity of some countries in renditions and torture (e.g., Poland, Romania, United Kingdom, and Canada). In such cases, countries abused personal or territorial distinctions to carve out human-rights–free zones beyond political, legal, or public scrutiny. Admittedly, in some (but very few) cases mechanisms of accountability and effective remedies have kicked in.[29] As with many other aspects of human rights protections, during the long decade there was first a backlash and then corrective measures[30] in favor of the extraterritorial application of human rights beyond state borders.

Beyond the state, counter-terrorism issues, particularly the listing of terrorist individuals and entities, have given rise to a rational discourse on the human rights obligations of international organizations, including the United Nations. Also, the role of private military and security contractors in counter-terrorism and counter-insurgency operations has become all too important a matter to be ignored by serious legal scholars. Further, the attribution of human rights violations to terrorist organizations is no longer just a defensive rhetorical trick by authoritarian governments faced with terrorism. Rather, something much more interesting is gradually emerging from efforts to address violence by non-state actors as a human rights violation. All in all, the debate on human rights and counter-terrorism has been useful in generating sophisticated and novel ideas about human rights extending beyond the territorial state as the sole duty-bearer. This wider approach, however, once again avoids old mistakes by contextualizing human rights in a broader, more complex way than they were immediately after 9/11, giving them greater force and broader application. Parallel to the counter-terrorism context, a rich discussion has emerged also in other fields concerning human rights obligations by non-territorial states and other actors besides states.[31]

CONCLUSION

As should be clear, these ten positive trends of the long decade largely overlap with each other. They could even be "re-packaged" into fewer trends, instead of ten. Also, each positive trend is a reaction to some negative countercurrent in the human rights backlash that appeared suddenly after 9/11. Nevertheless, many people might still think that these positive trends are just wishful thinking, and that the net effect of 9/11 and the long decade on human rights remains negative. However, such an alternative position may itself represent another form of wishful thinking, in the sense that what it depicts as the preferred state-of-affairs—a perceived pre-9/11 ideal of universal support for the idea of human rights—was in fact an illusion. Had all the state affirmations of human rights been genuine, there would have been no backlash. Yet, a backlash there was. Any effort to build a world with stronger human rights protections must therefore be aware of what went wrong and what are the building blocks for a better future.

NOTES

* Professor of International Law and Human Rights, European University Institute Department of Law; Former United Nations Special Rapporteur on Human Rights and Counter-Terrorism; former member of the United National Human Rights Committee.

1. U.N. Doc. CCPR/C/21/Rev.1/Add.11 (2001). I served as the Committee's rapporteur in the drafting of the general comment.

2. Since 1976 when the ICCPR entered into force, fewer than ten states have ever declared a state of emergency with reference to terrorism. See Martin Scheinin and Mathias Vermeulen, "Unilateral Exceptions to International Law: Systematic Legal Analysis and Critique of Doctrines to Deny or Reduce the Applicability of Human Rights Norms in the Fight against Terrorism," (2011) 8 *Essex Human Rights Review* 20 at section 3.10.1.
3. General Comment 29, *supra* note 1, paras. 3–4, 7, 13.
4. SC/RES/1373 (2001), para. 3(f), mentions human rights in the context of refugees, sending the double message that the human rights of refugees need to be respected but that asylum-seekers may be terrorists in disguise. The Resolution encourages that Member States "[t]ake appropriate measures in conformity with the relevant provisions of national and international law, including international standards of human rights, before granting refugee status, for the purpose of ensuring that the asylum-seeker has not planned, facilitated or participated in the commission of terrorist acts. . . ."
5. Sir Jeremy Greenstock. See U.N. Security Council, 4453rd meeting (18 January 2002), U.N. Doc. S/PV.4453, pp. 3–5.
6. UN Security Council, Counter-Terrorism Committee, Guidance Note of 26 October 2001 for Submission of Reports under Resolution 1373.
7. Office of the High Commissioner for Human Rights, Note to the Chair of the Counter-Terrorism Committee: A Human Rights Perspective on Counter-Terrorist Measures (23 September 2002), and Proposals for "Further Guidance" for the Submission of Reports Pursuant to Paragraph 6 of Security Council Resolution 1373 (2001) (intended to supplement the Guidance of 26 October 2001) (23 September 2002).
8. These insights are drawn from my direct experience, given my participation in the drafting of the "Further Guidance."
9. A/HRC/16/51 (2011): Ten areas of best practices in countering terrorism.
10. A/HRC/10/3 (2009): The role of intelligence agencies and their oversight in the fight against terrorism
11. A/HRC/13/37 (2010): The erosion of the right to privacy in the fight against terrorism; A/61/267 (2006): Freedom of association and peaceful assembly and counter-terrorism, and listing of terrorist individuals and entities.
12. A/HRC/4/26 (2007): Profiling in the context of countering terrorism, and suicide attacks as a form of terrorism.
13. A/63/223 (2008): Right to a fair trial in the context of prosecuting terrorist suspects.
14. Other topics included: A/65/258 (2010): Compliance by the United Nations with international human rights law while countering terrorism; A/HRC/14/46 (2010): Compilation of good practices on legal and institutional frameworks and measures that ensure respect for human rights by intelligence agencies, while countering terrorism, including their oversight; A/HRC/13/42 (2010): Joint study on secret detention with the Special Rapporteur on Torture and Other Cruel, Inhuman or Degrading Treatment or Punishment, and the two Working Groups on Arbitrary Detention, and Enforced or Involuntary Disappearances; A/64/211 (2009): A gender perspective on countering terrorism; A/HRC/6/17 (2008): Economic, social and cultural rights in the context of countering terrorism; A/62/263 (2007): Challenges to refugee protection caused by global measures to counter terrorism; E/CN.4/2006/98 (2006): Definitions of terrorism; Role of human rights in the review of Member State reports to the

Counter-Terrorism Committee; A/60/370 (2005) Conceptual framework of the mandate.

15. As one example of such agenda-shaping NGO projects, see International Commission of Jurists, *Assessing Damage, Urging Action, Report of the Eminent Jurists Panel on Terrorism, Counter-terrorism and Human Rights* (Geneva: International Commission of Jurists, 2009); See also, for example, Inter-American Commission on Human Rights, Report on Terrorism and Human Rights, OEA/Ser.L/V/II.116 (2002).
16. See, for example, A/HRC/RES/13/26 (2010), operative paras. 6–9 and 14–15, and A/RES/64/168 (2010), operative paras. 6, 9–10.
17. See Emmerson's first annual report to the General Assembly, U.N. Doc. A/66/310 (2011) and his first report to the Human Rights Council, U.N. Doc. A/HRC/20/14.
18. The formulation of the human rights clause in Resolution 1456 and some subsequent ones is based on the perception that securing compliance with human rights is a matter for Member States, even when they implement Security Council resolutions: "States must ensure that any measure taken to combat terrorism comply with all their obligations under international law, and should adopt such measures in accordance with international law, in particular international human rights, refugee, and humanitarian law. . . ," S/RES/1456 (2003), operative para. 6.
19. The formulation introduced in the preamble of Resolution 1822 implies that the United Nations itself also has a responsibility to comply with human rights by "[r]eaffirming the need to combat by all means, in accordance with the Charter of the United Nations and international law, including applicable international human rights, refugee, and humanitarian law, threats to international peace and security caused by terrorist acts, stressing in this regard the important role the United Nations plays in leading and coordinating this effort. . . ." S/RES/1822 (2008).
20. A/RES/60/288 (2006).
21. U.N. Doc. S/AC.40/2006/PG.2 (2006).
22. See generally United Nations, Counter-terrorism Implementation Task Force, online at http://www.un.org/en/terrorism/ctitf/index.shtml.
23. See pillar IV of the Strategy, *supra* note 21.
24. Ibid., pillar I.
25. See Scheinin and Vermeulen, *supra* note 2.
26. These included Turkey, the United States, Israel, Spain, and Peru. For the full list of country missions conducted or planned, see United Nations, Office of the High Commissioner for Human Rights, online at http://www.ohchr.org/EN/Issues/Terrorism/Pages/Visits.aspx (Last visited 7 November 2013); See U.N. Doc. A/HRC/16/51 (2011).
27. *Suresh* v. *Canada (Minister of Citizenship and Immigration)*, 2002 SCC 1. Notably, the case was heard before 9/11 and decided soon after 9/11. While Mr. Suresh was *not* to be sent to face the risk of torture, the Court compromised this outcome by explaining: "Deportation to torture . . . requires us to consider a variety of factors, including the circumstances or conditions of the potential deportee, the danger that the deportee presents to Canadians or the country's security, and the threat of terrorism to Canada. In contexts in which the most significant considerations are general ones, it is likely that the balance will be struck the same way in most cases. It would be impossible to say in advance, however, that the balance will necessarily be struck the same way in every case." Ibid. at para. 45.
28. A brief presentation of my position on the issue of "balancing," as an elaboration of Robert Alexy's theory of fundamental rights, can be found in Martin Scheinin, "Terrorism and the Pull of 'Balancing' in the Name of Security," in *Security and the*

Law—Facing the Dilemmas, Martin Scheinin, et al., eds., E.U.I. Working Papers in Law, (Nov. 2009), 55; See also Scheinin and Vermeulen, *supra* note 2.

29. The best example is the Maher Arar inquiry in Canada. Commission of Inquiry into the Actions of Canadian Officials in Relation to Maher Arar, Report of the Events Relating to Maher Arar: Analysis and Recommendations (Ottawa, 2006).
30. For the backlash, see *Banković and Others* v. *Belgium and Others*, European Court of Human Rights (App. no. 52207/99; 12 December 2001). This is very much a post-9/11 case where the European Court of Human Rights applied an overkill of justifications for declaring inadmissible a complaint that related to NATO bombings in Belgrade during the Kosovo war. As part of the collateral damage, it seemingly reduced the scope of extraterritorial human rights obligations close to nothing. Notably, the case was heard on 24 October 2001 and decided on 12 December 2001; Corrective measures are seen in, for example, *Al-Jedda* v. *United Kingdom*, European Court of Human Rights (App. No. 27021/08; 7 July 2011).
31. See, for instance Olivier De Schutter, Asbjørn Eide, Ashfaq Khalfan, Marcos Orellana, Margot Salomon, and Ian Seiderman, "Commentary to the Maastricht Principles on Extraterritorial Obligations of States in the Area of Economic, Social and Cultural Rights," (2012) 34 *Human Rights Quarterly* 1084–169, and Malcolm Langford, Wouter Vandenhole, Martin Scheinin, and Willem van Genugten, eds., *Global Justice, State Duties: The Extraterritorial Scope of Economic, Social, and Cultural Rights in International Law* (Cambridge: Cambridge University Press, 2013).

BIBLIOGRAPHY

JOURNAL ARTICLES

Aleinikoff, T. Alexander, "Constitutional Law in the Age of Balancing" (1987) 96 *Yale L. J.* 943.

Alexander, Larry and Frederick Schauer, "On Extrajudicial Constitutional Interpretation" (1997) 110 *Harv. L. Rev.* 1359.

Amoore, Louise and Marieke de Goede, "Governance, Risk and Dataveillance in the War on Terror" (2005) 43 *Crime, Law & Social Change* 149.

Atkinson, L. Rush, "Guns, Butter and Judges: Judicial Frameworks for Cases Implicating Security-Wealth Tradeoffs" (2010) 85 *N.Y.U. L. Rev.* 587.

Barak, Aharon, "The Supreme Court 2001 Term—Foreword: A Judge on Judging: The Role of a Supreme Court in a Democracy" (2002) 116 *Harvard L. Rev.* 16.

Barrett, Richard, "Time to Re-examine Regulation Designed to Counter the Financing of Terrorism" (2008) 41 *Case Western L. Rev.* 7.

Bernstein, Steven, "When Is Non-State Global Governance Really Governance?" (2010) 1 *Utah L. Rev.* 91.

Blasi, Vincent, "The Pathological Perspective and the First Amendment" (1985) 85(4) *Colum. L. Rev.* 449.

Bosniak, Linda, "Citizenship Denationalized" (2000) 7 *Ind. J. Global Legal Stud.* 447.

Búrca, Gráinne de, "The European Court of Justice and the International Legal Order after *Kadi*" (2010) 51 *Harv. Int'l L.J.* 1.

Cole, David, "No Reason to Believe: Radical Skepticism, Emergency Power, and Constitutional Constraint" (2008) 75 *U. Chi. L. Rev.* 1329.

Craig, Tony, "Sabotage!" (2010) 25(3) *Intelligence & Nat'l Sec.* 309.

Crocker, Thomas P., "Torture, with Apologies" (2008) 86(3) *Tex. L. Rev.* 569.

Dancy, Geoff, Hunjoon Kim, and Eric Wiebelhaus-Brahm, "The Turn to Truth: Trends in Truth Commission Experimentation" (2010) 9 *J. Hum. Rts.* 45.

Dragu, Tiberiu, "Is There a Tradeoff between Security and Liberty? Executive Bias, Privacy Protections, and Terrorism Prevention" (2011) 105(1) *Am. Political Sci. Rev.* 64.

Filler, Daniel M., "Terrorism, Panic, and Pedophilia" (2003) 10 *Va. J. Soc. Pol'y & L.* 345.

Finn, John, "Sunset Clauses and Democratic Deliberation" (2009) 48 *Colum. J. Transnat'l L.* 442.

Finucane, Melissa L., et al., "The Affect Heuristic in Judgments of Risks and Benefits" (2000) 13 *J. Behavioral Decision Making* 1.

Forcese, Craig, "Spies without Borders: International Law and Intelligence Collection" (2011) 5 *J. Nati'l Sec. L. & Pol'y* 179.

Furedi, Frank, "Fear and Security: A Vulnerability-Led Policy Response" (2008) 42(6) *Social Pol'y & Admin.* 645.

Gross, Oren, "Chaos and Rules: Should Responses to Violent Crises Always Be Constitutional?" (2003) 112 *Yale L.J.* 1011.

______, "'Once More unto the Breach': The Systemic Failure of Applying the European Convention on Human Rights to Entrenched Emergencies" (1998) 23 *Yale J. Int'l L.* 437.

______, "The Normless and Exceptionless Exception: Carl Schmitt's Theory of Emergency Powers and the 'Norm-Exception' Dichotomy" (2000) 21 *Cardozo L. Rev.* 1825.

______ and Fionnuala Ní Aoláin, "Emergency, War and International Law: Another Perspective" (2001) 70 *Nordic J. Int'l Law* 29.

______, "Words as Power: The Rhetoric of War" *J. Gender, Race and Justice* (forthcoming).

Guthrie, Chris, et al., "Inside the Judicial Mind" (2001) 86 *Cornell L. Rev.* 777.

Hamilton, Melissa, "The Child Pornography Crusade and Its Net Widening Effect" (2012) 33 *Cardozo L. Rev.* 1679.

Hanson, Jon and David Yosifon, "The Situational Character: A Critical Realist Perspective on the Human Animal" (2004) 93 *Geo. L.J.* 1.

Hayner, Priscilla B., "Truth Commissions: A Schematic Overview" (June 2006) 88 *ICRC* 295.

Holmes, Stephen, "In Case of Emergency: Misunderstanding Tradeoffs in the War on Terror" (2009) 97 *Cal. L. Rev.* 301.

Horwitz, Paul, "Free Speech as Risk Analysis: Heuristics, Biases, and Institutions in the First Amendment" (2003) 76 *Temple L. Rev.* 1.

Huq, Aziz Z., "What Good Is Habeas?" (2010) 26 *Constitutional Commentary* 385.

Ip, John, "Sunset Clauses and Counter-Terrorism Legislation" (2012) 2013 *Public L.* 74.

Issacharoff, Samuel, "Behavioral Decision Theory in the Court of Public Law" (2002) 87 *Cornell L. Rev.* 671.

Johns, Fleur, "Guantanamo Bay and the Annihilation of the Exception" (2005) 16(4) *Eur. J. Int'l L.* 613.

Kahneman, Daniel, "Maps of Bounded Rationality: Psychology for Behavioral Economics" (2003) 93(5) *Am. Econ. Rev.* 1449.

Kaplow, Louis, "Rules versus Standards: An Economic Analysis" (1992) 42 *Duke L.J.* 557.

Karst, Kenneth L., "Threats and Meanings: How the Facts Govern First Amendment Doctrine" (2006) 58 *Stan. L. Rev.* 1337.

Kingsbury, Benedict, Nico Krisch, and Richard B. Stewart, "The Emergence of Global Administrative Law" (2004–2005) 68 *Law & Contemp. Problems* 15.

Koh, Harold Hongju, "On American Exceptionalism" (2003) 55 *Stan. L. Rev.* 1479.

Komárek, Jan, "European Constitutionalism and the European Arrest Warrant: In Search of the Limits of 'Contrapunctual Principles'" (2007) 44 *Common Market L. Rev.* 9.

Korobkin, Russell B. and Thomas S. Ulen, "Law and Behavioral Science: Removing the Rationality Assumption from Law and Economics" (2000) 88 *Cal. L. Rev.* 1051.

Kuran, Timur and Cass R. Sunstein, "Availability Cascades and Risk Regulation" (1999) 51 *Stan. L. Rev.* 683.

Lepsius, Oliver, "Liberty, Security, and Terrorism" (2004) 5 *German L.J.* 436.

______, "Human Dignity and the Downing of Aircraft: The German Federal Constitutional Court Strikes Down a Prominent Anti-terrorism Provision in the New Air-Transport Security Act" (2006) 7 *German L.J.* 761. For the printed version, see *Jus Politicum*, vol. III (Éditions Dalloz, 2011).

Levinson, Sanford, "'Precommitment' and 'Postcommitment': The Ban on Torture in the Wake of September 11" (2003) 81 *Tex. L. Rev.* 2013.

________, and Jack M. Balkin, "Constitutional Dictatorship: Its Dangers and Its Design" (2010) 94 *Minn. L. Rev.* 1789.

Lipschutz, Ronnie D., "Terror in the Suites: Narratives of Fear and the Political Economy of Danger" (1999) 13(4) *Global Society* 411.

Lowenstein, George F., Elke U. Weber, Christopher K. Hsee and Ned Welch, "Risk as Feelings" (2001) 127 *Psychological Bulletin* 267 at 275–76.

Loewenstein, George and Ted O'Donoghue, "'We Can Do This the Easy Way or the Hard Way': Negative Emotions, Self-Regulation, and the Law" (2006) 73 *U. Chi. L. Rev.* 183.

Loewenstein, Karl, "Militant Democracy and Fundamental Rights, I" (1937) 31(3) *Am. Political Sci. Rev.* 417.

______, "Militant Democracy and Fundamental Rights, II" (1937) 31(4) *Am. Political Sci. Rev.* 638.

Macdonald, Stuart, "The Unbalanced Imagery of Anti-terrorism Policy" (2009) 18(2) *Cornell J.L. & Pub. Pol'y* 519.

Margulies, Peter, "The Ivory Tower at Ground Zero: Conflict and Convergence in Legal Education's Responses to Terrorism" (2011) 60 *J. Legal Educ.* 373.

Masur, Jonathan S., "Probability Thresholds" (2006–2007) 92 *Iowa L. Rev.* 1293.

Mazzone, Jason, "The Security Constitution" (2005) 53 *UCLA L. Rev.* 29.

McDonald, James, "Democratic Failure and Emergencies: Myth or Reality?" (2007) 93 *Va. L. Rev.* 1785.

Meron, Theodor, "The Humanization of Humanitarian Law" (2000) 94(2) *Am. J. Int'l L.* 239.

Mitten, Matthew J. and Hayden Opie, "'Sports Law': Implications for the Development of International, Comparative, and National Law, and Global Dispute Resolution" (2010) 85 *Tul. L. Rev.* 269.

Mokhtar, Aly, "Human Rights Obligations v. Derogations: Article 15 of the European Convention on Human Rights" (2004) 8 *Int'l J. Hum. Rts.* 65.

Note, "War, Schemas, and Legitimation: Analyzing the National Discourse about War" (2006) 119 *Harv. L. Rev.* 2099.

Nuotio, Kimmo, "Terrorism as a Catalyst for the Emergence, Harmonization and Reform of Criminal Law" (2006) 4(5) *J. Int'l. Crim. Justice* 998.

Okafor, Obiora C., "Newness, Imperialism, and International Legal Reform in Our Time: A Twail Perspective" (2005) 43 *Osgoode Hall L.J.* 171.

Paul, John and Sangyoub Park, "With the Best of Intentions: The Color Coded Homeland Security Advisory System and the Law of Unintended Consequences" (2009) 4(2) *Res. & Prac. in Social Sci.* 1.

Pearlstein, Deborah, "Form and Function in the National Security Constitution" (2009) 41(5) *Conn. L. Rev.* 1549.

Porras, Ileana M., "On Terrorism: Reflections on Violence and the Outlaw" (1994) *Utah L. Rev.* 119.

Pozen, David, "The Mosaic Theory, National Security, and the FOIA" (2005) 115 *Yale L.J.* 628.

Quarantelli, E.L. and Russell R. Dynes, "Community Conflict: Its Absence and Its Presence in Natural Disasters" (1976) 1(2) *Mass Emergencies* 139.

Rachlinski, Jeffrey J., et al., "Inside the Bankruptcy Judge's Mind" (2006) 86 *Bos. U. L. Rev.* 1227.

______, "The Uncertain Psychological Case for Paternalism" (2003) 97 *Nw.U. L. Rev.* 1165.
Ratner, Steven R., "Overcoming Temptations to Violate Human Dignity in Times of Crisis: On the Possibilities for Meaningful Self-Restraint" (2004) 5 *Theoretical Inquiries in Law* 81.
Repetto, Thomas, "Crime Prevention and the Displacement Phenomenon" (1976) 22 *Crime & Delinquency* 166.
Roach, Kent, "Judicial Review of the State's Anti-terrorism Activities" (2009) 3 *Indian J. Constitutional L.* 138.
Rostow, Eugene V., "The Japanese American Cases—A Disaster" (1945) 54(3) *Yale L.J.* 489.
Rothe, Dawn and Stephen L. Muzzatti, "Enemies Everywhere: Terrorism, Moral Panic, and US Civil Society" (2004) 12 *Critical Criminology* 327.
Scalia, Antonin, "The Rule of Law as a Law of Rules" (1989) 56 *U. Chi. L. Rev.* 1175 at 1186.
Scheinin, Martin and Mathias Vermeulen, "Unilateral Exceptions to International Law: Systematic Legal Analysis and Critique of Doctrines to Deny or Reduce the Applicability of Human Rights Norms in the Fight against Terrorism" (2011) 8 *Essex Hum. Rts. Rev.* 20.
Scheppele, Kim Lane, "Law in a Time of Emergency: States of Exception and the Temptations of 9/11" (2004) 6(5) *J. Constitutional L.* 1.
Schutter, Olivier De, Asbjørn Eide, Ashfaq Khalfan, Marcos Orellana, Margot Salomon, and Ian Seiderman, "Commentary to the Maastricht Principles on Extraterritorial Obligations of States in the Area of Economic, Social and Cultural Rights," (2012) 34(4) *Hum. Rts. Q.* 1084.
Schwinn, Steven D., "The State Secrets Privilege in the Post 9/11 Era" (2010) 30(2) *Pace L. Rev.* 778.
Shapiro, J.N. and D.K. Cohen, "Color Blind: Lessons from the Failed Homeland Security Advisory System" (2007) 32 *Int'l Sec.* 121.
Slovic, Paul, "What's Fear Got to Do with It? It's Affect We Need to Worry About" (2004) 69 *Mo. L. Rev.* 971.
Small, Deborah A. and George Loewenstein, "The Devil You Know: The Effects of Identifiability on Punishment" (2005) 18 *J. Behavioral Decision Making* 311.
Steyn, Lord, "Guantanamo Bay: The Legal Black Hole" (2004) 53 *I.C.L.Q.* 1.
Sunstein, Cass R., "Behavioral Law and Economics: A Progress Report" (1999) 1 *Am. L. & Econ. Rev.* 115.
______, "On the Divergent American Reactions to Terrorism and Climate Change" (2007) 107 *Colum. L. Rev.* 503.
______, "Probability Neglect: Emotions, Worst Cases, and Law" (2002) 112 *Yale L.J.* 61.
______, "The Laws of Fear" (2002) 115 *Harv. L. Rev.* 1119.
Tushnet, Mark, "Defending Korematsu?: Reflections on Civil Liberties in Wartime" (2003) *Wisc. L. Rev.* 273.
Tversky, Amos and Daniel Kahneman, "Availability: A Heuristic for Judging Frequency and Probability" (1973) 5 *Cognitive Psychol.* 207.
Ungar, Sheldon, "Moral Panic versus the Risk Society: The Implications of the Changing Sites of Social Anxiety" (2001) 52(2) *Brit. J. Sociology* 271.
Vermeule, Adrian, "A New Deal for Civil Liberties: An Essay in Honor of Cass R. Sunstein" (2008) 43 *Tulsa L. Rev.* 921.
Viscusi, W. Kip and Richard J. Zeckhauser, "Sacrificing Civil Liberties to Reduce Terrorism Risk" (2003) 26 *J. Risk & Uncertainty* 99.
Waldron, Jeremy, "Safety and Security" (2006) 85 *Neb. L. Rev.* 454.

______, "Security and Liberty: The Image of Balance" (2003) 11(2) *J. Polit. Phil.* 191.

Walker, Clive, "Neighbor Terrorism and the All-Risks Policing of Terrorism" (2009) 3 *J. Nat'l Sec. Law & Policy* 121.

______, "Political Violence and Commercial Risk" (2004) 56 *Current Legal Problems* 531.

______, "The Governance of the Critical National Infrastructure" (2008) *Pub. L.* 323.

Weiss, Joanna Cohn, "Tough on Crime: How Campaigns for State Judiciary Violate Criminal Defendants' Due Process Rights" (2006) 81 *N.Y.U. L. Rev.* 1101.

Wells, Christina E., "Fear and Loathing in Constitutional Decision-Making" (2005) *Wisc. L. Rev.* 115.

______, "Questioning Deference" (2004) 69 *Mo. L. Rev.* 903.

Wiecek, William M., "The Legal Foundations of Domestic Anti-communism: The Background of *Dennis v. United States*" (2001) *Sup. Ct. Rev.* 375.

Wilson, Molly, J. Walker and Megan P. Fuchs, "Publicity, Pressure, and Environmental Legislation: The Untold Story of Availability Campaigns" (2009) 30 *Cardozo L. Rev.* 2147.

Zedner, Lucia, "Securing Liberty in the Face of Terror: Reflections from Criminal Justice" (2005) 32 *J. L. & Society* 507.

Zizek, Slavoj, "Good Manners in the Age of WikiLeaks" (2011) 33(2) *London Rev. Books* 2.

BOOKS

Agamben, Giorgio, *State of Exception* (Chicago: University of Chicago Press, 2005).

Alam, Shawkat, Natalie Klein, and Juliette Overland, eds., *Globalisation and the Quest for Social and Environmental Justice: The Relevance of International Law in an Evolving World Order* (New York: Routledge, 2011).

Barzilai, Gad, *A Democracy in Wartime: Conflict and Consensus in Israel* (Tel-Aviv: Sifriat Polaim, 1992)

Bazerman, Max H., *Judgment in Managerial Decision Making*, 4th ed. (New York: Wiley, 1998).

______ and Michael D. Watkins, *Predictable Surprises* (Boston: Harvard Business School Press, 2004).

Beck, Ulrich, *Risk Society: Towards a New Modernity*, 1st ed. (London: Sage, 1992).

Bellamy, Richard, *Political Constitutionalism: A Republican Defence of the Constitutionality of Democracy* (New York: Cambridge University Press, 2007).

Berreby, David, *Us and Them: The Science of Identity*, 2d ed. (Chicago: University of Chicago Press, 2008).

Bobbitt, Philip, *Terror and Consent: The Wars for the Twenty-First Century*, 1st ed. (Anchor Books, 2009).

Bogdandy, Armin von, and Jürgen Bast, eds., *Principles of European Constitutional Law*, rev. 2d ed. (Oxford: Hart Publishing, 2010).

Brown, Rupert, ed., *Prejudice: Its Social Psychology* (Wiley-Blackwell, 1995).

Buzan, Harry, Ole Waever, and Jaap de Wilde, *Security: A New Framework for Analysis* (Boulder, CO: Rienner, 1998).

Chesterman, Simon, *One Nation under Surveillance* (Oxford: Oxford University Press, 2011).

Clarke, R.V. and G.R. Newman, *Outsmarting the Terrorists* (New York: Praeger, 2006).

Cohen, Stanley, *Folk Devils and Moral Panics: The Creation of the Mods and Rockers*, 1st ed. (London: MacGibbon and Kee, 1972).

Cole, David, *Enemy Aliens: Double Standards and Constitutional Freedoms in the War on Terrorism* (New York: The New Press, 2003).

Covello, Vincent T, et al., eds., *Effective Risk Communication: The Role and Responsibility of Government and Nongovernment Organizations* (New York: Plenum, 1989).
Cutler, A. Claire, *Private Power and Global Authority: Transnational Merchant Law in the Global Political Economy* (Cambridge: Cambridge University Press, 2003).
Daniels, Ronald J., Patrick Macklem, and Kent Roach, eds., *The Security of Freedom: Essays on Canada's Antiterrorism Bill* (Toronto: University of Toronto Press, 2001).
De Lege Årsbook 2009 (Uppsala: Iustus, 2010).
Delmas-Marty, Mireille, *Pour Un Droit Commun* (Éditions du Seuil, 1989).
Elster, Jon, *Ulysses and the Sirens: Studies in Rationality and Irrationality*, rev. ed. (Cambridge: Cambridge University Press, 1984).
Ely, John Hart, *Democracy and Distrust: A Theory of Judicial Review* (Cambridge, Mass.: Harvard University Press, 1980).
Enders, Walter and Todd Sandler, *The Political Economy of Terrorism*, 2d ed. (Cambridge: Cambridge University Press, 2006).
Erikson, Kai, *A New Species of Trouble: Explorations in Disaster, Trauma, and Community*, 1st ed. (W.W. Norton, 1994).
Evans, Jonathan and Keith Frankish, eds., *In Two Minds: Dual Processes and Beyond* (New York: Oxford University Press, 2009).
Farber, Daniel, ed., *Security v. Liberty: Conflicts between Civil Liberties and National Security in American History* (New York: Russell Sage Foundation, 2008).
Farer, Tom, *Confronting Global Terrorism and American Neo-conservatism* (Oxford: Oxford University Press, 2007).
Fatovic, Clement and Benjamin A. Kleinerman, *Extra-Legal Power and Legitimacy: Perspectives on Prerogative* (New York: Oxford University Press, 2013).
Fichera, Massimo, *The Implementation of the European Arrest Warrant in the European Union: Law, Policy and Practice* (Cambridge: Intersentia 2011).
Fiske, Susan T., and Shelley E. Taylor, *Social Cognition: From Brains to Culture*, 3d ed. (New York: McGraw-Hill, 2007).
Fukuyama, Francis, *The End of History and the Last Man* (London: Penguin Books, 1992).
Garland, David, *The Culture of Control: Crime and Social Order in Contemporary Society* (Oxford: Oxford University Press, 2001).
Goldsmith, Jack, *Power and Constraint: The Accountable Presidency after 9/11* (New York: W.W. Norton, 2012).
______ and Tim Wu, *Who Controls the Internet? Illusions of a Borderless World* (Oxford: Oxford University Press, 2006).
Goode, Erich, and Nachman Ben-Yehuda, *Moral Panics: The Social Construction of Deviance*, 2d ed. (Wiley-Blackwell, 2009).
Goold, Benjamin J., and Liora Lazarus, *Security and Human Rights* (Portland, OR: Hart, 2007).
Graham, Stephen, ed., *Cities, War and Terrorism* (Oxford: Blackwell, 2004).
Gray, Jesse Glenn, *The Warriors: Reflections on Men in Battle* (New York: Harper and Row, 1973).
Greenberg, Karen J. and Joshua L. Dratel, eds., *The Torture Papers: The Road to Abu Ghraib* (Cambridge: Cambridge University Press, 2005).
Gross, Oren and Fionnuala Ní Aoláin, *Law in Times of Crisis: Emergency Powers in Theory and Practice* (Cambridge: Cambridge University Press, 2006).

Guild, Elspeth, ed., *Constitutional Challenges to the European Arrest Warrant* (London: Wolf Legal Publishers, 2006).
Harris, David J., Michael O'Boyle, Edward P. Bates, and C.M. Buckley, *Harris, O'Boyle & Warbrick: Law of the European Convention on Human Rights*, 2d ed. (Oxford: Oxford University Press, 2009).
Hatfield, Elaine, et al., *Emotional Contagion* (Cambridge: Cambridge University Press, 1993).
Hegel, George, Wilhelm Friedrich, *Elements of the Philosophy of Right*, ed. Allen W. Wood (Cambridge: Cambridge University Press, 1991 (1821)).
Hobbes, Thomas, *Leviathan*, ed. Edwin Curley (Hackett, 1994 (1651)).
Holmes, Stephen, *Passions and Constraint: On the Theory of Liberal Democracy* (Chicago: University of Chicago Press, 1995).
______, *The Matador's Cape: America's Reckless Response to Terror* (New York: Cambridge University Press, 2007).
______ and Cass R. Sunstein, *The Cost of Rights: Why Liberty Depends on Taxes* (New York: W.W. Norton, 1999).
Ignatieff, Michael, ed., *American Exceptionalism and Human Rights* (Princeton, N.J.: Princeton University Press, 2005).
Janis, Irving L., *Groupthink: Psychological Studies of Policy Decisions and Fiascoes*, 2d ed. (New York: Houghton Mifflin, 1982).
Jareborg, Nils, ed., *Inkast i straffområdet* (Uppsala: Iustus, 2006).
Jellinek, Georg, *System der subjektiven öffentlichen Rechte* (J.C.B. Mohr, 1892).
Jessup, Philip C., *Transnational Law* (New Haven: Yale University Press, 1956).
Jones, C., *A "clean city": The Olympic Games and Civil Liberties* (London: Statewatch, 2012) available at http://www.statewatch.org/analyses/no-192-olympics.pdf.
Kahn, Paul W., *The Reign of Law:* Marbury *v.* Madison *and the Construction of America* (New Haven, Conn.: Yale University Press, 1997).
Kahnemann, Daniel, et al., eds., *Judgment under Uncertainty: Heuristics and Biases* (New York: Cambridge University Press, 1982).
______ and Amos Tversky, eds., *Choices, Values, and Frames* (Cambridge University Press, 2000).
Krisch, Nico, *Beyond Constitutionalism: The Pluralist Structure of Postnational Law* (Oxford: Oxford University Press, 2010).
Langford, Malcolm, Wouter Vandenhole, Martin Scheinin, and Willem van Genugten, eds., *Global Justice, State Duties: The Extraterritorial Scope of Economic, Social, and Cultural Rights in International Law* (Cambridge: Cambridge University Press, 2013).
Lev, Amnon, *Sovereignty and Liberty: A Study of the Foundations of Power* (Routledge, 2014).
Lipschutz, Ronnie D., ed., *On Security* (New York: Columbia University Press, 1995).
Londras, Fiona de, *Detention in the "War on Terror": Can Human Rights Fight Back?* (Cambridge: Cambridge University Press, 2011).
Milanovic, Marko, *Extraterritorial Application of Human Rights Treaties: Law, Principles, and Policy* (Oxford: Oxford University Press, 2011).
Omand, David, *Securing the State* (London: Hurst & Co., 2010).
Orakhelashvili, Alexander, ed., *Research Handbook on Theory and History of International Law* (Cheltenham, UK: Elgar Press, 2011).
Paustenbach, Dennis J., ed., *Human and Ecological Risk Assessment: Theory and Practice* (New York: Wiley-Interscience, 2002).

Plous, Scott, *The Psychology of Judgment and Decision Making* (New York: McGraw-Hill Series in Social Psychology, 1993).

Popper, Karl R., *The Open Society and Its Enemies*, 5th ed., vol. 1 of 2 (Princeton, N.J.: Princeton University Press, 1971).

Posner, Eric A., and Adrian Vermeule, *Terror in the Balance: Security, Liberty, and the Courts* (New York: Oxford University Press, 2007).

Posner, Richard A., *Not a Suicide Pact* (New York: Oxford University Press, 2006).

Ramraj, Victor V, Michael Hor, Kent Roach, and George Williams, eds., *Global Anti-terrorism Law and Policy*, 2d ed. (Cambridge: Cambridge University Press, 2012).

Rawls, John, *A Theory of Justice*, rev. ed. (Cambridge, Mass.: Harvard University Press, 1999).

Roach, Kent, *September 11: Consequences for Canada* (Montreal: McGill-Queen's University Press, 2003)

______, ed., *The 9/11 Effect: Comparative Counter-Terrorism* (Cambridge: Cambridge University Press, 2011).

Roberts, Alasdair, *Blacked Out: Government Secrecy in the Information Age* (Cambridge: Cambridge University Press, 2006).

Rossiter, Clinton L., *Constitutional Dictatorship: Crisis Government in the Modern Democracies* (Princeton, N.J.: Princeton University Press, 1948).

______,ed., *The Federalist Papers* (New York: New American Library, 1961).

Russett, Bruce, *Controlling the Sword: The Democratic Governance of National Security* (Cambridge, Mass.: Harvard University Press, 1990).

Sadurski, Wojciech, *Rights before Courts: A Study of Constitutional Courts in Postcommunist States of Central and Eastern Europe* (Dordrecht, The Netherlands: Springer, 2005).

Sifry, Micah L., *WikiLeaks and the Age of Transparency* (New Haven, Conn.: Yale University Press, 2011).

Simon, Herbert A., *Models of Man: Social and Rational*, 1st ed. (Wiley, 1957).

Slaughter, Anne-Marie, *A New World Order* (Princeton, N.J.: Princeton University Press, 2004).

Slovic, Paul, *The Perception of Risk* (London: Earthscan, 2000).

Smith, David Livingstone, *Less than Human: Why We Demean, Enslave, and Exterminate Others*, 1st ed. (New York: St. Martin's Press, 2011).

Staniforth, Andrew, eds., *Blackstone's Counter-Terrorism Handbook*, 2d ed. (Oxford: Oxford University Press, 2011).

Stanovich, Keith E., *The Robot's Rebellion: Finding Meaning in the Age of Darwin* (Chicago: University of Chicago Press, 2005).

Steele, Robert, *On Intelligence: Spies and Secrecy in an Open World* (Fairfax, Va.: AFCEA International Press, 2000).

Sunstein, Cass R., ed., *Behavioral Law and Economics* (Cambridge: Cambridge University Press, 2000).

______, *Laws of Fear: Beyond the Precautionary Principle* (New York: Cambridge University Press, 2005).

______, *Why Societies Need Dissent* (Cambridge, Mass.: Harvard University Press, 2003).

Tomkins, Adam, *Our Republican Constitution* (Portland, Oregon: Hart, 2005).

Suskind, Ron, *The One Percent Doctrine: Deep Inside America's Pursuit of Its Enemies Since 9/11* (New York: Simon and Schuster, 2007).

Tuori, Kaarlo, and Suvi Sankari, eds., *The Many Constitutions of Europe* (Aldershot: Ashgate, 2010).

Tushnet, Mark, *The Constitution of the United States: A Contextual Analysis* (Oxford: Hart, 2009).
Umphrey, Martha, ed., *Law and Secrets* (Palo Alto: Standford University Press, 2011).
Walker, Clive, *Terrorism and the Law* (Oxford: Oxford University Press, 2011).
Walker, Neil, ed., *Europe's Area of Freedom, Security and Justice* (Oxford: Oxford University Press, 2004).
Ward, Ian, *Law, Text, Terror* (Cambridge: Cambridge University Press, 2009).
Weber, Max, *Essays in Sociology*, H.H. Gerth and C. Wright Mills, eds. (New York: Oxford University Press, 1946).
Weiler, Joseph H. H., *The Constitution of Europe* (Cambridge: Cambridge University Press, 1999).
Wilkinson, Paul, ed., *Homeland Security in the UK* (Abingdon: Routledge, 2007).
Yoo, John, *War by Other Means: An Insider's Account of the War on Terror*, 1st ed. (New York: Atlantic Monthly Press, 2006).
Zamir, Eyal, and Barak Medina, *Law, Economics, and Morality* (New York: Oxford University Press, 2010).
Zedner, Lucia, *Security* (Abingdon: Routledge, 2009).

CHAPTERS IN BOOKS

Ashworth, Andrew, "Security, Terrorism and the Value of Human Rights," in *Security and Human Rights*, ed. Benjamin J. Goold and Liora Lazarus (Portland, Oregon: Hart, 2007) 203.
Asp, Petter and Iain Cameron, "Terrorism and Legal Security—a Swedish and European perspective," in *De Lege Årsbook 2009* (Uppsala: Iustus, 2010).
Dyzenhaus, David, "Deference, Security and Human Rights," in *Security and Human Rights*, ed. Benjamin J. Goold and Liors Lazarus (Oxford: Hart, 2007) 125.
Jareborg, Nils, "Vilken sorts straffrätt vill vi ha? Eller Om defensiv och offensiv straffrättspolitik," in *Inkast i straffområdet*, ed. Nils Jareborg (Uppsala: Iustus, 2006).
Kahn, Paul W., "American Exceptionalism, Popular Sovereignty, and the Rule of Law," in *American Exceptionalism and Human Rights*, ed. Michael Ignatieff (Princeton, N.J.: Princeton University Press, 2005) 207.
Kahneman, Daniel and Amos Tversky, "Prospect Theory: An Analysis of Decision under Risk," in *Choices, Values, and Frames*, ed. Daniel Kahneman and Amos Tversky (Cambridge: Cambridge University Press, 2000) 17.
Lev, Amnon, "The Transformation of International Law in the 19th Century," in *Research Handbook on Theory and History of International Law*, ed. Alexander Orakhelashvili (Cheltenham: Elgar Press, 2011) 121.
Madison, Jameas, "The Federalist No. 49," in *The Federalist Papers*, ed. Clinton Rossiter (New York: New American Library, 1961) 315.
Monar, Jörg, "The Area of Freedom, Security and Justice," in *Principles of European Constitutional Law*, ed. Armin von Bogdandy and Jürgen Bast, rev. 2d ed. (Oxford: Hart Publishing, 2010), 551.
Noll, Roger G. and James E. Krier, "Some Implications of Cognitive Psychology for Risk Regulation," in *Behavioral Law & Economics*, ed. Cass R. Sunstein (Cambridge: Cambridge University Press, 2000) 325.
Ramraj, Victor V., "The Impossibility of Global Anti-terrorism Law?," in *Global Anti-terrorism Law and Policy*, 2d ed., eds. Victor V. Ramraj, Michael Hor, Kent Roach, and George Williams (Cambridge: Cambridge University Press, 2012) 44.
Roach, Kent, "The Dangers of a Charter-Proof and Crime-Based Response to Terrorism," in *The Security of Freedom: Essays on Canada's Antiterrorism Bill*, ed.

Ronald J. Daniels, Patrick Macklem, and Kent Roach (Toronto: University of Toronto Press, 2001) 131.

Roberts, Alasdair, "Open Secrets and Dirty Hands," in *The Secrets of Law*, ed. Austin Sarat, Lawrence Douglas, and Martha Umphrey (Palo Alto, CA: Stanford University Press, 2012) 25.

Sandman, Peter, "Hazard versus Outrage in the Public Perception of Risk," in *Effective Risk Communication: The Role and Responsibility of Government and Non-government Organizations*, ed. Vincent T. Covello, et al. (New York: Plenum, 1989) 45.

Saul, Ben, "'Why Do They Hate Us?... They Hate our Freedoms': The Globalisation of Terrorism and Counter-Terrorism," in *Globalisation and the Quest for Social and Environmental Justice: The Relevance of International Law in an Evolving World Order*, ed. Shawkat Alam, Natalie Klein, and Juliette Overland (New York: Routledge, 2011) 207.

Simpson, John, "The UK and the Threat of Nuclear Terrorism," in *Homeland Security in the UK*, ed. Paul Wilkinson (Abingdon: Routledge, 2007) 159.

Stanovich, Keith E., "Distinguishing the Reflective, Algorithmic, and Autonomous Minds: Is It Time for a Tri-Process Theory?," in *In Two Minds: Dual Processes and Beyond*, ed. Jonathan Evans and Keith Frankish (New York: Oxford University Press, 2009) 55.

Tuori, Kaarlo, "The Many Constitutions of Europe," in *The Many Constitutions of Europe*, ed. Kaarlo Tuori and Suvi Sankari (Aldershot: Ashgate, 2010) 3.

Tversky, Amos and Daniel Kahneman, "Judgment under Uncertainty: Heuristics and Biases," in *Judgment under Uncertainty: Heuristics and Biases*, ed. Daniel Kahneman, et al. (New York: Cambridge University Press, 1982) 3.

Waever, Ole, "Securitization and Desecuritization," in *On Security*, ed. Ronnie D. Lipschutz (New York: Columbia University Press, 1995) 46.

Walker, Neil, "In Search of the Area of Freedom, Security and Justice: A Constitutional Odyssey," in *Europe's Area of Freedom, Security and Justice*, ed. Neil Walker (Oxford: Oxford University Press, 2004) 3.

Wiener, Jonathan, "Precaution in a Multi-Risk World," in *Human and Ecological Risk Assessment: Theory and Practice*, ed. Dennis J. Paustenbach (New York: Wiley-Interscience, 2002) 1509.

Wilkinson, Paul, "Enhancing UK Aviation Security Post 9/11," in *Homeland Security in the UK*, ed. Paul Wilkinson (Abingdon: Routledge, 2007) 256.

CASES

Canada:

Abdelrazik v Canadian Minister of Foreign Affairs [2009] FC 580.

Charkaoui v Canada [2007] 1 S.C.R.350.

Sagen v Vancouver Organizing Committee for the 2010 Olympic & Paralympic Winter Games [2009], BCCA 522.

Suresh v Canada (Minister of Citizenship and Immigration) [2002] 1 SCR 3, SCC 1.

United States v Khadr, [2011] ONCA. 358.

Walker v Baird [1892] AC 491 (P.C.).

Denmark:

Danish Supreme Court, 2 July 2008, in *Ugeskrift for Retsvæsen* 2008, 2394 *et seq*.

Danish Supreme Court, 19 November 2008, in *Ugeskrift for Retsvæsen* 2009, 426 *et seq*.

Danish Supreme Court, 24 June 2011, in *Ugeskrift for Retsvæsen* 2011, 2695 *et seq.*
Danish Supreme Court, 1 June 2012, Case 10/2011.

European Court of Justice:
Costa v ENEL (C-6/64) [1964] ECR 585.
European Parliament v Council of the European Union and European Parliament v Commission of the European Communities (joined cases C-317/04 and C-318/04) [2006].
Kadi & Al Barakaat International Foundation v Council and Commission (C-402/05 and C-415/05), [2008] ECR I-6351.
Kadi and Al-Barakaat v. Council of the European Union (3 September 2008), C-402/05 P & 415/15 P.
Kadi v Commission (T-85/09), [2010].
Van Gend en Loos v Netherlands Inland Revenue Administration (C-26/62) [1963] ECR 1.

European Court of Human Rights:
A and Others v United Kingdom [2009] App. no. 3455/05, ECHR 301.
Aksoy v Turkey [1996] App. no. 21987/93, 23 EHRR 553.
Al-Nashif v Bulgaria [2002] App. No. 50963/99, EHRR 655.
Al Jedda v United Kingdom [2011] App. No. 27021/08, ECHR.
Al Skeini & Others v United Kingdom [2011] App. No. 55271/07, ECHR.
Association for European Integration and Human Rights v Bulgaria [2007] App. No. 62540/00, ECHR 533.
Babar Ahmad & Others v United Kingdom [2010] App. Nos. 24027/07, 11949/08, 36742/08, 66911/09 and 67354/09, ECHR.
Banković and Others v Belgium and Others [2001] App. no. 52207/99, ECHR.
Brannigan and McBride v United Kingdom [1993] App. nos. 14553/89 and 14554/89, 17 EHRR 539.
Brogan and Others v United Kingdom [1988] App. Nos. 11209/84, 11234/84, 11266/84, 11386/85, 11 EHRR 117.
Chahal v United Kingdom [1996] App. No. 22414/93, 23 EHRR 413.
Demir and Others v Turkey [1998] App. Nos. 21380/93, 21381/93 and 21383/93, 33 EHRR 43.
Gäfgen v Germany [2010] App. No. 22978/05, 52 EHRR 1.
Gillan and Quinton v UK [2010] App. No. 4158/05, ECHR 28.
Ireland v United Kingdom [1978] App. No. 5310/71, 2 EHRR 25.
Kenedi v Hungary [2009] App. No. 31475/05, ECHR.
Klass and Others v Germany [1978] App. No. 5029/71, 2 EHRR 214.
Murray v United Kingdom [1994] App. No. 14310/88, 19 EHRR 193.
Nuray Sen v Turkey [2003] App. No. 41478/98, ECHR 297.
S and Marper v United Kingdom [2008] App. Nos. 30562/04 and 30566/04, ECHR 1581.
Saadi v Italy [2008] App. No. 37201/06, 49 EHRR 30.
TASZ v Hungary [2009], App. No. 37374/05, ECHR.
Weber and Saravia v Germany [2006] App. No. 54934/00, Admissibility, ECHR.

Germany:
Bundnisverfassungsgericht, Judgment of 12 October 1993: 2 BvR 2134.
Bundnisverfassungsgericht, Judgment of 30 June 2009: 2 BvE 2/08.
Bundesverfassungsgericht, Judgment of 15 February 2006, 1 BvR 357/05.

Inter-American Court of Human Rights:
Claude Reyes and others v. Chile, no. 151 (19 September 2006).

Norway:
Norwegian Supreme Court, Judgment of 8 November 2007, in *Norsk Retstidende* 2007, 1573.

Sweden:
Court of Appeal (Svea hovrätt), Judgment of 3 October 2005, No. B3687-05, ILDC 280 SE.
Court of Appeal for Skåne and Blekinge (Hovrätten över Skåne och Blekinge) Judgment of 9 November 2009, No. B685-09.
Court of Appeal for Western Sweden (Hovrätten för Västra Sverige), Judgment of 2 March 2009, No. B4645-10.
Swedish ombudsman (Riksdagens ombudsmän), JO Decision of 22 March 2005, No. 2169-2004.

United Kingdom:
A and Others v Secretary of State for the Home Department [2004] UKHL 56.
Attorney General v De Keyser's Royal Hotel Ltd [1920] UKHL 1, [1920] AC 508.
Austin v Commissioner of Police of the Metropolis [2009] UKHL 5.
Burmah Oil Company Ltd. v Lord Advocate [1965] AC 75 (H.L.).
Buron v Denman [1848] 154 ER 450.
Calvin's Case (1608) 7 Co Rep 1a.
H.M. Treasury v Ahmed [2010] UKSC 2.
Johnstone v Pedlar [1921] UKHL 1, 2 AC 262.
Liversidge v Anderson [1942] AC 206 (H.L.).
Netz v Chuter Ede [1946] 1 All E.R. 628.
Nissan v Attorney General [1970] AC 179 (H.L.).
R (Gillan) v Metropolitan Police Commissioner [2006] UKHL 12.
R (Singh) v Governor of Durham Prison [1984] 1 All ER 983 (Q.B.).
R. v Bottrill, ex parte *Kuechenmeister* [1947] KB 41.
R v Chief Constable of South Yorkshire Police ex parte *LS and Marper* [2004] UKHL 39.
R. v Home Secretary, ex parte *Greene* [1941] 3 All E.R. 104 (C.A.).
Re Clifford and O'Sullivan [1921] 2 AC 570 (H.L.).
Secretary of State for the Home Department v AF [2009] UKHL 28.
Secretary of State v Rehman [2001] UKHL 47.
Somerset v Stewart, 98 Eng. Rep. 499 [1772].

United States:
Abd Al Hakim Alhag v. *Obama*, case no. 08/5310, filed August 5, 2008 (D.C. Cir).
ACLU v. *U.S. Department of Defense*, 628 F.3d 612 (D.C. Cir. 2011).
ACLU v. *Department of State*, Memorandum Opinion, Civ. No. 11-01072 (D.D.C., July 23, 2012).
Al-Bihani v. *Obama*, 590 F.3d 866 (D.C. Cir. 2010).
Al Maqaleh v. *Gates*, 605 F.3d 84 (D.C. Cir. 2010).
Arar v. *Ashcroft*, 585 F.3d 559 (2d Cir. 2009).
Boumediene v. *Bush*, 553 U.S. 723, 128 S. Ct. 2229 (2008).
CIA v. *Sims*, 471 U.S. 159 (1985).
El-Masri v. *Tenet*, 437 F. Supp. 2d 530 (E.D. Va. 2006).

Fitzgibbon v. *CIA*, 911 F.2d 755 (D.C. Cir. 1990).
Hamdan v. *Rumsfeld*, 548 U.S. 557 (2006).
Hamdi v. *Rumsfeld*, 542 U.S. 507 (2004).
Holder v. *Humanitarian Law Project*, 561 U.S. __, 130 S. Ct. 2705 (2010).
Johnson v. *Eisentrager*, 339 U.S. 763 (1950).
Kiyemba v. *Obama*, 555 F.3d 1022 (D.C. Cir. 2009).
Kiyemba v. *Obama*, 561 F.3d 509 (D.C. Cir. 2009).
Miranda v. *Arizona*, 384 U.S.436 (1966).
Mohamed v. *Jeppesen Dataplan, Inc.*, 614 F.3d 1070 (9th Cir. 2010).
Rasul v. *Bush*, 542 U.S. 466 (2004).
Salahi v. *Obama*, 625 F.3d 745 (D.C. Cir. 2010).
United States v. *Progressive*, 467 F. Supp. 990 (W.D. Wisc. 1979).
United States v. *Verdugo-Urquidez*, 494 U.S. 259 (1990).
Youngstown Sheet & Tube Co. v. *Sawyer*, 343 U.S. 579, 635 (1952).

LEGISLATION AND REGULATIONS

European Union:

Directive 76/769/EEC.

Sweden:

Act on Assumed Identities, 2006:939.
Act on Communications Interception for Defence Intelligence Purposes, 2008:717.
Act on Criminal Responsibility for Terrorist Offences, 2003:148.
Act on Criminal Responsibility for the Financing of Particularly Serious Crime in some cases, 2002:444.
Act on Criminal Responsibility for Public Provocation, Recruitment and Training concerning Terrorist Offences and other Particularly Serious Crimes, 2010:299.
Act on Defence Forces' Assistance to the Police in Combating Terrorism, 2006:343.
Act on Covert Bugging, 2007:978.
Act on Measures to Prevent Certain Serious Crimes, 2007:979.
Act on Measures to Prevent Money Laundering and Terrorist Financing, 2009:62.
Act on Special Controls over Aliens, 1991:572.
Act on Supervision of Certain Crime-Fighting Activities, 2007:980.
Act on Surrender from Sweden, 2003:1156.
Bill 1994/95:23.
Defence Intelligence Activity Act 2000:130.
Defence Intelligence Activity Ordinance 2000:131.
Instrument of Government, SFS nr: 1974:152, reprinted 2003:593.
Security Protection Act 2009:966.
Security Protection Ordinance 2009:969.

United Kingdom:

Agreement Dated the 25th Day of January 1996 Between Her Majesty's Secretary of State for National Heritage and the British Broadcasting Corporation.
Anti-terrorism, Crime and Security Act 2001.
Civil Aviation Act 1982.
Control of Major Accident Hazards Regulations 1999 (COMAH), 1999 SI/743 as amended by 2005 SI/1088.
Communications Act 2003.
Critical Infrastructure Information Act of 2002.

Dangerous Substances (Notification and Marking of Sites) Regulations 1990 (SI 1990/304).
Harbours, Docks and Piers Clauses Act 1847.
Military Lands Act 1892.
Planning (Hazardous Substances) Act 1990.
Port of London Act 1968.
Prevention of Terrorism Act 2005.
Railway Regulation Act 1840.
Serious Organised Crime and Police Act 2005.
Telecommunications Act 1984.
Terrorism Act 2000 (Remedial) Order 2011, SI 2011/631.
Terrorism Act 2006.
Terrorism Prevention and Investigation Measures Act 2011.
The Data Retention (EC Directive) Regulations 2009 (SI 2009/859).
The Manufacture and Storage of Explosives Regulations 2005 (SI 2005/1082).
The Marking of Plastic Explosives for Detection Regulations 1996 (SI 1996/890) (Northern Ireland, SR 1996/262).

United States:
8 CFR 231, Arrival and Departure Manifests.
19 CFR 122.31, Notice of Arrival.
49 U.S.C. § 44909, Passenger Manifests.
Air Transportation Safety and System Stabilization Act 2001, Pub. L. No. 107-42.
Authorization for Use of Military Force, Pub. L. No. 107-40, 115 Stat. 224 (2001).
Designation under Executive Order 12958, Order of September 26, 2002, 67 Fed. Reg. 189.
Designation under Executive Order 12958, Order of May 6, 2002, 67 Fed. Reg. 90.
Designation under Executive Order 12958, Order of December 12, 2001, 66 Fed. Reg. 239.
Detainee Treatment Act of 2005, Pub. L. No. 109-148.
E-Government Act of 2002, Pub. L. No. 107-347, 116 Stat. 2899.
Executive Order 13224: Blocking Property and Prohibiting Transactions With Persons Who Commit, Threaten To Commit, or Support Terrorism. September 23, 2001. 66 Fed. Reg. 49079 (September 25, 2001).
Executive Order 13292: Further Amendment to Executive Order 12958, as Amended, Classified National Security Information. March 25, 2003. 68 Fed. Reg. 15315 (March 28, 2003).
Executive Order 13491: Ensuring Lawful Interrogations. January 22, 2009. 74 Fed. Reg. 4893 (January 27, 2009).
Executive Order 13492: Review and Disposition of Individuals Detained at the Guantanamo Bay Naval Base and Closure of Detention Facilities. January 22, 2009. 74 Fed. Reg. 4897 (January 27, 2009).
Executive Order 13493: Review of Detention Policy Options. January 22, 2009. 74 Fed. Reg. 4901 (January 27, 2009).
Executive Order 13526: Classified National Security Information. December 29, 2009. 75 Fed. Reg. 707 (January 5, 2010).
Executive Order 13567: Periodic Review of Individuals Detained at Guantanamo Bay Naval Station Pursuant to the Authorization for Use of Military Force. March 7, 2011. 76 Fed. Reg. 13277 (March 10, 2011).
Military Commissions Act of 2006, Pub. L. No. 109-366, 120 Stat. 2600.

Military Commissions Act of 2009, Pub. L. No. 111-84, 123 Stat. 2190.
National Defence Authorisation Act for Fiscal Year 2007, Pub. L. No. 109-364, 120 Stat. 2083.
National Defense Authorization Act for Fiscal Year 2011, Pub. L. No. 111-383, 124 Stat. 4137.
Military Order: Detention, Treatment, and Trial of Certain Non-Citizens in the War Against Terrorism. November 13, 2001. 66 Fed. Reg. 57831 (November 16, 2001).
National Defense Authorization Act for Fiscal Year 2012, Pub. L. No. 112-81, 125 Stat. 1298.
OPEN Government Act of 2007, Pub. L. No. 110-175, 121 Stat. 2524.
Presidential Policy Directive: Requirements of the National Defence Appropriations Act, February 28, 2012.
Uniform Code of Military Justice, Pub. L. No. 81-506, 64 Stat. 107 (1950), codified as amended at 10 U.S.C. § 801 *et seq.* (2000).
United Nations Participation Act of 1945, sec. 5, Pub. L. No. 79-264, 59 Stat. 619, as amended 22 U.S.C. § 287c.

LEGISLATIVE PROCEEDINGS

United Kingdom:

Hansard, House of Commons, HC 442 (7 June 2004).
Hansard, House of Commons, HC 467 (14 November 2007).
Hansard, House of Commons, HC 485 (8 December 2008).
Hansard, House of Lords, HL 703 (22 July 2008).

United States:

Congressional Record, Senate, v. 151, S12657 (November 10, 2005).

Sweden:

Bill 2008/09:201.
Bill 2009/10:78.

GOVERNMENT DOCUMENTS AND REPORTS

Canada:

Commission of Inquiry into the Actions of Canadian Officials in Relation to Maher Arar, *Report of the Events Relating to Maher Arar: Analysis and Recommendations* (Ottawa: Public Works and Government Services Canada, 2006).
Commission of Inquiry into the Investigation of the Bombing of Air India Flight 182, *Air India Flight 182: A Canadian Tragedy,* vol. 5 (Ottawa: Supply and Services, 2010).

Denmark:

Undersøgelseskommissionen vedrørende Politiets Efterretningstjeneste, *PET-kommissionens beretning, Vol. 4: PET's virkemidler* (Copenhagen: Schultz, 2009)

European Union:

European Commission, Communication from the Commission to the European Parliament and the Council, *A European Terrorist Finance Tracking System: Available Options,* COM(2011) 429 final.
European Commission, Communication from the Commission to the European Parliament and the Council, *On the Use of Security Scanners at EU Airports,* COM(2010) 311/4.

European Commission, Proposal for a Council Decision on the conclusion of the Agreement between the European Union and the United States of America on the processing and transfer of Financial Messaging Data from the European Union to the United States for purposes of the Terrorist Finance Tracking Program, COM(2010) 316 final.

European Commission, Proposal for a Council Framework Decision on the use of Passenger Name Record (PNR) for law enforcement purposes, COM(2007) 654 final.

European Commission, Proposal for a Directive of the European Parliament and of the Council on the use of Passenger Name Record data for the prevention, detection, investigation and prosecution of terrorist offences and serious crime, COM(2011) 32 final.

European Council, Council Decision 2004/496/EC on the conclusion of an Agreement between the European Community and the United States of America on the processing and transfer of PNR data by Air Carriers to the United States Department of Homeland Security, Bureau of Customs and Border Protection, L 183, 20.05.2004 P. 83.

European Council, Draft Agreement between the United States of America and the European Union on the use and transfer of Passenger Name Record data to the United States Department of Homeland Security, 10453/11, 20.5.2011.

European Council, Proposal for a Directive of the European Parliament and of the Council on the use of Passenger Name Record data for the prevention, detection, investigation and prosecution of terrorist offences and serious crime, 9941/11, 20.5.2011.

European Council, *Internal Security Strategy for the European Union—Towards a European Security Model* (Luxembourg: Publications Office of the European Union, 2010).

European Council, *Processing of EU Originating Personal Data by United States Treasury Department for Counter Terrorism Purposes—SWIFT*, 10741/2/07 (22 June 2007).

European Council, *The Hague Programme—Strengthening Freedom, Security and Justice in the European Union*, 2005/C 53/01.

European Council, *The Stockholm Programme—an Open and Secure Europe Serving and Protecting Citizens*, 2010/C 115/01.

European Parliament, Committee on Civil Liberties, Justice and Home Affairs, *First ECC report on the implementation of the EU-US SWIFT undertakings*, LIBE/6/73175 (16 February 2009).

Tampere European Council, *15* and *16 October 1999—Conclusions* of the *Presidency*, Bulletin of the European Union, No. 10/1999.

Sweden:

Polisens tillgång till signalspaning i försvarsunderrättelsearbete, Ds 2011:44.

Report of the Commission of Inquiry into Certain Police Methods, SOU 2010:103.

United Kingdom:

Cabinet Office, *Cyber Security Strategy of the United Kingdom—Safety, Security and Resilience in Cyber Space* (Cm.7642, London, 2009).

Cabinet Office, *The National Security Strategy—A Strong Britain in an Age of Uncertainty* (Cm.7953, London, 2010).

Cabinet Office, *The National Security Strategy of the United Kingdom—Security in an Interdependent World* (Cm.7291, London, 2008).

Centre for the Protection of National Infrastructure, *Protecting against Terrorism*, 3d ed, (London, 2010).
Lord Carlile, *Report on the Operation in 2001–2009 of the Terrorism Act 2000* (Home Office, London).
Lord Cullen, *The Public Inquiry into the Shootings at Dunblane Primary School on 13 March 1996* (Cm.3386, 1996).
Department for International Development, *Bilateral Aid Review* (London, 2010).
Department for Trade and Industry, *Managing the Nuclear Legacy—A Strategy for Action* (Cm.5552, London, 2002).
Department for Transport, *Draft Civil Aviation Bill: An Effective Regulatory Framework for UK Aviation* (Cm.8234-I, London, 2011).
Department for Transport, *Interim Code of Practice for the Acceptable Use of Advanced Imaging Technology (Body Scanners) in an Aviation Security Environment* (London, 2010).
Department for Transport, *Modernising the British Transport Police* (London, 2001).
Department for Transport, *TRANSEC annual report 2009/10.*
Felson, M. and R. V. Clarke, *Opportunity Makes the Thief*, Police Research Series Paper 98, Home Office (London, 1998).
HM Inspectorate of Constabulary, *Adapting to Austerity* (London, 2011) online at http://data.gov.uk/dataset/adapting-to-austerity.
HM Inspectorate of Constabulary, *Demanding Times* (London, 2011) online at http://library.npia.police.uk/docs/hmic/Demanding-times-2011.pdf.
Home Office, *Addressing Lessons from the Emergency Response to the 7 July 2005 London Bombings* (London, 2006).
Home Office, *Circular 24/2002: A protocol between the Ministry of Defence Police and Home Office Police Forces.*
Home Office, *CONTEST: The United Kingdom's Strategy for Countering Terrorism* (Cm.8123, London, 2011).
Home Office, *Countering International Terrorism* (Cm.6888, London, 2006).
Home Office, *Crowded Places: The Planning System and Counter Terrorism* (London, 2010).
Home Office, *National Policing Plan 2003–2006* (London, 2002).
Home Office, *National Policing Plan 2004–2007* (London, 2003).
Home Office, *Operation of police powers under the Terrorism Act 2000 and subsequent legislation*, HOSB 15/11 (London, 2011).
Home Office, *Policing in the 21st Century* (Cm.7925, London, 2010).
Home Office, *Prevent Strategy* (Cm.8092, London, 2011).
Home Office, *Protecting Crowded Places: Design and Technical Issues* (London, 2010).
Home Office, *Pursue, Prevent, Protect, Prepare—The United Kingdom's Strategy for Countering International Terrorism* (Cm.7547, London, 2009).
Home Office, *Safer Places* (London, 2009).
Home Office, *Transposition of Directive 2006/24/EC* (London, 2008).
Home Office, *Working Together to Protect Crowded Places* (London, 2009 and 2010).
House of Commons, Committee of Public Accounts, *The budget for the London 2012 Olympic and Paralympic Games* (2007–08 HC 85).
House of Commons, European Scrutiny Committee, *Seventh Report* (2007–08 HC 16-vii).
House of Commons, Home Affairs Committee, *Counter Terrorism Measures in British Airports* (2009–10 HC 311).
House of Commons, Home Affairs Committee, *Policing in the 21st Century* (2007–08 HC 364).

House of Commons, Transport Committee, *UK Transport Security* (2005–06 HC 637).
House of Lords, European Union Committee, *Government Reply* (Cm.7461, London, 2008).
House of Lords, European Union Committee, *The Passenger Name Record (PNR) Framework Decision* (2007–08 HL 106).
Lord Lloyd, *Inquiry into Legislation against Terrorism* (Cm.3420, London, 1996).
Lord Macdonald of River Glaven, *Review of Counter-Terrorism and Security Powers* (Home Office, Cm.8003, January 2011).
Pitt, Michael, *Learning Lessons from the 2007 Floods Final Report*, Cabinet Office (London, 2008).
Ministry of Defence Police and Guarding Agency, *Annual Report and Accounts 2007–2008* (2007–08 HC 699).
Privy Counsellor Review Committee, *Anti-terrorism, Crime and Security Act 2001 Review Report* (2003–04 HC 100).
Wheeler, John, *Report on Airport Security,* Department for Transport (London, 2002).

United States:
CIA Inspector General, "Special Review, Counterterrorism Detention and Interrogation Activities" (May 7, 2004).
Commission on Protecting and Reducing Government Secrecy, Report (March 3, 1997).
Department of Army, Field Manual FM 2-22.3, Human Intelligence Collector Operations, Appendix M (September 2006).
Department of Defense, Memorandum from Secretary of Defense Donald Rumsfeld to the Pentagon (January 15, 2003), online at http://www.fas.org/sgp/news/2003/01/dodweb.html.
Department of Defense, The National Defense Strategy of the United States of America 6 (2005).
Department of Justice, "Decision Regarding Application of the Geneva Convention on Prisoners of War to the Conflict with Al-Qaeda and the Taliban." Draft Memorandum from Attorney General Alberto R. Gonzales to President George W. Bush (January 25, 2002), online at http://news.lp.findlaw.com/hdocs/docs/torture/gnzls12502mem2gwb2.html.
Department of Justice, Executive Office for Immigration Review, "Cases Requiring Special Procedure." Internal memorandum from Chief Immigration Judge Michael Creppy (September 21, 2001), online at http://fl1.findlaw.com/news.findlaw.com/wp/docs/aclu/creppy092101memo.pdf.
Department of Justice, Office of the Inspector General, *A Review of the FBI's Involvement in and Observations of Detainee Interrogations in Guantanamo Bay, Afghanistan, and Iraq* (May 2008).
Department of Justice, Office of the Inspector General, *A Review of the FBI's Use of National Security Letters* (March 9, 2007).
Department of Justice, Office of Legal Counsel, "Standards of Conduct for Interrogation under 18 U.S.C. §§ 2340–2340A," Memorandum from Assistant Attorney General Jay S. Bybee to Acting General Counsel of the Central Intelligence Agency John Rizzo (August 1, 2002).
Department of State, *Report of the United States of America: Submitted to the U.N. High Commissioner for Human Rights in Conjunction with the Universal Periodic Review* (2010).
Director of National Intelligence, *Vision 2015: A Globally Networked and Integrated Intelligence Enterprise* (July 22, 22 2008).

Gallis, Paul, "NATO in Afghanistan: A Test of the Transatlantic Alliance," Congressional Research Service, RL33627 (2006).

Garcia, Michael John and Charles Doyle, CSR Report for Congress, "Extradition to and from the United States: Overview of the Law and Recent Treaties," Congressional Research Service (March 17, 2010), available online at http://www.fas.org/sgp/crs/misc/98-958.pdf.

Garcia, et al., CRS Report for Congress, "Closing the Guantanamo Detention Center: Legal Issues," Congressional Research Service, R40139 (July 6, 2011).

Government Accountability Office, *Report on Information Sharing, GAO-06-385* (March 17, 2006).

Guantanamo Review Task Force, *Final Report* (Department of Justice, Washington DC, 2010).

House of Representatives, Committee on Government Reform – Minority Staff Special Investigations Division, *Secrecy in the Bush Administration* (September 14, 2004).

Information Security Oversight Office [Annual] *Report to the President* (2001–2010).

Information Security Oversight Office, *Audit of the Withdrawal of Records from Public Access at the National Archives and Records Administration for Classification Purposes* (April 26, 2006).

Moteff, John, *Critical Infrastructure: The National Asset Database*, CRS Report for Congress, RL33648 (Washington, DC, 2007).

National Commission on Terrorist Attacks Upon the United States, *The 9/11 Commission Report* (New York: Norton, 2004).

Senate, Committee on Foreign Rel., 111th Cong., *Afghanistan's Narco-War: Breaking the Link between Drug Traffickers and Insurgents* (Comm. Print 2009).

United States Intelligence Community, *Information Sharing Strategy* (February 22, 2008).

White House, "Humane Treatment of al Qaeda and Taliban Detainees." Memorandum from President George W. Bush to Vice-President Richard B. Cheney, et al., (February 7, 2002), online at http://www.dia.mil/publicaffairs/foia/pdf/detainee/Humane Treatment of al Qaeda and Taliban Detainees.pdf.

White House, "Transparency and Open Government." Memorandum from President Barack Obama to Heads of Executive Departments and Agencies (January 12, 2009).

INTERNATIONAL DOCUMENTS

African Commission and Human and People's Rights, 32nd Session Declaration of Principles on Freedom of Expression in Africa (October 2002).

Financial Action Task Force on Money Laundering, "FATF Public Statement" (25 February 2011), online at http://www.fatf-gafi.org/topics/high-riskandnon-cooperativejurisdictions/documents/fatfpublicstatement-25february2011.html.

Financial Action Task Force on Money Laundering, *History of the FATF*, online at http://www.fatf-gafi.org/pages/aboutus/historyofthefatf/ (last visited date November 17, 2013).

Financial Action Task Force on Money Laundering, "Improving Global AML/CFT Compliance: on-going process" (25 February 2011), online at http://www.fatf-gafi.org/topics/high-riskandnon-cooperativejurisdictions/documents/improvingglobalamlcftcomplianceon-goingprocess-25february2011.html.

Inter-American Commission on Human Rights, *Report on Terrorism and Human Rights*, OEA/Ser.L/V/II.116 (2002).

International Commission of Jurists, *Assessing Damage, Urging Action, Report of the Eminent Jurists Panel on Terrorism, Counter-Terrorism and Human Rights* (Geneva, 2009).

International Committee of the Red Cross, *Interpretive Guidance on the Notion of Direct Participation in Hostilities under International Humanitarian Law* (May 2009) (prepared by Nils Melzer), available online at http://www.icrc.org/eng/assets/files/other/icrc-002-0990.pdf.

International Committee of the Red Cross, *Report on the Treatment of Fourteen 'High Value Detainees' in CIA Custody* (14 February 2007).

International Court of Justice, *Legality of the Threat or Use of Nuclear Weapons, Advisory Opinion*, 1996 ICJ Rep. 226.

International Data Corporation, *The Digital Universe Decade—Are You Ready?* (May 2010).

International Data Corporation, *The Diverse and Exploding Digital Universe: An Updated Forecast of Worldwide Information Growth through 2011* (March 2008).

International Data Corporation, *The Expanding Digital Universe: A Forecast of Worldwide Information Growth through 2010* (March 2007).

International Telecommunication Union, *The World in 2010: Facts and Figures* (20 October 2010).

Joint Declaration of the U.N. Special Rapporteur on Freedom of Opinion and Expression, the OAS Special Rapporteur on Freedom of Expression and the OSCE Representative on Freedom of the Media (26 November 1999).

Joint Declaration of the U.N. Special Rapporteur on Freedom of Opinion and Expression, the OAS Special Rapporteur on Freedom of Expression and the OSCE Representative on Freedom of the Media (6 December 2004).

Siracusa Principles on the Limitation and Derogation Provision in the International Covenant on Civil and Political Rights (1984).

U.N.Commission on Human Rights, Promotion and Protection of Human Rights, Report of the Special Rapporteur on the promotion and protection of human rights and fundamental freedoms while countering terrorism, Martin Scheinin, 28 December 2005, UN doc. E/CN.4/2006/98.

U.N.Committee Against Torture, Ahmed Hussein Mustafa Kamil Agiza v. Sweden, Communication No. 233/2003, UN doc. CAT/C/34/D/233/2003, (24 May 2005).

U.N.General Assembly, Promotion and protection of human rights and fundamental freedoms while countering terrorism, Note by the Secretary-General, 21 September 2005, UN doc. A/60/370.

U.N.General Assembly, Promotion and protection of human rights and fundamental freedoms while countering terrorism, Note by the Secretary-General, 16 August 2006, UN doc. A/61/267.

U.N.General Assembly, Promotion and protection of human rights and fundamental freedoms while countering terrorism, Note by the Secretary-General, 15 August 2007, UN doc. A/62/263.

U.N.General Assembly, Promotion and protection of human rights and fundamental freedoms while countering terrorism, Note by the Secretary-General, 6 August 2008, UN doc. A/63/223.

U.N.General Assembly, Promotion and protection of human rights and fundamental freedoms while countering terrorism, Note by the Secretary-General, 3 August 2009, UN doc. A/64/211.

U.N.General Assembly, Promotion and protection of human rights and fundamental freedoms while countering terrorism, Note by the Secretary-General, 6 August 2010, UN doc. A/65/258.

U.N.General Assembly, Promotion and protection of human rights and fundamental freedoms while countering terrorism, Note by the Secretary-General, 18 August 2011, UN doc. A/66/310.

U.N.General Assembly, Resolution: The United Nations Global Counter-Terrorism Strategy, 8 September 2006, UN doc. A/RES/60/288.

U.N.General Assembly, Resolution: Protection of human rights and fundamental freedoms while countering terrorism, 22 January 2010, UN doc. A/RES/64/168.

U.N.Human Rights Committee, CCPR General Comment No. 29: Article 4: Derogations during a State of Emergency, 31 August 2001, UN doc. CCPR/C/21/Rev.1/Add.11.

U.N.Human Rights Council, Implementation of General Assembly Resolution 60/251 of 15 March 2006 entitled "Human Rights Council," Report of the Special Rapporteur on the promotion and protection of human rights and fundamental freedoms while countering terrorism, Martin Scheinin, 29 January 2007, UN doc. A/HRC/4/26.

U.N.Human Rights Council, Promotion and protection of all human rights, civil, political, economic, social and cultural rights, including the right to development; Joint study on global practices in relation to secret detention in the context of countering terrorism of the Special Rapporteur on the Promotion and Protection of Human Rights and Fundamental Freedoms while Countering Terrorism, 19 February 2010, UN doc. A/HRC/13/42.

U.N.Human Rights Council, Promotion and protection of all human rights, civil, political, social and cultural rights, including the right to development; Report of the Special Rapporteur on the promotion and protection of human rights and fundamental freedoms while countering terrorism, Martin Scheinin, 21 November 2007, UN doc. A/HRC/6/17.

U.N.Human Rights Council, Promotion and protection of all human rights, civil, political, social and cultural rights, including the right to development, Report of the Special Rapporteur on the promotion and protection of human rights and fundamental freedoms while countering terrorism, Martin Scheinin, 4 February 2009, UN doc. A/HRC/10/3.

U.N.Human Rights Council, Promotion and protection of all human rights, civil, political, economic, social and cultural rights, including the right to development, Report of the Special Rapporteur on the promotion and protection of human rights and fundamental freedoms while countering terrorism, Martin Scheinin, 28 December 2009, UN doc, A/HRC/13/37.

U.N.Human Rights Council, Report of the Special Rapporteur on the promotion and protection of human rights and fundamental freedoms while countering terrorism, Compilation of good practices on legal and institutional frameworks and measures that ensure respect for human rights by intelligence agencies while countering terrorism, including on their oversight, Martin Scheinin, 17 May 2010, UN doc. A/HRC/14/46.

U.N.Human Rights Council, Report of the Special Rapporteur on the promotion and protection of human rights and fundamental freedoms while countering terrorism, Framework principles for securing the human rights of victims of terrorism, Ben Emmerson, 4 June 2012 UN doc. A/HRC/20/14.

U.N.Human Rights Council, Report of the Special Rapporteur on the promotion and protection of human rights and fundamental freedoms while countering terrorism, Ten areas of best practices in countering terrorism, Martin Scheinin, 22 December 2010, UN doc. A/HRC/16/51.

U.N.Human Rights Council, Resolution 13/26, Protection of human rights and fundamental freedoms while countering terrorism, 15 April 2010, UN doc. A/HRC/RES/13/26.

U.N.Office of the High Commissioner for Human Rights, Note to the Chair of the Counter-Terrorism Committee: A Human Rights Perspective On Counter-Terrorist Measures (23 September 2002).

U.N.Office of the High Commissioner for Human Rights, Proposals for "Further Guidance" for the Submission of Reports Pursuant to Paragraph 6 of Security Council Resolution 1373 (2001) (intended to supplement the Guidance of 26 October 2001)—Compliance with International Human Rights Standards, (23 September 2002).

U.N.Security Council, 4453rd meeting, 18 January 2002, UN doc. S/PV.4453.

U.N.Security Council, Conclusions for policy guidance regarding human rights and the CTC, 25 May 2006, UN doc. S/AC.40/2006/PG.2 (2006).

U.N.Security Council, Security Council Resolution 1373 (2001) [on threats to international peace and security caused by terrorist acts], 28 September 2001, UN doc. S/RES/1373 (2001).

U.N.Security Council, Security Council Resolution 1456 (2003) on combating terrorism, 20 January 2003, S/RES/1456 (2003).

U.N.Security Council, Security Council Resolution 1822 (2008) [on continuation of measures imposed against the Taliban and Al-Qaida], 30 June 2008, S/RES/1822 (2008).

U.N.Security Council, Counter-Terrorism Committee, Guidance Note for Submission of Reports under Resolution 1373 (26 October 2001).

TREATIES AND INTERNATIONAL CONVENTIONS

Agreement between the European Union and the United States of America on the processing and transfer of passenger name record (PNR) data by air carriers to the United States Department of Homeland Security (13668/06) OJ L 298, 27.10.2006, at 29–31.

Agreement between the European Union and the United States of America on the processing and transfer of Passenger Name Record (PNR) data by air carriers to the United States Department of Homeland Security (11304/07), OJ L 204, 4.8.2007, at 18–25.

Agreement between the United States and Cuba for the Lease of Lands for Coaling and Naval Stations, February 23, 1903, U.S.-Cuba, Article III, T.S. No. 418.

Convention Against Torture and Other Cruel, Inhuman or Degrading Treatment or Punishment, opened for signature Dec. 10, 1984, S. Treaty Doc. No. 100-20 (1988), 1465 U.N.T.S. 85.

Geneva Convention (III) Relative to the Treatment of Prisoners of War (12 August 1949), 6 U.S.T. 3316, 75 U.N.T.S.

American Convention on Human Rights (18 July 1978) 1144 U.N.T.S. 123.

International Committee of the Red Cross (ICRC), Protocol Additional to the Geneva Conventions of 1949 and relating to the Protection of Victims of International Armed Conflict (Protocol I), (8 June 1977) 1125 U.N.T.S. 3.

International Committee of the Red Cross (ICRC), Protocol Additional to the Geneva Conventions of 12 August 1949 and relating to the Protection of Victims of Non-International Armed Conflicts, (8 June 1977) 1125 U.N.T.S. 609.

International Covenant on Civil and Political Rights, G.A. res. 2200A (XXI), 21 U.N. GAOR Supp. (No. 16) at 52, U.N. Doc. A/6316 (1966), 999 U.N.T.S. 171 (entered into force 23 March 1976).

Rome Statute of the International Criminal Court (1998), U.N. Doc. A/Conf. 183/9th, available online at http://untreaty.un.org/cod/icc/statute/romefra.htm.

Treaty Defining Relations with Cuba (29 May 1934), U.S.-Cuba, 48 Stat. 1683, T.S. No. 866.

NEWS AND MEDIA REPORTS

"After the Attacks: Bush's Remarks to Cabinet and Advisors" New York Times (13 September 2011), online at http://www.nytimes.com/2001/09/13/us/after-the-attacks-bush-s-remarks-to-cabinet-and-advisers.html.

Alarkon, Walter, "Congress Uses Spending Bills to Halt Closing of Guantanamo Bay" The Hill (4 October 2009), online at http://thehill.com/homenews/house/61549-congress-uses-spending-bills-to-halt-gitmo-closing.

Apuzzo, Matt, "U.S., Canada Are Close Allies. That's Classified?" Associated Press (9 December 2010), online at http://seattletimes.com/html/politics/2013631961_apwikileaksthatsclassified.html.

"Britain 'at War with Terrorism'" BBC News (16 September 2001), online at BBC News, http://news.bbc.co.uk/2/hi/uk_news/politics/1545411.stm.

Burke, Jason, "Secret World of U.S. Jails" Observer (12 June 12 2004), online at http://www.guardian.co.uk/world/2004/jun/13/usa.terrorism.

"Bush Admits to CIA Secret Prisons" BBC (7 September 2006), online at http://news.bbc.co.uk/2/hi/americas/5321606.stm.

Calabresi, Massimo, "Ex-CIA Counterterror Chief: 'Enhanced Interrogation' Led U.S. to bin Laden" TIME (4 May 2011), online at, http://swampland.time.com/2011/05/04/did-torture-get-the-us-osama-bin-laden.

"Canada Court Denies Khadr Terror Extradition Appeal" BBC (6 May 2011), online at http://www.bbc.co.uk/news/world-us-canada-13319957.

Carter, Jimmy, Op-ed., "Obama's Human Rights Opportunity" The Washington Post (10 December 2008), online at http://www.cartercenter.org/news/editorials_speeches/obamas_human_rights_opportunity.html.

Claiborne, William, "FBI Gives Reward to Unabomber's Brother" The Washington Post (21 August 1998), online at http://www.washingtonpost.com/wp-srv/national/longterm/unabomber/trialstory.htm.

CNN Political Unit, "Poll: WikiLeaks Has Few Fans in U.S." CNN (30 December 2010), online at http://politicalticker.blogs.cnn.com/2010/12/30/cnn-poll-wikileaks-has-few-fans-in-u-s/.

CNN Wire Staff, "Freed Hikers Recount 2 years of 'Lies and False Hope'" CNN (25 September 2011), online at http://articles.cnn.com/2011-09-25/us/us_us-iran-hikers_1_sarah-shourd-iranian-authorities-iranian-prison?_s=PM:US.

Condon, Stephanie, "Poll: Americans Concerned WikiLeaks Dump Will Hurt the U.S." CBS News (3 December 2010), online at http://www.cbsnews.com/8301-503544_162-20024619-503544/poll-americans-concerned-wikileaks-dump-will-hurt-the-u-s-/.

De Borchgrave, Arnaud, "The High Cost of Intelligence Secrecy" Newsmax (16 January 2008), online at http://www.newsmax.com/deBorchgrave/secrecy/2008/01/16/id/322664.

De Sola, David, "U.S. agencies warn unauthorized employees not to look at WikiLeaks" CNN (3 December 2010), online at http://edition.cnn.com/2010/US/12/03/wikileaks.access.warning/index.html.

Editorial, "An Exit Strategy for Guantanamo" New York Times (3 May 2007), online at http://www.nytimes.com/2007/05/03/opinion/03thu2.html.

Feinberg, Russ "Secret Laws" L.A. Times (8 May 2008).

Frontline, "Extraordinary Rendition" PBS (4 November 2007), online at http://www.pbs.org/frontlineworld/stories/rendition701/.

Greenwald, Glenn, "When Presidential Sermons Collide" Salon (25 March 2010), online at http://www.salon.com/news/opinion/glenn_greenwald/2010/03/25/obama.

Grimes, William, "Louis Henkin, Leader in Field of Human Rights Law, Dies at 92" New York Times (17 October 2010), online at http://www.nytimes.com/2010/10/17/us/17henkin.html.

Jeffery, Simon, "The Rules of the Game Are Changing" The Guardian (5 August 2005), online at http://www.guardian.co.uk/uk/2005/aug/05/july7.uksecurity5.

Johnston, David and Charlie Savage, "Obama Reluctant to Look Into Bush Programs" New York Times (12 January 2009), online at http://www.nytimes.com/2009/01/12/us/politics/12inquire.html?pagewanted=all.

Kayyem, Juliette, Op-ed., "The War on Terror is Over" Boston Globe (10 September 2011), online at http://articles.boston.com/2011-09-10/bostonglobe/30139939_1_terror-war-homeland-security-adviser.

Keith, Tamara, "Pentagon Papers Declassified after 40 Years" NPR (13 June 2011), online at http://www.npr.org/2011/06/13/137150344/after-40-years-pentagon-papers-declassified-in-full.

McNeal, Greg, "Obama's Self-Serving Leaks, His Selective Outrage and the Need for a Special Counsel" Forbes (8 June 2012), online at http://www.forbes.com/sites/gregorymcneal/2012/06/08/obamas-self-serving-leaks-his-selective-outrage-and-the-need-for-a-special-counsel/.

Perens, Bruce, "Why Security through Obscurity Won't Work" Slashdot (20 July 1998), online at http://slashdot.org/features/980720/0819202.shtml.

Perez-Rivas, Manuel, "Bush Vows to Rid the World of 'Evil-Doers'" CNN (16 September 2001), online at http://edition.cnn.com/2001/US/09/16/gen.bush.terrorism/.

Perrin, Chad, "Security through Visibility: The Secrets of Open Source Security" TechRepublic (25 April 2006), online at http://www.techrepublic.com/article/security-through-visibility-the-secrets-of-open-source-security/6064734.

Priest, Dana, "CIA Holds Terror Suspects in Secret Prisons" The Washington Post (2 November 2005), online at http://www.washingtonpost.com/wp-dyn/content/article/2005/11/01/AR2005110101644.html.

______ and William M. Arkin, "Top Secret America" The Washington Post (19 July 2010), online at http://projects.washingtonpost.com/top-secret-america/articles/a-hidden-world-growing-beyond-control/.

Raju, Manu and Elana Schor, "Feinstein, Harkin Aim to Shut Guantanamo through Defence Authorisation Bill" The Hill (21 June 2007), online at http://thehill.com/leading-the-news/feinstein-harkin-aim-to-shut-guantnamo-through-defense-authorization-bill-process-2007-06-21.html.

Risen, James and Eric Lichtblau, "Bush Lets U.S. Spy on Callers without Courts" N.Y. Times (16 December 2005), online at http://www.nytimes.com/2005/12/16/politics/16program.html?pagewanted=all&_r=0.

Ross, Brian and Richard Esposito, "Exclusive: Only Three Have Been Waterboarded by CIA" ABC News (2 November 2007), online at http://abcnews.go.com/blogs/headlines/2007/11/exclusive-only/.

Shachtman, Noah, "Open Source Intel Rocks—Sorry, It's Classified" Wired (17 September 2008), online at http://www.wired.com/dangerroom/2008/09/download-hayden/.

Shane, Scott, "Keeping Secrets WikiSafe" New York Times (11 December 2010), online at http://www.nytimes.com/2010/12/12/weekinreview/12shane.html?pagewanted=all.

______, "Secrets in Plain Sight in Censored Book's Reprint" New York Times (17 September 2010), online at http://www.nytimes.com/2010/09/18/us/18book.html.

______ and Benjamin Weiser, "U.S. Drops Plan for a 9/11 Trial in New York City" New York Times (29 January 2010) A1, online at http://www.nytimes.com/2010/01/30/nyregion/30trial.html?pagewanted=all&_r=0.

Smith, Craig S. and Souad Mekhennet, "Algerian Tells of Dark Term in U.S. Hands" New York Times (7 July 2006), online at http://www.nytimes.com/2006/07/07/world/africa/07algeria.html?pagewanted=all&_r=0.

Sniffen, Michael J. and John Solomon, "Thousands of Federal Trials Kept Secret" USA Today (5 March 2006).

Stark, Holger, "Germany Limits Information Exchange with US Intelligence" Der Spiegel (17 May 2011) (Christopher Sultan, trans.), online at http://www.spiegel.de/international/germany/0,1518,druck-762873,00.html.

"The Leaky Corporation: Digital Information Is Easy Not Only to Store but also to Leak. Companies Must Decide What They Really Need to Keep Secret, and How Best to Do So" The Economist (26 February 2011), online at http://www.economist.com/node/18226961.

"This Week: Jake Tapper Interviews CIA Director Leon Panetta" Transcript of Television Broadcast, ABC News (27 June 2010), online at http://abcnews.go.com/ThisWeek/week-transcript-panetta/story?id=11025299&page=4.

"US 'Erodes' Global Human Rights" BBC (13 January 2005), online at http://news.bbc.co.uk/2/hi/americas/4171177.stm.

Weisberg, Joseph, "The CIA's Open Secrets" New York Times (27 August 2007), online at http://www.nytimes.com/2007/08/27/opinion/27weisberg.html.

Wintour, Patrick, "Blair Vows to Root Out Extremism" The Guardian (6 August 2005), online at, http://www.guardian.co.uk/politics/2005/aug/06/terrorism.july7.

Worthington, Andy, "Seven Years of Torture: Binyam Mohamed Tells His Story" (8 March 2009), online at http://www.andyworthington.co.uk/2009/03/08/seven-years-of-torture-binyam-mohamed-tells-his-story/.

Yoo, John, "The Supreme Court Goes to War" Wall Street Journal (17 June 2008), online at http://online.wsj.com/article/SB121366596327979497.html.

WORKING/RESEARCH PAPERS

Coglianese, Cary, "The Transparency President? The Obama Administration and Open Government," University of Pennsylvania Public Law and Legal Theory Research Paper Series, Paper No. 09-18, online at Social Science Research Network, http://papers.ssrn.com/sol3/papers.cfm?abstract_id=1433815.

Davis, Kevin and Benedict Kingsbury, "Obligation Overload: Adjusting the Obligations of Fragile or Failed States" (Fall 2010) (unpublished draft), presented at the Hauser Globalization Colloquium, New York University School of Law.

Elster, Jon, "Emotions and Behavioral Economics," (2006) (unpublished manuscript), online at Ragnar Frisch Centre for Economic Research, University of Oslo, online at http://www.frisch.uio.no/behave_seminar/papers/Elster.pdf at 18.

Gross, Oren, "Security vs. Liberty: An Imbalanced Balancing," (2009) (unpublished manuscript), online at Social Science Research Network, http://papers.ssrn.com/sol3/papers.cfm?abstract_id=1471634.

McAdams, Richard H., "Present Bias and Criminal Law," John M. Olin Law and Economics Working Paper No. 562 (2d Series), The University of Chicago Law School (2011), online at Social Science Research Network, http://ssrn.com/abstract=1893008.

Scheinin, Martin, "Terrorism and the Pull of 'Balancing' in the Name of Security," in *Security and the Law—Facing the Dilemmas*, ed. Martin Scheinin, et al., E.U.I. Working Papers in Law (Nov. 2009).

Sunstein, Cass R. and Reid Hastie, "Four Failures of Deliberating Groups" (April 2008), John M. Olin Law & Economics Working Paper no. 401 (2d Series); Public Law and Legal Theory Working Paper no. 215, online at Social Science Research Network, http://ssrn.com/abstract=1121400).

Zimbardo, Philip G., "The Political Psychology of Terrorist Alarms" (2003), available online at, American Psychological Association, http://www.zimbardo.com/downloads/2002%20Political%20Psychology%20of%20Terrorist%20Alarms.pdf.

SPEECHES/TESTIMONIES/STATEMENTS

Benjamin, Daniel, U.S. Department of State, "U.S. Counterterrorism Strategy in Yemen: Remarks to the U.S. Institute of Peace, Washington D.C." (8 September 2010), online at http://www.state.gov/j/ct/rls/rm/2010/147296.htm.

Blair, Dennis C., Director of National Intelligence, Statement for the Record, Hearing Before House Permanent Select Committee on Intelligence, 111th Congress at 74 (2 February 2010).

Blanton, Thomas, Statement to the Committee on the Judiciary, U.S. House of Representatives, Hearing on the Espionage Act and the Legal and Constitutional Implications of Wikileaks (16 December 2010).

Bush, President George W., "Remarks by the President at Connecticut Republican Committee Luncheon" (9 April 2002), online at http://georgewbush-whitehouse.archives.gov/news/releases/2002/04/20020409-8.html.

Center for Human Rights and Global Justice, "Surviving the Darkness: Testimony from the Secret 'Black Sites'" (2007).

Clinton, Hilary, "Remarks to the Press on Release of Purportedly Confidential Documents by WikiLeaks" (29 November 2010), online at http://www.state.gov/secretary/rm/2010/11/152078.htm.

Crowe, June and Thomas S. Davidson, "The 'Grey' Intersection of Open Source Information and Intelligence," GL10 Conference in Amsterdam (8 December 2008).

Graham, Lindsey, U.S. Senator "Comments at Carnegie Endowment for International Peace" (15 June 2011), available online at http://carnegieendowment.org/files/0615carnegie-graham.phf (at 00:46:07 of transcript).

Holder, Eric, Declaration, *Fazaga v. FBI*, 8:11-cv-00301-CJC –VBK, Cir.D. Ca. (1 August 2010).

Holder, Eric, Testimony to the Senate Judiciary Committee (18 November 2009), online at http://www.justice.gov/ag/testimony/2009/ag-testimony-091118.html.

Koh, Harold Hongju, U.S. Department of State, "Remarks at Annual Meeting of the American Society of International Law" (25 March 2010), online at http://www.state.gov/s/l/releases/remarks/139119.htm.

Obama, President Barack, "Remarks by the President at the Pentagon Memorial," (11 September 2010), online at http://www.whitehouse.gov/the-press-office/2010/09/11/remarks-president-pentagon-memorial.

Pope John Paul II, "Address of Pope John Paul II to the Honorable George W. Bush President of the United States of America (4 June 2004)," Insegnamenti di Giovanni Paolo II, XXVII, online at http://www.vatican.va/holy_father/john_paul_ii/speeches/2004/june/documents/hf_jp-ii_spe_20040604_president-usa_en.html.

Rona, Gabor, Remarks at the Eminent Jurists Panel on Terrorism, Counter-Terrorism and Human Rights (19 September 2006), online at http://www.humanrightsfirst.org/wp-content/uploads/pdf/06922-usls-icj-ej-panel-hrf-pres.pdf.

Waxman, Matthew, Opening Statement of Matthew Waxman, Head of U.S. Delegation before the UN Human Rights Committee (17 July 2006), available online at http://2001-2009.state.gov/g/drl/rls/70392.htm.

MISCELLANEOUS

Advertising Standards Authority, Complaint Ref: 122211, Ruling on The Association of Chief Police Officers (11 August 2010).

Article 19, "*Five Billion Now Have Right to Information*" (28 September 2010).

Bank for International Settlements, *History of the Basel Committee and Its Membership*, online at www.bis.org/bcbs/history.htm.

Bybee, Jay S., Office of Legal Counsel, Department of Justice, Memorandum to Alberto R. Gonzales, Counsel to the President, "Standards of Conduct for Interrogation under 18 U.S.C. §§ 2340–2340A," (1 August 2002).

European Court of Human Rights, Press Unit, "Factsheet—Expulsions and Extraditions" (June 2011).

Eviatar, Daphne, "High Stakes for an Administration Battle: A National Security Nightmare" Human Rights First Blog (16 September 2011), online at http://www.humanrightsfirst.org/2011/09/16/high-stakes-for-an-administration-battle-a-national-security-nightmare/.

Fellmeth, Aaron, "International Law and Foreign Laws in the U.S. State Legislatures," Insights by American Society of International Law (26 May 2011), *available at* http://www.asil.org/insights110526.cfm (last visited Sept. 22, 2011).

Forestry Stewardship Council, www.fsc.org/about-fsc.html.

Goldschmidt, Jack, "Realism 101 on Wikileaks," The Lawfare Blog (1 December 2010), online at http://www.lawfareblog.com/2010/12/realism-101-on-wikileaks/.

Human Rights First, "Assessing the Obama Administration's Record of Compliance with the Rule of Law and Human Rights in National Security Policy" (2011), available online at http://www.humanrightsfirst.org/wp-content/uploads/HRF-Natl-Sec-Rep-Card.pdf.

Human Rights First, "Detained and Denied in Afghanistan: How to Make U.S. Detention Comply with the Law" (May 2011), available online at http://www.humanrightsfirst.org/wp-content/uploads/pdf/Detained-Denied-in-Afghanistan.pdf.

Human Rights First, "The U.S. Army Field Manual on Interrogation: A Strong Document in Need of Careful Revision," available online at http://www.humanrightsfirst.org/wp-content/uploads/pdf/Army_Field_Manual.pdf.

Hurri, Ssamuli, *The Birth of the European Individual*, academic dissertation, (Helsinki: 2011).

Husayn v. *Gates*, Petitioner's Memorandum in Support of Motion for Relief from Improper Classification, 08-cv-1360, D.D.C. (11 May 2009).

Khan v. *Gates*, Respondent's Opposition to the Motion of the New York Times Company, the Associated Press, and USA Today to Unseal Classified Documents, Civ. No. 07-1324, D.C. Cir. (28 March 2008).

OpenTheGovernment.org, [Annual] "Secrecy Report Card" (2007-2010), online at http://www.openthegovernment.org/press_room/reports.

Paracha v. *Obama*, Respondents' Response to Petitioner's Emergency Application for Immediate Access to All Publicly Available WikiLeaks Documents Relevant to Petitioner's Case, Civ. No. 04-2002, D.C. Cir. (15 June 2011).

Scheinkman, Andrei, et al., "The Guantánamo Docket," interactive database, New York Times, online at http://projects.nytimes.com/guantanamo (last visited November 17, 2013).

Swedish Judicial Cooperation: The Ordinance on Surrender to Sweden according to the European Arrest Warrant, 2003:1178.

U.K.National Counter Terrorism Security Office, *Project Argus*, online at http://www.nactso.gov.uk/our-services.

U.K.National Counter Terrorism Security Office, *Secure Your Fertiliser*, online at http://www.secureyourfertiliser.gov.uk.

UN Office of the High Commissioner for Human Rights, Full list of country missions conducted or planned, online at http://www.ohchr.org/EN/Issues/Terrorism/Pages/Visits.aspx (last visited November 7, 2013).

Vleugels, Roger, "Overview of All FOIA laws" (20 September 2010).

Witte, Benjamin, "Updated Habeas Numbers," The Lawfare Blog (2 August 2011), available online at http://www.lawfareblog.com/2011/08/updated-habeas-numbers-2/.

WL Central, "Debunked: 'Wikileaks Did Not Redact the Afghanistan War Logs'" (28 November 2010), online at http://wlcentral.org/node/379.

Zabel, Richard B. and James J. Benjamin, Jr., "In Pursuit of Justice: Prosecuting Terrorism Cases in the Federal Courts: 2009 Update and Recent Developments," Human Rights First (2009), available online at http://www.humanrightsfirst.org/wp-content/uploads/pdf/090723-LS-in-pursuit-justice-09-update.pdf.

INDEX

www.ingramcontent.com/pod-product-compliance
Ingram Content Group UK Ltd.
Pitfield, Milton Keynes, MK11 3LW, UK
UKHW020849150926
475595UK00003B/94

9 780199 368327